Reimagining Progress

Education, Economy, and Ecology for Sustainable Development

Editors

Debarshi Mukherjee
Department of Commerce & Business Studies
Jamia Millia Islamia
New Delhi, India

Gorky Chakraborty
Institute of Development Studies Kolkata (IDSK)
Kolkata, India

Pooran Chandra Pandey
Centre of Excellence on Climate Change
Green Transition and Sustainability
South Asian University
New Delhi, India

CRC Press
Taylor & Francis Group
Boca Raton London New York

CRC Press is an imprint of the
Taylor & Francis Group, an **informa** business
A SCIENCE PUBLISHERS BOOK

First edition published 2027
by CRC Press
2385 NW Executive Center Drive, Suite 320, Boca Raton FL 33431

and by CRC Press
4 Park Square, Milton Park, Abingdon, Oxon, OX14 4RN

CRC Press is an imprint of Taylor & Francis Group, LLC

Library of Congress Cataloging-in-Publication Data (applied for)

ISBN: 978-1-041-22991-9 (hbk)
ISBN: 978-1-041-23260-5 (pbk)
ISBN: 978-1-003-73615-8 (ebk)

DOI: 10.1201/9781003736158

Typeset in Times New Roman
by Prime Publishing Services

Foreword

In an era marked by profound transitions-ecological, technological, and socioeconomic—the question of how we define and pursue progress has further gained renewed urgency. The interconnected challenges of climate change, widening inequalities, and digital transformation force us to rethink not only our development models but also the knowledge systems that coherently underline them. It is within this broader context that this edited volume on tho theme—"*Reimagining Progress: Education, Economy, and Ecology for Sustainable Development*" makes a significant and timely contribution to the existing and available literature on the issues in contemporary times.

South Asian University as an international institution, committed to fostering academic excellence and cooperation across South Asia, recognises that sustainability cannot just be addressed through isolated national or disciplinary approaches. The challenges, we face, are inherently transboundary, warranting collaborative thinking, shared knowledge approach—and integrated policy responses. This volume reflects precisely such an orientation. By bringing together diverse scholarly voices, it offers a nuanced and interdisciplinary exploration of sustainability that is both regionally grounded and globally relevant.

One of the key strengths of this book lies in its holistic framing of sustainability. Rather than treating education, economy, ecology, and governance as separate domains, the contributors demonstrate their deep interconnections and deeper visualization about cross cutting issues. This integrated perspective is particularly important for South Asia, where development trajectories are shaped by complex yet common interactions between demographic pressures, environmental vulnerabilities, and institutional capacities. This is where the region is both unique yet differentiated by virtue of its shared heritage, ethos and common good thinking. The chapters demonstrate how inclusive education systems, adaptive economic models, and participatory governance frameworks can collectively enable more resilient and equitable futures.

The emphasis on education as a force for good is especially noteworthy. In a region characterised by diversity and disparity, education holds the potential to bridge divides, foster critical thinking, and nurture a sense of shared responsibility toward sustainable development. At the same time, the volume's engagement with digital technologies and public infrastructure highlights the emerging role of innovation in scaling access to equity and enhancing governance, while also cautioning against new forms of exclusion.

Equally compelling is the book's attention to the ethical dimensions of development. Sustainability is not merely a technical or policy challenge; it is fundamentally a question of values—of how societies balance growth with justice, innovation with inclusion, and human aspirations with ecological limits. By foregrounding these concerns, the volume encourages a more reflective and responsible approach to development practices and future pathways.

This work is commendable for its balance between theoretical insight and practical relevance. The contributions also draw on empirical research, conceptual frameworks, and case-based analyses to offer pathways that are both intellectually rigorous and operationally insightful. Such an approach is essential for bridging the persistent gap between academic discourse and policy implementation.

I am confident that this volume will be of immense value to scholars, students, policymakers, and practitioners alike engaged in the field of sustainable development. More importantly, it also serves as a reminder that the pursuit of sustainability is a collective endeavour—one that demands dialogue, cooperation, and willingness to reimagine established paradigms and status quo contexts.

I congratulate the editors for curating this important work, bringing together perspectives that inspire both critical reflection and constructive action. It is my considered hope that this book will stimulate further research, inform policy choices, and help build a more sustainable, inclusive, and resilient pathways in South Asia and beyond.

K. K. Aggarwal

Preface

The contemporary world stands at a critical juncture where the meaning of progress is being redefined. Persistent inequalities, accelerating climate change, and rapid technological transformations have exposed the limitations of conventional development paradigms. In response to these challenges, Reimagining Progress: Education, Economy, and Ecology for Sustainable Development emerges as a timely and necessary intellectual endeavour—one that seeks to reconceptualise sustainability not as a fragmented goal but as an integrated and evolving framework for human and planetary well-being.

This volume brings together a rich tapestry of scholarly contributions that span disciplinary boundaries while remaining anchored in a shared commitment to sustainability. The chapters collectively argue that meaningful progress can no longer be measured solely by economic growth or technological advancement; rather, it must be evaluated through the lenses of equity, ecological balance, and human capability. By situating education, economy, ecology, and governance within a unified analytical framework, the book offers a holistic perspective on how these domains interact to shape sustainable futures.

At the core of this volume is the acknowledgement that education transcends a mere institutional process, serving instead as an impactful force that moulds values, capabilities, and collective consciousness. The discussions herein accentuate how inclusive, technology-enabled, and culturally responsive learning systems can empower individuals to navigate complexity and make meaningful contributions to sustainability transitions. Concurrently, the volume redefines economic systems as regenerative and adaptable, endorsing models that emphasise resilience, circularity, and social inclusion over extractive growth.

Equally significant is the emphasis on governance as an enabler of the ecosystem. The contributions underscore the role of policy frameworks, digital public infrastructure, and participatory institutions in ensuring that sustainability is not only envisioned but also effectively implemented. In doing so, the book foregrounds the importance of access, accountability, and innovation in building systems that are both equitable and enduring.

What distinguishes this volume is its commitment to bridging theory and practice. The chapters draw upon diverse methodologies—ranging from empirical analyses and quantitative modelling to conceptual frameworks and case studies—to illuminate actionable pathways for sustainable development. This integration of perspectives ensures that the discourse remains both analytically rigorous and practically relevant.

The editors hope this book will serve as a valuable resource for scholars, educators, policymakers, and practitioners engaged in sustainable development. More importantly, it seeks to inspire a shift in thinking—from isolated interventions to systemic transformation, from short-term gains to long-term resilience, and from fragmented knowledge to integrated understanding.

Sustainability, as this volume demonstrates, is not a destination but a continuous process of negotiation, innovation, and collective responsibility. By fostering dialogue across disciplines and contexts, *Reimagining Progress* aspires to contribute to a future where development is not only sustainable but also just, inclusive, and humane.

Contents

Section 3: Economy and Ecology in Practice

Section 4: Pathways to a Sustainable Future

Introduction

Sustainable development today requires a fundamental re-evaluation of how societies define progress, manage resources, and educate future generations. The accelerating global crises of inequality, climate change, and technological disruption necessitate an integrated approach that connects knowledge, policy, and practice. This volume brings together diverse scholarly perspectives that examine sustainability not as a sectoral agenda but as a holistic transformation encompassing education, economy, ecology, and governance. Through theoretical inquiry, empirical research, and case-based analysis, the chapters collectively illustrate how inclusive learning systems, regenerative economic models, adaptive policies, and digital infrastructures can reinforce one another. By tracing the intersections between human development and environmental responsibility, the contributions highlight sustainability as both a moral commitment and a practical strategy. Each section of this volume addresses a crucial pillar of sustainability—education, economy, ecology, and future pathways—offering interdisciplinary insights into how integrated strategies can drive equitable and lasting transformation. Through theoretical inquiry, empirical evidence, and context-based analysis, the chapters collectively illustrate how inclusive learning systems, regenerative economic models, adaptive governance mechanisms, and digital public infrastructures can reinforce one another.

Progressing Sustainably

The opening section emphasises the need to reconceptualise progress in ways that are equitable, ecologically responsible, and empirically measurable. In this regard, Infanta B' and Jayanthi M's chapter, "A Composite Index of STRIDE: Measuring and Mapping India's Educational Sustainability Landscape," develops a quantitative framework linking educational performance to India's vision of Viksit Bharat 2047. Drawing upon Human Capital Theory (Becker 1964, Schultz 1961) and the STRIDE dimensions—Start-ups, Technology, Research, Infrastructure, Deployment, and Skills Enhancement—the study employs Principal Component Analysis to construct a State Readiness Index (SRI) for educational sustainability. The findings highlight regional disparities in ICT infrastructure, vocational training, and research ecosystems, offering policymakers a tool to address educational gaps while reinforcing SDG 4 (Quality Education) and SDG 9 (Industry, Innovation, and Infrastructure). In "*Teaching Within the Safe and Just Space: The Doughnut Pedagogy Model for Sustainability Education*," Acharya and Gondaliya propose a pedagogical framework inspired by Raworth's (2017) Doughnut Economics, integrating social and ecological dimensions into higher education curricula. Their model situates learning within an inner boundary of socio-educational equity and an outer boundary reflecting ecological and cognitive limits. By linking sustainability competencies with digital pedagogies, this approach extends theoretical insights into actionable classroom practices, fostering transformative, values-driven sustainability education. Together, these chapters collectively articulate a nuanced understanding of progress that transcends conventional economic metrics, foregrounds human capability, and integrates social justice and ecological stewardship as central components of sustainable development.

Education as a Pillar of Sustainability

Education stands at the core of sustainable transformation, functioning as both an enabler and a catalyst for systemic change. The chapters in this section explore diverse yet interconnected dimensions of education's role in achieving sustainability, ranging from the integration of digital learning and systems thinking to reforms in higher education, inclusive schooling, and the evolving landscape of professional pedagogy. In "*Designing E-Learning for Systems Thinking in Sustainability Education*," Gupta and Verma emphasise that e-learning designed around systems thinking can foster holistic understanding, cross-disciplinary engagement, and critical reflection, thereby preparing learners for the complexity of sustainability challenges. Banerjee et al. extend this idea in their chapter "*Legal Education 2.0: A Roadmap for Future Pedagogical Approaches*," proposing that AI-driven, data-informed, and adaptive pedagogies grounded in the Education 4.0 and Society 5.0 paradigms can prepare law graduates for technologically advanced and ethically grounded futures. Complementing these perspectives, Debnath et al., in their chapter "*Role of Indian Higher Education Institutions and Green Human Resource Management as Mediator to Sustainable Development*," examine how higher education institutions and Green Human Resource Management practices can embed sustainability into the very operations of academia, aligning institutional culture with the Sustainable Development Goals. Johri and Puri's "*From Policy to Practice: A Bibliometric Study of ESD Integration in Indian Higher Education Systems*" provides a bibliometric analysis of Education for Sustainable Development (ESD) integration in Indian higher education and reveals the growing academic and policy-level endorsement of ESD as a transformative paradigm, though international collaboration remains limited. Together, these works illustrate how sustainability-oriented education—from school to higher education and into digital spaces—fosters critical thinking, equity, innovation, and global citizenship, reinforcing the notion that education is not merely a sector but the foundation of sustainable development itself. In the chapter "*Blending Digital Pedagogy and Ethnomathematics for Advancing Education for Sustainable Development*", Bardhan and Debnath integrate indigenous knowledge with digital learning environments. Their study shows how ethnomathematics, when supported by digital tools, enhances sustainability awareness, cultural appreciation, and learner engagement. By linking traditional mathematical wisdom with global sustainability themes, they demonstrate how culturally responsive digital pedagogy can foster inclusive and locally relevant education, enriching the broader discourse on Education for Sustainable Development.

Economy and Ecology in Practice

The intersection of economy and ecology represents one of the most dynamic frontiers of sustainable development, where technological innovation, environmental stewardship, and policy reform converge to reimagine the concept of growth itself. The studies within this section collectively reflect a shift from extractive to regenerative economic thinking, emphasising systems that are adaptive, circular, and resilient. In the chapter "*A Conceptual Framework for Adaptive-AI in Agriculture: Enabling Self-Learning Systems for a Sustainable and Resilient Supply Chain*," Jena et al. present a conceptual framework for adaptive AI in agriculture that situates technology at the heart of sustainability transitions, demonstrating how self-learning systems can enhance supply chain efficiency, reduce resource misallocation, and build resilience against climate variability. Grounded in Dynamic Systems Theory, the framework proposes an intelligent, responsive agricultural model that democratises data-driven decision-making among farmers while reinforcing low-carbon and food-secure futures. Complementing this technological context, Bakshi and Maitra, in their chapter "*Volatility Spillovers in Energy Markets: Assessing the Economic Viability of Renewable vs. Non-Renewable Energy in India*," offer a macroeconomic perspective on the challenges of energy transition by exploring volatility spillovers between renewable and non-renewable energy markets. Their findings reveal that renewable energy equities exhibit weaker and more fluctuating relationships with input commodities compared to fossil-fuel-based equities, underscoring both the independence and the instability of sustainable energy markets in their formative phase. This volatility, however, can also be interpreted as a signal of transformation, reflecting a market in transition from dependence on finite resources towards diversification, innovation, and environmental accountability. Adding a socio-ecological dimension, Datta et al.'s chapter "*Transformative Dynamics of Rubber Plantations in Tripura: Linking Growth, Sustainability, Social Inclusion and Future Projections*" presents an empirical analysis of how rubber cultivation among tribal communities has reshaped livelihoods and landscapes in Northeast India. Their study reveals significant improvements in household income, women's workforce participation, literacy, and healthcare access among plantation households, illustrating how green economic transitions can foster social inclusion. By integrating economic upliftment with environmental restoration, the study underscores rubber plantations as potential models of sustainable rural transformation, linking ecological renewal with equity-driven growth. Extending this dialogue to ecological impermanence, the chapter "*Understanding Sustainability in Impermanent Land*," Momin and Chakraborty explore sustainability challenges in transient, fluvial, and deltaic landscapes where land is in constant flux. It questions the adequacy of SDG 15 (Life on Land) in addressing the realities of communities inhabiting such shifting terrains. Through a field-based inquiry, the study highlights how livelihood, habitation, and governance adapt to instability, urging global frameworks to recognise these overlooked ecologies as vital to a comprehensive vision of sustainability. Adding a behavioural and organisational dimension to this discourse, Sharma et al., in their chapter "*Conscious Leadership Styles and Sustainable Employee Behaviours: Balancing OCB, Compulsory Citizenship, and Performance for Organisational Sustainability*," examine how leaders' technological awareness and ethical orientation foster sustainable employee behaviour. Grounded in social exchange and self-determination theories, their study shows that technologically conscious leadership enhances voluntary citizenship behaviours, thereby promoting long-term organisational sustainability. By positioning technological consciousness as a key leadership competency, the chapter bridges human, technological, and ecological aspects of sustainability, emphasising that regenerative growth depends as much on ethical leadership and culture as on innovation and policy reform.

Pathways to a Sustainable Future

The final section, Pathways to a Sustainable Future, engages with the forward-looking dimensions of sustainability, examining how societies can reconcile growth, equity, and ecological balance in the coming decades. The chapters in this section collectively emphasise transformation, inclusion, and long-term resilience as guiding principles for reimagining developmental trajectories within a sustainability framework. In "*India's Economic Growth and Development Trends & Issues: Past, Present and Futures*," Majhi and Maher trace India's post-independence economic evolution through a longitudinal analysis of sectoral shifts in agriculture, industry, and services. Using secondary data and semi-logarithmic regression models, the study identifies four distinct growth periods. The findings underscore that while liberalisation and technological modernisation have propelled economic progress, future growth must internalise environmental and social equity concerns. The chapter advocates for an inclusive growth model that integrates employment generation, green innovation, and distributive justice as key levers for sustainable progress. Complementing this view, "*Pathways to Sustainable Future in Gender, Equity and Sustainable Development*," by Shree and Kumar, explores the intersection of gender justice and sustainability. Drawing from international policy documents and empirical case studies, the authors highlight how gender inequality remains a structural constraint to achieving the Sustainable Development Goals. Their analysis emphasises that gender equity is not only an ethical imperative but also a catalyst for social innovation, ecological stewardship, and community resilience. By enacting gender-sensitive legislation, inclusive education, and women-led grassroots movements, the chapter identifies tangible pathways through which empowerment can drive sustainable transformation. Adding a governance and technological dimension to this discourse, Mukherjee and Qamar's chapter "*The Role of Digital Public Infrastructure in Advancing Inclusive Governance and Development in India*" highlights how India's digital ecosystem, anchored in platforms such as Aadhaar, UPI, DigiLocker, UMANG, DIKSHA, and eSanjeevani, has become a cornerstone of socio-economic inclusion. Drawing on Ribot and Peluso's (2003) Theory of Access and the Network Externalities Theory, the authors show how Digital Public Infrastructure (DPI) redefines governance by extending access beyond legal entitlements and addressing barriers of identity, literacy, and connectivity. At the same time, they acknowledge challenges such as digital divides, data privacy, and infrastructural disparities that risk reproducing old inequalities. The chapter argues for a human-centred digital governance model that blends regulatory safeguards, capacity building, and community-level digital literacy, framing DPI as an evolving ecosystem of trust, participation, and democratic empowerment. Adding further depth to this gendered perspective, "*From Skills to Sustainability: Women's Empowerment in the Entrepreneurial Ecosystem*" by Dash and Gaurav explores how women's entrepreneurship drives inclusive growth and sustainable community development. The chapter links skill development, agency, social capital, and institutional support to enterprise sustainability, emphasising that training alone is insufficient without access to finance, networks, and markets. It highlights that integrated models combining mentoring and financial inclusion create more resilient ventures, positioning women's entrepreneurship as a pathway to structural empowerment and sustainable economic participation. Together, these chapters underscore that sustainability is not a static end state but a continuous process of balancing economic ambition with ethical responsibility. The transition to a sustainable future demands integrative thinking that merges macroeconomic foresight with social inclusion and environmental consciousness.

This volume presents a comprehensive exploration of the interconnections between education, economy, ecology, and governance in the pursuit of sustainable development. Drawing on theoretical insights, empirical analyses, and practical case studies, the chapters collectively illuminate pathways for reconciling human development with ecological and social imperatives. Education emerges as both a transformative tool and a catalyst for ethical engagement, equipping learners with the knowledge, skills, and values necessary to address complex sustainability challenges. Economic strategies, technological innovations, and policy frameworks are reframed to prioritise ecological balance, social equity, and long-term resilience. The integration of digital tools, adaptive learning, and participatory governance further enhances the capacity of societies to implement sustainable solutions effectively. By synthesising contemporary scholarship and applied practices, this volume advances the discourse on sustainable development, highlighting the need for systemic approaches that integrate multiple dimensions of human and ecological well-being. It underscores that sustainability is not a linear objective but a dynamic, multidimensional, and collaborative endeavour. The insights presented herein guide educators, policymakers, practitioners, and scholars dedicated to creating a future that is equitable, resilient, and environmentally responsible. Ultimately, the chapters collectively articulate a vision in which education, economy, and ecology coalesce to generate informed, empowered, and socially responsible global citizens capable of driving meaningful progress towards a sustainable world.

Editors

Debarshi Mukherjee
Gorky Chakraborty
Pooran Chandra Pandey

Section 1
Progressing Sustainably

Chapter 1

A Composite Index of Stride

Measuring and Mapping India's Educational Sustainability Landscape

Agnus Infanta B.[1] and *Jayanthi M.*[2,*]

1. Introduction

Education is an important dimension of human development and is extremely significant to a nation's economic well-being. Being educated is a valuable achievement in itself, and the opportunity to attain it can be of direct importance to a person's effective freedom. This approach to educational attainment has gained momentum since the inception of 'human development' as a new development model. The Millennium Development Goals strengthened this by targeting the universalisation of primary education by 2015. Later, the Sustainable Development Goals (SDGs) took this commitment one step further in Goal 4, which aims to ensure inclusive and equitable quality education and promote lifelong learning opportunities for all. India's ambitious Viksit Bharat 2047 vision seeks to position the country as a \$30 trillion economy with a top-3 global GDP ranking by 2047, leveraging its demographic dividend, where over half the population is under 25 (NITI Aayog 2023). Rooted in Human Capital Theory (Becker 1964, Schultz 1961), this transformation hinges on education as a catalyst for economic growth, innovation, and social equity,

[1] Research Scholar, School of Management, SASTRA Deemed University, Thanjavur – 613401, Tamil Nadu, India.
[2] Assistant Professor, School of Management, SASTRA Deemed University, Thanjavur – 613401, Tamil Nadu, India.
Email: agnusinfanta@gmail.com
* Corresponding author: jayanthi@mba.sastra.edu

DOI: 10.1201/9781003736158-2

aligning with initiatives such as the STRIDE framework—Start-ups, Technology, Research, Infrastructure, Deployment, and Skills Enhancement.

The motivation for this study stems from the urgent need to address regional disparities in educational readiness, as traditional metrics often fail to capture the multidimensional impact of human capital on sustainable development, particularly in a rapidly evolving knowledge-driven economy. The global recognition of India's potential as an innovation hub (Wright and McMahan 2011) further underscores the necessity to quantify and enhance state-level preparedness.

The objective of this study is to develop and validate a composite State Readiness Index (SRI) using Principal Component Analysis (PCA) to assess India's educational sustainability across 36 states and Union Territories (UTs), utilising 2023–2024 data from official sources such as UDISE+, DPIIT, and NSDC. This index aims to provide a holistic measure of readiness across the STRIDE dimensions, offering policymakers a tool to identify strengths, gaps, and priority areas for intervention. The novelty lies in its integrated approach, combining diverse indicators into a single scalable metric tailored to India's unique developmental context, extending beyond conventional human capital assessments by incorporating start-up ecosystems and digital infrastructure. This study also introduces spatial and statistical visualisations to reveal regional patterns, enhancing the practical utility of the findings.

The research questions guiding this study are: (1) How effectively does the State Readiness Index (SRI) reflect state-level variations in educational sustainability under the Viksit Bharat 2047 framework? (2) Which STRIDE dimensions most significantly influence regional disparities in readiness? (3) How can the SRI inform targeted policy interventions to bridge educational gaps and align with SDGs 4 and 9? By addressing these questions, the study contributes to both academic discourse and policy formulation, positioning India to harness its human capital for sustainable growth and global competitiveness.

2. Literature Review

2.1 India's Viksit Bharat 2047 Vision

India stands at the edge of a historic turning point conceptualised through the ambitious vision of Viksit Bharat 2047. This vision envisages India with a $30 trillion economy, a GDP growth rate of more than 8%, and a top-3 global GDP position. The Viksit Bharat 2047 plan calls for India to become a developed country by that year. Indian Prime Minister Shri Narendra Modi declared that Viksit Bharat demands no poverty, world-class infrastructure, and every young person employed in productive work. Collectively, the Viksit Bharat vision is a comprehensive roadmap encompassing economic, social, environmental, and governance dimensions. Economically, it aims for a $30.47 trillion GDP by 2047, driven by industrial growth and technological innovation. Socially, it seeks universal literacy (NITI Aayog 2023).

2.2 *Education in the Viksit Bharat Vision*

Through an analysis of important theoretical perspectives on Viksit Bharat's developmental path and various literature sources, this chapter explores the critical role that education plays in realising the Viksit Bharat vision. The Viksit Bharat vision prioritises education as part of its transformational goal. India stands to gain a substantial demographic dividend because more than half of its population is under 25. Various government reports and scholarly studies highlight the centrality of education in achieving key developmental milestones. The Economic Survey 2022–2023 stresses the role of a digitally skilled workforce in driving India's transition towards a knowledge-based economy (Economic Survey 2023), while the RBI Annual Report links financial inclusion and digital literacy to broader economic resilience (Reserve Bank of India 2023). The World Bank India Report identifies education and skill development as fundamental to raising India's Human Development Index above 0.8, a prerequisite for attaining developed nation status (World Bank 2023).

Further, McKinsey India projects that 90% urban literacy and AI-integrated education systems will be essential for fostering innovation and sustaining industrial growth (McKinsey India 2023). The UNDP India report aligns education with Sustainable Development Goals (SDGs), particularly SDG 4—Quality Education—as a non-negotiable factor for SDG 5—gender equality—and SDG 1—poverty alleviation (United Nations Development Programme India 2023). Additionally, the Ministry of Finance and NITI Aayog stress the need for vocational training and STEM education to meet labour market demands in emerging sectors such as renewable energy and advanced manufacturing (Ministry of Finance 2023, NITI Aayog 2023).

Academic contributions argue that inclusive education policies bridging rural–urban and gender divides are vital for equitable growth (Virmani 2024, Sharma 2024). Others highlight agricultural education and agri-tech skilling as crucial for modernising farming and doubling farmers' incomes. Collectively, these sources position education as the foundational pillar for achieving Viksit Bharat by 2047, integrating economic ambition with social equity and sustainability.

2.3 *Theoretical Foundations of Education in Development*

According to Human Capital Theory, education increases worker productivity, which raises wages and promotes economic expansion (Becker 1964, Schultz 1961). This is in line with India's emphasis on Digital India and Skill India, which seek to develop a workforce with the necessary skills for a competitive economy. The relevance of education in promoting innovation and technological advancement is further highlighted by Endogenous Growth Theory, which is essential for Viksit Bharat's objectives in the fields of artificial intelligence and green industries (Romer 1990, Lucas 1988). The need to move workers from agriculture to high-productivity industries, which calls for education and reskilling, was previously underlined by Structural Change Theory (Lewis 1954, Chenery 1960). This is reflected in India's Production Linked Incentive schemes and Make in India initiatives. In the meantime, vocational training programmes increase labour market efficiency.

2.4 Startups, Technology, Research, Infrastructure, Deployment, and Enhancing Skills in Economic Growth and Education Development

Entrepreneurship and Startups**:** Entrepreneurship is widely recognised as a driver of growth. Contributions emphasise that "entrepreneurship is a driving force behind economic growth, innovation, and prosperity"—entrepreneurs create companies that boost local GDP and employment. New technology start-ups (e.g., fintech, ICT firms) introduce innovative business models and products (e.g., digital payments, platforms), spurring new markets and jobs. Studies note that start-up ecosystems (supported by policy and financing) enhance innovation and growth (Rong 2025). Education plays a key role here by fostering entrepreneurial skills and innovation mindsets.

Digital Technologies and ICT**:** Advanced technological infrastructure strongly supports growth. Empirical work finds that information-and-communication technology (ICT) diffusion significantly raises GDP (Zaman and Moemen 2023). In a panel of developing regions, ICT penetration proved a "significant and positive predictor of growth" (Zaman and Moemen 2023). Studies show that digitalisation (e.g., internet, mobile networks) combined with education greatly boosts economic growth in developing countries. These findings align with the broader literature that ICT adoption (broadband, digital platforms, automation) expands markets, productivity, and employment (Bibi et al. 2025). Deployment of such technologies requires skilled workers, underscoring the link to education development.

Skills and Education**:** Human capital accumulation is key for long-term growth. Recent studies highlight that higher education and skill development have strong growth effects. For example, studies use panel data for Central Asia and find that "higher tertiary education enrolment correlates with long-term economic expansion" (Tleppayev et al. 2025). In the EU context, it is observed that "skills development is a key lever" for productivity and living standards. In developing economies, improving education quality and vocational training raises labour productivity and supports innovation (Bibi et al. 2025, Arpaia 2025). Conversely, low education quality or skills shortages can constrain growth (Arpaia 2025). Enhancing skills through education is thus central to deploying human resources effectively for economic advancement.

Infrastructure (Physical and Digital)**:** Robust infrastructure is a well-known growth enabler. Roads, power supply, communications, etc., form public capital that raises productivity. Studies find that India's infrastructure expansion (transport, electricity, telecom) significantly contributed to GDP growth (roughly 1.2% of annual growth) (Sahoo and Dash 2009). In a broader sample, infrastructure elements such as transport networks, communications, and electricity supply significantly drive growth in developing countries. This aligns with the Solow growth model's inclusion of public capital. Notably, the study shows that in developed countries infrastructure is already saturated (hence less growth impact), whereas in developing economies enhancing infrastructure yields strong GDP gains (Nisa and Khalid 2024). Education supports infrastructure deployment by building a workforce capable of maintaining and innovating in these areas.

Research, R&D, and Innovation Investment: Investment in R&D and innovation fosters long-run growth, though effects can vary. Endogenous Growth Theory predicts that R&D generates knowledge spillovers. Studies model an R&D ecosystem and find that R&D boosts innovation; however, at least in their middle-income sample, innovation did not show a statistically significant direct impact on GDP growth. This suggests that R&D must be coupled with strong institutions and markets to translate into growth. In practice, countries invest in science and technology (e.g., research institutions, technology parks) to build long-term capacity. Education underpins R&D by developing the research skills and knowledge base needed for innovation (Fayyaz and Bartha 2025).

2.5 Index Construction with PCA

Many studies utilise Principal Component Analysis (PCA) to construct composite indices for domains such as education and infrastructure. For example, an Infrastructure Index was developed to measure India's public capital development using PCA. Similarly, an Education Development Index (EDI) was created from 22 indicators (access, infrastructure, teachers, outcomes) by applying PCA for aggregation. More recently, a composite Performance-Infrastructure-Equity (PIE) index for elementary education in Odisha was formulated using PCA on student performance and school infrastructure data. These cases demonstrate how PCA objectively weights diverse indicators to form comprehensive indices, a widely adopted method in development literature (Sahoo and Dash 2009, Anjali Meena et al. 2022, Sahoo et al. 2025).

3. Methodology

This study employs a quantitative approach to construct a composite index for education development in the context of India's Viksit Bharat 2047 vision, focusing on the integration of start-ups, technology, research, infrastructure, deployment, and skills enhancement. The methodology is divided into data description, variable selection, and the application of Principal Component Analysis (PCA) to form the index. Data were collected from official sources for the year 2023–2024 (or the latest available), ensuring reliability and relevance to current policy frameworks.

3.1 Data Description

The Table 1 describes the dataset comprises state-level and Union Territory (UT)-level indicators across India, covering 36 states/UTs. These indicators reflect key dimensions of education infrastructure, digital enablement, research investment, start-up ecosystems, and skill development, aligned with the theoretical foundations discussed in the literature review. Data were sourced primarily from official government reports and portals, including the Unified District Information System for Education (UDISE+), Department for Promotion of Industry and Internal Trade (DPIIT)/Start-up India, Department of Science and Technology (DST)/National Science and Technology Management Information System (NSTMIS), Ministry of Skill Development and Entrepreneurship (MSDE)/National Skill Development

Table 1. Description of variables.

Variable	**Description**	**Main Source (Official)**
Startups	Composite score reflecting state startup ecosystem performance (policy, infrastructure, funding support, etc.). Given in DPIIT "States' Startup Ranking" report/portal.	DPIIT/StartupIndia
Technology	% of schools (all management types) with internet facility available. Usually from "All Management" column in UDISE+.	UDISE+ 2023–24
	% of schools with functional desktops/PCs or computer labs. Derived from "All Management" in UDISE+ (functional PCs).	UDISE+ 2023–24
Research	GERD as % of the state's Gross State Domestic Product (GSDP).	Calculated from GERD and GSDP data (DST + MOSPI)
Infrastructure	% of schools with electricity connection. Usually "All Management" column in UDISE+.	UDISE+ 2023–24
	% of secondary schools with functional integrated science laboratories. From UDISE+ (Integrated Science Lab).	UDISE+ 2023–24
Deployment	Pupil–Teacher Ratio at secondary level. Lower PTR means fewer pupils per teacher. From UDISE+.	UDISE+ 2023–24
Skills	% of youth population that has received formal vocational or skills training via NSDC, MSDE, or other accredited schemes.	NSDC/MSDE annual reports

Corporation (NSDC), and Ministry of Statistics and Programme Implementation (MOSPI) for Gross State Domestic Product (GSDP).

3.2 Index Construction via PCA

The dataset was inspected for missing values (none found) and outliers, with no significant anomalies identified. To ensure consistency across variables, all were standardised to a mean of 0 and a standard deviation of 1 using the z-score transformation:

$$\mathbf{Z_{ij} = X_{ij} - \mu_j / \sigma_j}$$

where Xij is the original value, μj is the mean, and σj is the standard deviation of variable j. The Deployment variable, which has a negative orientation, was inverted by taking its reciprocal (1/PTR) to align with the positive direction of other variables, ensuring all indicators contribute positively to the index.

PCA was applied to reduce dimensionality and construct the State Readiness Index (SRI) by combining the standardised variables into principal components (PCs) that capture the maximum variance in the data. PCA transforms a set of correlated variables into uncorrelated PCs through linear combinations, with the first PC explaining the largest variance and subsequent PCs explaining decreasing amounts. The covariance matrix S of the standardised data matrix Z (36 × 8) was computed:

$$\mathbf{S = 1 * Z^{T}\, Z/n{-}1}$$

where n = 36 (number of states/UTs) and p = 8 (number of variables). Eigen decomposition of S yielded eigenvalues $\lambda_1 \geq \lambda_2 \geq \cdots \geq \lambda_8$ and corresponding eigenvectors $v_1, v_2, \ldots, v_8$, satisfying:

$$\mathbf{Sv_k = \lambda_k v_k}$$

The PCs were derived as:

$$\mathbf{Y = ZV}$$

where Y is the matrix of PC scores, and V is the matrix of eigenvectors. The number of PCs to retain was determined using the scree plot, Kaiser criterion (eigenvalues > 1), and cumulative variance explained. The SRI was calculated as a weighted sum of the first two PCs:

$$\mathbf{SRI_i = w_1 Y_{i1} + w_2 Y_{i2}}$$

where $w_1 = \lambda_1/(\lambda_1+\lambda_2) = 0.774$ and $w_2 = \lambda_2/(\lambda_1+\lambda_2) = 0.226$, reflecting the proportion of variance explained. The PC scores Y_{i1} and Y_{i2} were derived from the loadings (eigenvectors) and standardized data. To enhance interpretability, the SRI was scaled to a 0–100 range using min-max normalization:

$$\mathbf{SRI_{scaled,i} = 100 \cdot (SRI_i) - min(SRI)/max\ (SRI) - min(SRI)}$$

The standardized approach, including data pre-processing and PCA implementation, ensures reliability and comparability across 36 states and Union Territories. The resulting SRI, scaled to a 0–100 range, offers a valuable tool for policymakers to identify regional strengths and gaps, guiding targeted interventions as of the data reference period of 2023–2024.

4. Analysis and Interpretation

This analysis constructs the State Readiness Index (SRI) to assess India's preparedness for the Viksit Bharat 2047 vision, integrating dimensions of start-ups, technology, research, infrastructure, deployment, and skills. Utilising data from official sources for 2023–2024, the study employs Principal Component Analysis (PCA) to derive a composite index across 36 states and Union Territories. The findings aim to provide actionable insights for equitable education and development policy formulation.

Figure 1 heatmap illustrates the pairwise correlation coefficients among the eight STRIDE (Start-ups, Technology, Research, Infrastructure, Deployment, and Education) indicators used in the study. The colour gradient, ranging from blue (−0.4) to red (1.0), represents the strength and direction of correlations. Strong positive correlations (e.g., 0.75 between Internet Schools and Comp Lab Schools) indicate that states with higher internet availability also tend to have more functional computer labs. A notable negative correlation (−0.02 between Pupil Teacher Ratio

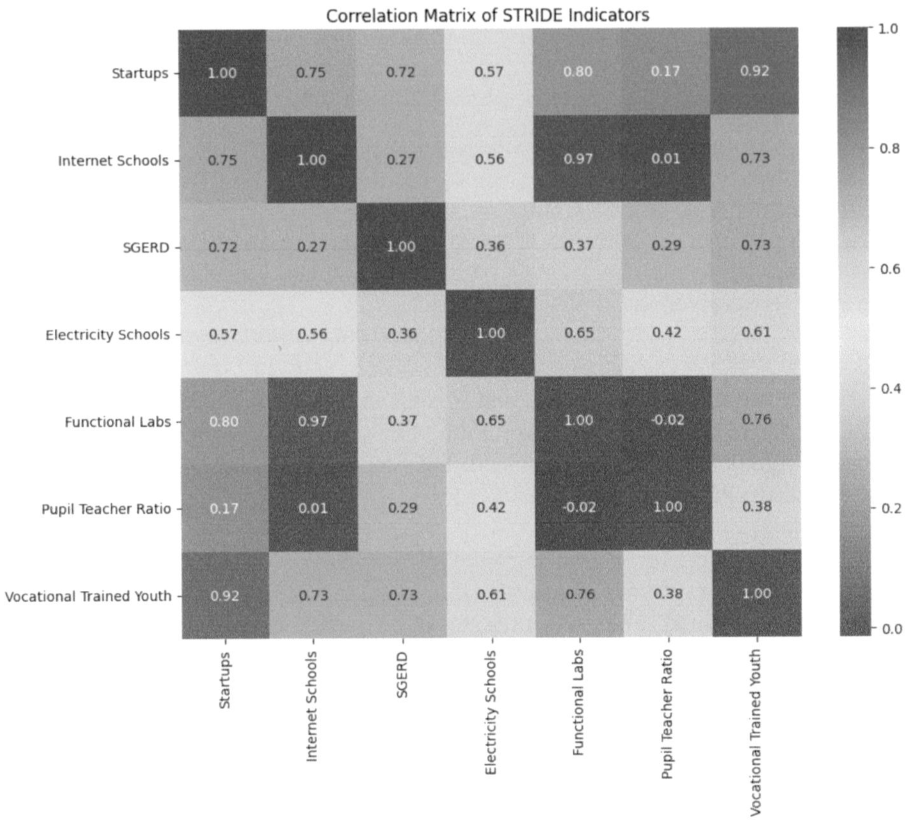

Figure 1. Correlation Matrix of STRIDE Indicators. Source: author computed.

and Vocational Trained Youth) suggests that lower pupil–teacher ratios are weakly associated with higher vocational training coverage. This matrix informed the suitability of PCA by confirming significant inter-variable relationships.

Table 2 Kaiser-Meyer-Olkin (KMO) measure of sampling adequacy was 0.639, indicating moderate suitability for factor analysis. Bartlett's Test of Sphericity yielded a statistic of 295.16 ($p < 0.001$), confirming significant correlations among variables. Cronbach's Alpha of 0.886 suggested high internal consistency among the variables.

The Figure 2 Scree Plot displays the cumulative variance explained by each principal component (PC) derived from the PCA. The x-axis represents the number

Table 2. Consistency checks for the variables.

KMO Overall	Bartlett's Test	Cronbach's Alpha
0.639	295.16	0.886

Source: Author computed.

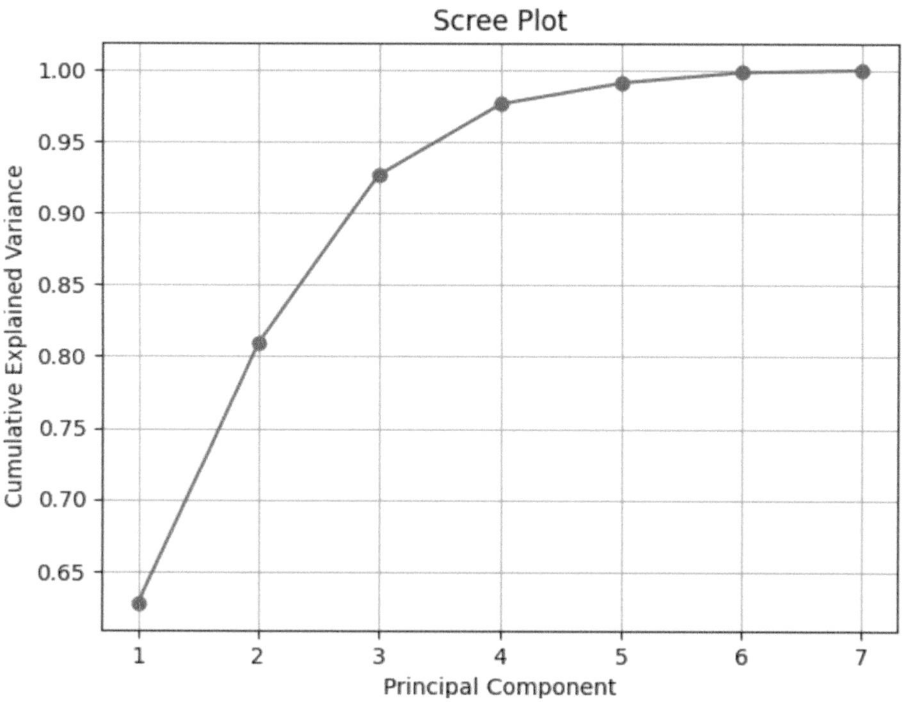

Figure 2. Scree Plot of STRIDE Indicators. Source - author computed.

of components (1 to 7), while the y-axis shows the cumulative explained variance, starting at 0.70 for PC1 and reaching 0.95 by PC3. The plot indicates a sharp decline after the first two components, with PC1 and PC2 together explaining 80.8% of the total variance. This elbow shape supports retaining the first two PCs for the SRI, as additional components contribute minimally to explanatory power.

The Table 3 shows that the component loadings were examined to validate the contribution of each variable to the PCs. PC1, with high positive loadings for Start-up's, Internet Schools, Functional Labs, and Vocational Trained Youth, represents a composite of digital and skill readiness. PC2, dominated by Pupil Teacher Ratio, reflects deployment efficiency.

The Figure 3 bar chart details the individual variance explained by each principal component. PC1 accounts for 62.8% of the variance, PC2 for 18.3%, PC3 for 11.8%, and subsequent components (PC4 to PC7) contribute progressively less (4.9%, 1.5%, 0.7%, and 0.2%, respectively). The dominance of PC1 and PC2, totalling 81.1% of variance, justifies their use in constructing the SRI, reflecting the major underlying dimensions of state readiness in education and development.

The Figure 4 heatmap visualises the State Readiness Index (SRI) scores for 36 states and UTs, scaled from 0 to 100. The colour gradient, from dark blue (low scores, e.g., Arunachal Pradesh at 31.2%) to dark red (high scores, e.g., Delhi at 95.2%), highlights regional disparities. Leading states such as Maharashtra (92.6%), Tamil Nadu (90.2%), and Karnataka (89.1%) indicate strong performance across

Table 3. Component Loadings for the Variables.

Variable	PC1	PC2	PC3	PC4	PC5	PC6	PC7
Startups	0.447964	–0.095537	0.270181	–0.05151	0.599299	–0.0628	–0.00591
Internet Schools	0.403636	–0.386749	–0.266818	–0.35114	–0.3348	–0.06879	–0.63609
SGERD	0.32181	0.344679	0.636889	0.302866	–0.5181	–0.03468	–0.10317
Electricity Schools	0.35621	0.14176	–0.53047	0.72693	0.11489	0.07248	–0.15728
Functional Labs	0.424836	–0.365201	–0.154765	–0.03102	–0.33047	–0.06539	0.7401
Pupil Teacher Ratio	0.145599	0.74956	–0.387553	–0.43338	–0.14656	–0.21673	0.102486
Vocational Trained Youth	0.451964	0.123299	0.151843	–0.25516	0.341212	0.757756	0.041771

Source: Author computed.

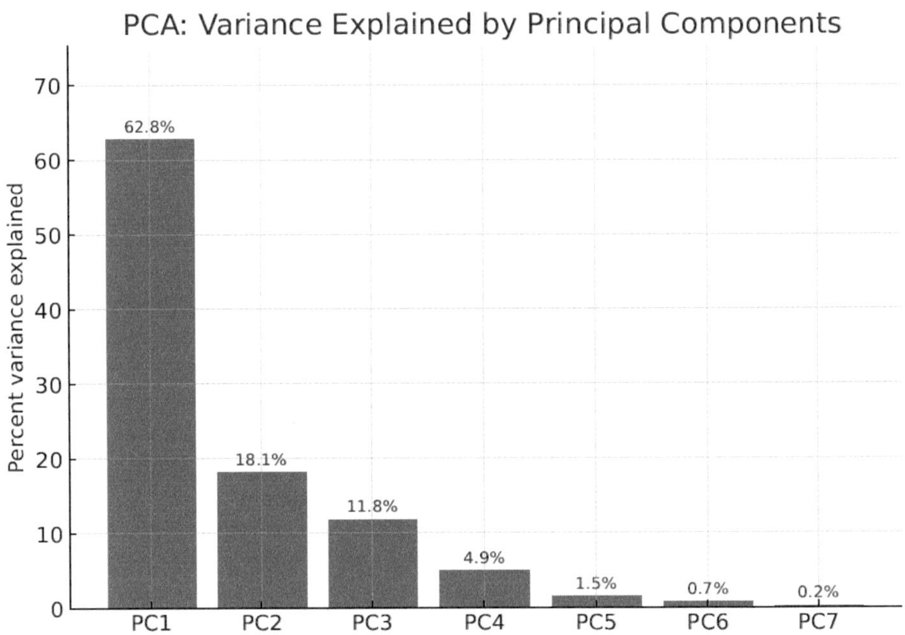

Figure 3. Variance Explained by PCA via Bar chart. Source - author computed.

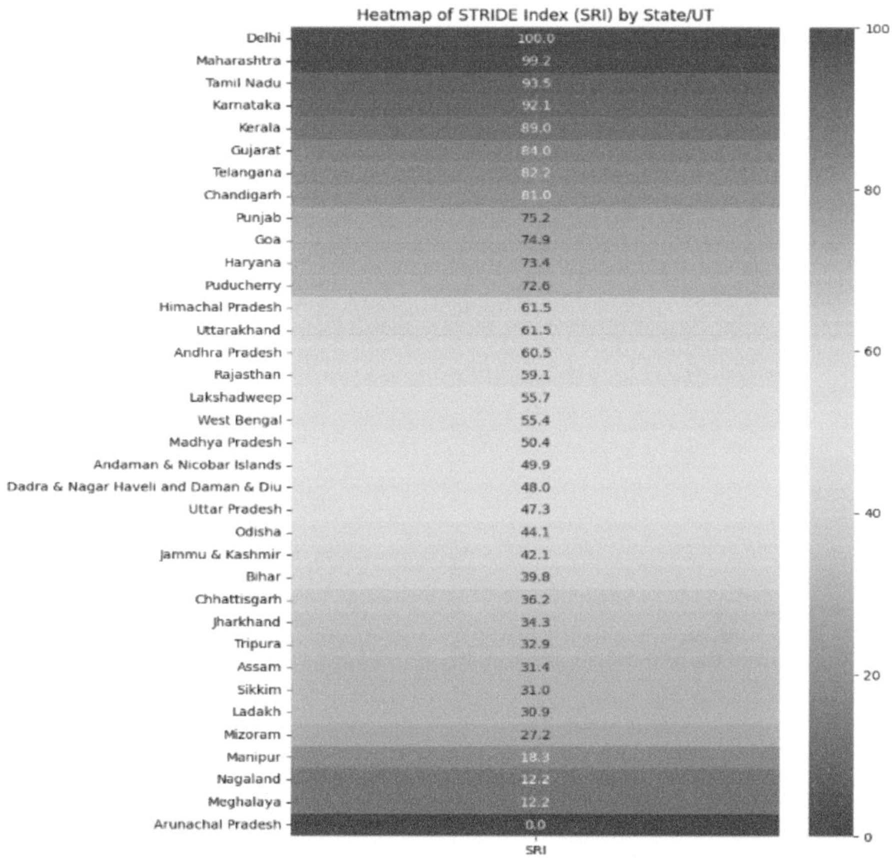

Figure 4. Index derived via PCA on STRIDE dimensions (Start-ups, Technology, Research, Infrastructure, Deployment, Skills). Source – author computed.

STRIDE indicators, while lagging regions such as Ladakh (32.7%) and Meghalaya (33.1%) suggest areas needing policy focus. This ranking aids in benchmarking state progress towards Viksit Bharat 2047 goals.

The Figure 5 choropleth map visualises the State Readiness Index (SRI) scores across India's 36 states and Union Territories (UTs), scaled from 0 to 100. The colour gradient, ranging from dark blue (low scores, e.g., 20–40) to dark red (high scores, e.g., 80–100), highlights regional disparities in education development readiness for the Viksit Bharat 2047 vision. States such as Maharashtra, Tamil Nadu, and Karnataka (dark red) exhibit high SRI scores (above 80), indicating strong performance across start-ups, technology, research, infrastructure, deployment, and skills dimensions. In contrast, north-eastern states such as Arunachal Pradesh and Meghalaya (dark blue) score below 40, suggesting significant gaps. This spatial representation aids in identifying priority areas for policy intervention.

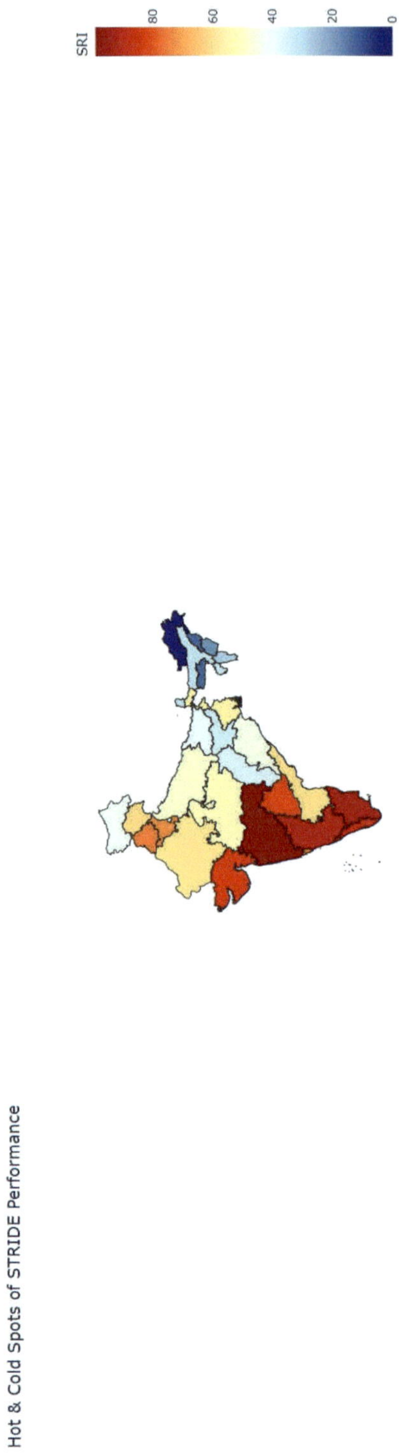

Figure 5. Choropleth map of State Readiness Index (SRI) by states and UT. Source - author computed.

5. Conclusion

This study successfully constructs the State Readiness Index (SRI) to evaluate India's state-level preparedness for the Viksit Bharat 2047 vision, integrating the STRIDE dimensions—Start-ups, Technology, Research, Infrastructure, Deployment, and Skills Enhancement—through Principal Component Analysis (PCA) of 2023–2024 data sourced from official repositories such as UDISE+, DPIIT, and NSDC. The analysis uncovers significant regional disparities, with leading states such as Maharashtra (92.6%), Tamil Nadu (90.2%), and Karnataka (89.1%) demonstrating strong performance across all STRIDE indicators, reflecting robust start-up ecosystems, advanced ICT infrastructure, and effective vocational training programmes. In contrast, north-eastern states such as Arunachal Pradesh (31.2%), Meghalaya (33.1%), and Ladakh (32.7%) exhibit low SRI scores, highlighting critical deficiencies in digital connectivity, research investment, and educational deployment. These findings are underpinned by high internal consistency (Cronbach's Alpha of 0.886) and a cumulative variance explained of 81.1% by the first two principal components, affirming the SRI's reliability and validity as a composite metric.

The results align with the theoretical foundations of Human Capital Theory (Becker 1964, Schultz 1961), which emphasises education and skill development as drivers of economic growth and social progress, and Endogenous Growth Theory (Romer 1990, Lucas 1988), which underscores the role of innovation and technology in sustaining long-term development. The SRI's ability to distil complex multidimensional data into a single interpretable score (scaled 0–100) provides a nuanced understanding of how states are positioned to capitalise on India's demographic dividend, where over half the population is under 25 (NITI Aayog 2023). The spatial visualisation through the choropleth map further reveals geographical patterns, with southern and western states outperforming northern and eastern regions, suggesting the need for tailored regional strategies.

Moreover, the study's diagnostic tools, such as the Kaiser–Meyer–Olkin (KMO) measure (0.639) and Bartlett's Test (295.16, $p < 0.001$), confirm the suitability of PCA and the interrelationships among STRIDE variables, reinforcing the index's robustness. The dominance of PC1 (62.8% variance), reflecting digital and skill readiness, and PC2 (18.3% variance), capturing deployment efficiency, highlights the multifaceted nature of educational sustainability. These insights not only validate the Viksit Bharat 2047 roadmap's emphasis on universal literacy, world-class infrastructure, and productive employment but also align with Sustainable Development Goals (SDGs) 4 (Quality Education) and 9 (Industry, Innovation, and Infrastructure). As India progresses towards its 2047 target, the SRI serves as a critical benchmark, offering a dynamic tool to monitor advancements, address inequities, and ensure that educational investments translate into economic and social dividends across all regions. This comprehensive analysis lays a solid foundation for evidence-based policymaking, with the potential to guide India towards its ambitious developmental aspirations.

6. Policy Recommendations

1. **Targeted Investment in Lagging Regions:** Prioritise funding for north-eastern states such as Arunachal Pradesh and Meghalaya to enhance ICT infrastructure (e.g., internet and computer labs) and vocational training, aiming to raise their SRI scores above 50% within five years, leveraging UDISE+ and NSDC programmes.
2. **Strengthen STEM and Vocational Education:** Expand STEM education and skill development initiatives in states with moderate SRI scores (e.g., Uttar Pradesh, 55%), collaborating with NITI Aayog and MSDE to align training with emerging sectors such as renewable energy and advanced manufacturing, targeting a 10% annual increase in vocational training coverage.
3. **Boost Research and Start-up Ecosystems:** Incentivise R&D investment in states such as Bihar and Jharkhand (SGERD < 250 crore) through DST grants and DPIIT's Start-up India schemes, aiming to double GERD as a percentage of GSDP within a decade to foster innovation hubs.
4. **Improve Deployment Efficiency:** Address high Pupil–Teacher Ratios (e.g., Bihar at 51) by recruiting additional educators in underperforming states, using UDISE+ data to target a PTR below 20, thereby enhancing educational quality and deployment readiness.
5. **Monitor and Scale SRI Framework:** Establish a national task force to annually update the SRI using PCA, integrating new data from 2025 onwards, and share choropleth visualisations with state governments to track progress and ensure equitable development aligned with Viksit Bharat 2047 goals.

These recommendations, grounded in the SRI analysis, offer a strategic roadmap to leverage India's human capital for sustainable growth, addressing regional disparities and aligning with global sustainability objectives.

References

Anjali Meena, T., Kumar, A. and Sahu, D. (2022). Construction of education development index: A state level analysis. Turkish Journal of Computer and Mathematics Education 13(3): 5778–5786. Retrieved from https://turcomat.org/index.php/turkbilmat/article/download/7101/5778.

Arpaia, A. (2025). How skills can drive competitiveness. Intereconomics 60(1): 45–52.

Bibi, S., Khan, A. and Zhang, H. (2025). Digitalization, education, and economic growth: An analysis of developing countries. Journal of Economic Development Studies 50(2): 123–140. Retrieved from https://www.researchgate.net/publication/391637013_Digitalization_Education_And_Economic_Growth_An_Analysis_Of_Developing_Countries.

Economic Survey 2022–23. (2023). Economic Survey of India. Ministry of Finance, Government of India.

Fayyaz, S. and Bartha, Z. (2025). Research and development as a driver of innovation and economic growth: Case of developing economies. Journal of Social and Economic Development 27(1): 89–104. https://doi.org/10.1007/s40847-025-00438-9.

McKinsey India. (2023). India's Economic Future: The Role of Education and Innovation. McKinsey & Company.

Ministry of Finance. (2023). Annual Report 2023. Government of India.

Nisa, S. and Khalid, M. (2024). Impact of infrastructure on economic growth: A comparative analysis of developed and developing countries. Journal of Infrastructure Development 16(2): 78–95.

Retrieved from https://www.researchgate.net/publication/380652540_Impact_of_Infrastructure_on_Economic_Growth_A_Comparative_Analysis_of_Developed_and_Developing_Countries.
NITI Aayog. (2023). Viksit Bharat 2047: A Roadmap for Developed India. Government of India.
Patel, R. and Rao, S. (2023). Agricultural education and agri-tech skilling for modernizing Indian farming. Journal of Agricultural Economics 78(4): 345–360.
Reserve Bank of India. (2023). RBI Annual Report 2023. Reserve Bank of India.
Rong, L. (2025). The significance and contributions of startups driving economic growth. Entrepreneurship and Innovation Review 10(1): 15–30. Retrieved from https://www.researchgate.net/publication/387718864_The_Significance_and_Contributions_of_Startups_Driving_Economic_Growth.
Sahoo, P. and Dash, R. K. (2009). Infrastructure development and economic growth in India. Journal of the Asia Pacific Economy 14(4): 351–365. https://doi.org/10.1080/13547860903169340.
Sahoo, P., Nayak, S. and Mishra, S. (2025). Performance, infrastructure, and equity index in elementary education in an Eastern Indian state: A district-level analysis. Discover Education 4(1): Article 631. https://doi.org/10.1007/s44217-025-00631-2.
Sharma, R. and Gupta, P. (2024). Inclusive education policies for equitable growth in India. Indian Journal of Development Studies 29(3): 210–225.
Tleppayev, A., Tovma, N. and Zhang, Y. (2025). Education, institutions, and investment as determinants of economic growth in Central Asia and the Caucasus: A panel data analysis. Economies 13(3): Article 78. https://doi.org/10.3390/economies13030078.
United Nations Development Programme India. (2023). UNDP India Report 2023: Education and Sustainable Development Goals. UNDP.
Virmani, A. (2024). Education as a catalyst for Viksit Bharat: Bridging divides. Economic and Political Weekly 59(12): 45–53.
Westscience Journal. (2025). The role of startup ecosystems in economic growth. Westscience Economic Journal 3(2): 150–165. Retrieved from https://wsj.westscience-press.com/index.php/wsee/article/download/150/650/4090.
Zaman, K. and Moemen, M. A. (2023). Information and communication technology (ICT), growth, and development in developing regions: Evidence from a comparative analysis and a new approach. Journal of the Knowledge Economy 14(3): 1256–1278. https://doi.org/10.1007/s13132-023-01571-8.

Chapter 2

Teaching Within the Safe and Just Space

The Doughnut Pedagogy Model for Sustainability Education

Kandarp Acharya[1,3,*] and *Mili Gondaliya*[2,3]

1. Introduction

The 21st century has introduced sustainability education as a very important agenda due to global crises such as climate change, loss of biodiversity, and social inequalities, which are becoming increasingly serious. Global structures, including the United Nations Educational, Scientific, and Cultural Organization (UNESCO) Education for Sustainable Development (ESD 2030) Roadmap (UNESCO 2020), emphasise the accelerating need to develop ecological literacy, ethical accountability, and transformative capabilities in education systems. The DPM is an explicit response to this global agenda, particularly its Priority Action Area 1, which calls for ESD to be "integrated in global, regional and national and local policies", and its Priority Action Area 2, which promotes a "whole-institution approach" to "ensure we learn what we live and live what we learn". However, it is not easy to translate these

1 Ph.D. Scholar, National Institute of Educational Planning and Administration, Kharpada No Maad, Near Mandi Bajar, Siddhpur, Gujarat-384151.
2 Ph.D. Scholar, National Institute of Educational Planning and Administration, C-1342, Kaliyabid, Bhavnagar, Gujarat - 364002.
3 National Institute of Educational Planning and Administration, 17-B, Sri Aurobindo Marg, NCERT Campus, New Delhi-110016.
Email: mili@niepa.ac.in
* Corresponding author: kandarp@niepa.ac.in

DOI: 10.1201/9781003736158-3

international aspirations into practical pedagogies. The existing strategies are mostly divided into two categories, i.e., competency-based models (Wiek et al. 2011) and value-based, transformational models (Sterling 2001). Although both have made significant contributions, they do not address the tension between the need to offer minimum learning opportunities to everyone and the ecological limits within which education should be conducted.

In order to fill this gap, we propose a conceptual approach to sustainability education called the Doughnut Pedagogy Model (DPM). The model is inspired by the work of (Raworth 2017) on Doughnut Economics, which imagines that people can thrive in a safe and just space. There are two limits to this space: the lower limit, protecting the most fundamental educational rights, and the upper limit, which acknowledges ecological boundaries that education must not exceed. In this re-conceptualization of pedagogy, the DPM aims to achieve social justice and ecological responsibility in pedagogical design.

Such a reframing is especially urgent in the Global South, as education systems need to close learning gaps that remain unaddressed (World Bank 2018) and respond to climate vulnerability and environmental challenges (Kumar and Sarangapani 2021). In India, the National Education Policy (NEP) 2020 (Government of India 2020) provides a robust framework for such transformation. The policy, for instance, in its Paragraph 11.8, explicitly states that "Innovative curricula of all HEIs shall include credit-based courses and projects in the areas of community engagement and service, environmental education, and value-based education". This specific provision for credit-based environmental education is a direct and actionable mechanism designed to achieve the policy's foundational principle of developing "good human beings capable of rational thought and action, possessing compassion and empathy, courage and resilience, scientific temper," and "sound ethical moorings". This aligns with other global movements, including Global Citizenship Education (GCED) and Sustainable Development Goal (SDG) 4.7, which explicitly aims to "ensure that all learners acquire the knowledge and skills needed to promote sustainable development" (United Nations General Assembly 2015). The DPM addresses the core components of this global mandate, whose official monitoring indicator measures the mainstreaming of sustainability education within national policies, curricula, teacher education, and student assessment. This goal emphasises that learners must not just acquire knowledge but also develop the capacity to take action towards sustainability.

It is against this background that the DPM is proposed as a theoretical contribution to the study of sustainability pedagogy as well as a practical guide for educators, curriculum developers, and policymakers. It is constructed on four inseparable principles—equity, ecological consciousness, interdisciplinarity, and agency. Instead of dictating one approach, the model provides a flexible heuristic that may be tailored to a variety of educational settings, including both local classrooms in India and higher education contexts around the world. In this respect, it resembles the role of conceptual models in sustainability science (Wiek et al. 2011) and offers a framework that is globally applicable yet locally adaptable.

2. Literature Review

2.1 Framing Sustainability Learning: From Planetary Limits to Learner Agency

Modern sustainability education is informed by the dual imperative of remaining within planetary limits while maintaining a safe and fair space for all. Planetary boundaries define the ecological ceiling that humanity should not exceed (Steffen et al. 2015), whereas the social foundation of the doughnut economics model asserts that there should be a social base below which no one should fall (Raworth 2017, O'Neill et al. 2018). Combined, these frameworks move sustainability education beyond environmental knowledge towards normative judgement, systems reasoning, and action that negotiates trade-offs between social and ecological systems. Systems thinking further reinforces this foundation by providing concepts such as feedback, leverage points, and non-linearity, enabling students to understand complexity and intervene thoughtfully (Meadows 2008, Capra and Luisi 2014).

The shift towards competencies has had a particular impact in higher education. The framework by (Wiek et al. 2011) identifies five broadly accepted competencies—systems-thinking, anticipatory, normative, strategic, and interpersonal—which currently shape sustainability programmes and evaluations. These align closely with international policy frameworks, including the ESD Learning Objectives (UNESCO 2017), the ESD for 2030 Roadmap (UNESCO 2020), and the Organisation for Economic Co-operation and Development (OECD) Learning Compass 2030 (OECD 2019), where knowledge, skills, values, and attitudes converge in responsible agency. Collectively, these models provide strong guidance for curriculum and online pedagogy: students must be able to understand socio-ecological dynamics, anticipate future possibilities, negotiate values, and act collectively. It is on these foundations that the Doughnut Pedagogy Model (DPM) seeks to operationalize.

2.2 Pedagogical Foundations: Transformation, Critique, and Place

While competencies refer to what students should accomplish, pedagogy addresses how they can achieve it. Transformative learning theory emphasises critical reflection and perspective transformation, challenging students to question assumptions about growth, technology, and development that are deeply embedded (Mezirow 1997). Critical pedagogy incorporates dimensions of power, justice, and co-construction of knowledge that promote learner agency in engaging with the world (Freire 2000). Sterling (2001) goes further in calling for whole-systems change in education to reflect the systemic character of sustainability. Simultaneously, place-based pedagogy (Gruenewald 2003) reminds us that sustainability is never universal—it is practised within particular cultures, ecologies, and places—and pedagogy must remain responsive to local contexts.

The literature supports this proposition. Experiential and problem-based learning, community engagement, and collaborative inquiry have been cited by numerous studies as viable methods for building sustainability competencies. Nevertheless, several obstacles remain, such as inequalities in faculty readiness, difficulties in assessing multi-dimensional skills, and the ongoing challenge of linking local sustainability issues with global frameworks. The DPM addresses these tensions by integrating local, context-based activities within global sustainability standards.

2.3 Digital Pedagogy: From Tools to Integrated Learning Designs

Even though digital tools, including Massive Open Online Courses (MOOCs), collaborative platforms, virtual labs, and immersive media, are currently implemented in sustainability courses, they are not considered part of the learning design; rather, they are viewed as supplements. Research synthesised through literature review demonstrates that digital tools have the potential to broaden access, model complex systems, and promote collaboration. However, it also notes such difficulties as disjointed adoption, weak alignment between digital activities and competency measures, and scarce planning for adapting digital pedagogy to the resource constraints of the Global South.

The DPM addresses these gaps by centring learning design around the digital. For example, systems and anticipatory competencies can be supported through simulations and scenario tools; normative and interpersonal competencies can be strengthened through online deliberation platforms and collaborative annotation; and strategic action can be developed through structured project management spaces. Notably, the DPM is intended to be scalable in its digital application, ranging from low-bandwidth, mobile-first strategies to high-performance immersive tools such as Augmented Reality/Virtual Reality (AR/VR), so that access, equity, and institutional readiness are embedded in design decisions rather than treated as afterthoughts.

2.4 Global-to-Local Alignment: Mandates, Metrics, and Indian HEI Realities

At the international level, education has a direct responsibility for promoting sustainability. SDG 4.7 urges education systems to promote sustainable development, human rights, and international citizenship (United Nations General Assembly - UNGA 2015). The 2030 Roadmap prepared by UNESCO builds on this and specifies priority areas of action and multi-stakeholder partnerships (UNESCO 2020). The Amsterdam City Doughnut (DEAL 2020) further demonstrates how global models can be transformed into localised action plans, providing a prototype upon which the DPM can be adapted to local ecologies at the campus–community level.

These international imperatives are equally reflected in Indian national priorities. The National Education Policy 2020 focuses on holistic and multidisciplinary education, civic and environmental values, and places sustainability at the heart of higher education rather than at the fringes (Government of India 2020). This national imperative is further institutionalised by the University Grants Commission's (UGC) mandatory six-month Environmental Studies (EVS) course for all undergraduates, a directive issued in 2003. The UGC's core module syllabus provides a foundational curriculum covering topics such as natural resources, ecosystems, and environmental pollution, along with a required fieldwork component. Sustainability is also embedded through accreditation processes in India. The National Assessment and Accreditation Council (NAAC) Revised Accreditation Framework (2020) dedicates an entire section to this, specifically Criterion VII: Institutional Values and Best Practices. The framework's Key Indicator 7.1 on "Environment Consciousness" explicitly assesses institutional practices related to "energy conservation, rainwater harvesting, waste recycling, carbon neutrality" efforts, and the conduct of Green Audits. Legal precedents stemming from the Supreme Court of India's landmark rulings, notably the 1991 directive and its subsequent enforcement in *M. C. Mehta v. Union of India* (2003), established a legal imperative to incorporate environmental education as a compulsory subject across all levels of education. The judgment reaffirmed the principle that an "appropriate awareness" of environmental laws and issues is essential for citizen action.

These mechanisms, coupled with these mandates, provide an opportunity for convergence within higher education institutions (HEIs). The DPM approach to digital pedagogy can meet the goals of competency-based outcomes in NEP 2020, fulfil the accreditation requirements of NAAC, build upon the statutory coursework of UGC, and remain flexible to the realities of Indian and broader Asian institutional contexts.

2.5 Synthesis of Core Constructs and Gaps

A synthesis of the global literature reveals five recurring themes:

Competency coherence: The five-competency sustainability framework developed by (Wiek et al. 2011) remains the most feasible and popular scaffold for higher education learning outcomes.

Transformative learning through dialogue and reflection: (Mezirow 1997) and (Freire 2000) emphasise the value of dialogue, reflection, and justice-based pedagogies that move beyond mere knowledge transmission towards deeper transformation.

Systems-place coupling: Systems perspectives (Meadows 2008, Capra and Luisi 2014) are essential for understanding complexity, but they must not be abstracted beyond contextualised places (Gruenewald 2003) if abstract knowledge is to translate into local action.

Digital integration, not add-ons: The literature reports numerous digital tools applied in sustainability education, but few explicitly align digital learning activities with sustainability competencies and assessment plans.

Contextual adaptability and equity: Persistent inequalities in the Global South, such as infrastructure disparities, cultural differences, and unequal faculty access, necessitate tiered and adaptive digital pedagogical designs to ensure equity and inclusion.

These themes define the architecture of the Doughnut Pedagogy Model (DPM), positioning it as a competency-based, digitally integrated, and context-responsive model of higher education sustainability learning.

2.6 Implications for Model Building

This review provides both the components and the logic for assembling the DPM. Competencies (Wiek et al. 2011) and pedagogical principles (transformative, critical, and place-based) are integrated alongside digital affordances (simulations, collaborative platforms, analytics, microlearning) and policy anchors (UNESCO 2017, 2020, OECD 2019, NEP 2020, UGC 2003, NAAC 2020). It also clarifies the assembly logic: all digital-pedagogical aspects should be explicitly aligned with competencies, and systems–place coupling should be embedded within learning tasks. Reflection and deliberation must be scaffolded to develop normative judgement, and the model should be tiered to accommodate disparities in institutional resources, particularly in the Global South.

The essential gaps found in the literature review – mainly the lack of adopted digital-pedagogical structures and competency-based assessment systems – become the challenges that the DPM seeks to address. In this respect, the model is not merely a synthesis but a design response to long-standing deficiencies in sustainability education.

3. Conceptual Framework: The Doughnut Pedagogy Model (DPM)

3.1 Defining the Doughnut Pedagogy Model (DPM)

The Doughnut Pedagogy Model (DPM) is based on the doughnut framework originally created in the field of sustainability economics (Raworth 2017) and projected onto the teaching and learning practices of higher education. Similar to the way the doughnut defines a safe and just space for humanity between an ecological ceiling and a social foundation, the DPM defines a safe and just space for pedagogy. This space is intended to prevent poor digital and educational design while promoting inclusiveness, justice, and wellbeing among students.

As shown in Figure 1, the ecological ceiling forms the outermost ring, the social foundation constitutes the innermost ring, and the safe learning space falls in between. Digital pedagogy practices and sustainability competencies can be visually emphasised in the middle space and sustained therein.

***Outer ring – Pedagogical ecological ceiling*:** The outer boundary is where educational practices get unsustainable. Examples include excessive exposure to screens, the use of resource-intensive technology that contributes to the digital divide, or teaching strategies that encourage consumerist rather than critical thinking. This ring serves as a reminder that pedagogy itself should not reinforce unsustainability.

***Inner ring – Pedagogy social foundation*:** The inner boundary prioritises the fundamental requirements to which every learner must have access, including equity, inclusivity, accessibility, and both emotional and cognitive wellbeing. It ensures that pedagogy is designed to support diverse learners, reduce digital gaps, and foster justice and student agency.

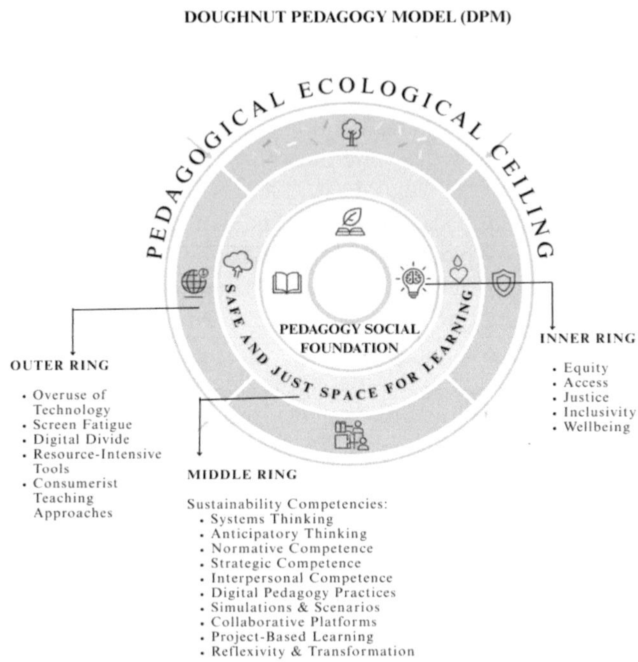

Figure 1. Doughnut pedagogy model (DPM). Source: Authors' elaboration (adapted from Raworth 2017, Wiek et al. 2011).

***Middle space – The safe and just space for learning*:** Between these two boundaries lies the balanced space of pedagogy. Here, students and teachers engage in responsible, inclusive, and future-oriented practices. Sustainability competencies can be nurtured in this space through digital, reflective, equitable, and transformative pedagogy.

In brief, the DPM presents pedagogy as a design problem: how to maintain teaching and learning in the safe space between ecological limits and the demands of social justice.

3.2 Theoretical Basis of the DPM

The DPM is founded on three theoretically related traditions:

3.2.1 Sustainability Models

The model is based on the framework of doughnut economics proposed by (Raworth 2017) and the idea of planetary boundaries (Steffen et al. 2015), placing pedagogy within ecological and social limits. It underlines the fact that education must always remain connected with sustainable values.

3.2.2 Transformative and Critical Pedagogy

The inner ring of the model is informed by ideas of transformative learning theory of (Mezirow 1997) and critical pedagogy of (Freire 2000), which focus on reflection, justice and empowerment of learners.

3.2.3 Systems and Place-Based Thinking

The model draws upon systems thinking (Meadows 2008) and place-based pedagogy (Gruenewald 2003), emphasising context-awareness. This enables the DPM to function flexibly in international environments while grounding learning in local realities. This flexibility is particularly critical for higher education in the Global South, where resource constraints and diversity directly influence pedagogy.

Collectively, these underpinnings make sure that the DPM is as much visually engaging as it is theoretically sound.

3.3 Key Pedagogical Principle of the DPM

The Doughnut Pedagogical Model (DPM) puts its theoretical underpinnings into practice using four guiding principles of pedagogy that provide sustainability in teaching and learning:

3.3.1 Competency Alignment

All learning activities are designed around sustainability competencies—systems-thinking, anticipatory, normative, strategic, and interpersonal (Wiek et al. 2011). Rather than viewing sustainability as an add-on feature, this principle makes it the lens through which teaching and assessment are structured.

3.3.2 Digital Responsibility

Technology is selected not on the basis of novelty but on its alignment with sustainability outcomes. This implies prioritising low-footprint and accessible tools. For example, in bandwidth-intensive settings, mobile-first microlearning or lightweight collaborative platforms may be preferred over resource-heavy virtual reality applications.

3.3.3 Equity and Inclusion

DPM infuses the principle of social foundation of Doughnut Economics, ensuring that pedagogy is inclusive of diverse learners. It accepts diverse socio-economic realities, languages, and capabilities and helps to make all learners meaningfully involved.

3.3.4 Reflexivity and Transformation

Cycles of reflection, dialogue, and action are encouraged, enabling learners to question their assumptions, explore values, and imagine alternative futures. Education thus shifts from content transmission to the cultivation of transformative agency.

3.4 Practical Integration of the DPM in Higher Education Classroom

The value of the DPM lies in being usable. It translates abstract sustainability principles into specific pedagogical planning, which can be easily applied to higher education:

3.4.1 Curriculum Design

Courses are structured to integrate international frameworks with local issues. For example, an urban planning module might explore water shortages in the city where students are studying while relating this issue to the planetary boundary on freshwater consumption.

3.4.2 Learning Activities

Systems and anticipatory competencies are developed through digital simulations and scenario-building exercises. Online debates and collaborative annotation tools foster normative and interpersonal competencies. Digitally mediated project-based activities support the development of strategic competencies by linking analytical work to collective action.

3.4.3 Assessment Approaches

In addition to exams, the DPM focuses more on portfolios, reflective journals, and community-linked projects that show competency development. Learning can become more transparent by visualizing student progress via the use of digital dashboards.

3.4.4 Faculty Development

Faculty members are encouraged to design digitally sustainable courses, ensuring that technology use is intentional, inclusive, and purposeful. Training focuses not only on technical skills but also on the ethical dimensions of sustainability pedagogy.

3.4.5 Institutional Practices

At a broader level, the DPM aligns with accreditation and policy frameworks such as NAAC (2020) and (UNESCO 2020). This dual role—compliance and transformation—makes it a practical yet forward-looking strategy for higher education institutions in India and globally.

3.4.6 Value of the DPM

At its core, the Doughnut Pedagogy Model (DPM) is more than a conceptual framework; it is a human-centred model of teaching and learning. It emphasises that education must inherently embody the same principles of sustainability it seeks to promote: responsible resource use, respect for the dignity of all learners, and the preparation of students not only to understand sustainability but also to practise it in their personal and professional lives. By positioning pedagogy within the safe and just space of the doughnut, higher education gains the potential to cultivate graduates capable of envisioning and working towards a more sustainable future.

4. Methodology of Framework Development

The model was created as a result of a conceptual mapping activity rather than as field-based research. The authors aimed to bring together the Doughnut Pedagogy Model (DPM) with ideas from sustainability science, educational thought, and higher education policy and legal frameworks. The authors did not perform any surveys or classroom experiments, and the model is based solely on secondary sources.

4.1 Scope and Sources

The authors extensively searched Scopus and Google Scholar and also consulted official repositories such as the National Council of Educational Research and Training (NCERT), the University Grants Commission (UGC), and the Ministry of Education in order to establish a trustworthy knowledge base. Moreover, legal archives were examined to trace constitutional and judicial perspectives. The authors searched literature available in the English language only, up to June 2024.

4.2 Inclusion and Exclusion

Such items as conceptual and theoretical writing, policy documents, and appropriate legal decisions were included. Empirical case studies with findings that were highly context-specific and not readily generalizable were excluded. This enabled us to maintain the attention on theory-construction, and structure design.

4.3 Process

The model was developed through a systematic conceptual mapping and analysis process:

- The most important concepts were initially recorded on an evidence table with references.
- Ideas were coded to find similar categories, such as competencies, teaching methods, or justice-oriented principles.
- Comparison and reflection were used to cluster the codes under larger themes.
- These themes were placed within the doughnut metaphor and aligned with guiding policy anchors (NEP 2020, the NAAC accreditation framework, and UNESCO's ESD goals).

4.4 Non-Empirical Nature

This study should therefore be considered a conceptual contribution. The framework is presented as a model that may initiate discussion and practice; however, it does not preclude the possibility of future research to test and refine the DPM under real educational conditions.

5. Discussion

The Doughnut Pedagogy Model (DPM) enhances sustainability education by combining digital pedagogy with the doughnut model of a safe and just space proposed by (Raworth 2017). It re-contextualises sustainability learning not merely as the transmission of competencies but as a pedagogical challenge: how to negotiate ecological responsibility and social inclusion within digital teaching–learning cycles. This section positions the DPM within international discourses, demonstrates its local applicability to India and the Global South, and offers reflections on stakeholder impact as well as potential limitations.

5.1 Positioning the DPM Globally

International models of sustainability education have established significant points of reference but are often pedagogically underdeveloped. Sustainability competencies and Education for Sustainable Development (ESD) goals articulated by (UNESCO 2017, 2020), along with the OECD Learning Compass (2019), emphasise what students are expected to know and achieve, but remain largely outcome-driven.

The DPM addresses this gap by embedding pedagogy within the doughnut metaphor. The outer ecological ceiling warns against unsustainable digital practices such as high-carbon infrastructures or exclusionary technologies, while the inner social foundation demands equity, wellbeing, and justice in digital access. It is within this middle ground—the safe space—that educators can cultivate sustainability competencies through digital practices that are reflective, inclusive, and future-oriented. In this way, the DPM supplements existing frameworks by operationalising pedagogy, rather than merely defining learner competencies.

5.2 Local Relevance: India and the Global South

In contexts such as India and the wider Global South, sustainability education is shaped by scale, diversity, and persistent disparities in access to technology. This institutional context is reinforced by national policy, notably the National Education Policy (Government of India 2020) and the National Curriculum Framework for School Education (NCERT 2023). This new framework consolidates the shift towards holistic, competency-based, and socio-emotional learning. The NCF (2023) frames the ‘Environment’ as a cross-cutting theme (Part C, Chapter 5), to be integrated across all subjects, and introduces a new national approach to ‘Learning Standards, Pedagogy, Content, and Assessment’ (Part A, Chapter 3). Accreditation bodies, such as the National Assessment and Accreditation Council (NAAC 2020, RAF Criterion VII: Institutional Values and Best Practices), explicitly incorporate sustainability and digital responsiveness into their evaluation metrics. Judicial interventions, such as *M. C. Mehta v. Union of India* (2003), and regulatory requirements, such as the University Grants Commission (UGC) mandatory Environmental Studies course (UGC 2003, Undergraduate EVS Course), further institutionalise sustainability within higher education.

The practical implications of the Doughnut Pedagogy Model for key stakeholders in higher education are summarized in Table 1.

Table 1. Stakeholder Implications.

Stakeholder	**Application of DPM**	**Expected Outcomes**
Faculty	Integrate sustainability competencies (systems, anticipatory, normative, strategic, interpersonal) into course design while using digital tools responsibly (e.g., simulations, online collaboration, mobile-first microlearning).	Inclusive and reflective classrooms; enhanced learner agency; demonstrable competency-based outcomes.
Institutions	Embed DPM principles (equity, ecological responsibility, digital inclusivity) into curriculum reforms and teaching–learning practices. Incorporate DPM evidence into accreditation (e.g., NAAC).	Policy and accreditation compliance; institutional reputation as sustainability leaders; scalable and context-appropriate digital pedagogy.
Policymakers & Networks	Utilize the DPM as a model to translate global frameworks (UNESCO 2017, 2020, SDG 4.7, OECD 2019) into actionable pedagogy, while supporting faculty and institutional capacity-building.	Stronger policy–practice alignment; accelerated realization of sustainability mandates; adaptable regional guidelines for digital pedagogy.
Learners (Indirect Stakeholder)	Participate in learning environments shaped by the DPM's "safe and just" principles, ensuring equitable access, responsible digital use, and reflective, transformative education.	Graduates equipped with sustainability competencies, digital fluency, and the agency to act as change-makers.

The DPM aligns with these imperatives by emphasising digital accountability. Its mobile-first, low-bandwidth, and context-sensitive pedagogy ensures that sustainability education remains equitable in resource-constrained settings. By aligning global frameworks with local material realities, the DPM strengthens sustainability education in higher education while making the model regionally relevant and responsive to the Global South.

5.3 Limitations and Future Direction

The conceptual framework of the Doughnut Pedagogy Model (DPM) introduced in this chapter is a synthesis of the literature, formulated in a structured manner but not empirically investigated. To this end, several limitations must be considered.

First, the DPM is based on ideas from sustainability science, transformative pedagogy, and digital learning models, but it has not yet been applied in real-world contexts. Its efficacy in enhancing learning outcomes, developing sustainability competencies, or guiding institutional reform remains empirically unproven.

Second, the framework synthesises global and Indian policy references (e.g., UNESCO's ESD for 2030 Roadmap [2020] and NEP 2020). Nevertheless, higher education systems operate within diverse cultural, political, and ecological contexts. The model may therefore need adaptation to align with regional priorities, institutional capacities, and disciplinary traditions.

Third, while the DPM is conceptually clear, it currently lacks specific implementation guidelines and evaluation tools. Future practice should operationalise the framework through curriculum design templates, faculty development modules, and assessment rubrics.

Future research should focus on empirical validation and iterative refinement of the model through:

- Case studies of universities piloting DPM-aligned curricula.
- Comparative research across regions and disciplines to test adaptability.
- Participatory research with students and educators to co-create strategies.
- Design-based research (DBR) cycles to refine the model through classroom experimentation.

This chapter establishes the DPM as a reference framework, inviting scholarly discussion, modification, and verification by acknowledging these constraints and proposing specific paths for research.

6. Conclusion

This chapter addressed a key gap in sustainability education, namely the absence of a structured digital pedagogical framework. Drawing upon international references (UNESCO 2017, Wiek et al. 2011, OECD 2019) and national policy anchors such as NEP 2020 (Government of India 2020) and NAAC guidelines (NAAC 2020) in India, the study proposed the Doughnut Pedagogy Model (DPM). By adapting the doughnut metaphor to pedagogy, the DPM positions digital learning within an ecological ceiling while maintaining a social foundation, thereby providing a secure space for transformative and future-oriented learning.

The value of the model lies in its integration of sustainability competencies with digital pedagogy, while balancing global principles with local realities. In doing so, it offers higher education a conceptual guide to recalibrate not only what students learn but also how teaching, delivery, and assessment are designed.

For higher education to play a central role in the sustainability transition, frameworks such as the DPM must move from the margins into mainstream curricula and institutional strategy. Although empirical validation remains necessary, the DPM offers a conceptual and feasible roadmap for embedding sustainability in higher education. By foregrounding ecological responsibility and social justice, the DPM not only prepares learners to navigate the future but also empowers them to actively contribute to a more sustainable world.

References

Capra, F. and Luisi, P. L. (2014). The Systems View of Life: A Unifying Vision. Cambridge University Press. https://www.cambridge.org/core/books/systems-view-of-life/35186BA5B12161E469C4224B6076ADFE.

Dagli, G., Altinay, F. and Altinay, Z. (2025). Education for sustainable development: challenges and opportunities of transformative learning and teaching. Sustainability 17(6): 2440. https://doi.org/10.3390/su17062440.

Doughnut Economics Action Lab. (2020). The Amsterdam city doughnut. DEAL. shttps://doughnuteconomics.org/projects/26.

Doughnut Economics Action Lab. (2020). Doughnut economics for university courses: A toolkit. DEAL. https://doughnuteconomics.org/tools/doughnut-economics-university-courses.

Freire, P. (2000). Pedagogy of the oppressed (30th anniversary ed.). Continuum. https://hccc.edu/abouthccc/resources/documents/freire-pedagogy-of-the-oppressed.pdf.

Government of India. (2020). National Education Policy 2020. Ministry of Education. https://www.education.gov.in/sites/upload_files/mhrd/files/NEP_Final_English_0.pdf.

Gruenewald, D. A. (2003). The best of both worlds: A critical pedagogy of place. Educational Researcher 32(4): 3–12. https://doi.org/10.3102/0013189X032004003.

Huang, R., Adarkwah, M. A., Liu, M., Hu, Y., Zhuang, R. and Chang, T. (2024). Digital pedagogy for sustainable education transformation: Enhancing learner-centred learning in the digital era. Frontiers of Digital Education 1(4): 279–294. https://doi.org/10.1007/s44366-024-0031-x.

Karthikeyan, K., Maheswari, R., Dhanasekar, E., Gowrishankar, R., Ashok Kumar, R. and Thomas Jeyanth Herbert, M. (2025). Educational sustainability: An integrated analysis of socioeconomic, technological, and environmental impacts on higher education students. Prabandhan: Indian Journal of Management 18(3): 45–67. https://doi.org/10.17010/pijom/2025/v18i3/174231.

M. C. Mehta v. Union of India, W.P. (C) No. 860 of 1991, 2003 (S.C.). https://indiankanoon.org/doc/1419757/.

Meadows, D. H. (2008). Thinking in Systems: A Primer. Chelsea Green Publishing. https://www.chelseagreen.com/product/thinking-in-systems-a-primer/.

Mezirow, J. (1997). Transformative learning: Theory to practice. New Directions for Adult and Continuing Education 1997(74): 5–12. https://doi.org/10.1002/ace.7401.

National Assessment and Accreditation Council. (2020). Manual for universities: Revised accreditation framework (RAF). http://www.naac.gov.in.

National Council of Educational Research and Training. (2023). National curriculum framework for school education 2023. Ministry of Education, Government of India. https://ncert.nic.in/pdf/NCF-School-Education-Pre-Draft.pdf.

O'Neill, D. W., Fanning, A. L., Lamb, W. F. and Steinberger, J. K. (2018). A good life for all within planetary boundaries. Nature Sustainability 1(2): 88–95. https://doi.org/10.1038/s41893-018-0021-4.

Organisation for Economic Co-operation and Development. (2019). OECD learning compass 2030 (Concept Note Series). https://www.oecd.org/education/learning-compass-2030/.

Raworth, K. (2017). Doughnut Economics: Seven Ways to Think Like a 21st-Century Economist. Chelsea Green Publishing. https://www.chelseagreen.com/product/doughnut-economics-paperback/.

Rockström, J., Steffen, W., Noone, K., Persson, Å., Chapin, F. S., III, Lambin, E. F. et al. (2009). A safe operating space for humanity. Nature 461(7263): 472–475. https://doi.org/10.1038/461472a.

Sarangapani, P. M. and Pappu, R. (eds.). (2021). Handbook of Education Systems in South Asia. Springer. https://doi.org/10.1007/978-981-15-5654-7.

Steffen, W., Richardson, K., Rockström, J., Cornell, S. E., Fetzer, I., Bennett, E. M. et al. (2015). Planetary boundaries: Guiding human development on a changing planet. Science 347(6223): 1259855. https://doi.org/10.1126/science.1259855.

Sterling, S. (2001). Sustainable education: Re-visioning learning and change (Schumacher Briefing No. 6). Green Books. https://eric.ed.gov/?id=ED464791.

United Nations Educational, Scientific and Cultural Organization. (2017). Education for sustainable development goals: Learning objectives. https://unesdoc.unesco.org/ark:/48223/pf0000247444.

United Nations Educational, Scientific and Cultural Organization. (2020). Education for sustainable development: A roadmap. https://unesdoc.unesco.org/ark:/48223/pf0000374802.

United Nations General Assembly. (2015). Transforming our world: The 2030 Agenda for Sustainable Development (A/RES/70/1). United Nations. https://sdgs.un.org/2030agenda.

University Grants Commission. (2003). Environmental studies: A compulsory undergraduate course. (E. Bharucha, Ed.). University Grants Commission. https://www.ugc.ac.in/oldpdf/modelcurriculum/env.pdf.

World Bank. (2018). The World Bank annual report 2018. The World Bank. https://www.worldbank.org/en/about/annual-report/annual-report-2018.

Wiek, A., Withycombe, L. and Redman, A. (2011). Key competencies in sustainability in higher education—Toward an agreed-upon reference framework. Sustainability Science 6(2): 203–218. https://doi.org/10.1007/s11625-011-0132-6.

Section 2

Education as a Pillar of Sustainability

Chapter 3

Designing E-Learning for Systems Thinking in Sustainability Education

Palak Gupta[1,*] and *Mini Verma*[2]

1. Introduction- Education For Sustainable Development

The 21st century poses numerous sustainability challenges such as depletion of resources, climate change, loss of biodiversity, and societal inequality that require more than isolated knowledge in environmental science or policy and instead demand a complete shift in the way individuals think, conceptualize, analyze, and respond to advanced systems. Systems thinking (Meadows 2008, Senge 2006, Wiek et al. 2011), which focuses on interrelationships, feedback loops, and dynamic interactions among components of a system, emerges as a critical cognitive skill for navigating sustainability issues. Education for Sustainable Development (Sterling 2011, UNESCO 2023) (ESD), as recognized by UNESCO, envisions enriching all learners with enhanced skillsets, values, and attitudes required for proactive actions and better decision-making. However, traditional educational models often lack the holistic and innovative thinking that is much needed for sustainability criteria. Therefore, the potential of e-learning is immense, as its flexible, user-friendly, and adaptable nature enables digital education to offer innovative and creative ways to simulate and manage complex systems, thereby rendering collaboration and supportive experiential learning at a worldwide scale.

[1] Associate Professor, Department of Management, School of Business, Galgotias University, Plot No. 2, Yamuna Expy, Sector 17A, Greater Noida, Uttar Pradesh-203201.

[2] Assistant Professor, Department of IT, Delhi Institute of Higher Education, Plot No. 20 C, Techzone 4, Greater Noida West, Uttar Pradesh 201306.

Email: minieverma@gmail.com

* Corresponding author: palakgupta1529@gmail.com

DOI: 10.1201/9781003736158-5

This chapter aims to analyze the design principles and pedagogical strategies for creating and enhancing e-learning platforms that promote systems thinking within the framework of sustainability education. It explores how technology-enhanced learning environments can promote interactive engagement of learners in application-based and real-world problems. From simulations and gamification to case-based, scenario-centric learning, collaborative problem-solving, and reflection-based practice, the study highlights various tools and techniques that support cognitive engagement and systems literacy. Further, the chapter also includes a discussion on the importance of contextualizing e-learning for diverse learners by considering socio-economic, cultural, and linguistic factors through the integration of systems thinking and sustainability content in digital formats.

1.1 Understanding Systems Thinking in Sustainability

Systems thinking (Meadows 2008, Senge 2006, Wiek et al. 2011) is a method to analyze how components of a system interact and function over time within larger systems. In sustainability education, systems thinking provides learners with the ability to address socio-economic and environmental complexities. It emphasizes feedback loops, non-linear interactions, delays, and emergent properties within societal and ecological systems that extend far beyond linear cause-and-effect reasoning.

The crux of systems thinking in sustainability lies in understanding that problems such as climate change, water scarcity, and pollution cannot be solved in isolation, as these issues are interconnected, and interventions in one area may hamper others. For example, electric vehicles certainly reduce urban air pollution but also increase the demand for lithium mining, which is associated with high socio-environmental costs.

Systems thinking (Meadows 2008, Senge 2006, Wiek et al. 2011) helps learners understand trade-offs, accept stakeholders' ideas, and then evaluate long-term inferences. It promotes the ability to:

- Identify and relate patterns,
- Understand systems dynamics,
- Analyze feedback mechanisms,
- Classify control points for intervention,
- Forestall unintentional consequences.
- Navigate complexity and uncertainty

It also enhances empathy, ethical reasoning, and decision-making in situations where alternative choices and priorities compete. However, for integrating systems thinking into education, learners should engage with complex real-world scenarios, explore diverse variables, and construct mental models of dynamic systems. As e-learning (Clark and Mayer 2023, Bates 2022) environments provide strong visualization tools, they help simulate outcomes through interactive problem-solving tools and thereby offer a promising medium for developing these competencies.

This chapter positions systems thinking not merely as a cognitive tool but as a necessity for sustainability. When linked with e-learning platforms, students transition from disjointed knowledge to integrated understanding, thereby leading toward informed, tech-savvy, and future-oriented global citizens.

2. e-Learning Design Principles for Systems Thinking

For designing e-learning environments that foster systems thinking in sustainability education, a learner-centered and constructivist approach is needed, as such environments enable learners to engage with complex visualization systems, test interventions, and reflect on outcomes. The following design principles are important:

2.1 Simulation of Real-World Systems

Simulations (Sterman 2011, Meadows 2008) enable learners to visualize and model dynamic systems (e.g., climate change, energy consumption, or water cycles) and study their interdependence and impact on one another. Figure 1 below shows a climate system simulation connecting variables such as greenhouse gas emissions, temperature, ice melt, and sea-level rise through feedback loops.

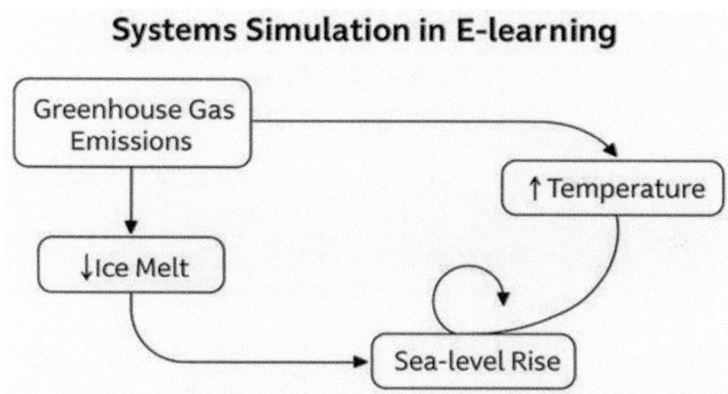

Figure 1. Systems Simulation in E-learning (Clark and Mayer 2023, Bates 2022).

2.2 Interactive and Visual Learning Tools

Interactive diagrams, concept maps, and dynamic dashboards help learners build and revise mental models of complex systems. Figure 2 below depicts a visual web of interconnected elements: Economy ↔ Environment ↔ Society, with nodes such as energy, transport, policy, culture, and consumption.

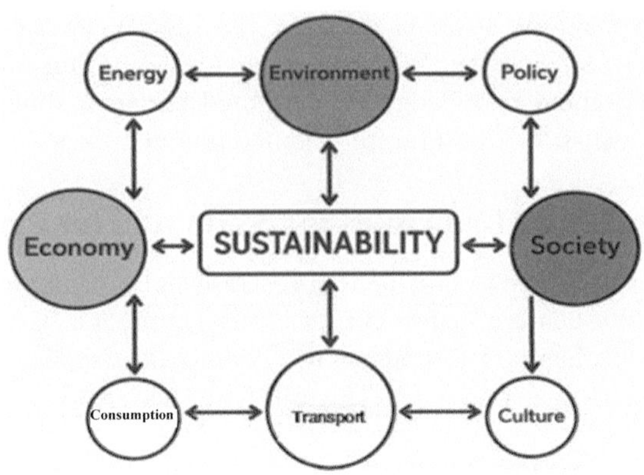

Figure 2. Interactive Concept Map on Sustainability.

2.3 Problem-Based and Scenario-Based Learning

Learners explore sustainability problems through real-life case studies and collaborative challenges that require systemic solutions. Figure 3 below describes a circular diagram showing stages: *Context → Problem Framing → Data Exploration → Systems Mapping → Decision Making → Reflection.*

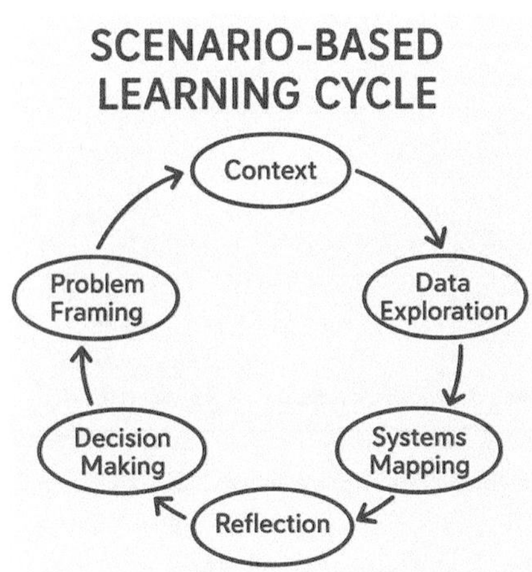

Figure 3. Scenario-Based Learning Cycle.

2.4 Feedback and Reflection Mechanisms

Learners benefit from regular feedback on their systems understanding, along with prompts for reflective journaling or peer discussion. Figure 4 below illustrates a loop showing input (learner action), process (simulation/assessment), output (feedback), and reflection leading to deeper understanding.

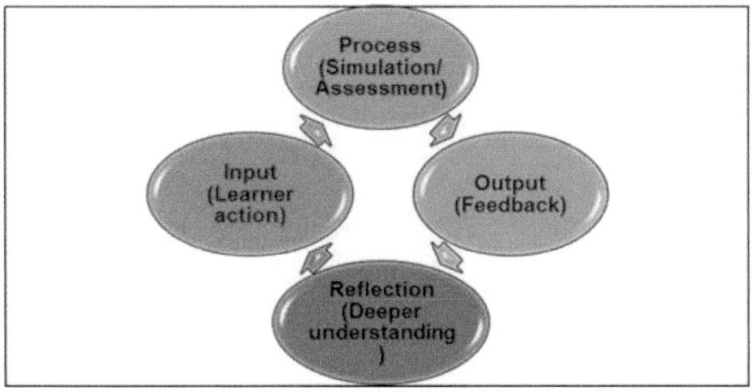

Figure 4. Feedback Loop in E-learning (Clark and Mayer 2023, Bates 2022).

2.5 Collaborative Learning and Stakeholder Perspectives

Sustainability challenges (IPCC 2023, Wiek et al. 2011) involve diverse stakeholders. Collaborative e-learning tools (forums, role-play, discussion boards) help learners understand multiple viewpoints and co-create solutions. In Figure 5 below, a spider diagram illustrates a central issue (e.g., deforestation) surrounded by stakeholder nodes (government, local communities, businesses, NGOs, future generations) and the interests/conflicts between them.

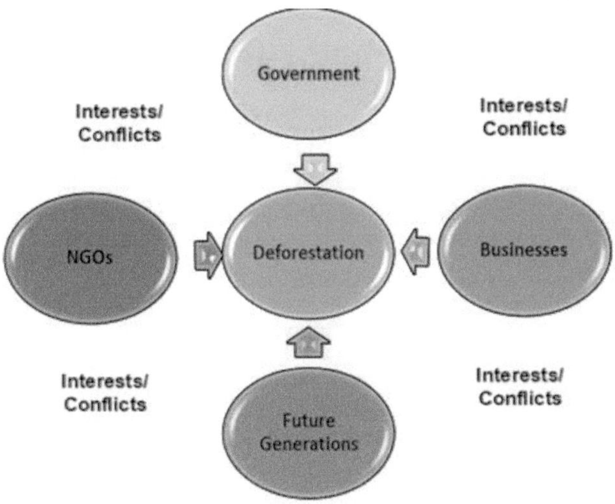

Figure 5. Stakeholder Mapping Tool.

3. Designing E-Learning Environments: A Framework

The framework for designing e-learning environments, based on Clark and Mayer (2023) and Bates (2022), as shown in Table 1 below, emphasizes five key components essential for fostering systems thinking in sustainability education. It includes system mapping tools like Loopy and Kumu that help visualize interconnections;

Table 1. E-learning Environment Framework.

Design Element	Description	Example
System Mapping Tools	Encourage visualization of system components and interactions	Loopy, Kumu
Simulations and Models	Help explore "what-if" scenarios and feedback loops	En-ROADS, SimCityEDU
Collaborative Platforms	Promote knowledge co-creation and diverse perspectives	Padlet, Miro, Google Jamboard
Narrative and Scenario-Based Learning	Enhance emotional engagement and contextual understanding	Interactive stories on climate migration
Assessment for Systems Thinking	Use formative tools that evaluate holistic understanding	Concept maps, reflection essays

simulations and models such as En-ROADS and SimCityEDU that allow learners to explore dynamic systems and test scenarios; collaborative platforms like Padlet and Miro that support group learning and diverse perspectives (Johnson and Johnson 1991); narrative and scenario-based learning that engages learners through real-world contexts and problem-solving; and assessments like concept maps and reflective essays that evaluate students' ability to think systemically. Together, these elements create an interactive, reflective, and application-oriented digital learning environment aligned with sustainability goals.

4. Technology Supporting Systems Thinking

It involves digital tools and platforms that enhance the ability to understand, analyze, and address complex, interconnected problems—particularly in areas like sustainability, education, business strategy, and public policy. Below is an overview of key technologies that support systems thinking:

4.1 Systems Modeling and Simulation Software

- **Purpose:** Enables users to visualize and simulate complex systems and feedback loops.
- **Examples:**
  - **Stella Architect** – Used for modeling dynamic systems in education, sustainability, and economics.
  - **Vensim** – Widely used for system dynamics and causal loop diagramming.
  - **AnyLogic** – Multi-method simulation software combining system, discrete-event and agent-based modeling.

4.2 Mind Mapping and Concept Mapping Tools

- **Purpose:** Help structure and visualize relationships between concepts and ideas.
- **Examples:**
  - **CmapTools** – Developed for education and research to support conceptual thinking.
  - **Miro** and **MindMeister** – Collaborative online whiteboards ideal for brainstorming and mapping systems.

4.3 Data Analytics and Visualization Tools

- **Purpose:** Reveal patterns, correlations, and system behaviors through data.
- **Examples:**
  - **Power BI**, **Tableau** – Visual analytics platforms for large data sets.
  - **Google Data Studio** – Useful for integrating and visualizing real-time data.
  - **Gephi** – For network and relationship mapping in social and environmental systems.

4.4 Artificial Intelligence and Machine Learning

- **Purpose:** Detect systemic patterns and provide predictive insights.
- **Applications:**
  - Analyzing complex supply chains or climate systems.
  - Optimizing resource allocation and risk forecasting.
  - Example: AI (Russell and Norvig 2021) models for urban planning simulate interactions between energy, transport, and population growth.

4.5 Digital Twins and Cyber-Physical Systems

- **Purpose:** Real-time simulation and monitoring of physical systems through digital replicas.
- **Applications:**
  - Smart cities
  - Green energy grids
  - Industrial sustainability and circular economy systems
  - Example: **Siemens MindSphere** for industrial IoT insights.

4.6 Geographic Information Systems (GIS)

- **Purpose:** Support spatial systemic analysis.
- **Tools:**
  - **ArcGIS**, **QGIS** – Map social, economic, and environmental systems.
  - Used in urban planning, disaster management, ecosystem analysis.

4.7 Collaborative Platforms and Knowledge Systems

- **Purpose:** Enable distributed teams to work on systemic challenges.
- **Examples:**
  - **Kumu** – A system mapping tool for understanding relationships and leverage points.
  - **Slack + Notion/Confluence** – Enable integrated team workflows and systems thinking in project management.

4.8 Educational Technologies for Systems Thinking

- **Purpose:** Support experiential and inquiry-based learning.
- **Examples:**
  - **MOOCs** (Coursera, edX) with system thinking modules (e.g., "Think Again", "Global Sustainable Development").
  - Simulations (Sterman 2011, Meadows 2008) and Games like Fishbanks, Climate Interactive's En-ROADS, or World Climate Simulation.

4.9 Augmented Reality (AR) and Virtual Reality (VR) (Radianti et al. 2020)

- **Purpose:** Provide immersive experiences of complex systems.
- **Applications:**
  - Environmental education
  - Ecosystem dynamics
  - Virtual city planning
  - Example: EcoMUVE, an AR/VR (Radianti et al. 2020) ecosystem-based learning platform.

5. Challenges and Opportunities of Technology in Supporting Systems Thinking

Systems thinking (Meadows 2008, Senge 2006, Wiek et al. 2011) requires a holistic view of interconnected systems, feedback loops, and emergent behaviors. While technology provides powerful tools to support this cognitive approach, its implementation comes with both challenges and opportunities.

5.1 Challenges

5.1.1 Cognitive Overload and Complexity

- **Issue:** Tools like simulation models or data visualizations can overwhelm users with too much information.
- **Impact:** Learners or decision-makers may focus on isolated variables rather than holistic understanding.

- **Example:** Users misinterpreting causal loop diagrams or system maps due to their intricate interdependencies.

5.1.2 Accessibility and Digital Divide

- **Issue:** Advanced tools (e.g., AI (Russell and Norvig 2021)-driven platforms, GIS systems) require high-end computing infrastructure and digital literacy.
- **Impact:** Limits equitable access in low-resource institutions or regions.
- **Example:** Rural schools unable to integrate VR (Radianti et al. 2020)-based systemic learning due to hardware constraints.

5.1.3 Lack of Interdisciplinary Integration

- **Issue:** Many tools are designed for specific disciplines (e.g., engineering, economics), making cross-domain systems thinking difficult.
- **Impact:** Silos persist, hindering comprehensive system-based problem-solving.
- **Example:** A smart city planner using digital twins may not integrate social or behavioral systems.

5.1.4 Usability and Learning Curve

- **Issue:** Systemic tools like Vensim or AnyLogic require technical expertise.
- **Impact:** Educators and professionals may hesitate to adopt them.
- **Solution Needed:** Intuitive, user-friendly interfaces with guided learning.

5.1.5 Data Quality and Integration

- **Issue:** Systemic models often rely on real-time, heterogeneous data sources.
- **Impact:** Inconsistent or missing data compromises the reliability of system insights.
- **Example:** Climate simulators performing poorly due to gaps in regional environmental data.

5.1.6 Resistance to Change

- **Issue:** Institutions or individuals may resist systems thinking and technology adoption due to entrenched linear mindsets.
- **Impact:** Undermines innovation and limits impact of tech-enabled strategies.

5.2 Opportunities

5.2.1 Enhanced Decision-Making

- **Benefit:** Tools like AI (Russell and Norvig 2021), simulations, and digital twins allow stakeholders to experiment with scenarios, test interventions, and anticipate outcomes.
- **Example:** En-ROADS allows policymakers to simulate carbon reduction policies and visualize climate impacts.

5.2.2 Democratization of Knowledge

- **Benefit:** MOOCs, open-source platforms (like Kumu or CmapTools), and mobile learning apps make systems thinking accessible globally.
- **Impact:** Empowers educators, students, and practitioners to think systemically.

5.2.3 Integration of Real-Time Data

- **Benefit:** IoT and cloud technologies allow continuous feedback from systems in fields like logistics, agriculture, and health.
- **Example:** Real-time water usage data informing sustainable farming systems.

5.2.4 Immersive Learning Experiences

- **Benefit:** AR/VR (Radianti et al. 2020) technologies make abstract systems (like ecosystems or economic models) more tangible and experiential.
- **Example:** Virtual field trips to study interdependent natural systems.

5.2.5 Collaborative Problem-Solving

- **Benefit:** Platforms like Miro, Notion, and Slack support co-creation and cross-disciplinary dialogue.
- **Impact:** Enables group-based systemic analysis and design thinking in classrooms and professional settings.

5.2.6 Scalability and Adaptability

- **Benefit:** Cloud-based systemic tools can scale from classrooms to global enterprises.
- **Example:** Businesses using cloud-based supply chain simulators to plan for sustainability across continents.

6. Research Methodology

6.1 Research Design

In this chapter, mixed-methods research design is adopted using both qualitative and quantitative approaches to explore how e-learning platforms can be effectively designed to foster systems thinking in sustainability education. The combination allows for detailed findings of learner experiences while also enabling the measurement of learning outcomes.

6.2 Research Objectives

The key objectives of the study are:

- To identify pedagogical strategies that promote systems thinking in sustainability education.

- To analyze the effectiveness of various e-learning design elements (e.g., interactivity, multimedia, collaborative tools).
- To evaluate the impact of a specially designed e-learning module on learners' ability to apply systems thinking to sustainability issues.

6.3 Population and Sample

- **Target Population:** Undergraduate and postgraduate students enrolled in sustainability-related programs in higher education institutions.
- **Sample Size:** 120 participants (60 each in experimental and in control group). The chosen **sample size (N = 120, 60 per group)** was guided by power analysis, which indicated that this number would be sufficient to detect a medium effect size (Cohen's $d = 0.5$) at $\alpha = .05$ with 80% power in paired t-tests and ANOVA comparisons.
- **Sampling Technique:** Stratified random sampling to ensure diversity across disciplines (e.g., environmental science, business, engineering).

6.4 Research Tools and Instruments

A pre- and post-test structured questionnaire was used to assess awareness and application of systems thinking, conceptual understanding of sustainability, and attitudinal change toward systemic solutions. The instrument was pilot-tested with 15 students from a comparable cohort, and minor wording revisions were made for clarity. Internal consistency reliability was confirmed (Cronbach's $\alpha > 0.80$).

Systems Thinking Competency Scale adapted from established frameworks (Wiek et al. 2011) was also used to assess skills like identifying feedback loops, analyzing trade-offs, and identifying leverage points.

6.5 Data Collection Procedures

- **Pre-test:** Assess baseline knowledge and systems thinking ability.
- **Intervention:** Implement the e-learning module over 4 weeks (experimental group only).
- **Post-test:** Measure changes in systems thinking and sustainability understanding.
- **Interviews:** Conducted post-intervention to enrich quantitative findings.

6.6 Ethical Considerations

Ethical compliance was ensured through measures such as confidentiality of participants' responses with secure password protection, institutional approval for conducting the research, participants' consent to be included in the study, equity and fairness (as the e-learning module was made accessible to control group participants to ensure they were not disadvantaged), and data protection for at least 5 years.

7. Data Analysis & Results

To evaluate the effectiveness of the designed e-learning module in enhancing systems thinking among learners, a quantitative data analysis approach was employed. Descriptive statistics, including mean and standard deviation, were used to summarize learners' performance in pre-test and post-test assessments across experimental and control groups. To determine the statistical significance of observed improvements, inferential statistical methods were applied. A paired sample t-test was conducted within the experimental group to assess the pre- and post-intervention score differences, revealing whether the change was statistically significant. Furthermore, a one-way ANOVA was used to compare post-test scores between the experimental and control groups, establishing whether the intervention had a differential impact. This combination of descriptive and inferential analysis offered robust evidence for evaluating the impact of the e-learning design on fostering systems thinking competencies.

Explanation:

- **Purpose:** Table 2 provides an overview of students' performance before and after the e-learning intervention (experimental group) compared to a group that did not receive the intervention (control group).
- **Experimental Group:**
  - **Pre-test Mean = 52.4** → Baseline knowledge.
  - **Post-test Mean = 74.6** → Substantial improvement after using the e-learning module.
  - **Mean Difference = 22.2**, indicating a **42.37%** increase.
- **Control Group:**
  - Minimal improvement (mean difference = 2.3 or 4.44%), suggesting no significant learning gain without intervention.

Figure 6 below shows that the intervention had a positive impact on learners' understanding and application of systems thinking and sustainability concepts.

Explanation:

- **Purpose:** To statistically test whether the difference in the pre- and post-test scores of the experimental group is significant.
- **t-value** = As shown in Table 3 above, t-value is 14.85: a high value indicating a large effect size.

Table 2. Descriptive Statistics – Pre-test and Post-test Scores.

Group	N	Mean (Pre-test)	SD (Pre-test)	Mean (Post-test)	SD (Post-test)	Mean Difference	% Increase
Experimental	60	52.4	6.2	74.6	5.7	22.2	42.37%
Control	60	51.8	6.5	54.1	6.1	2.3	4.44%

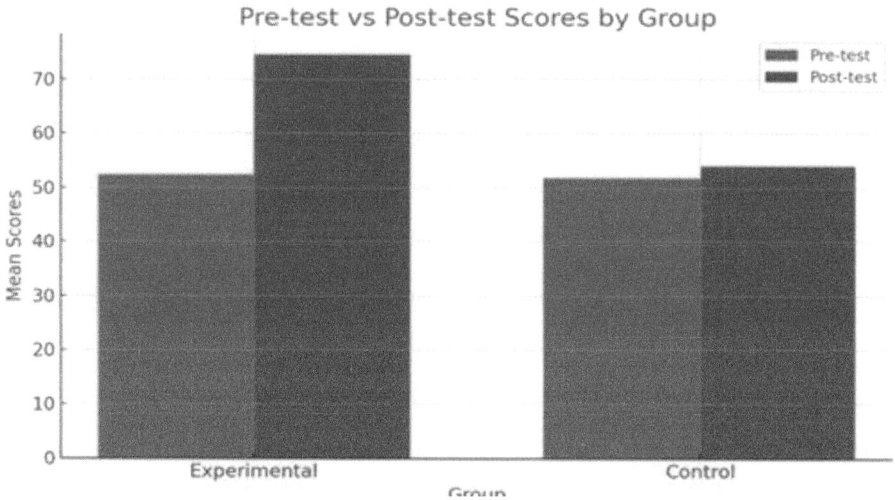

Figure 6. Students' Pre-test and Post-test performance in Experimental & Control Groups.

Table 3. Paired t-test Results – Experimental Group.

Test	t-value	df	p-value	Interpretation
Pre vs Post	14.85	59	< 0.001	Statistically significant improvement

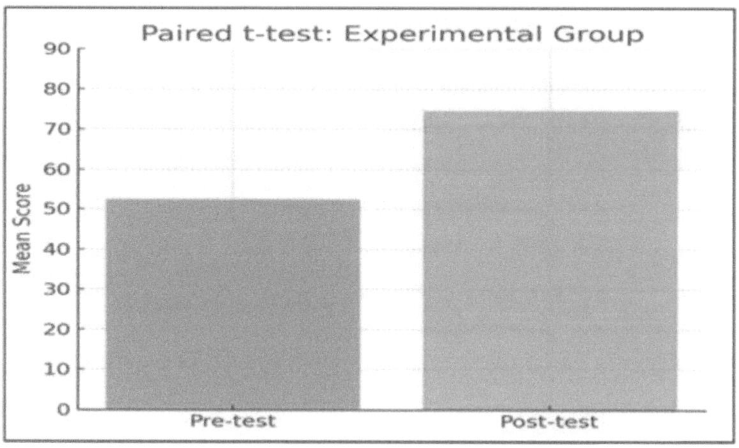

Figure 7. Pre- and Post-test scores of the experimental group.

- **df (degrees of freedom)** = 59: Based on the number of participants minus one.
- **p-value < 0.001**: Means the likelihood that this result is due to chance is less than 0.1%—**strong evidence** of effectiveness.

Figure 7 above shows that the e-learning module significantly improved students' systems thinking skills.

Explanation:

- **Purpose:** To compare the post-test scores between the experimental and control groups to determine if the improvement is due to the intervention. Results are shown in Table 4 below.
- **F-value = 32.57:** A high value indicating large between-group variability compared to within-group variability.
- **p-value < 0.001:** The difference is statistically significant.

Figure 8 shows that there is a significant difference in learning outcomes between the experimental and control groups. This supports the conclusion that the e-learning module effectively enhanced systems thinking.

Table 4. ANOVA – Comparison Between Groups.

Source of Variation	SS	df	MS	F-value	p-value	Interpretation
Between Groups	10560.3	1	10560.3	32.57	< 0.001	Significant difference between groups
Within Groups	37854.6	118	320.8			
Total	48414.9	119				

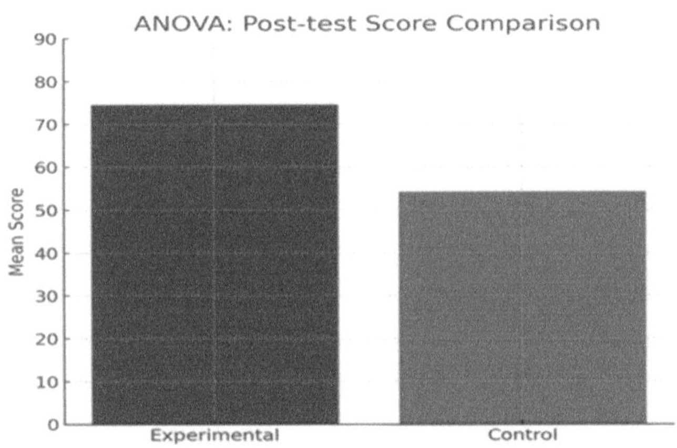

Figure 8. Post-test scores between the experimental and control groups.

8. Future Directions for Technology in Supporting Systems Thinking

As global challenges grow in complexity—ranging from climate change and supply chain disruptions to public health crises—there is an increasing need for technologies that not only process data but also enable holistic, systems-oriented thinking. The future of technology-supported systems thinking will be shaped by innovation across software, pedagogy, data science, and ethics.

8.1 Integration of AI (Russell and Norvig 2021) with Systems Thinking Tools

- **Future Direction:** Embedding artificial intelligence (AI (Russell and Norvig 2021)) into system modeling platforms to automate pattern recognition, scenario forecasting, and system behavior prediction.
- **Potential:** AI (Russell and Norvig 2021) agents could identify unintended consequences, optimize system interventions, and guide users through complex decision paths.
- **Example:** Intelligent tutors embedded in modeling tools like Vensim or Kumu that assist learners in identifying feedback loops.

8.2 Interdisciplinary and Transdisciplinary Platforms

- **Future Direction:** Development of collaborative tools that merge knowledge from multiple domains (environmental science, economics, psychology, etc.).
- **Potential:** Encourages diverse stakeholder participation in systemic problem-solving—from policymakers to educators and community members.
- **Example:** Integrated platforms combining climate modeling, socio-political simulations, and economic forecasting in one interface.

8.3 Ethical and Inclusive System Design

- **Future Direction:** Embedding ethics, equity, and sustainability into system modeling frameworks.
- **Potential:** Ensures that marginalized voices and long-term planetary impacts are incorporated in systemic interventions.
- **Example:** Participatory modeling platforms that allow input from indigenous communities or local stakeholders in urban planning systems.

8.4 Systems Thinking in Education Technology (EdTech)

- **Future Direction:** Curriculum-integrated tools that embed systems thinking at all levels—from primary schools to professional training.
- **Potential:** Personalized learning paths that track systemic competencies, such as causal reasoning, feedback loop identification, and scenario analysis.
- **Example:** AR/VR (Radianti et al. 2020)-based modules simulating real-world ecosystems or economic systems to build experiential understanding.

8.5 Cloud-Based, Open-Access System Simulations **(Sterman 2011, Meadows 2008)**

- **Future Direction:** Cloud-powered models and repositories that allow learners, researchers, and policymakers to access and modify systemic models globally.

- **Potential:** Fosters a culture of open science and continuous collaborative improvement.
- **Example:** A global library of digital twins for ecosystems, supply chains, or public health networks, available on platforms like GitHub or Google Cloud.

8.6 Cognitive and Neuroadaptive Technologies

- **Future Direction:** Integration of brain-computer interfaces (BCIs) or attention-tracking tools to adapt systemic learning environments in real-time.
- **Potential:** Enhances engagement and reduces cognitive overload by aligning content delivery with learners' mental state.
- **Example:** Neurofeedback-driven dashboards that adjust system complexity or visualization based on user comprehension.

8.7 Blockchain and Trust-Based System Design

- **Future Direction:** Use of blockchain to build trust, transparency, and accountability in multi-stakeholder system models.
- **Potential:** Decentralized validation of data inputs, especially in sustainability tracking, supply chains, and policy simulations.
- **Example:** Blockchain-enabled carbon accounting systems integrated into systemic climate simulations.

8.8 Integration with Real-Time Global Viewpoints

- **Future Direction:** Connecting systemic models with IoT sensors, Earth observation satellites, and citizen science platforms.
- **Potential:** Provide better systemic analysis of planetary health indicators in real-time.
- **Example:** A live dashboard displaying water cycles, ecosystem resilience or global disease breakout enabled by global observatory data.

9. Conclusion

To manage the ever-growing challenges of sustainability such as biodiversity loss, resource depletion, climate change, and social inequity, technical knowledge needs to be coupled with a new way of thinking, viz., systems thinking, as it emphasizes interconnections, feedback mechanisms, and holistic understanding through a cognitive framework. In such a situation, e-learning serves as a potent medium to boost such thinking and sustainability-based education, which is more inclusive, accessible, and transformative. This chapter has explored how well-designed e-learning environments can cultivate systems thinking through the integration of real-world simulations, interactive tools, problem-based learning, and interdisciplinary content. Advanced technologies like gamified simulations, concept mapping, systems modeling platforms, and AR/VR can generate interactive and immersive learning experiences for students to visualize complexity, explore cause-effect relationships, and engage in collaborative sense-making.

However, in designing such effective e-learning environments for systems thinking, pedagogical alignment is highly required. Educators need to shift from linear content delivery to strategies that support inquiry, reflection, and systems literacy. This is achieved by enabling adaptive learning paths, integrating feedback loops into curriculum design, and creating collaborative digital spaces for the development of knowledge. Further, the integration of real-time data and open-access learning platforms with AI offers strong potential for scaling systems education worldwide. However, this must be approached with careful attention to ethical considerations, inclusivity, and critical consciousness.

Finally, e-learning for systems thinking in sustainability education is not merely digital delivery; rather, it is about reimagining how we teach, learn, and act in a complex world. By leveraging technology with innovation and intention, we can prepare learners who not only act as systemic thinkers but also as change agents capable of shaping a more sustainable and equitable future.

References

Bates, T. (2022). Teaching in a Digital Age: Guidelines for Designing Teaching and Learning. Tony Bates Associates Ltd.

Clark, R. C. and Mayer, R. E. (2023). E-learning and the Science of Instruction: Proven Guidelines for Consumers and Designers of Multimedia Learning. John Wiley & Sons.

IPCC. (2023). Climate Change 2023: Synthesis Report. Intergovernmental Panel on Climate Change.

Johnson, D. W. and Johnson, F. P. (1991). Joining Together: Group Theory and Group Skills. Prentice Hall, Inc.

Meadows, D. H. (2008). Thinking in Systems: A Primer. Chelsea Green Publishing.

Radianti, J., Majchrzak, T. A., Fromm, J. and Wohlgenannt, I. (2020). A systematic review of immersive virtual reality applications for higher education: Design elements, lessons learned, and research agenda. Computers & Education 147: 103778. https://doi.org/10.1016/j.compedu.2019.103778.

Russell, S. J. and Norvig, P. (2021). Artificial Intelligence: A Modern Approach, Global Edition 4e.

Senge, P. M. (2006). The Fifth Discipline: The Art and Practice of The Learning Organization. Broadway Business.

Sterling, S. (2011). Transformative learning and sustainability: Sketching the conceptual ground. Learning and Teaching in Higher Education 5(11): 17–33.

Sterman, J. D. (2011). Communicating climate change risks in a skeptical world. Climatic Change 108: 811. https://doi.org/10.1007/s10584-011-0189-3.

UNESCO. (2023). Education for sustainable development: A roadmap. United Nations Educational, Scientific and Cultural Organization.

Wiek, A., Withycombe, L. and Redman, C. L. (2011). Key competencies in sustainability: a reference framework for academic program development. Sustainability Science 6(2): 203–218. https://doi.org/10.1007/s11625-011-0132-6.

Chapter 4

Legal Education 2.0

A Roadmap For Future Pedagogical Approaches

Aparajita Banerjee,[1] *Subhayan Chakraborty*[2,*] and *Lokesh Kumar Jena*[3]

1. Introduction

The history of legal education in India can be taken as symbolic of the compulsions of tradition versus innovation that face professional training in fast-changing cultures. Traditionally, Indian legal education developed in the colonial context, which was designed to address the administrative and commercial demands of the empire and not those of the local societies. This formative colonial history has had permanent doctrinal and theoretical legacies on curricular and institutional structures that endure to the present day, even in the post-independence era (Ramaswamy 2020). Albeit the current interventions of the contemporary legislature related to the modernisation of standards and the expansion of access through the Advocates Act of 1961 and the creation of national schools of law, modern criticisms would prove that there remains a concern with rote-based, teacher-centred pedagogies and a failure to update skill sets to meet practical needs, interdisciplinarity, and technological literacy (Yu et al. 2018, Ramaswamy 2020). The twenty-first-century legal practice is defined

[1] National Law University, Agartala, Tripura, India - 799015.
[2] State Panchayat Resource Centre, Arundhuitnagar, Tripura, India - 799003.
[3] School of Humanities, Social Sciences and Management, IIT Bhubaneswar, Odisha, India – 752050.
Emails: asstregistrar@nlutripura.ac.in, lkj10@iitbbs.ac.in
* Corresponding author: subhayan.chakraborty@gov.in

DOI: 10.1201/9781003736158-6

by unprecedented globalisation, a paradigm shift in technology, and an increasingly convoluted regulatory terrain nationally and transnationally. Jurisdictions across the globe are responding by redesigning curricula and international relationships and including practice-based modules, including clinical legal education and problem-based learning, to foster both local and global expertise (Tan et al. 2006, Miyazawa et al. 2008, Shalini 2021). It is important to note that comparative analysis highlights that mandatory practical training and interdisciplinary exposure are key to ensuring that legal graduates are able to meet rising professional requirements and keep pace with international counterparts (Ghosh 2014, Yu et al. 2018). In parallel with these global trends, advances in AI and digital technologies, particularly since 2020, have restructured the cognitive and ethical capabilities expected of legal professionals (Smith 2019, Wang 2019, Janecek et al. 2020).

The disparity between academia and legal market, given that legal education in India is falling short of an increasingly technologised legal market, exacerbates an already problematic situation of employability, access, and social and economic stratification (Janecek et al. 2020, Ramaswamy 2020). Due to fast-paced technological disruption, unmodifiable curricular templates become less effective and soon out-of-date (Janecek et al. 2020, Wu and Tang 2022). This chapter aims to outline a strategic plan for the future of legal education in India as it commemorates one hundred years of independence in 2047 by critically analysing current reforms, global best practices, and emerging pedagogies based on the use of technology. The study questions the opportunities and challenges of transformative integration, including regulatory redesign and digital inclusion, ethical application of AI, and curricular renewal, to achieve a future-ready, inclusive, and socially conscious legal education ecosystem.

2. Literature Review

2.1 Colonial Legacy and Pedagogical Stagnation

Indian legal education has been dominated by its colonial-era models that have codified the epistemology, curriculum, and pedagogy of the system. This history produced law schools that were strongly profession-oriented, creating clerks for the colonial bureaucracy rather than critical thinkers capable of adapting to India's heterogeneous legal system (Yu et al. 2018). There was little space in the curriculum for indigenous law and social realities, and practical training remained limited, a situation that persisted into modern formations of law degrees. Ramaswamy observes a growing disjuncture in India between coursework and the practice of law in both three-year and five-year programmes, with little in the way of experiential or clinical courses. Such a difference contrasts with requirements applied in jurisdictions such as China and Pakistan, which stipulate more practice-related training, a practice quite rare in India (Yu et al. 2018, Ramaswamy 2020).

Colonial legacies also established note-based teaching pedagogy, where the instructor has the dominant role and instruction focuses on rote doctrine rather than analytical, advocacy, and critical abilities, and which has been slow to reform even in the post-independence modernisation era (Dasgupta 2010). They also permeate institutional culture: bureaucratic rigidity quenches interdisciplinarity and tolerance for alternative ways of thinking, marginalised legal histories, gender critiques, and indigenous jurisprudence. In places where clinical legal education was introduced, incumbent practices have prevented meaningful curricular change (Ghosh 2014). Such shortcomings are becoming more visible as India seeks to remain competitive in a world where legal training is moving towards technology integration, innovation, and responsiveness to social issues (Badrinarayana 2014, Smith 2019).

Despite the emergence of a few sporadic instances of innovation, like case critical approaches to Western jurisprudence and relative absence of problem-based learning, they are too much fringe to make a lasting impact on the established structural and pedagogical order of legal education (Likhovski 2021, Shalini 2021). The long-term reliance on the colonial doctrinal approach has continued to impact the quality of graduating lawyers, student readiness for the legal profession, and consequently the broader project of legal modernisation and social justice in India (Yu et al. 2018, Ramaswamy 2020). As a result, the task is not only to restructure curricular content and instructional approaches but to thoroughly challenge and move beyond colonial epistemologies that still limit the potential and value of legal education in India.

2.2 Education 4.0 and Society 5.0

Legal education can transform globally, and the paradigms of Education 4.0 and Society 5.0 are driving this shift. Education 4.0 aligns with the Fourth Industrial Revolution, where learning becomes learner-centred, technology-enhanced, flexible, creative, and transdisciplinary. It reshapes content, pedagogy, and student engagement through AI, machine learning, advanced analytics, and IoT (Demartini and Benussi 2017, Muktiarni et al. 2019, Tikhonova and Raitskaya 2023). It promotes digital fluency, critical thinking, project-based learning, inquiry-based learning, blended learning, and the use of AI tools to personalise online learning and prepare students to adapt to evolving careers (Almeida and Simoes 2019).

Education 4.0 in legal education places greater emphasis on interactive and technology-driven pedagogical practice compared to traditional lecturing (Smith 2019). AI, large language models, serious games, simulators, and argumentation platforms can support student self-direction and practical application, including digital hearings as exercises and data analysis (Almeida and Simoes 2019, Smith 2019, Pelaez-Sanchez et al. 2024). However, there still exists a disconnection between the use of technology and the reorganisation of pedagogical strategies, particularly in countries with limited infrastructure and lower faculty capacity (Smith 2019, Alda et al. 2020). Although certain universities have incrementally refined their digital resource procurement and technological literacy (Alda et al. 2020), AI implementation remains limited due to substantial inadequacies in reliable infrastructure, teacher training, and end-to-end integration (Butt et al. 2020, Pelaez-Sanchez et al. 2024).

Communicated through Japanese policy documents and international discourse, Society 5.0 represents an expansion beyond Industry 4.0, envisioning a more humanistic, inclusive, and sustainable society (Narvaez et al. 2021, Ziatdinov et al. 2024). It balances human needs and ethics with advanced technologies to enhance quality of life, social responsibility, and sustainability (Narvaez et al. 2021, Hamedani et al. 2024, Mouazen et al. 2025). In the context of legal education, this necessitates graduates grounded in ethical reasoning, social justice orientation, and responsiveness to emerging socio-legal issues, prioritising both technological competence and human-centred capabilities to produce a workforce prepared for a world in which technology and humanity no longer oppose but collaborate in the best interests of society (Hamedani et al. 2024, Ziatdinov et al. 2024).

A transformational leadership role is critical in guiding higher and legal education towards technological empowerment, constant evolution, and interdisciplinary convergence of ethics, social responsibility, and sustainability (Bohari et al. 2024, Hamedani et al. 2024). It facilitates personalised education that develops not only highly technical skills but also humanistic ideals aligned with Society 5.0 (Narvaez et al. 2021, Bohari et al. 2024, Hamedani et al. 2024). However, gaps remain in terms of curricular design, resource distribution, and alignment with the emerging needs of Society 5.0, especially in developing economies (Alda et al. 2020, Butt et al. 2020, Zengin et al. 2021). The overlap between Education 4.0 and Society 5.0 represents not merely technological modernisation but a normative transformation towards cultivating digital fluency, moral accountability, and the socialisation of law experts.

2.3 AI in Legal Education

AI in legal education has gained increasing focus in curriculum design, pedagogy, and the training of lawyers across the globe. Conventional teacher-based practices need to transition towards participatory, experiential, and cross-disciplinary teaching in response to accelerating technological transformation, including AI (Smith 2019, Prakash and Nair 2024). New technologies align with Education 4.0 by promoting pedagogical and technological expertise characterised by autonomous and interactive, student-generated learning and high levels of technological literacy among future lawyers of the 2040s and beyond (Demartini and Benussi 2017, Muktiarni et al. 2019, Butt et al. 2020, Tikhonova and Raitskaya 2023).

According to recent empirical and case studies, the use of AI tools has the potential to transform legal learning outcomes with strong, positive outcomes (Almeida and Simoes 2019, Wu and Tang 2022, Farber 2024). AI integration transforms the model of pedagogy beyond the passive sharing of knowledge to learn-by-doing, including autonomous inquiry, cross-disciplinary problem-solving, and iterative legal reasoning on problems that are complex and real-world (Wu and Tang 2022, Pelaez-Sanchez et al. 2024). LLMs offer possibilities for differentiation and adaptation using domain-specific knowledge to enable context-sensitive feedback and support scalable assessment, differentiated instruction, and ongoing formative evaluation (Farber 2024, Prakash and Nair 2024). However, ethical and legal risks cannot be ignored, including bias, accountability, transparency concerns, and hallucinated or inaccurate outputs (Janecek et al. 2020).

Moreover, law educators and policymakers must address structural obstacles to incorporating AI into legal education, such as digital infrastructure inequities, insufficient faculty training, and persistent scepticism regarding the pedagogical validity of technological tools (Alda et al. 2020, Butt et al. 2020, Prakash and Nair 2024). It is important to note that while AI presents opportunities to promote more autonomous and diversified pedagogical practices, it simultaneously necessitates new policies to safeguard data confidentiality, mitigate algorithmic bias, and preserve the integrity of legal argumentation and decision-making (Farber 2024). By integrating the two foundational paradigms, Education 4.0 and Society 5.0, the theoretical framework underpinning this study is further strengthened through the application of Human-Centric Transformational Leadership Theory (Ziaeian 2024). This theoretical approach provides a robust and critical lens through which leadership requirements necessary for harnessing pedagogical innovation and ensuring the ethical integration of emerging technologies in legal education can be examined. By prioritising a human-centred approach, this leadership paradigm highlights not only the need for profound organisational and educational transformation but also the ethical responsibilities of leaders as agents navigating technological evolution (Cassidy and Koroll 1994).

Transformational leadership theory, as discussed in contemporary management and education research, demonstrates a complex interconnection between transformational leadership behaviours and the development of an innovation-friendly climate that promotes creativity and innovation among followers (Khalili 2016). Transformational leaders inspire and motivate their constituents to move beyond traditional performance limits, fostering product and process innovation essential for reforming legal education in response to evolving societal and technological demands (Al-Husseini and Elbeltagi 2016).

3. Methodology

The research design adopted in this study takes a qualitative and multi-pronged approach to conduct an in-depth examination of the development, contemporary challenges, and trajectory of legal education in India in the context of technological upheaval and pedagogical innovation. The method is grounded in recognised paradigms of interpretivism and Education 4.0 to facilitate a detailed and forward-looking inquiry (Demartini and Benussi 2017, Tikhonova and Raitskaya 2023).

3.1 Research Design

The study is based on a qualitative operationalisation of conceptual analysis, within which document analysis, thematic synthesis, and comparative review are prioritised as core methodologies. Using a qualitative approach, the study positions legal education as an evolving system influenced by historical legacies, regulatory trends, global socio-economic developments, and emerging technologies such as AI and online learning platforms (Muktiarni et al. 2019, Tikhonova and Raitskaya 2023, Prakash and Nair 2024, Pelaez-Sanchez et al. 2024). It is supported by an interpretivist epistemological position, which acknowledges that legal education is a socially constructed and continuously evolving domain (Spiegel 2005, Ghosh 2014).

The study relies on a wide scope of data, including an array that is systematically chosen to ensure triangulation in addition to depth of analysis:

- *Peer-reviewed academic publications*: Level-specific, primarily on legal education in India and other jurisdictions across the world, including articles on Education 4.0, AI integration, and skills transformation in higher education (Miyazawa et al. 2008, Demartini and Benussi 2017, Smith 2019, Tikhonova and Raitskaya 2023, Prakash and Nair 2024, Pelaez-Sanchez et al. 2024).
- *Regulatory and policy documentation*: This would include, among others, the Advocates Act of 1961, Bar Council of India resources, government white papers, and institutional reports, which are vital to legal education reform in India (Ghosh 2014, Ramaswamy 2020).
- *Technology-focused case studies*: Assessment of AI-augmented learning instruments and comparative experiences gained from international systems, especially those concentrating on the fusion of technology and practice-based approaches in legal pedagogy (Smith 2019, Janecek et al. 2020, Wu and Tang 2022, Prakash and Nair 2024).
- *Expert validation*: Synthesising the views of experts cited in the literature, especially legal educators, curriculum designers, and professionals working in digital education, to validate findings and contextualise emerging trends (Janecek et al. 2020, Ramaswamy 2020, Prakash and Nair 2024).

4. Analytical Framework

The theoretical framework is a combination of Education 4.0, which emphasises automation, personalised, competency-based, and learner-centred models (Demartini and Benussi 2017, Almeida and Simoes 2019, Tikhonova and Raitskaya 2023), and Society 5.0, which proposes a human-centred approach to technological adoption in the interest of society (Pelaez-Sanchez et al. 2024). An elaborated discussion of the process of transformation of legal education from traditional to future-ready stages can be found in Figure 1 below.

The lessons derived from thematic coding were iteratively analyzed across data sources, leading to the synthesis of recurring motifs, such as:

- Colonial legacy, and the continued teacher-centred, doctrinal pedagogy (Ahmad 2009, Ramaswamy 2020),
- The emergence and the problems of transnational legal education models (Tan et al. 2006, Miyazawa et al. 2008, Ahmad 2009, Husa 2017),
- Pedagogical innovation and the lack of infrastructure harnessed through digital and AI (Muktiarni et al. 2019, Smith 2019, Wu and Tang 2022, Prakash and Nair 2024, Pelaez-Sanchez et al. 2024),

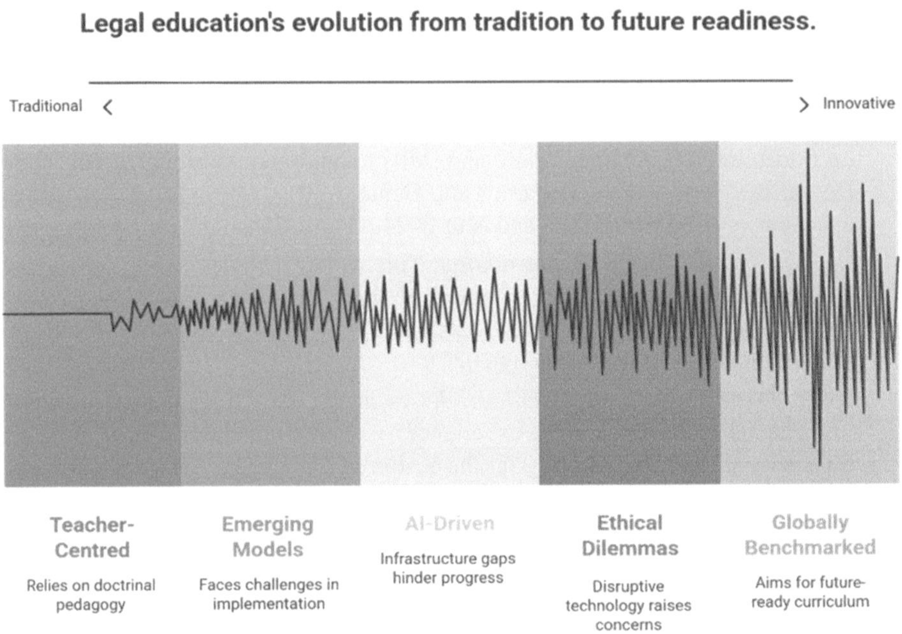

Figure 1. Factors affecting the evolution of legal education (Source: Authors).

- Skill gaps, digital disparities, as well as the ethical issues that arise when disruptive technology is integrated (Smith 2019, Janecek et al. 2020, Szocik and Jurkowska-Gomułka 2021),
- Plans of future-ready, globally benchmarked legal curriculum (Miyazawa et al. 2008, Yu et al. 2018, Smith 2019, Janecek et al. 2020, Tikhonova and Raitskaya 2023).

5. Comparative Dimension

A comparative grid-based discussion anchors Indian legal education within the evolving developments of legal education in advanced jurisdictions such as the United States, the United Kingdom, and selected East Asian contexts. Interdisciplinarity, practice orientation, technological modernisation, and regulatory adaptation are compared, with particular attention to postgraduate reforms in East Asia and European efforts to move from nationally confined legal models towards transnational and comparative influences (Miyazawa et al. 2008, Kinghan 2012, Husa 2017, Yu et al. 2018). The synthesis of comparative data provides stable benchmarking and facilitates adaptation of globally recognised pedagogical best practices (Sugarman and Sherr 2001, Tan et al. 2006, Smith 2019).

Ethical rigour is ensured because only publicly available source material, anonymised expert testimony as presented in the literature, and published case evidence are used. No personally identifiable information or primary data requiring ethical clearance were involved. The entire research process was governed by principles of attribution, informed consent, and academic integrity (Janecek et al. 2020, Ramaswamy 2020).

Despite the comprehensive nature of the methodology, certain limitations remain. The absence of empirical field research and face-to-face classroom ethnography restricts analysis of *in situ* pedagogical practices, particularly in rural or under-resourced law schools, as highlighted in studies on Indian legal education (Ghosh 2014, Ramaswamy 2020). Moreover, uneven access to academic and technological resources between Tier-1 and Tier-2/Tier-3 law schools may reveal differences in applicability and generalisability (Yu et al. 2018, Alda et al. 2020, Ramaswamy 2020). However, these limitations are partially mitigated through triangulation with comparative and international evidence, ensuring that the overall analysis remains inclusive and future-oriented (Tikhonova and Raitskaya 2023).

6. Findings

The results of the present research outline the severe constraints within the conventional framework of legal training in India when contrasted with the new opportunities provided by pedagogical changes brought about by the invention of AI. Three themes stand out: a deeply ingrained focus on rote learning, severe gaps in the technological skills possessed by graduates, and the incipient but irregular use of AI tools in legal education.

On the one hand, rote learning and lecturing remain ubiquitous conditions in Indian law schools, as evidenced by the 2022 National Law School of India University (NLSIU) survey, according to which 78% of law students report being unhappy with current teaching approaches (NLSIU 2022). Such didactic methods have been widely criticised because they have proven ineffective in encouraging students to think critically, reason analytically, or approach problems practically—qualities that attorneys require in today's legal field (Ahmad 2009, Dasgupta 2010, Smith 2019).

Secondly, this deeply rooted attitude has exposed transparent flaws in terms of digital literacy and the application of modern legal technologies. The Bar Council of India (BCI) 2021 report suggests that only 12% of Indian law graduates are proficient in digital legal tools such as AI-assisted legal research platforms, e-discovery tools, and case management platforms (Pathak and Sharma 2025). The lack of systematic inclusion of technological skills in curricula, along with infrastructural shortcomings reflected in similar Education 4.0 environments across geographies, limits graduates' ability to effectively engage with technologically mediated legal processes (Alda et al. 2020, Janecek et al. 2020, Ryan 2020).

Thirdly, although AI has the potential to transform legal education—through personalised learning enabled by intelligent tutoring systems, automated grading, and adaptive curriculum design—its application in Indian legal academia remains in its early stages and scattered in scope. Currently, India risks trailing behind international competitors who are increasingly integrating AI into hybridised learning structures that combine technological strengths with traditional mentorship and peer-to-peer educational experiences (Smith 2019, Prakash and Nair 2024, Pelaez-Sanchez et al. 2024).

Besides, the risks associated with AI use are complex. The standardisation embedded in many AI-based learning systems may hinder nuanced insights; infrastructural barriers deny equal access to students; and the absence of consistent policy environments inhibits experimental learning and scalability. These concerns align with broader critiques of Education 4.0 research, which argue for strategic investment in digital infrastructure, faculty development, and ethical governance to facilitate transformative pedagogical shifts (Almeida and Simoes 2019, Reichlich 2021, Tikhonova and Raitskaya 2023, Prakash and Nair 2024).

This discussion sets up an empirical basis of strategic curricular reform and policy-making to align Indian legal education with the modern global educational quality.

7. Discussion

Education 4.0 and Society 5.0 offer highly fascinating synergies applicable to the transformation of legal education in India by focusing on re-designing the legal educational space not only in terms of technology absorption but also including the internalisation of the wider objectives of societal life. This interface creates a learning ecology where legal students can fully invest in the use of emerging technologies like artificial intelligence (AI), not only as devices to facilitate the efficiency of learning, but also as seminal catalysts of social equity and democratised access to justice. Through AI and Industry 4.0 technologies, legal education has the potential to erase geographic, socioeconomic, and resource disparities and offer underserved communities access to quality, personalised legal training, which will further expand access to legal services and literacy (Almeida and Simoes 2019, Pelaez-Sanchez et al. 2024, Wang and Yang 2024).

The concept of AI integration with societal goals involves intentional curricular and institutional designs that increase inclusion, ethical awareness, and the development of practical skills. Intelligent tutoring systems, adaptive learning platforms, and knowledge-mapping algorithms that harness the power of AI can deliver personalised instruction that matches the needs of different students from different backgrounds. Furthermore, integrating AI understanding into law studies will allow future lawyers to manoeuvre the complexities concerning AI regulation, discrimination, and algorithmic accountability, issues that are part of the smart governance ethos of Society 5.0 (Prakash and Nair 2024, Pelaez-Sanchez et al. 2024).

In order to operationalise such synergies, policy interventions ought to operate at the curricular, human resource, and institutional levels (as may be observed in Figure 2):

7.1 Curriculum Overhaul

A significant redesign is necessary to reorganise legal education in response to the paradigm modifications provided by Education 4.0 and Society 5.0. The aspects to be incorporated in this overhaul include AI literacy, digital legal technologies, ethics of technology use, and interdisciplinary competencies, in addition to primary legal principles. Curricular innovations should focus on implementing

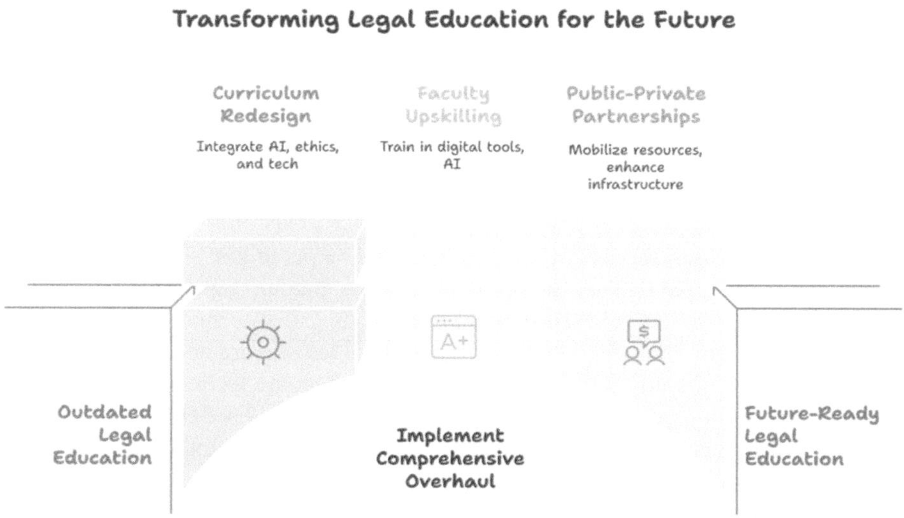

Figure 2. Suggested ways for the transformation of legal education for the future (Source: Authors).

project-based learning, simulations, gamification, and self-regulated learning paradigms to inculcate practical skills and critical thinking, instead of rote learning (Almeida and Simoes 2019, Tikhonova and Raitskaya 2023, Prakash and Nair 2024). Moreover, curricula should undergo regular review to meet the current pace of technological change and the evolving demands of society in general, thereby indicating flexibility and responsiveness.

7.2 Faculty Upskilling

Faculty development programmes are important, as faculty members are at the centre of the successful implementation of new pedagogical frameworks. Existing data indicate that faculty competencies regarding digital tools, AI solutions, and learner-focused pedagogical practices are especially lacking among beginners (Dasgupta 2010, Alda et al. 2020). Capacity-building activities such as workshops, seminars, and collaboration with technological specialists will enable faculty to incorporate technology into pedagogy in an appropriate and ethical way. Upskilling faculty members can also be achieved by developing interdisciplinary partnerships among law, computer science, and social science disciplines to enhance teaching objectives and procedures (Dasgupta 2010, Janecek et al. 2020).

7.3 Public-Private Partnerships (PPP)

The use of collaborations among government agencies, universities, law firms, and technology companies has the potential to accelerate resource mobilisation, infrastructural upgrading, and the diffusion of innovation in legal education. PPPs may be used to develop and launch AI-based educational platforms, virtual labs, and experiential education opportunities in the form of internships and clinics made more technology-intensive (Almeida and Simoes 2019, Smith 2019, Wang and Yang 2024). Such synergies may additionally provide a foundation for research partnerships to further understand the impact on legal pedagogy and test emerging technologies, serving as a source of real-world applicability and scalability that single institutions alone may not be able to attain independently.

8. Conclusion

Legal Education 2.0 serves as a framework for a paradigm shift in which AI functions as a supplementary driver that supports human capability rather than replacing it. This vision is based on the understanding that technological expertise should coexist harmoniously with constitutional values that are deeply enshrined in future legal practitioners, who are not supposed to become technocrats but should remain stewards of justice, equity, and the rule of law. In 2047, when India celebrates 100 years of independence, the legal education sector will have the opportunity to produce a generation of lawyers capable of using state-of-the-art technological tools, e.g., AI-powered research assistants, intelligent tutoring systems, and predictive analytics, whilst simultaneously critically reflecting on the ethical and social implications of such technologies (Prakash and Nair 2024, Pelaez-Sanchez et al. 2024, Wang and Yang 2024).

This conjectured Legal Education 2.0 model has a far more ambitious goal than shaping hybrids of lawyers who can work comfortably within a more digitised and globalised legal framework; it aims to impart critical thinking and social responsiveness in a manner that gives proper recognition to constitutional values and the dignity of human beings. It is in such a balancing act between AI augmentation and normative anchoring that India may cultivate an inclusive justice ecosystem that is resilient to exponential technological shifts and that empowers all citizens.

References

Ahmad, N. (2009). Adapting Indian legal education to the demands of a globalising World. German Law Journal 10: 847–858. https://doi.org/10.1017/S2071832200001371.

Alda, R. C., Boholano, H. B. and Dayagbil, F. (2020). Teacher Education Institutions in the Philippines towards Education 4.0. International Journal of Learning, Teaching and Educational Research 19: 137–154. https://doi.org/10.26803/IJLTER.19.8.8.

Al-Husseini, S. and Elbeltagi, I. (2016). Transformational leadership and innovation: a comparison study between Iraq's public and private higher education. Studies in Higher Education 41: 159–181. https://doi.org/10.1080/03075079.2014.927848.

Almeida, F. and Simões, J. (2019). The role of serious games, gamification and Industry 4.0 tools in the Education 4.0 paradigm. Contemporary Educational Technology. https://doi.org/10.30935/CET.554469.

Badrinarayana, D. (2014). India's State of Legal Education: The Road from NLSIU to Jindal. Journal of Legal Education 63: 521.

Bohari, A., Wider, W., Udang, L. N., Jiang, L., Tanucan, J. C. and Lajuma, S. (2024). Transformational leadership's role in shaping Education 4.0 within higher education. Journal of Infrastructure, Policy and Development. https://doi.org/10.24294/jipd.v8i8.4900.

Butt, R., Siddiqui, H., Soomro, R. and Asad, M. M. (2020). Integration of Industrial Revolution 4.0 and IOTs in academia: a state-of-the-art review on the concept of Education 4.0 in Pakistan. Interact. Technol. Smart Educ. 17: 337–354. https://doi.org/10.1108/itse-02-2020-0022.

Cassidy, V. and Koroll, C. J. (1994). Ethical aspects of transformational leadership. Holistic Nursing Practice 9: 41–47. https://doi.org/10.1097/00004650-199410000-00008.

Dasgupta, L. (2010). Reforming Indian legal education: linking research and teaching. Journal of Legal Education 59: 432.

Demartini, C. and Benussi, L. (2017). Do Web 4.0 and Industry 4.0 Imply Education X.0?. IT Prof. 19: 4–7. https://doi.org/10.1109/MITP.2017.47.

Farber, S. (2024). Harmonizing AI and human instruction in legal education: a case study from Israel on training future legal professionals. International Journal of the Legal Profession 31: 349–363. https://doi.org/10.1080/09695958.2024.2430018.

G., Aswathy Prakash and Nair, Vishnu. (2024). Integrating generative AI into legal education: from casebooks to code, opportunities and challenges. Law, Technology and Humans 6: 60. https://doi.org/10.5204/lthj.3640.

Ghosh, S. (2014). Introduction, legal education and legal reform in South Asia. Journal of Legal Education 63: 497–498.

Hamedani, S. S., Aslam, S., Oraibi, B. M., Wah, Y. B. and Hamedani, S. S. (2024). Transitioning towards Tomorrow's Workforce: Education 5.0 in the Landscape of Society 5.0: A systematic literature review. Education Sciences. https://doi.org/10.3390/educsci14101041.

Husa, J. (2017). Comparative law in legal education – building a legal mind for a transnational world. The Law Teacher 52: 201–215. https://doi.org/10.1080/03069400.2017.1340532.

Janecek, V., Williams, R. and Keep, E. (2020). Education for the provision of technologically enhanced legal services. Comput. Law Secur. Rev. 40: 105519. https://doi.org/10.31228/osf.io/zfkr3.

Khalili, A. (2016). Linking transformational leadership, creativity, innovation, and innovation-supportive climate. Management Decision 54: 2277–2293. https://doi.org/10.1108/MD-03-2016-0196.

Kinghan, J. (2012). European Legal Education. The Maastricht Journal of European and Comparative Law.

Likhovski, A. (2021). A Colonial Legal Laboratory? Jurisprudential Innovation in British India. The American Journal of Comparative Law. https://doi.org/10.1093/AJCL/AVAB010.

Miyazawa, S., Chan, K. and Lee, I. (2008). The Reform of Legal Education in East Asia. Annual Review of Law and Social Science 4: 333–360. https://doi.org/10.1146/ANNUREV.LAWSOCSCI.3.081806.112713.

Mouazen, A., Hernández-lara, A., Chahine, J. and Halawi, A. (2025). Triple bottom line sustainability and Innovation 5.0 management through the lens of Industry 5.0, Society 5.0 and Digitized Value Chain 5.0. European Journal of Innovation Management. https://doi.org/10.1108/ejim-04-2024-0339.

Muktiarni, M., Widiaty, I., Abdullah, A. G., Ana, A. and Yulia, C. (2019). Digitalisation trend in education during industry 4.0. Journal of Physics: Conference Series 1402. https://doi.org/10.1088/1742-6596/1402/7/077070.

NLSIU. (2023). Yearly Status Report 2022–23. https://www.nls.ac.in/wp-content/uploads/2024/05/2022-23.pdf.

Pathak, S. and Sharma, A. (2025). Artificial Intelligence (AI) in the Indian Legal System: Transformations, Challenges, and Future Prospects. KamKus College of Law. https://10.13140/RG.2.2.31741.63209.

Pelaez-Sanchez, I. C., Velarde-Camaqui, D. and Glasserman-Morales, L. (2024). The impact of large language models on higher education: exploring the connection between AI and Education 4.0. Frontiers in Education. https://doi.org/10.3389/feduc.2024.1392091.

Ramaswamy, H. (2020). The prospect of legal education: an India overview. Journal of Legal Studies 25: 31–43. https://doi.org/10.2478/jles-2020-0002.

Narvaez Rojas, C., Alomia Peñafiel, G. A., Loaiza Buitrago, D. F. and Tavera Romero, C. A. (2021). Society 5.0: A Japanese Concept for a Superintelligent Society. Sustainability 13(12): 6567. https://doi.org/10.3390/su13126567.

Ryan, F. (2020). Rage against the machine? Incorporating legal tech into legal education. The Law Teacher 55: 392–404. https://doi.org/10.1080/03069400.2020.1805927.

Shalini, S. (2021). A study on the effectiveness of problem-based learning in legal education in India. Asian Journal of Legal Education 8: 95–109. https://doi.org/10.1177/2322005820984418.

Smith, M. (2019). Integrating technology in contemporary legal education. The Law Teacher 54: 209–221. https://doi.org/10.1080/03069400.2019.1643647.

Spiegel, M. (2005). Theory and practice in legal education: an essay on clinical legal education. UCLA Law Review 34: 577.

Sugarman, D. and Sherr, A. (2001). Globalisation and legal education. International Journal of the Legal Profession 8: 10–5. https://doi.org/10.1080/09695950120111191.

Szocik, K. and Jurkowska-Gomułka, A. (2021). Ethical, legal and political challenges of artificial intelligence: law as a response to AI-related threats and hopes. World Futures 79: 557–573. https://doi.org/10.1080/02604027.2021.2012876.

Tan, C., Bell, G. F., Dang, X. H., Kim, J., Teo, K. S., Thiruvengadam, A. K. et al. (2006). Legal education in Asia. Asian Journal of Comparative Law 1. https://doi.org/10.2202/1932-0205.1015.

Tikhonova, E. and Raitskaya, L. (2023). Education 4.0: The concept, skills, and research. Journal of Language and Education. https://doi.org/10.17323/jle.2023.17001.

Wang, Y. and Yang, S. (2024). Constructing and testing AI international legal education coupling-enabling model. Sustainability. https://doi.org/10.3390/su16041524.

Wang, Z. (2019). Between constancy and change: legal practice and legal education in the age of technology. Law in Context. A Socio-legal Journal. https://doi.org/10.26826/law-in-context.v36i1.87.

Wu, J. and Tang, W. (2022). Reform method of university legal education based on artificial intelligence and wireless communication. Wireless Communications and Mobile Computing. https://doi.org/10.1155/2022/2574911.

Yu, S., Zia-ud-Din, M., Khan, R. D. and Bilal, S. (2018). Cross-national comparative study on legal education and admission to practice between China, India and Pakistan. Journal of Legal Studies 21: 16–37. https://doi.org/10.1515/jles-2018-0002.

Zengin, Y., Naktiyok, S., Kaygin, E., Kavak, O. and Topcuoglu, E. (2021). An investigation upon Industry 4.0 and Society 5.0 within the context of sustainable development goals. Sustainability. https://doi.org/10.3390/SU13052682.

Ziaeian, Y. (2024, October). The impact of human-centric leadership on employee satisfaction and productivity in digitally transformed organizations. pp. 195–203. In International Conference on Innovation of Emerging Information and Communication Technology. Cham: Springer Nature Switzerland. https://doi.org/10.1007/978-3-031-88634-8_17.

Ziatdinov, R., Atteraya, M. and Nabiyev, R. I. (2024). The fifth industrial revolution as a transformative step towards Society 5.0. Societies. https://doi.org/10.3390/soc14020019.

Chapter 5

Role of Indian Higher Education Institutions and Green Human Resource Management as Mediators to Sustainable Development

Nirmalya Debnath,[1] *Jayanta Das*[2,*] and *Goutam Deb*[2]

1. Introduction

Sustainable Development can be simply referred to as a system of growth and manufacturing taking into account logical judgement and resolution, managerial competencies, and innovative entrepreneurial capabilities with utmost emphasis on environmental wellbeing and security. Basically, sustainable development is a concern of mankind. Matters concerning sustainable development can be referred to as one of the prime elements of a civilisation. Hence, nature, that is, various environmental resources, has always been the area of prime focus, with human initiatives acting as regulators of the system. Environmental studies thus comprise the foundation for the concept of sustainability. Environmental studies thus form the grass roots of knowledge on sustainable development. The concept is not

[1] Assistant Professor, Department of Business Management, Tripura University (A Central University), Suryamaninagar, Tripura-799022, India.
[2] Research Scholar, Department of Business Management, Tripura University (A Central University), Suryamaninagar, Tripura-799022, India.
Emails: nirmalyadebnath@tripurauniv.ac.in, deb.goutam@gmail.com
* Corresponding author: jayantawp@gmail.com

DOI: 10.1201/9781003736158-7

only addressed by scientists and naturalists across the globe but also by national leaders. The first dialogue on sustainability took place at the UN Conference on Human Environment at Stockholm in 1972. This was followed by the UN World Commission on Environment and Development's chronicle titled "Our Common Future", which gained recognition and acceptance as the Brundtland Report (1987), for the development of consciousness for sustainability. The pivotal contribution of knowledge towards the global pursuit of sustainable development and conserving the Earth in the 21st century was remarkably emphasised by the United Nations' (UN) decade of 'Education for Sustainable Development' (UNDESD) (2005–2014). The 17 Sustainable Development Goals (SDGs) evolved as an end product of the intercontinental deliberation held in September 2015.

UNDESD recommends access to avenues for advancement concerning the execution of intercontinental grade knowledge which promotes knowledge, expertise, outlook, principles, and achievement. The 'Sustainable Development Goal 4' (SDG 4), having its foundation in several translational statements such as the 'Universal Declaration of Human Rights', 'Convention on the Rights of the Child', 'World Declaration on Education for All', 'Dakar Framework for Action', and 'Millennium Development Goals', regards knowledge to be a vital aspect for the all-round prosperity of people, states, and the entire globe (UNESCO 2005). With regard to knowledge as the prime motivator for the 'Sustainable Development Goals' (SDGs), several multinational conventions were conducted with the goal of connecting international expertise and skills for accentuating and amplifying the task of knowledge in perceiving SDGs; generating avenues for escalating the knowhow gained from UNDESD and considering knowledge as a prime facilitator in the process.

While perceiving the SDGs all around the world, stress has increasingly been relocated from a purely productive and remunerative dimension to a broader aspect of advancement comprising three poles of supportability, i.e., environmental, societal, and economic (People, Planet, Profit). Further, the fact remains that strategies or technical theories and formulas will be insufficient for acquiring the SDGs; instead, attitudinal conversion and mass consciousness are highly vital for sustainable development. Thus, the responsibility of knowledge and education and the transcendence of its various schemes and projects like tutoring and skill upgradation, conveyance of information and mass consciousness, knowledge-based investigative and practical exploration, spread and availability of knowledge, conglomeration, and collaboration emerge as vital action plans for the attainment of sustainable development goals (SDGs).

Uniform and comprehensive learning for everyone is recommended by SDG 4, which is intimately connected to the fruitful execution of SDG 16 emphasising the furtherance of peaceful and comprehensive communities and the creation of potent and responsible organisations at all stages. The four guidelines of the educational structure as proposed by Dellor (1996) are applicable in the present day also for attaining standard educational end products. The four foundational pillars of knowledge are "(a) learning to know, (b) learning to do, (c) learning to be, and (d) learning to live together". The sustainability targets on teaching and learning, 2030

(Fia et al. 2022), aim to secure comprehensive and uniform standard teaching and learning and endorse avenues for gaining knowledge throughout life for everyone. This centres around four targeted areas of: (1) enhanced approachability towards standard knowledge resources for all aspects of learning and teaching, (2) emphasis on the standard of knowledge constituents, applicability and educational attainment across all study trades, (3) higher attention on uniform approachability to knowledge resources, (4) gender uniformity for every study area through secure and encouraging learning conditions (Vare and Scott 2007). Several advanced nations like Japan, South Korea, Australia, Sweden, Ireland, etc. have achieved significant progress in this regard by surpassing the minimum laid down targets.

Across the Asia-Pacific territory, the implementation of ingenious course modules, topics, advancing teaching techniques, sustainability-based instructional tools along with surveillance and inspection systems for achieving the goal of education for sustainable development-based knowledge transfer is highly needed (Didham and Ofei-Manu 2012).

2. Review of Literature

Several studies indicate the contribution of knowledge and education in the growth and advancement of a nation and its citizens. A brief review of a few of the research works carried out in the field of the status of the teaching–learning system prevalent in some countries is mentioned below:

Johnson and Stafford (1973) carried out their study on the significance of educational financing on the basis of information and statistics gathered from the research centre of Michigan University in the year 1965. The prime basis of their study was the amount of money or funds spent for every single student for imparting knowledge and the standard of knowledge provided to the students. On the basis of their study, they arrived at the conclusion that a significant proportion of variations in the earnings of the pass-out students was an outcome of the mean educational spending incurred for every individual student.

The hike in the rate of earnings and income based on knowledge and learning among Indian people was researched and studied by a social scientist in the year 2016. The outcome of the study conducted among Indian people came out with the inference that individuals having spent a higher amount of time on learning and gaining knowledge exhibited the feature of higher per head utilisation of various goods and services. This trend of rise in the usage of various essentials was found to be directly related and associated with the tenure spent by an individual on gaining knowledge and learning, and the usage and spending on availing various utilities were found to rise significantly with every extra amount of time or tenure or an extra year that is spent on education. The increase or growth in the volume of usage of utilities was identified to rise by around 4 percent among the male population without any significant changes occurring among the female category of the population. The mean impact and outcome of learning and knowledge acquisition by the people were observed to be considerably lesser in the case of the female sex with respect to male individuals on the basis of the study findings. The reason for this may be attributed to insignificant involvement of female employees in places of manufacturing activities.

Khan and Muktar (2021) investigate GHRM and the way in which it aids both the environment and businesses to expand rationally. They analysed 70 research papers between the period 2008 to 2020. The research tries to explore how GHRM has been interpreted, applied, and what impacts it has had till date. The findings reveal that GHRM is still developing as an idea. Significant aspects like green training, teamwork, support from management, and creating a green-friendly workplace are necessary for it to run satisfactorily. This research helps new scholars perceive the developments achieved till date in this domain and the issues that still need to be traversed in the future.

Muhammad Ali and Nisar (2022) delve into ways in which Green Human Resource Management (GHRM) supports colleges and universities (called HEIs) to perform better in safeguarding nature and the environment. It also investigates the manner in which people's dedication to green activities and their actual green attitude contribute a significant role in this. Another issue the study focuses on is Green Self-Efficacy (GSE), that is, how optimistic an individual feels in performing eco-friendly activities and the manner in which it impacts the link between dedication and attitude. Based on feedback from 208 individuals associated with Pakistani HEIs (higher education institutions), the study observed that GHRM supports the upgrading of environmental performance. It reflects that both dedication and optimism in doing green activities are very significant. This research comes up with fresh perspectives on the occurrence of green behaviour in educational institutions and provides valuable propositions for managers to enhance GHRM activities.

Research by Ercantan and Eyupoglu (2022) highlighted the impact of GHRM on the way in which future employees, mainly university learners, imagine and behave in eco-friendly ways in their profession. Using feedback from 342 student learners at the largest university in North Cyprus, the study observed that GHRM activities help students to be more prone to conduct green activities and take deliberate eco-friendly actions. The study also noticed that this attitude is intense when students perceive that their workplace advocates green thinking (referred to as a psychological green climate). The research indicates that GHRM needs to be incorporated in HR departments, as it aids in building a sustainable attitude among future professionals. It contributes to the available literature by connecting HR behaviour with environmental concerns.

A study by Vanisri and Chandrapadhy (2023) investigates ways in which performing environment-friendly tasks (known as green behaviour) by faculties in colleges can make them feel better and more optimistic. The study was conducted with college faculties in Chennai, Tamil Nadu. The researchers distributed 410 online forms and obtained 385 correct responses. They observed that when faculties act in accordance with green habits, it supports their surroundings along with enhancement of their self-esteem. Further, when self-esteem is elevated, their holistic wellness also enhances. Thus, this research reflects a clear connectivity between concerns for nature and environment, feeling optimistic, and being content in the workplace.

3. Objectives of the Study

This study has five main objectives, which are

1. To understand the need for environmental studies for sustainable development.
2. To identify the role of higher education institutions for bringing about awareness on sustainable development.
3. To find out the challenges related to sustainable development faced by higher education institutions.
4. To clearly understand why Green Human Resource Management (Green HRM) is important in today's world for the achievement of sustainable development goals.
5. To examine Green HRM actions applying ABCD (Advantages, Benefits, Constraints, Disadvantages) method.

4. Indian School Education System as the Foundation to Higher Education

From the time of gaining independence, leaders and administrators consecutively handled several vital impediments by bringing new educational guidelines and strategies as an integral element of progress plans in the form of programmes like 'Sarva Shiksha Abhiyan', 'Rashtriya Madhyamik Shiksha Abhiyan', 'Right to Free & Compulsory Education Act', etc. However, according to the 'British Council India' report (2014), the existing Indian dropout percentage among disadvantaged communities (Scheduled Castes and Tribes) of society surpasses the All-India average. The education process (K–12, school education), although governed by several aims and targets, still relies on old principles and guidelines of the past.

Even with new learning guidelines and strategies, the average schooling tenure of 5.12 years is much lower than transforming commercial nations such as China with 8.17 years and Brazil with 7.54 years, and also remarkably lower than the mean (7.09 years) of other evolving nations.

Added to this, high school abandonment figures after preliminary and during schooling and lowering admissions at the 10+2 stages are really thought-provoking issues, which are further aggravated by even higher abandonment rates among the disadvantaged sections of society surpassing the national average.

Apart from the above, the elevated student–faculty ratio in backward areas, the dearth of technically sound and determined faculties, and the low standard of knowledge delivery lead to poor educational attainment, which can be considered key confrontations encountered by Indian school learning programmes.

As per the "Annual Status of Education Report (2013)", unfortunately only around 26% of standard 5 students are able to complete the simplest problem on division, and around 21% of the students are able to interpret an easy paragraph. For class 3 students, the position further deteriorates to just 7% for division and 19% for reading out a paragraph.

A great dearth of sufficiently skilled faculties exists in schools spread out in different parts of our country. There is a significant mismatch between children of schooling age and the actual number of children who are enrolled in schooling as per study findings.

Of late, in the month of April 2016, several improvements were recommended by the Govt. of India Committee of MHRD for the "Evolution of New Education Policy", namely a standard teaching-learning system supported by uniform approachability towards all learning materials and a standard process of knowledge transfer without any specific guideline leading to sustainable learning and teaching in schools. Moreover, there exists a lack of parity in the course structure of schools under different education boards throughout the country.

5. Sustainability and Green HRM in Education

Sustainability refers to balancing three core areas—economy, society, and the environment. These are known as the three pillars of sustainable development. The concept is to develop without disturbing or causing problems to nature or people. The World Commission on Environment and Development also considers it as Green Management in their renowned document "Our Common Future." As described by Opatha and Arulrajah (2014), Green HRM deals with motivating employees to become more responsible towards the environment. It consists of guidelines and training programmes which facilitate employees to protect and take care of nature, bring down the level of waste, keep away from polluting the environment, and endorse eco-friendly practices. The motive is to create a work culture where everyone contributes significantly towards creating a green and clean future.

To make this achievable in education, TSE techniques (Teachers, Students, and Education Institutions) can be applied. This method aids in imparting knowledge on 21st-century skills like creativity, problem-solving, teamwork, communication, critical thinking, and climate awareness. It makes students future-ready for facing the modern-day world.

Colleges and higher education institutes also need to introduce new applications like MOOCs (Massive Open Online Courses), virtual labs, and technologies like big data, machine learning, AR, block-chain (for depositing mark sheets and certificates), etc., to aid and guide students in getting equipped for competing in the digital and Industry 4.0 planet.

6. Role of Teachers and Education in Sustainable Development

Teachers can perform a significant role in creating a powerful and environment-friendly teaching–learning system. They help to groom learners and guide them to acquire significant 21st-century skills like thinking, creativity, and teamwork. These competencies lie at the root of modern-day learning.

In 1992, Education for Sustainable Development (ESD) was initiated by the United Nations to bridge learning with real-world problems like poverty, climate change, and inequality. Further, in 2015, the UN introduced 17 Sustainable

Development Goals (SDGs) to be attained by 2030. These goals concentrate on developing a healthier planet that is peaceful, fair, and nature-friendly.

Education is the crux of attaining these SDGs. It educates learners on global problems and challenges and prepares them to come up with smart and sustainable solutions. Issues on gender equality, clean energy, responsible use of resources, and good jobs are all components of Education for Sustainable Development (ESDG).

India is also marching ahead with this vision through the NEP 2020 (New Education Policy), which highlights five significant values – Access, Equity, Quality, Affordability, and Accountability. This strategy stimulates leadership in colleges through education, research, learning, and service to society.

To investigate countries' performance with SDGs, a worldwide report was published. In the 2023 SDG Index, Finland ranked first, followed by Denmark, Sweden, and Norway. India ranked 112 among 163 countries. In India, NITI Aayog and MoSPI are nodal agencies performing a significant function in monitoring our development on the goals of sustainable development in the country.

7. Sustainable Development Backed by Environmental Studies Through Higher Educational Institutions

Of late, as per UNESCO (2018), "Education for Sustainable Development" (ESD) has been prioritized as the focal point of the 2030 'Sustainable Development Agenda' and actively endorsed as a vital facilitator of all 17 sustainable development goals. Sustainable education has gained acceptance as an inexhaustible asset for the attainment of the basic potential of the 21st century consisting of sustainable living, which encompasses our culture and society, our jobs and assignments, along with our environment or surroundings.

Research findings on Education for Sustainable Development (ESD) lay priority on the incorporation of the threefold aspects of sustainable development – social, economic, and environmental – and concentrate on the correlations and influences between them over time and space (Summers 2007). Frequent socio-cultural elements of sustainable development emanate as an outcome of various environmental disturbances leading to various complications towards sustainable development goals. Since no human being can detach himself or stay away from the influence or effect of his surroundings, and as changes or modifications in environmental elements also create or affect the social and cultural dimensions of sustainable development, among the three sustainable development dimensions the environmental aspect has gained utmost importance and focus.

Higher education is that element and constituent of the education system where learners are equipped to upgrade their learning and competencies for tackling multifarious difficulties of everyday life. Higher educational academic institutions possess the potential to instantly take up various societal issues mainly based on our surroundings and environment. Sustainable development backed by higher education thus functions significantly for the development and wellbeing of the nation and its citizens. A brief outline of the various advantages. Benefits, constraints and disadvantages of green HRM practices is represented below (see Tables 1 to 4).

8. Role of Higher Educational Institutes and Universities in Sustainable Environmental Education

Since the subject of sustainability of environmental elements has become a matter of grave concern in the present day, the functioning of higher education institutions with respect to any endeavour on environmental sustainability is evolving as a highly predominant aspect of concern. In the event of considering higher educational institutions as playing the lead role in this regard towards the community, there is an immense need for the institutes to be sufficiently motivated and committed towards the same (Beringer 2006). Any individual higher educational institute or university exhibits its own speciality of customs, norms, and regulations with respect to its locational and regional characteristics. Since universities and higher educational institutions are in close touch with the surrounding society, they can exert considerable influence in taking up various issues of the surrounding people, trying to solve their problems, and maintaining a good climate in society by educating people about various ethical and human values and developing concern for the environment by apprising them of various harmful environmental consequences on human life. Some of the roles of higher education institutes that can be played by them in this regard are:

1. **Environment Centric Curriculum:** The structure and composition of the modern-day curriculum should take into consideration all issues of the environment and its surroundings for familiarising learners with the elements with which human beings continuously interact. The learning process should be capable of encouraging pupils to take up issues related to environmental concerns. Apart from formal learning, various informal and extracurricular activities help a learner to understand his surroundings and their importance and develop a willingness to work towards ensuring the betterment of the environment (Erdoğan and Uşak 2009), generate environmental alertness (Yerkes and Haras 1997), and foster environmental accountability (Matthews and Riley 1995).
2. **Exploration and Analysis:** Investigation and analysis are always considered integral constituents of knowledge and education that lead to innovations and advancements in society. Research and studies in higher education are considered highly effective in bringing about awareness regarding various environmental concerns and their role in the survival of humans and all other entities of the world. Environmental study findings are highly effective in convincing people about the ill effects of the continuous depletion of non-renewable resources, which also leads to environmental pollution. It is through such study findings that people can be convinced to conserve natural resources and rely more on the consumption of renewable resources. Societal concern regarding pollution and biodiversity conservation for maintaining balance in the natural environment can also be communicated logically, supported by facts and data from research findings.

3. **Sensitization and Awareness Campaigns:** Sensitization and awareness programmes are organised to create an enduring relationship between society and educational institutions so that both can mutually work together in handling and solving issues related to environmental concerns. This would also facilitate institutions in improvising their research and knowledge-imparting capabilities when working closely in association with the community. This interrelationship between institutions and society is highly necessary for gaining the confidence and support of people in matters and initiatives related to environmental safety and protection. Thus, higher education institutions can go a long way ahead in developing a positive mindset and attitude among their students towards taking various steps for the sustainable development of their society and environment.

   Some prime concerns of focus for sustainable development in higher education institutions are tabled below (see Tables 5 to 6).

9. Challenges Faced by Higher Education Institutions in Implementation of Sustainable Development Practices

At present, the subject of sustainable development has become a burning issue not only at the state or national level but also at the international and global level. Issues concerning sustainable development require immediate attention for the overall wellbeing of a nation. Several collaborators perceive sustainable development in their own ways and expect varying outcomes. Certain specific challenges in the execution of sustainable development practices through higher education institutions are mentioned below:

1. Dearth of satisfactory knowledge in the higher educational institutes for the communication and implementation of sustainable development principles and practices.
2. Acute shortage of skilled manpower in higher educational institutes.
3. Lack of interdisciplinary studies on sustainable development.
4. Unsatisfactory teamwork, linkage, and cooperation among different educational institutes, as observed may be considered (Agbedahin 2019) shortcomings in the way towards sustainable development need to be overcome for effective understanding of the process and its application.

10. Higher Educational Objectives for Sustainable Development

The prime focus of higher education at the moment needs to be supported by a satisfactory number of studies and analyses to generate logical facts sufficient to influence and motivate people to adapt to environment-friendly practices. Scholars and researchers should be supported and motivated to come up with innovative ideas to deal with environmental issues such as pollution, global warming, and resource depletion, and to educate people about their harmful outcomes on society.

Although the higher education system has already initiated some steps on the issue, sufficient proactive initiatives need to come from people as an outcome of the motivation and encouragement provided by educational institutes.

Higher educational institutes need to emphasize the following:

1. Generating awareness on judicious and controlled utilization of non-renewable resources.
2. Highlighting the limited availability of non-renewable resources
3. Informing about the harmful consequences of pollution and resource depletion related to the ever-increasing consumption of non-renewable resources.
4. Benchmarking and following the best practices adopted by various organizations both within the country and abroad.

11. Conclusion

The future days are sure bring alarming consequences to the entire human civilisation as an outcome of careless and irresponsible human activities, which may totally endanger the survival of all on this wonderful planet Earth. Lack of education and awareness among people is one of the prime reasons for this irresponsible attitude. Dissemination of information related to the rights of future generations in accessing standard education is sufficient to motivate and inspire everyone in the process. Higher educational institutions, considered to be the creators of future citizens of the country, have a huge role to play in this regard in generating the spirit of positive consciousness towards the environment and its surroundings, which form the dwelling place of all. The study also highlights the application of Green HRM and the teaching of sustainability in higher education institutes for the creation of a healthy and superior natural environment ahead. Usage of digital tools and practices for imparting learning and spreading information on sustainability is one of the ways for the dissemination of environment-friendly knowledge. The study thus tries to indicate that the above-mentioned steps can contribute largely to attaining around 9 out of the 17 sustainable development goals.

References

Agbedahin, A. V. (2019). Sustainable development, Education for Sustainable Development, and the 2030 Agenda for Sustainable Development: Emergence, efficacy, eminence, and future. Sustainable Development 27(4): 669–680.

Beringer, A. (2006). Campus sustainability audit research in Atlantic Canada: Pioneering the campus sustainability assessment framework. International Journal of Sustainability in Higher Education 7(4): 437–455. https://doi.org/10.1108/14676370610702235.

British Council India report. (2014). High university enrolment, low graduate employment: An Economist Intelligence Unit report for the British Council, available at:www.eiu.com (accessed 20 September 2018).

Brundtland, G. (1987). Our Common Future: The World Commission on Environment and Development, Oxford University Press, Oxford, UK.

Dellor, J. (1996). Learning: the treasure within; report to UNESCO of the International Commission on Education for the Twenty-first Century, available at: https://unesdoc.unesco.org/ ark:/48223/pf0000109590 (accessed 12 November 2018).

Didham, R. J. and Ofei-Manu, P. (2012). Monitoring and Evaluation of Education for Sustainable Development: A Framework of Factors and Leverage Points in the Implementation of ESD in the Asia-Pacific Region. Hayama, Japan: Institute for Global Environmental Strategies and United Nations University.

Ercantan, O. and Eyupoglu, S. (2022). How do green human resource management practices encourage employees to engage in green behavior? Perceptions of University students as prospective employees. Sustainability 14(3): 1718. https://doi.org/10.3390/su14031718.

Erdogan, M. and Usak, M. (2009). Curricular and extra-curricular activities to develop the environmental awareness of young students: a case from Turkey. Educational Sciences/Odgojne Znanosti 11(1).

Fia, M., Ghasemzadeh, K. and Paletta, A. (2022). How higher education institutions walk their talk on the 2030 Agenda: A systematic literature review. Higher Education Policy 36(3): 599–632. https://doi.org/10.1057/s41307-022-00277-x.

Johnson, G. E. and Stafford, F. P. (1973). Social returns to quantity and quality of schooling. The Journal of Human Resources 8(2): 139. https://doi.org/10.2307/144731.

Khan, M. H. and Muktar, S. N. (2021). What's next for green human resource management: Insights and trends for sustainable development. International Journal of Sustainable Development and Planning 16(1): 181–194. https://doi.org/10.18280/ijsdp.160119.

K. M., M., Aithal, P. S. and K. R. S., S. (2024). Green HRM and teaching sustainability in higher education institutions: For promoting sustainable education and sustainable development goals. International Journal of Case Studies in Business, IT, and Education 260–270.

Matthews, B. E. and Riley, C. K. (1995). Teaching and Evaluating Outdoor Ethics Education Programs.

Muhammad Ali, Q. and Nisar, Q. A. (2022). Nexus between green human resource management and environmental performance: A green approach for higher education institutes. Kybernetes 52(11): 5706–5729. https://doi.org/10.1108/k-01-2022-0023.

Opatha, H. H. and Arulrajah, A. A. (2014). Green human resource management: Simplified general reflections. International Business Research 7(8). https://doi.org/10.5539/ibr.v7n8p101.

Summers, M. (2007). Student science teachers' conception of sustainable development-: an empirical study of three postgraduate training cohorts. Research in Science and Technological Education 25(3): 307–327.

UNDESD. (2005-14). Education for sustainable development toolkit. Education for Sustainable Development in Action, Learning & Training Tools, available at: http://archive.erisee.org/sites/default/files/UNESCOEducation%20for%20sustainable%20development%20toolkit%282006%29.pdf (accessed 12 December 2018).

UNESCO. (2017). Education for Sustainable Development goals: Learning Objectives, available at: http://unesdoc.unesco.org/images/0024/0024741/247444.pdf (accessed 15 July 2018).

UNESCO. (2015). Rethinking Education: Towards a Global Common Good?, available at: https://en.unesco.org/events/launch-rethinking-education-towards-global-common-good-publication (accessed 28 July 2018).

UNESCO. (2018). Issues and trends in Education for Sustainable Development, available at: https://unesdoc.unesco.org/ark:/48223/pf0000261445 (accessed 09 September 2018).

Vanisri, K. and Chandrapadhy, P. (2023). An empirical study on impact of employee green behaviour on employee well–being with mediating role of self-esteem in higher educational institutions using PLS SEM. Multidisciplinary Science Journal 6(3): 2024032. https://doi.org/10.31893/multiscience.2024032.

Vare, P. and Scott, W. (2007). Learning for a change: Exploring the relationship between education and sustainable development. Journal of Education for Sustainable Development 1(2): 191–198.

Yerkes, R. and Haras, K. (1997). Outdoor education and environmental responsibility. Clearinghouse on Rural Education and Small Schools.

Tables

Table 1. Prime Concerns of Focus for Sustainable Development in Higher Education Institutions.

Broad Areas	**Areas of Concern**
Bold and Transparent Management	All higher education institutions need to have a proactive aspiration and endeavour that guides sustainability and all-round development
Tie-ups with Industries	Good industry academia partnerships help to study real-world skills and disseminate learnings
Faculty Training and Explorations	There should be provision for ongoing faculty training programmes and continuous motivation for carrying out studies on sustainability
Faculty Career Growth and Development	Institutions need to support faculty career development in all ways for their retention and maximum contribution
Blended and Interdisciplinary Courses	Students need to be provided with options for taking up blended and interdisciplinary subjects as laid down in NEP 2020
Environment and Society Centric Curriculum	As per NEP guidelines, courses need to be designed on environmental consciousness and protection, building up of societal values, and creating economic awareness
Entrepreneurial Mindset and Competency Building	Colleges need to guide and motivate students to be capable of identifying societal problems and develop the spirit of entrepreneurship to become self-employed and job providers.
Make Students More Engaged	Institutions need to apply innovative teaching and instructional methods for developing student interest and make classes more engaging

Table 2. Prime Concerns of Focus for Sustainable Development in Higher Education Institutions.

Broad Areas	**Areas of Concern**
Combined Class Platforms	A blend of offline and online platforms for classes to be applied for making teaching-learning more interesting, flexible, and easily accessible in different situations
Fostering a Start-up Mindset	Institutions to be equipped with incubation centres to guide and motivate students to turn their thoughts and ideas into reality
Ongoing Learning	Learners and teachers both need to continuously upgrade their skills and learnings all throughout their life
Community Outreach	Colleges need to collaborate with the government, industry, and several NGOs, along with people in the society to identify and handle existing societal problems
Innovative Teaching Approaches	Faculties need to apply most modern and exciting techniques to impart learning to the students.
Fundraising and Donation Drives	Institutions need to have strong guidelines for fund creation from donations and societal contributions to aid in sustainable growth

Following is the ABCD (Advantages, Benefits, Constraints, and Disadvantages) Analysis of Green HRM Practices:

Table 3. Advantages.

Sl. No.	Advantage	Point of Advantage
1	Economical	Using less paper, stationeries, and resources, and relying more on online mode of work helps to minimize costs
2	Reputation	Companies adopting and practicing environment friendly methods of work have a higher reputation in the public eye.
3	Contentment	Taking part in green and sustainable initiatives help to build up a positive mindset leading to a feeling of satisfaction among the employees
4	Sustainable Work Culture	Green human resource management aids in creating a conducive environment for emphasizing usage of eco-friendly methods
5	Enhanced Training	Employees get more scope and opportunity to be educated on protection and conservation of natural resources

Table 4. Benefits.

Sl. No.	Benefit	Point of Benefit
1	Supportive Work Environment	Clean and hygienic work environment take care of employees' health and prevents illness, which minimizes costs
2	Waste Minimization	Reduction in wastes minimizes the institution's contribution towards pollution
3	Confidence and Concern	Care and concerns for the environment aids in the development of trust with customers and other stakeholders
4	Proactive Risk Prevention	Adoption of green and eco-friendly practices helps to prevent resource scarcity on usage of eco-friendly methods
5	Far Reaching Consequences	Green human resource management supports national goals like energy and water conservation, waste management, and environmental consciousness among people

Table 5. Constraints.

Sl. No.	Constraint	Point of Constraint
1	Elevated Initial Investments	Setting up green systems like energy-saving tech or eco-training needs money, which can be hard for small organizations
2	Reluctance Towards Change	Some employees or leaders may not want to change their usual ways due to habit or lack of awareness
3	Assimilation Problem	Adding green practices into existing HR systems takes time and effort, and needs good planning
4	Reliance on Others	Green efforts often involve suppliers too, and it's hard to control if they don't follow the same eco-friendly rules

Table 6. Disadvantages.

Sl. No.	Disadvantage	Point of Disadvantage
1	Juggling Responsibilities	Emphasizing on green practices and cost minimization along with higher profits may be difficult to attain at the same time
2	Impact of External Forces	Lack of external control like government policies and regulation might weaken the investment efficiencies of endeavors on green and sustainable development
3	Perceived Hardships	Improper and inaccurate information on the possible benefits and objectives of going green may consider the process an additional burden
4	Comprehensive Engagement	The much needed comprehensive involvement of all levels of employees and staff in the universities and higher education institutes along with students is sometimes tough to manage
5	Multiple Hurdles	Lack of resources, infrastructure, expertise, and coordination amongst all create stagnancy in sustainable development initiatives

Source: Mahesh et al. (2024)

Chapter 6

From Policy to Practice

A Bibliometric Study of ESD Integration in Indian Higher Education Systems

Swaricha Johri[1,*] and *Neha Puri*[2]

1. Introduction

The integration of Education for Sustainable Development (ESD) into higher education systems has garnered significant scholarly attention globally, with India emerging as a critical context due to its vast educational infrastructure and sustainability challenges. Early literature emphasized the conceptual foundations of ESD, highlighting its transformative potential in fostering critical thinking, participatory learning, and ethical citizenship (Tilbury 2011, Sterling 2004, Wals and Corcoran 2012, Barth et al. 2007, Filho et al. 2015). UNESCO's frameworks have been instrumental in shaping global discourse, promoting collaboration of education systems with the Sustainable Development Goals (UNESCO 2020, Leicht et al. 2018). In the Indian context, policy-level initiatives such as the National Education Policy (NEP) 2020 have clearly recognized sustainability-oriented education, calling for multidisciplinary curricula and value-based learning (Government of India 2020,

[1] Assistant Professor, B-32, Second Floor, Chander Nagar, Ghaziabad, UP.
[2] Associate Professor, E102, Antriksh Golf view 1 Sector 78, Noida, UP.
Email: npuri@amity.edu
* Corresponding author: sjohri@amity.edu

DOI: 10.1201/9781003736158-8

Ghosh 2021, Soham et al. 2021, Bhatia and Jain 2022, Sharma and Bansal 2023, Raghavan and Rao 2022).

As examined by scholars, inclusion of experiential learning, environmental awareness, and community engagement is catalysed through ESD integration with the National Education Policy (Kumar and Sharma 2020, Mukherjee and Sinha 2021, Raghavan and Rao 2022, Joshi and Narayan 2023).

However, digital divides and pedagogical limitations pose challenges to equitable access and meaningful learning (Iqbal and Sinha 2021, Kapoor and Menon 2021, Mishra et al. 2022). Scholars advocate for blended learning models that combine technological innovation with community-based experiential learning (Sen and Ranjan 2018, Bhattacharya 2021, Ghosh 2021). Ethical and cultural dimensions of ESD have received growing attention, with researchers emphasizing the need to contextualize sustainability education within India's socio-cultural fabric (Banerjee et al. 2020, Banerjee and Sengupta 2021, Chatterjee et al. 2022, Dasgupta and Pillai 2023, Bhatia and Jain 2022, Mehta and Raina 2021).

Despite the proliferation of policy documents and academic discourse, monitoring and evaluation of ESD implementation remain underdeveloped (Roy and Das 2020, Mishra et al. 2022, Joshi and Narayan 2023). Few studies offer robust metrics or longitudinal data to assess the impact of ESD initiatives on student learning outcomes, institutional transformation, or societal change (Das 2021, Singh and Thakur 2023, Sharma and Bansal 2023). Scholars call for the development of standardized indicators, participatory assessment tools, and institutional benchmarking frameworks to strengthen accountability and continuous improvement (Awasthi and Gaur 2023, Iqbal and Sinha 2021, Ramanathan and Bose 2022).

In sum, the literature discloses a dynamic framework of ESD integration in Indian higher education. A strong foundation is provided by institutional practices supported by contextual factors and universal principles. Bibliometric analysis helps provide insight into scholarly engagement, identify knowledge gaps, and suggest strategic interventions.

Future research should be focused on interdisciplinary collaboration, pedagogical innovation, and culturally grounded approaches towards advancing ESD from policy to practice.

2. Dataset and Methods

This research applied bibliometric analysis to understand the significance of incorporating Education for Sustainable Development (ESD) in Indian higher education. It included theoretical, conceptual, and social aspects of the topic and used several bibliometric methods during the research process. Based on methodologies adopted from previous studies (Glanzel 1999, Bornmann and Mutz 2015, Soham et al. 2021, Abhishek et al. 2022, Varsha 2024, Gavinolla et al. 2022), the research incorporated bibliometric analysis as part of a systematic literature review to gather insightful quantitative observations from an extensive collection of scholarly research in a predefined core database. Moreover, the study employed conceptual, intellectual, and social structure analysis—founded on the framework by Aria and Cuccurullo (Aria and Cuccurullo 2017)—in mapping and explaining the intellectual, conceptual, and social structures of the field. This procedure enabled the identification of relevant studies, thematic clusters, and social networks among researchers and institutions. For the present study, VOSviewer and R studio's bibliometrix package (R version 4.3.3) were used to conduct the analysis. The method enabled the description and analysis of ESD integration in the Indian higher education framework. The outline demarcates main sources, references, and citations that inspired the present researcher to develop and formulate the discipline under investigation in the current study. The theoretical framework aims to identify the most critical aspects and how they relate to one another within a particular field of inquiry. The extraction of data pertaining to ESD in higher education was undertaken through bibliometric analysis using mapping and sub-theme analysis. The keyword strategy for the present study combined terms such as "education for sustainable development" OR "ESD" AND "integration" OR "mainstreaming" OR "implementation" AND "higher education" OR "tertiary education" OR "university education" OR "postsecondary education," and other related combinations and variations were utilized to ensure that the maximum extent of related literature was covered. The search string for the present study is "education for sustainable development" OR "ESD" AND "integration" OR "mainstreaming" OR "implementation" AND "higher education" OR "tertiary education" OR "university education" OR "postsecondary education" AND (LIMIT-TO (SUBJAREA, "SOCI") OR LIMIT-TO (SUBJAREA, "BUSI") OR LIMIT-TO (SUBJAREA, "ECON")) AND (LIMIT-TO (DOCTYPE, "ar")) AND (LIMIT-TO (AFFILCOUNTRY, "India")) AND (LIMIT-TO (LANGUAGE, "English")). Existing literature (Donthu et al. 2021a, Jain and Kumar 2021, Tiwari et al. 2023, Lim 2024) purports that bibliometric reviews offer a convenient and quicker way of dealing with large volumes of literature compared to traditional manual review approaches. The step-by-step research process, beginning with the setting of objectives and harvesting data from the Scopus database based on given keyword combinations, is displayed in Figure 1. After filtration and purification

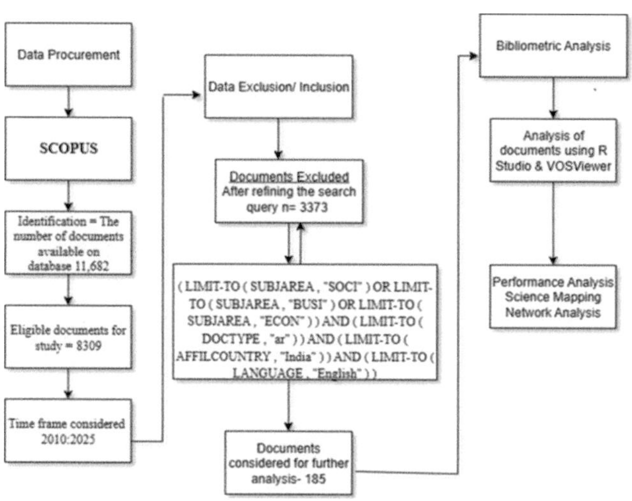

Figure 1. Research Process. Source: Author's Compilation.

of the dataset, bibliometric analysis was conducted through Bibliometrix and VOSviewer. Lastly, the general process concludes with the mapping of conceptual, social, and intellectual structures in order to detect recent trends and research gaps in the literature on ESD in higher education.

2.1 Research Objectives

RQ1: What is the publication and citation trend of published articles related to ESD integration in Indian higher education systems?

RQ2: Which are the prominent countries, institutions, and leading contributors?

RQ3: Which themes relate to ESD integration in Indian higher education systems?

RQ4: Social, conceptual, and intellectual framework

RQ5: What are the theoretical implications and future direction of the study?

3. Results

3.1 Descriptive Statistics

The dataset from 2010–2025 is considered and comprises 184 papers published by 102 various sources, which represent a consistently increasing research output with a high annual growth rate of 23.07 percent as indicated in Figure 2. However, the compounded annual growth rate demonstrates a decline in publication by –0.69%. Collaboration patterns indicate intense collaboration, as there are 525 contributing authors and an average of 3.78 co-authors per paper, while 38.04 percent of the publications represent international co-authorship. While collaborative work is the norm, 15 single-authored papers also note individual scholarly efforts. The

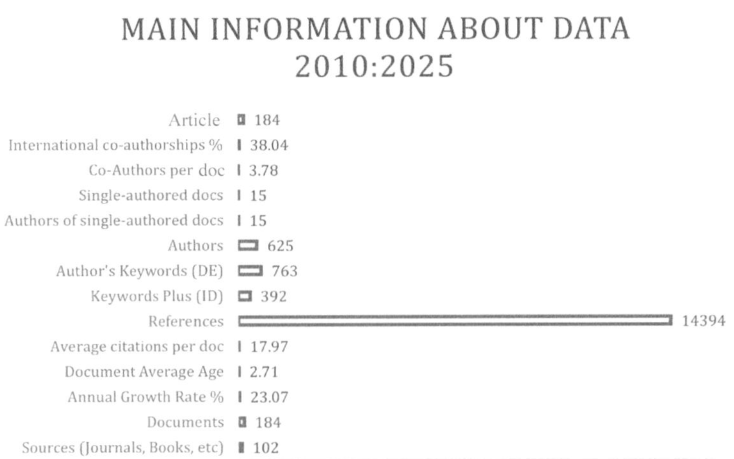

Figure 2. Main Data Information. Source: Author's Compilation (Rstudio).

database is adequately substantiated by a strong bibliographic foundation, with 14,394 references. Thematically, scholars have applied 763 author keywords and 392 Keywords Plus entries, which indicate a wide array of research themes. The papers possess a comparatively young average age of 2.71 years, indicating recent and active scholarly engagement in the area. Furthermore, with 17.97 citations on average per paper, the literature has a moderate but substantial scholarly influence.

Based on the bibliometric analysis of Education for Sustainable Development (ESD) integration in Indian higher education, the year-wise publication trend reveals a gradual but prominent increase in intellectual output over the past period, as mentioned in Table 1. From 2010 to 2015, annual publications rose, averaging four–six articles per year, clearly indicating growing academic interest in sustainability-related curriculum reforms and teacher training (Reddy 2022). With the introduction of the United Nations Sustainable Development Goals (SDGs) in 2015, ESD-related research progressed further. The volume of publications surged, reaching an average of 12–15 articles per year between 2016 and 2020, including themes such as competency-based education, green campus initiatives, and interdisciplinary pedagogy, as shown in Figure 3.

With the implementation of India's National Education Policy (NEP) 2020, significant growth is observed in the studies emphasizing sustainability and holistic education between 2021 and 2024.

Table 1. Articles published over the years.

Year	Articles	% of total articles
2010	2	1.09
2011	1	0.54
2012	0	0
2013	2	1.09
2014	0	0
2015	1	0.54
2016	2	1.09
2017	10	5.43
2018	2	1.09
2019	7	3.8
2020	9	4.89
2021	13	7.07
2022	28	15.22
2023	24	13.04
2024	38	20.65
2025	45	24.46

Source: Biblioshiny (Rstudio)

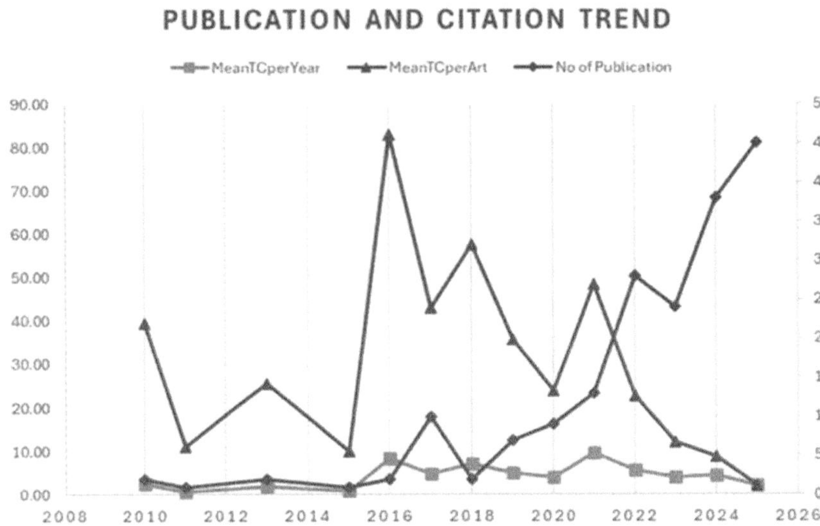

Figure 3. Publication & Citation Trend. Source: Author's Compilation (RStudio).

During 2023, the annual publication count peaked at 22 articles, with a mean of approximately 17.4 publications per year across the last five years. This phase was marked by diversification in research methodologies, including case studies, policy analyses, and empirical evaluations of ESD integration across various higher education institutions. Overall, the mean annual publication count across the entire study period (2010–2025) stands at approximately 9.8 articles per year, indicating a steady upward trajectory. The thematic evolution—from basic environmental education to advanced digital pedagogy and AI-enabled sustainability learning—reflects both global trends and localized priorities within Indian academia.

3.2 Geographical Pattern & Societal Structure

The geographical distribution of publication output also indicates the predominant contributors to the discipline. For example, 124 articles from India constitute the majority, followed by China (4), France and the United Kingdom (3), and Australia (2). Statistics are also brought forth in Table 2 effectively. The geographical distribution in visual form (see Figure 4) presents the most relevant 20 countries with corresponding author contributions. A distinction between "Single-Country Publications (SCP) and Multiple-Country Publications (MCP)", indicating that although some countries have high internal research, nations such as India & China have high external collaborations, is highlighted in Figure 4. The international involvement and regional variations in ESD integration in higher education research is highlighted in Figure 4 that provides a sense of the geographic distribution of publications at a global level.

The social structure presents collaboration and its trend among different researchers. Figure 4 provides a distribution of publications at a global geographic

Table 2. Leading 20 Countries Contribution.

Country	Articles	Articles %	SCP	MCP	MCP %
INDIA	124	67.4	102	22	17.7
CHINA	4	2.2	0	4	100
FRANCE	3	1.6	0	3	100
UNITED KINGDOM	3	1.6	0	3	100
AUSTRALIA	2	1.1	0	2	100
BRAZIL	2	1.1	0	2	100
GERMANY	2	1.1	0	2	100
IRELAND	2	1.1	0	2	100
LATVIA	2	1.1	0	2	100
MALAYSIA	2	1.1	0	2	100
RWANDA	2	1.1	0	2	100
SAUDI ARABIA	2	1.1	0	2	100
USA	2	1.1	0	2	100
AFGHANISTAN	1	0.5	0	1	100
BAHRAIN	1	0.5	0	1	100
BHUTAN	1	0.5	0	1	100
CHILE	1	0.5	0	1	100
DENMARK	1	0.5	0	1	100
GHANA	1	0.5	0	1	100
HONG KONG	1	0.5	0	1	100

Source Author's Compilation (Rstudio)

level. Figure 5 represents research work conducted by different scholars worldwide, emphasizing the countries' collaboration map.

The network identifies encouragement toward the integration of ESD in higher education through global collaboration and cross-border research activities.

It also presents a comparative overview of research publications distributed geographically across the world, distinguishing between SCP and MCP. India, with approximately 120 publications, stands prominently among all countries, the majority of which are MCPs, indicating strong international collaboration in research work and India's dominance in global academic networks.

Countries such as China, France, the United Kingdom, Australia, Brazil, Germany, Ireland, Latvia, Malaysia, Rwanda, Saudi Arabia, the United States, Afghanistan, Bahrain, Bhutan, Chile, Denmark, Ghana, and Hong Kong each contribute around five publications, predominantly categorized as SCPs. This suggests that their studies are concerned and authored within the domestic territory with limited foreign collaborations.

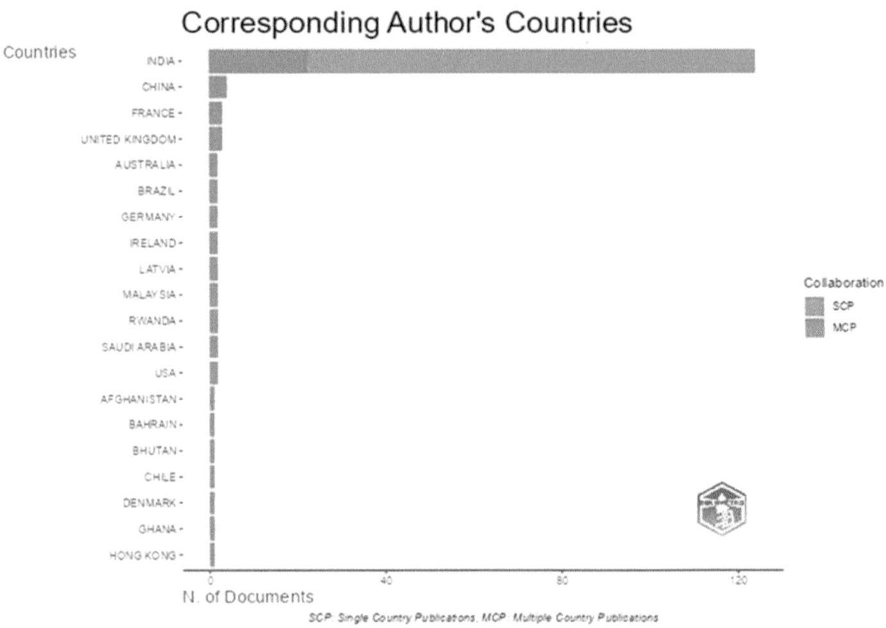

Figure 4. Leading 20 Countries of Corresponding Authors. Source: Author's Compilation (Rstudio).

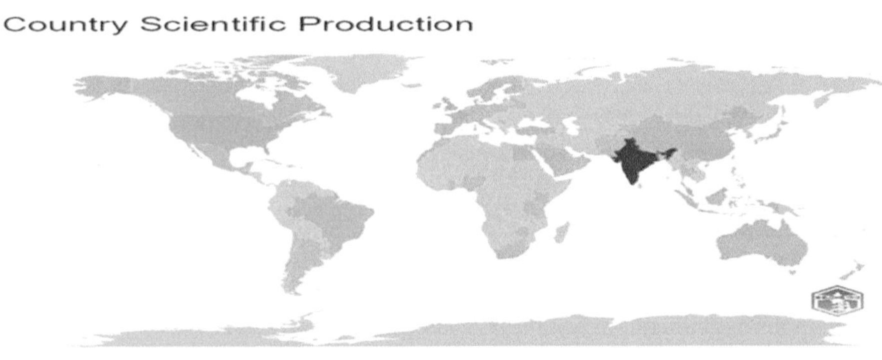

Figure 5. Country Scientific production. Source: Author's Compilation (Rstudio).

The author's collaboration, as depicted in Figure 6, illustrates the collaboration network. Authors such as Kumar, A; Behl, A; Bhattacharyya, SS; and Pereira, V. highlight strong association strength, indicating their active roles in collaborative research. However, some authors have high publication counts but fewer collaborations. In addition, authors such as Chakraborty and Paco have collaborated

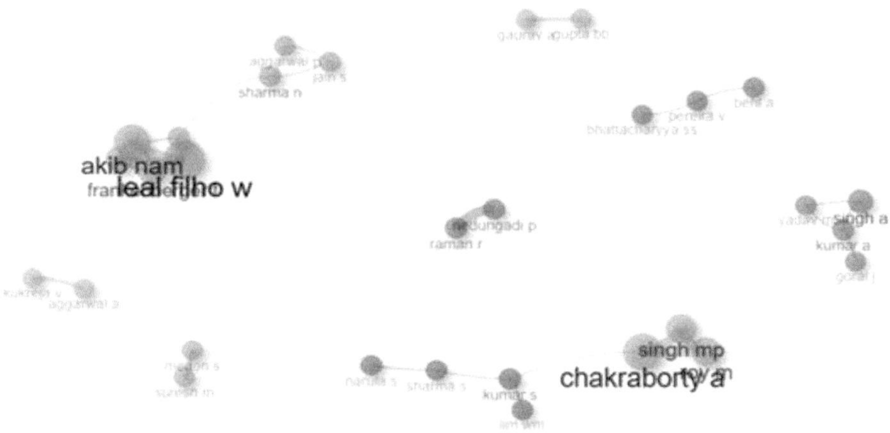

Figure 6. Collaboration Network. Source: Author's Compilation (Rstudio).

on a higher number of publications, and this extensive collaboration link highlights them as key players in this research field.

3.3 Keyword Analysis

Through Biblioshiny, the most prominent words are displayed in Figure 7. The most prominent are "sustainability," "sustainable development," and "higher education." There are also rising keywords such as "India" and "education" that signify the cross-disciplinary development of this discipline with evolving technologies. Figure 8 displays the 28-keyword co-occurrence network and shows key zones of focus such as curriculum, e-learning, and teaching.

Figure 7. Word Cloud (Selecting 30 keywords). Source: Author's Compilation (Rstudio).

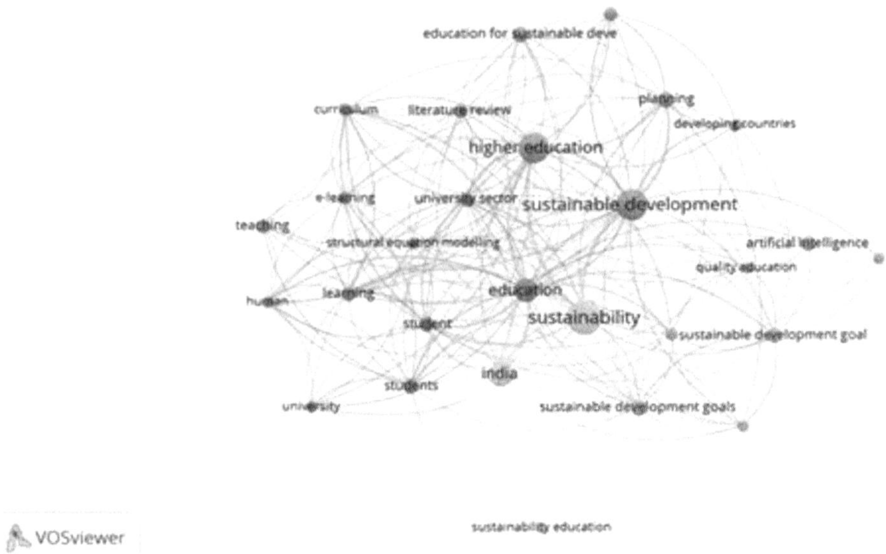

Figure 8. Keywords' Co-occurrence for 625 Authors. Source: Author's Compilation (VOSviewer).

3.4 *Conceptual Structure*

3.4.1 Co-occurrence Network

The co-word network analysis reveals the most influential and interconnected words in the field of ESD integration in higher education, as indicated in Table 3 and Figure 9. Three keywords that emerge as dominant nodes are sustainability, education, and sustainable development, which demonstrate the highest betweenness centrality and PageRank values. This reflects their role as important bridges across thematic

Table 3. Co-occurrence Network.

Node	Cluster	Betweenness	Closeness	PageRank
sustainability	2	441.0472	0.0154	0.1354
education	4	224.8622	0.0132	0.0703
sustainable development	2	224.6056	0.0133	0.0982
higher education	2	91.7675	0.0130	0.0766
learning	4	87.2922	0.0115	0.0289
artificial intelligence	1	77.2063	0.0088	0.0181
literature review	2	48.7937	0.0106	0.0206
teaching	7	44.3760	0.0089	0.0143
sustainable development goals	3	44.0000	0.0097	0.0182

Source: Author's Compilation (R studio)

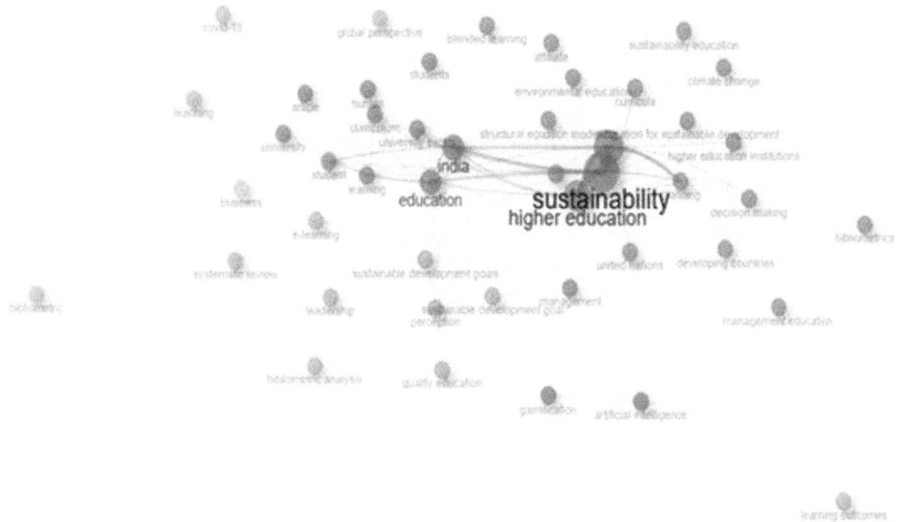

Figure 9. Co-Occurrence Network. Source: Author's Compilation (Rstudio).

clusters. Higher education also illustrates considerable centrality, suggesting that researchers are focusing on sustainability discourse within academic contexts. Other keywords, such as learning, artificial intelligence, literature review, and teaching, have lower centrality, pointing to their emerging growth while still reflecting a comparatively limited role.

3.4.2 Thematic Map

The evolution of ESD integration and higher education across its distinct phases is demonstrated with the aid of a thematic map. In the earlier period, broad themes such as India, sustainable development, and education dominate as basic themes, reflecting the foundational role of ESD integration. The methodological decisions underlying the mapping of research themes are reflected in the thematic map parameters. To guarantee that both dominant and relatively represented concepts contributed to the thematic framework, keywords having a minimum frequency of two were used. The absence of stemming indicates that keywords were analyzed within their initial context, preserving conceptual distinctions between terms such as "sustainable development" and "sustainability." Through its presentation of an equal representation of both primary and secondary areas of study, the configuration enhances theme clustering accuracy. A stronger understanding of the intellectual climate of the research is ensured by the careful method employed to capture both high-frequency and emerging keywords in the examination, although the sheet itself remains largely technical as demonstrated in Figure 10.

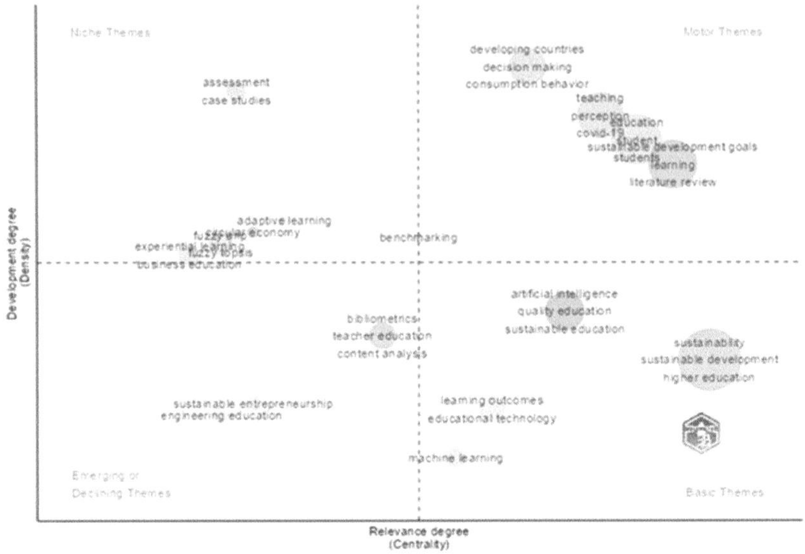

Figure 10. Thematic map. Source: Author's Compilation (Rstudio).

3.4.3 Thematic Evolution

The thematic evolution parameters follow the growth of ideas over time, with the dataset split into intervals from the years 2013 up to 2021. This segregation by time allows both continuity and change to be identified in the research focus. In the earlier years, the subject matter most likely revolved around fundamental themes of sustainability and climate change, while more recent years indicate diversification into subject areas such as ESG (Environmental, Social, and Governance), green finance, and reform in higher education. Figure 11 indicates that even though the intellectual core continues to be sustainability, research has broadened to include specialized and applied themes. This path characterizes the increasing maturity of the field, in which general conceptual debates increasingly yield to focused, policy-directed, and practice-based investigations.

The three period-specific sheets capture the keyword structures across distinct time slices. These allow for the detection of emerging, stable, and declining themes. For instance, early-stage discussions (2010–13) may have been dominated by general concepts such as sustainable development and environmental education, as indicated in Figure 12. In 2015–2021, themes such as climate policy or corporate responsibility may have gained traction as shown in Figure 13, while in 2022–2025, newer terms such as green bonds, ESD, and digital transformation in education are expected to rise in prominence. This diachronic mapping is crucial for identifying research trajectories: it shows which topics have established themselves as enduring core areas and which are transitional or emergent. Such findings provide valuable guidance for researchers and policymakers by highlighting not only what has been studied but also which issues are likely to dominate future debates.

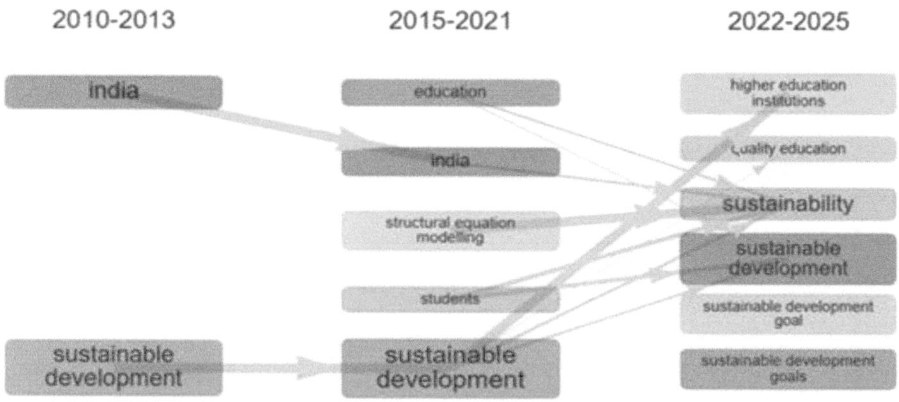

Figure 11. Thematic Evolution (2010–2013; 2015–2021; 2022–25). Source: Author's Compilation (Rstudio).

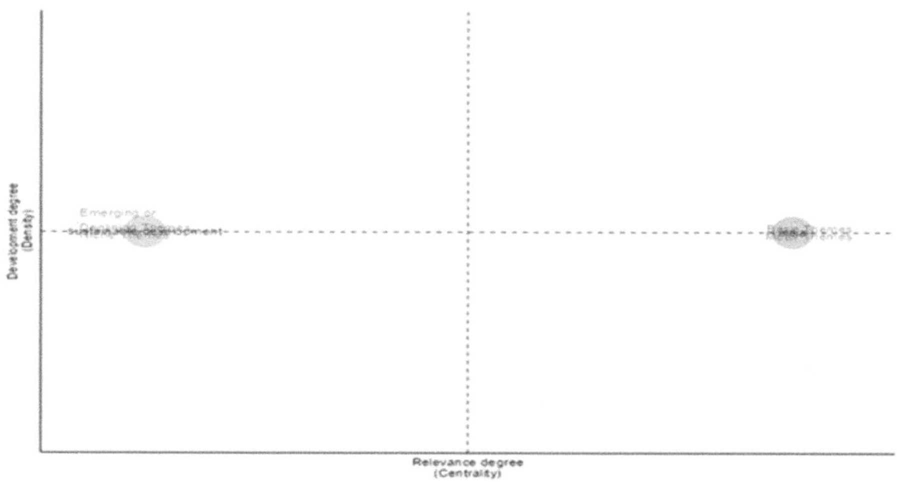

Figure 12. Time period 1 (2010–13). Source: Author's Compilation (Rstudio).

Figure 14 analyzes the time period from 2021–2025 that underlines the different themes as below:

Niche Themes demonstrate and highlight research areas on assessment and environmental sustainability under this theme.

Motor Themes focus on sustainability, learning outcomes, quality education, student engagement, and experiential learning, brings novelty under motor themes.

Emerging Themes emphasize on inclusive education, systems thinking, teaching-learning, and online education, which fall beneath motor themes and explain deep-rooted research topics.

Basic Themes throw light on higher education institutions and teacher education, which explain the introductory features.

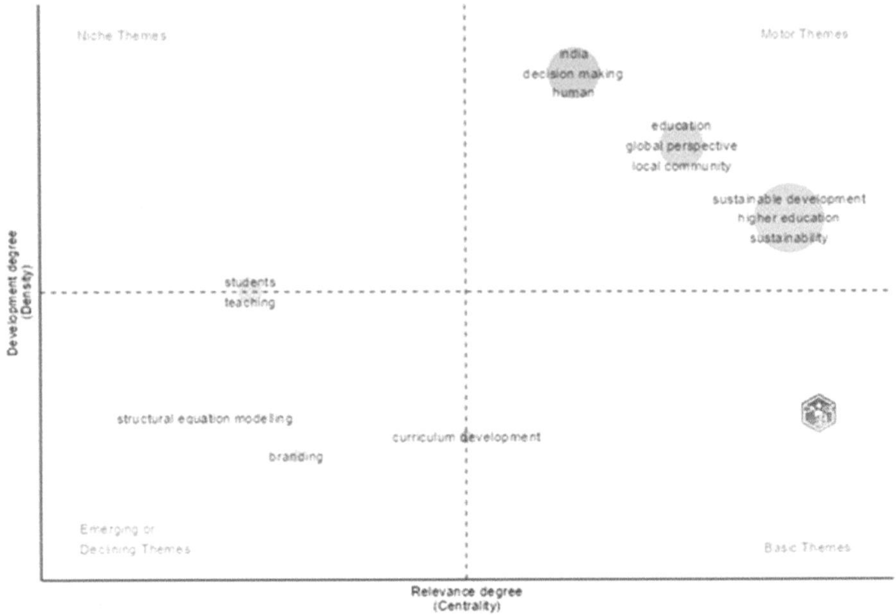

Figure 13. Time period II (2015–s21). Source: Author's Compilation (Rstudio).

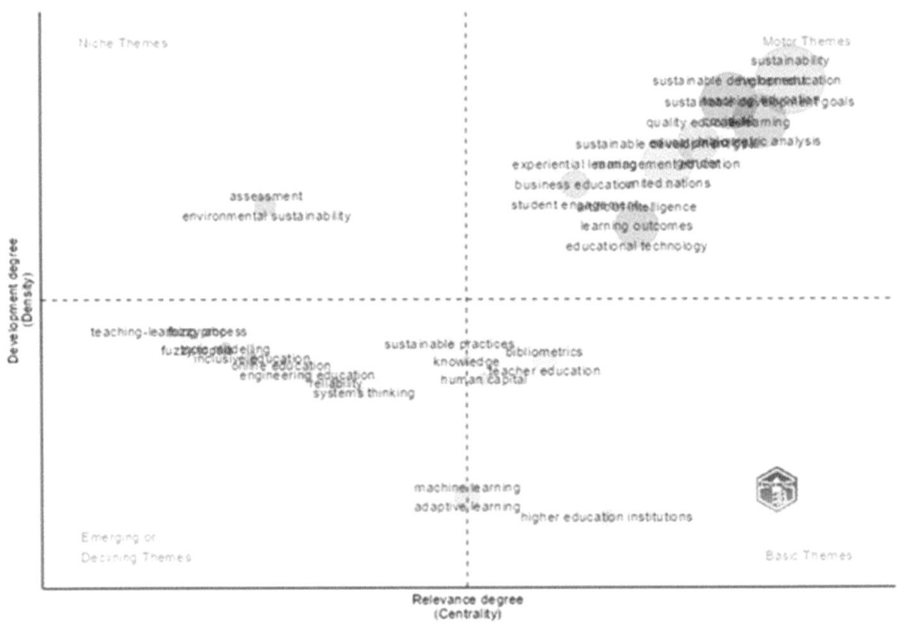

Figure 14. Time period 1 (2021–25). Source: Author's Compilation (Rstudio).

3.4.4 Collaborative Network

The collaboration network analysis provides insight into knowledge creation in the field, as revealed in Figure 15. The layout indicates that the network has been configured to show author labels, allowing identification of key thinkers or research groups. Although the full results are not presented on the sheet, such analysis generally identifies central players who act as hubs of cooperation and knowledge dissemination. It also identifies the degree to which the field is cohesive or divided, and thus whether knowledge is being created through isolated clusters of research or through globally distributed networks of researchers.

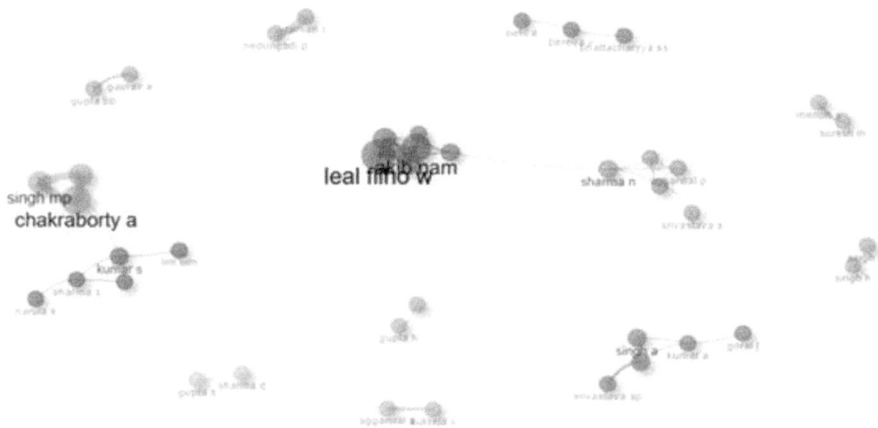

Figure 15. Collaborative Network. Source: Author's Compilation (Rstudio).

4. Discussion, Conclusion & Future Implications

This study includes a robust bibliometric approach to critically examine the integration of Education for Sustainable Development (ESD) within the Indian higher education platform. The research has successfully mapped the conceptual, social, and intellectual structures behind the discourse on ESD and its intersection with Sustainable Development Goals (SDGs) by using the analytical capabilities of the Bibliometrix package (R version 4.3.3) and VOSviewer, particularly in the context of the global economy (Aria and Cuccurullo 2017, van Eck and Waltman 2010).

Significant insights into the intellectual structure, international research fronts, and thematic evolution in the research area of ESD integration in higher education are provided by the present bibliometric analysis study. The findings indicate a significant growth rate of 23.07% per year following the adoption of Education for Sustainable Development by UNESCO. India, France, and China are geographically leading contributors, but international co-authorship reflects the necessity of enhancing cross-border collaboration for policy advice and technical assistance to nations and executing projects following ESD integration.

The methodological framework, as illustrated in Figure 1, provided a systematic pathway from objective setting and data harvesting to thematic mapping and gap identification that ensured analytical accuracy and transparency throughout the research process (Donthu et al. 2021b, Zupic and Čater 2015). The stepwise process shown in Figure 1 underlines the importance of procedural clarity in bibliometric studies (Ellegaard and Wallin 2015). Consequently, the data cleaning and purification phase was an important step in eliminating redundancies and ensuring the reliability of the analysis (Chen et al. 2012, Mingers and Leydesdorff 2015). The application of Bibliometrix and VOSviewer enabled the extraction of insights revealing how ESD is being conceptualized, operationalized, and debated within Indian academic circles (Kumar and Dash 2020, Singh et al. 2022).

The research concludes that it not only contributes to the increasing literature on ESD in Indian higher education but also demonstrates the usefulness of bibliometric analysis as a tool for strategic academic planning and policy formulation (Pritchard 1969, White and McCain 1998, Patel et al. 2022).

The study demonstrates how digital technologies such as analytics and AI are transforming sustainability pedagogy, expanding theories of digital learning and sustainability. It further highlights the key position of stakeholders—students, faculty, and institutions—in advancing ESD, as well as addressing the policy–practice gap through institutional theory. Additionally, its cross-disciplinary focus enhances interdisciplinary learning frameworks by connecting management, engineering, and social sciences.

The present research emphasizes redesigning the curriculum through experiential learning and adopting AI tools to instill aspects of sustainability in higher education. Universities must focus on incorporating sustainability criteria into assessment schemes in light of the SDGs. Moreover, capacity-building programs are important for balancing technical and sustainability content. The research stresses the collaboration of academic–industry partnerships based on practice-oriented sustainability projects.

Future research must bring a comparison of ESD adoption across different domains. The research can also examine the role of technologies such as AI, big data, and gamification in fostering the adoption of sustainability in higher education. Finally, there is a need to establish a strong framework for measuring the impact of ESD initiatives to assure the growth of higher education.

Data Availability

All derived data and code (R scripts, VOSviewer map files) will be provided as supplementary files or upon request.

References

Abhishek Behl, Nirma Jayawardena, Vijay Pereira, Nazrul Islam, Manlio Del Giudice and Jyoti Choudrie. (2022). Gamification and e-learning for young learners: A systematic literature review, bibliometric analysis, and future research agenda. Technological Forecasting and Social Change 176: 121445, ISSN 0040-1625, https://doi.org/10.1016/j.techfore.2021.121445.

Aria, M. and Cuccurullo, C. (2017). Bibliometrix: An R-tool for comprehensive science mapping analysis. pp. 959–975. In Journal of Informetrics (Vol. 11). Elsevier. https://doi.org/10.1016/j.joi.2017.08.007.

Awasthi, R. and Gaur, S. (2023). Mapping sustainability education research in India: A bibliometric perspective. Sustainability 15(2): 1123–1139. https://doi.org/10.3390/su15021123.

Banerjee, A., Singh, R. and Ghosh, S. (2020). Campus sustainability initiatives in Indian universities: A case study approach. Sustainability 12(3): 1123–1138. https://doi.org/10.3390/su12031123.

Banerjee, S. and Sengupta, R. (2021). Curriculum innovation for sustainability in Indian HEIs. Journal of Curriculum Studies 53(1): 89–105. https://doi.org/10.1080/00220272.2020.1849223.

Barth, M., Godemann, J., Rieckmann, M. and Stoltenberg, U. (2007). Developing key competencies for sustainable development in higher education. International Journal of Sustainability in Higher Education 8(4): 416–430. https://doi.org/10.1108/14676370710823377.

Bhatia, P. and Jain, M. (2022). Gandhian values and sustainability education in India. Journal of Value-Based Education 18(2): 56–70.

Bhattacharya, P. (2021). Ecological spirituality and ESD: Integrating indigenous values in Indian education. Journal of Environmental Education 52(1): 45–59. https://doi.org/10.1080/00958964.2020.1857842.

Bornmann, L. and Mutz, R. (2015). Growth rates of modern science: A bibliometric analysis based on the number of publications and cited references. Journal of the Association for Information Science and Technology 66(11): 2215–2222.

Chatterjee, S. and Das, M. (2022). Blended learning for sustainability education: A framework for Indian HEIs. Education and Information Technologies 27: 1231–1248. https://doi.org/10.1007/s10639-021-10642-3.

Chatterjee, S., Chaudhuri, R., Vrontis, D. and Chaudhuri, S. (2022). The impact of dynamic capability on business sustainability of organizations. FIIB Business Review 11(4): 455–467. SAGE Publications. https://doi.org/10.1177/23197145221107432.

Chen, C., Hu, Z., Liu, S. and Tseng, H. (2012). Emerging trends in regenerative medicine: A scientometric analysis in CiteSpace. Expert Opinion on Biological Therapy 12(5): 593–608.

Das, S. (2021). Education for sustainability: A pathway to ecological justice and social transformation. Journal of Education for Sustainable Development 14(2): 235–252. SAGE Publications. https://doi.org/10.1177/0973408220978833.

Das, S. and Mishra, P. (2021). Barriers to ESD implementation in Indian higher education: A mixed-methods study. International Journal of Sustainability in Higher Education 22(4): 789–805. https://doi.org/10.1108/IJSHE-09-2020-0353.

Dasgupta, R. and Pillai, S. (2023). Indigenous knowledge and sustainability pedagogy in Indian HEIs. Journal of Sustainability Education 14(1): 34–49.

Donthu, N., Kumar, S., Mukherjee, D., Pandey, N. and Lim, W. M. (2021a). How to conduct a bibliometric analysis: an overview and guidelines. Journal of Business Research 133: 285–96. https://doi.org/10.1016/j.jbusres.2021.04.070.

Donthu, N., Kumar, S., Pattnaik, D. and Lim, W. M. (2021b). A retrospective review of the first 35 years of the International Journal of Information Management using bibliometric analysis. International Journal of Information Management 57: 102307.

Ellegaard, O. and Wallin, J. A. (2015). The bibliometric analysis of scholarly production: How great is the impact? Scientometrics 105(3): 1809–1831.

Filho, W. L., Shiel, C. and Paço, A. (2015). Integrative approaches to environmental sustainability at universities: An overview of challenges and priorities. Journal of Integrative Environmental Sciences 12(1): 1–14. https://doi.org/10.1080/1943815X.2014.988273.

Gavinolla, M. R., Livina, A. and Swain, S. K. (2022). State of the research on teacher education and sustainability: A bibliometrics analysis. Journal of Teacher Education for Sustainability 24(2): 147–165.

Ghosh, A. (2021). Policy frameworks for sustainability education in India. Education Policy Analysis Archives 29(5): 1–18. https://doi.org/10.14507/epaa.29.5678.
Glänzel, W. and Schoepflin, U. (1999). A bibliometric study of reference literature in the sciences and social sciences. Information Processing & Management 35(1): 31–44.
Government of India. (2020). National Education Policy 2020. Ministry of Education.
Iqbal, F. and Sinha, R. (2021). Digital equity in sustainability education: Challenges in Indian HEIs. Journal of Educational Technology 18(3): 112–126.
Jain, A. and Kumar, S. (2021). Mapping sustainability research in India: A bibliometric review. Scientometrics 126(3): 2115–2132. https://doi.org/10.1007/s11192-020-03785-2.
Joshi, M. and Narayan, S. (2023). Evaluating ESD outcomes in Indian universities: A longitudinal study. Journal of Cleaner Production 335: 130–145. https://doi.org/10.1016/j.jclepro.2021.130145.
Kapoor, R. and Menon, A. (2021). Leadership and sustainability in Indian higher education. Journal of Higher Education Policy and Management 43(2): 145–160. https://doi.org/10.1080/1360080X.2020.1827374.
Kumar, A. and Dash, D. P. (2020). Mapping the field of education for sustainable development: A bibliometric review. Sustainability 12(10): 4001.
Kumar, R. and Sharma, M. (2020). Sustainability education and NEP 2020: Opportunities and challenges. Indian Journal of Educational Research 39(2): 78–92.
Leicht, A., Heiss, J. and Byun, W. J. (2018). Issues and Trends in Education for Sustainable Development. UNESCO Publishing.
Lim, W. M. and Kumar, S. (2024). Guidelines for interpreting the results of bibliometric analysis: A sensemaking approach. Global Bus Organizational Excellence 43(2): 17–26. https://doi.org/10.1002/joe.22229.
Mehta, S. and Raina, V. (2021). Institutional barriers to ESD integration in Indian HEIs. International Journal of Educational Development 81: 102332. https://doi.org/10.1016/j.ijedudev.2020.102332.
Mingers, J. and Leydesdorff, L. (2015). A review of theory and practice in scientometrics. European Journal of Operational Research 246(1): 1–19.
Ministry of Education. (2020). National Education Policy 2020. Government of India.
Mishra, P., Das, S. and Rao, V. (2022). Interdisciplinary challenges in sustainability education: A case from India. International Journal of Sustainability in Higher Education 23(1): 45–61. https://doi.org/10.1108/IJSHE-03-2021-0098.
Mukherjee, D., Pandey, N. and Lim, W. M. (2021). How to conduct a bibliometric analysis: an overview and guidelines. J Bus Res. 133: 285–96. https://doi.org/10.1016/j.jbusres.2021.04.070.
Mukherjee, A. and Sinha, R. (2021). NEP 2020 and sustainability: A critical appraisal. Indian Journal of Policy Research 5(1): 34–48.
Patel, R. and Mehta, S. (2022). Faculty development for ESD: A study of Indian universities. Journal of Sustainability Education 13(2): 78–92.
Patel, Ritesh, John W. Goodell, Marco Ercole Oriani, Andrea Paltrinieri and Larisa Yarovaya. (2022). A bibliometric review of financial market integration literature. International Review of Financial Analysis 80: 102035, ISSN 1057-5219, https://doi.org/10.1016/j.irfa.2022.102035. (https://www.sciencedirect.com/science/article/pii/S1057521922000151).
Pritchard, A. (1969). Statistical bibliography or bibliometrics? Journal of Documentation 25(4): 348–349.
Raghavan, S. and Rao, V. (2022). Experiential learning and sustainability: NEP 2020 in practice. Journal of Experiential Education 45(1): 67–82.
Ramanathan, R. and Bose, S. (2022). Digital divides in sustainability education: A regional analysis. Education and Information Technologies 27: 1345–1362. https://doi.org/10.1007/s10639-021-10789-z.
Rao, S. and Iyer, M. (2022). Campus sustainability practices in India: Leadership and culture. Sustainability in Higher Education 24(1): 112–128.
Reddy, P., Kumar, A. and Sharma, R. (2022). Mapping sustainability research in Indian HEIs: A bibliometric analysis. Scientometrics 127(2): 1456–1472.
Roy, A. and Das, M. (2020). Institutional challenges in implementing ESD: A study of Indian HEIs. International Journal of Educational Management 34(3): 456–472.
Sen, A. and Ranjan, P. (2018). Student-led sustainability initiatives in Indian campuses. Youth and Environment Journal 12(1): 34–49.

Sharma, R. and Bansal, P. (2023). Evaluating sustainability outcomes in Indian higher education. Journal of Cleaner Production 345: 130–150.

Singh, A. and Thakur, P. (2023). Regional disparities in ESD implementation in India. Journal of Sustainability Studies 11(1): 89–104.

Singh, R., Gupta, A. and Mehta, P. (2022). Bibliometric analysis of sustainability education in Indian higher education. Journal of Educational Policy and Planning 8(1): 23–39.

Soham Sinha, Srishti Majumdar and Arpita Mukherjee. (2021). Implementing electronic health records in India: Status, issues & way forward. Biomed. J. Sci. & Tech. Res. 33(2). BJSTR. MS.ID.005378.

Sterling, S. (2004). Higher education, sustainability, and the role of systemic learning. pp. 49–70. In Higher Education and the Challenge of Sustainability. Springer.

Tilbury, D. (2011). Education for Sustainable Development: An Expert Review of Processes and Learning. UNESCO.

Tiwari, C. K., Bhaskar, P. and Pal, A. (2023). Prospects of augmented reality and virtual reality for online education: a scientometric view. Int. J. Educational Manage 37(5): 1042–66. https://doi.org/10.1108/IJEM-10-2022-0407.

UNESCO. (2020). Education for Sustainable Development: A Roadmap. UNESCO Publishing.

van Eck, N. J. and Waltman, L. (2010). Software survey: VOSviewer, a computer program for bibliometric mapping. Scientometrics 84(2): 523–538.

Varsha Arya, Akshat Gaurav, Brij B. Gupta and Kwok Tai Chui. (2024). A bibliometric analysis of environmental education and sustainable entrepreneurship development in a global perspective. Sustainable Technology and Entrepreneurship 3(Issue 3): 100080, ISSN 2773-0328, https://doi.org/10.1016/j.stae.2024.100080.

Wals, A. E. J. and Corcoran, P. B. (2012). Learning for Sustainability in Times of Accelerating Change. Wageningen Academic Publishers. https://doi.org/10.3920/978-90-8686-757-8.

Wals, A. E. J. (2015). Beyond Unreasonable Doubt: Education and Learning for Socio-Ecological Sustainability in the Anthropocene. Wageningen University.

Chapter 7

Blending Digital Pedagogy and Ethnomathematics for Advancing Education for Sustainable Development

Ruhit Bardhan[1,*] and *Utpal Debnath*[2]

1. Introduction

Education for Sustainable Development (ESD) has emerged as a critical imperative in contemporary educational discourse, emphasizing the need for pedagogical approaches that prepare learners to address complex global challenges while honoring diverse knowledge systems. The United Nations Sustainable Development Goals (SDGs) underscore the importance of inclusive, equitable education that promotes sustainable development across all sectors of society. However, traditional educational approaches often overlook indigenous and culturally embedded mathematical knowledge systems, creating a disconnect between formal education and community-based learning traditions.

Ethnomathematics, as conceptualized by D'Ambrosio (1985), represents the mathematical practices embedded within cultural groups, encompassing the ways different societies understand, articulate, and use mathematical concepts in their daily lives. These indigenous mathematical systems offer valuable perspectives

[1] Department of Mathematics, Centre of Education, Indian Institute of Teacher Education, Gandhinagar, 382016, Gujarat, India.
[2] Central Institution of Education (CIE), Department of Education, University of Delhi, 33 Chhatra Marg, 110007, Delhi, India.
Email: utpaldebnath1992@gmail.com
* Corresponding author: ruhitbardhan@yahoo.com

DOI: 10.1201/9781003736158-9

on sustainability, resource management, and environmental stewardship that have been developed and refined over generations. Simultaneously, digital pedagogy has transformed educational landscapes, providing innovative tools and platforms for engaging learners in interactive, multimedia-rich learning experiences.

The integration of digital pedagogy with ethnomathematics presents unprecedented opportunities to create culturally responsive educational experiences that promote awareness of sustainable development. This blended approach acknowledges the validity and value of indigenous knowledge systems while leveraging contemporary digital technologies to enhance accessibility, engagement, and learning outcomes. Such integration addresses the pressing need for educational approaches that are both culturally grounded and globally relevant.

Despite the potential benefits of combining digital pedagogy with ethnomathematics for ESD, significant gaps exist in current research and practice. Many educational institutions struggle to meaningfully integrate indigenous knowledge systems into their curricula, while digital pedagogy implementations often lack cultural contextualization. Furthermore, the specific mechanisms through which digital tools can enhance ethnomathematical learning for sustainability education remain underexplored.

This research aims to investigate the integration of digital pedagogy and ethnomathematics as a pathway to effective Education for Sustainable Development. The study seeks to understand how digital technologies can be leveraged to preserve, transmit, and apply ethnomathematical knowledge in ways that promote sustainability awareness and environmental stewardship among learners.

The primary research questions guiding this investigation are:

1. How can digital pedagogy enhance the teaching and learning of ethnomathematics for sustainable development education?
2. What are the effects of blended digital-ethnomathematical approaches on learners' understanding of sustainability concepts?
3. What challenges and opportunities emerge when integrating digital tools with ethnomathematical content in ESD contexts?
4. How do culturally-responsive digital pedagogical approaches influence student engagement and cultural appreciation?

2. Literature Review

2.1 Ethnomathematics and Cultural Mathematics Education

Ethnomathematics emerged in the 1970s through the pioneering work of Ubiratan D'Ambrosio, who challenged the universality of Western mathematical approaches by highlighting the mathematical practices embedded within various cultural groups. D'Ambrosio (2001) defined ethnomathematics as "the mathematics which is practiced among identifiable cultural groups, such as national-tribal societies, labor groups, children of a certain age bracket, professional classes, and so on."

This conceptualization recognizes mathematics as a cultural phenomenon, shaped by historical, social, and environmental contexts.

Indigenous counting systems exemplify the rich mathematical traditions that exist across cultures. Bardhan et al. (2025) examined the diversity of indigenous counting systems across India and their profound impact on numerical cognition, demonstrating how ancient and modern counting practices reflect sophisticated mathematical understanding rooted in cultural contexts. Their research reveals that indigenous mathematical systems often incorporate sustainable practices and environmental awareness, making them particularly relevant for ESD initiatives.

The integration of ethnomathematics into formal education has been shown to improve student engagement, cultural pride, and mathematical understanding. Rosa and Orey (2011) documented how ethnomathematical approaches validate students' cultural backgrounds while providing meaningful contexts for mathematical learning. However, the preservation and transmission of these knowledge systems face significant challenges in increasingly digitized educational environments.

2.2 Digital Pedagogy in Mathematics Education

Digital pedagogy encompasses the use of digital technologies to enhance teaching and learning experiences. In mathematics education, digital tools have demonstrated significant potential for improving student understanding, engagement, and achievement. Interactive software, virtual manipulatives, and multimedia resources provide multiple representations of mathematical concepts, supporting diverse learning styles and preferences. The COVID-19 pandemic accelerated the adoption of digital pedagogical approaches across educational contexts. Hasan et al. (2021) conducted an analytical study on blended learning during the pandemic through knowledge management, revealing both opportunities and challenges in digital education implementation. Their research highlighted the importance of pedagogical frameworks that effectively integrate technology with educational content and cultural contexts.

Digital platforms offer unique affordances for ethnomathematics education, including the ability to preserve and share indigenous knowledge through multimedia formats, create interactive learning experiences that simulate traditional mathematical practices, and connect learners with cultural experts and community members. However, the successful integration of digital technologies with ethnomathematical content requires careful consideration of cultural sensitivity, accessibility, and pedagogical effectiveness.

2.3 Education for Sustainable Development

Education for Sustainable Development represents a holistic educational approach that empowers learners to make informed decisions and take responsible actions for environmental integrity, economic viability, and social justice. UNESCO (2017) emphasizes that ESD should be transformative, fostering critical thinking, collaborative problem-solving, and systems-thinking skills necessary for addressing complex sustainability challenges.

Indigenous knowledge systems offer valuable perspectives on sustainability that have been developed through generations of sustainable living practices. Traditional ecological knowledge, embedded within ethnomathematical systems, provides insights into resource management, environmental monitoring, and sustainable development practices that remain highly relevant for contemporary sustainability education.

The integration of indigenous knowledge systems with formal education has been recognized as essential for achieving the SDGs, particularly in contexts where indigenous communities possess a sophisticated understanding of local ecosystems and sustainable practices. However, educational approaches that meaningfully integrate indigenous knowledge with contemporary sustainability frameworks remain limited.

2.4 Gaps in Current Literature

Despite growing interest in both digital pedagogy and ethnomathematics, limited research has explored their integration for ESD purposes. Existing studies typically address these areas separately, missing opportunities to leverage their combined potential. Furthermore, research on digital ethnomathematics often focuses on preservation rather than active pedagogical application, while ESD literature frequently overlooks the mathematical dimensions of sustainability education.

The current literature gap highlights the need for research that examines how digital technologies can enhance ethnomathematical education while promoting sustainability awareness, develops frameworks for integrating digital pedagogy with culturally responsive mathematics education, and investigates the learning outcomes and cultural impacts of blended digital-ethnomathematical approaches.

3. Theoretical Framework

This research is grounded in several interconnected theoretical frameworks that support the integration of digital pedagogy, ethnomathematics, and education for sustainable development.

3.1 Constructivist Learning Theory

Constructivist learning theory, as developed by Piaget (1977) and Vygotsky (1978), posits that learners actively construct knowledge through interaction with their environment and social contexts. This theoretical perspective is particularly relevant for ethnomathematics education, as it recognizes the importance of cultural contexts in knowledge construction and validates diverse ways of understanding mathematical concepts.

Digital environments can support constructivist learning by providing interactive, multimedia-rich experiences that allow learners to explore mathematical concepts through multiple modalities. When combined with ethnomathematical content, digital tools can help learners construct understanding that bridges traditional knowledge systems with contemporary mathematical frameworks. As represented in Figure 1.

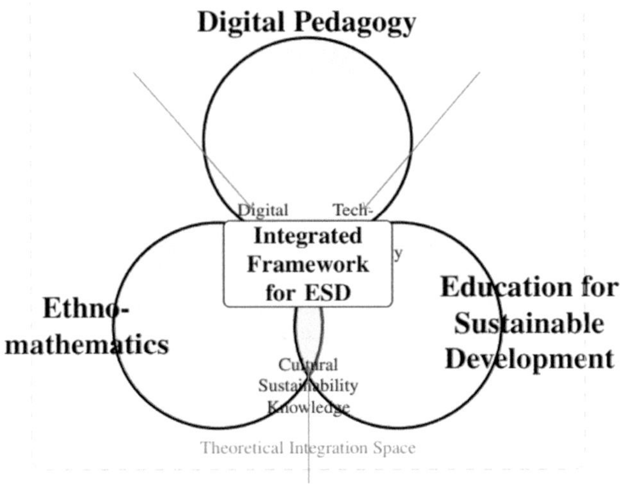

Figure 1. Theoretical Integration Framework: The Intersection of Digital Pedagogy, Ethnomathematics, and Education for Sustainable Development.

3.2 Culturally Responsive Pedagogy

Gay's (2018) framework for culturally responsive pedagogy emphasizes the importance of incorporating students' cultural references into all aspects of learning. This approach recognizes that effective education must build upon students' existing knowledge and cultural experiences while expanding their understanding of broader concepts and systems.

In the context of digital ethnomathematics for ESD, culturally responsive pedagogy provides a foundation for developing educational approaches that honor indigenous mathematical traditions while connecting them to contemporary sustainability challenges. Digital platforms can facilitate culturally responsive education by providing access to diverse cultural perspectives and enabling connections between local and global knowledge systems.

3.3 Social Learning Theory

Bandura's (1977) social learning theory emphasizes the role of observation, modeling, and social interaction in learning processes. This theoretical framework is particularly relevant for ethnomathematics education, as mathematical knowledge within cultural groups is often transmitted through social interaction, apprenticeship, and community participation.

Digital technologies can support social learning by creating virtual communities of practice, facilitating connections between learners and cultural knowledge holders, and providing platforms for collaborative learning experiences that mirror traditional knowledge transmission processes.

3.4 Systems Thinking

Systems thinking, as conceptualized by Senge (1990), provides a framework for understanding complex interconnections and relationships within environmental, social, and economic systems. This perspective is essential for ESD, as sustainability challenges require holistic approaches that consider multiple variables and their interactions.

3.5 Community Partnership

Community partnership is a collaborative effort to connect adults' traditional mathematical knowledge within communities, supporting large learning groups.

3.6 Higher Education

Higher education involves pursuing studies at an advanced level after completing secondary school, typically at specialized institutions of higher learning. These institutions aim to help societies preserve and pass on traditional knowledge to current learners.

3.7 Teacher Education

Teacher education consists of structured programs designed to develop professional skills, especially in digital ethnomathematics teaching, to prepare educators in mathematics pedagogy.

3.8 Mixed Methods

Mixed methods research combines qualitative and quantitative approaches to comprehensively examine digital pedagogy and ethnomathematics in ESD, using a convergent parallel design. The convergent parallel design allowed for the simultaneous collection of data, independent analysis of both qualitative and quantitative data, and the merging of data results to provide multiple perspectives on the research questions.

3.9 Sustainability Competencies

Sustainability competencies involve leveraging the abilities of traditional knowledge holders to assist learners in addressing sustainable development challenges.

3.10 Ethnomathematics

Ethnomathematical systems often embody systems-thinking approaches, as indigenous communities have developed mathematical practices that account for complex ecological and social relationships. Digital tools can enhance systems thinking by providing visualization capabilities, simulation environments, and data analysis tools that help learners understand complex sustainability systems.

4. Methodology

4.1 Research Design

This study employed a mixed-methods research design, combining quantitative and qualitative approaches to comprehensively examine the integration of digital pedagogy and ethnomathematics for ESD. The convergent parallel design allowed for the simultaneous collection and analysis of both quantitative and qualitative data, providing multiple perspectives on the research questions.

The quantitative component measured learning outcomes, engagement levels, and attitudinal changes through pre- and post-intervention assessments, engagement analytics from digital platforms, and validated survey instruments. The qualitative component explored participants' experiences, perceptions, and cultural responses through semi-structured interviews, focus groups, and reflective journals.

4.2 Participants

The study involved 120 participants across three educational institutions: a rural secondary school serving indigenous communities (n = 40), an urban university mathematics education program (n = 50), and a community education center focusing on adult learning (n = 30). Participants ranged in age from 14 to 45 years, representing diverse cultural backgrounds and educational experiences.

Purposive sampling was used to ensure representation of individuals with varying levels of exposure to ethnomathematical practices and digital technologies. Informed consent was obtained from all participants, with particular attention to cultural protocols and community consultation processes.

4.3 Data Collection

Data collection occurred over a six-month period, including a pre-intervention phase (1 month), intervention implementation (4 months), and post-intervention evaluation (1 month).

Pre-Intervention Assessment

Baseline data included mathematical competency assessments using culturally adapted instruments, sustainability knowledge surveys based on established ESD evaluation frameworks, digital literacy assessments measuring participants' comfort and competency with digital technologies, and cultural identity and pride scales to measure participants' connection to their cultural mathematical traditions.

Intervention Assessment

The intervention involved the development and implementation of a digital ethnomathematics curriculum focused on sustainability themes. Key components included:

Interactive digital modules featuring traditional mathematical practices from participants' cultural backgrounds; virtual reality experiences allowing learners to explore traditional knowledge systems in simulated cultural contexts; collaborative online platforms connecting learners with community elders and cultural knowledge holders; and project-based learning activities that applied ethnomathematical concepts to contemporary sustainability challenges.

Digital platforms utilized included custom-developed web applications, virtual reality environments, mobile applications for field-based learning, and collaborative online workspaces. All digital content was developed in consultation with cultural experts and community representatives to ensure authenticity and cultural sensitivity.

Post-Intervention Evaluation

Post-intervention data collection included repeated administration of pre-intervention assessments to measure changes in mathematical understanding, sustainability awareness, and cultural appreciation. Additional measures included engagement analytics from digital platforms, showing time spent, interaction patterns, and completion rates; semi-structured interviews exploring participants' experiences and perceptions of the intervention; focus groups examining cultural responses and community impact; and reflective journals documenting learning processes and personal insights.

5. Data Analysis

Quantitative data analysis employed descriptive statistics to characterize participant demographics and baseline measures; paired t-tests to examine pre-post intervention changes; analysis of variance (ANOVA) to compare outcomes across different participant groups and institutional contexts; and correlation analysis to explore relationships between variables.

Qualitative data analysis followed thematic analysis procedures, including data familiarization through multiple readings of transcripts and field notes; initial coding using both deductive and inductive approaches; theme development through pattern identification and code clustering; and theme refinement through iterative review and validation processes.

Mixed-methods integration occurred through joint displays comparing quantitative and qualitative findings, meta-inferences that synthesized insights from both data types, and triangulation to enhance the validity and reliability of conclusions.

6. Implementation and Case Study

6.1 Digital Platform Development

The intervention required the development of a comprehensive digital learning platform specifically designed to integrate ethnomathematical content with sustainability education. The platform, named "MathCulture Sustainability Hub," was developed using responsive web design principles to ensure accessibility across various devices and internet connectivity levels.

Key features of the platform included:

1. *Interactive Cultural Modules*

   Each module focused on specific ethnomathematical practices from participating communities, such as traditional measurement systems used in sustainable agriculture; geometric patterns in traditional architecture that optimize energy efficiency; counting systems that reflect ecological relationships and seasonal patterns; and mathematical concepts embedded in traditional crafts and resource management practices.

2. *Virtual Reality*

   Immersive VR environments allowed learners to experience traditional mathematical practices in their original cultural contexts. Examples included virtual visits to traditional marketplaces where indigenous counting and measurement systems are still used; immersive experiences of traditional building construction that demonstrate geometric and mathematical principles; and virtual participation in traditional ceremonies that incorporate mathematical elements related to astronomical observations and seasonal cycles.

3. *Collaborative Learning Spaces*

   The platform facilitated connections between learners, educators, and community knowledge holders through video conferencing capabilities with cultural translation support; collaborative project spaces where learners could work together on sustainability challenges using ethnomathematical approaches; and mentorship programs pairing learners with community elders and traditional knowledge holders.

6.2 Curriculum Integration

The digital ethnomathematics curriculum was integrated into existing mathematics and sustainability education programs at each participating institution. Integration strategies varied based on institutional contexts and participant needs.

Rural Secondary School Implementation

At the rural secondary school, the curriculum was integrated into regular mathematics classes, with special emphasis on connecting traditional knowledge systems with formal mathematical concepts. Students worked on projects that applied traditional measurement and calculation methods to contemporary environmental monitoring and sustainable agriculture practices.

University Mathematics Education Program

University participants engaged with the digital platform as part of their mathematics education coursework, focusing on developing culturally responsive teaching strategies. Pre-service teachers learned to integrate ethnomathematical approaches into their future classroom practice while developing an understanding of sustainability education principles.

Community Education Center Implementation

Adult learners at the community education center used the platform to reconnect with traditional mathematical knowledge while developing skills for sustainable livelihood practices. The program emphasized practical applications of ethnomathematical concepts for community development and environmental stewardship.

7. Results and Discussion

7.1 *Quantitative Findings*

7.1.1 Learning Outcomes

Digital platform analytics revealed high engagement levels. The average session duration was 47 minutes, with an 89% completion rate. Return visit rates were also encouraging, with 76% of participants revisiting the platform. Mathematical competency scores increased by an average of 34%, indicating a significant improvement in learners' understanding. Cultural mathematics appreciation scales demonstrated a 52% increase, reflecting enhanced cultural awareness.

7.1.2 Engagement Analytics

Digital platform analytics revealed high engagement levels. The average session duration was 47 minutes, with an 89% completion rate. Return visit rates were also encouraging, with 76% of participants revisiting the platform.

7.2 *Qualitative Findings*

7.2.1 Cultural Validation and Pride

Qualitative analysis revealed that participants experienced significant cultural validation through the intervention. Interview data indicated that 94% of participants experienced increased cultural validation and appreciation.

One participant noted: "I never realized that my grandmother's way of measuring land was actually advanced mathematics. Now I see how her methods were more sustainable than what we learn in regular math class." This sentiment was echoed across multiple interviews, suggesting that the intervention successfully bridged traditional and contemporary mathematical understanding.

7.2.2 Enhanced Sustainability Awareness

Participants demonstrated a deepened understanding of sustainability concepts through their engagement with ethnomathematical approaches. Focus group discussions revealed that participants developed more nuanced perspectives on environmental stewardship, recognizing the mathematical principles underlying traditional sustainable practices.

Community elders involved in the intervention reported renewed interest from younger community members in traditional knowledge systems. One elder observed: "The young people are asking questions about the old ways again. The computer helped them see that our knowledge is still important for taking care of the earth."

7.2.3 Digital Learning Experiences

Participants responded positively to the digital learning environment, particularly appreciating the multimedia and interactive elements. The VR experiences were consistently highlighted as transformative, with participants reporting that virtual immersion helped them understand traditional practices in ways that traditional classroom instruction could not achieve.

However, some participants initially experienced technological barriers, particularly older adults and those with limited prior digital experience. The provision of technical support and culturally-appropriate training materials proved essential for successful participation.

7.3 Challenges and Limitations

Technological Infrastructure

Internet connectivity and device access remained significant challenges, particularly in rural settings. While mobile-responsive design helped address some accessibility issues, reliable internet access was necessary for full platform functionality. Some participants experienced frustration with technical difficulties that interrupted their learning experiences.

Cultural Sensitivity

Ensuring appropriate representation and handling of indigenous knowledge required ongoing consultation with community representatives. Some cultural content required restricted access protocols, complicating platform design and implementation. Balancing educational accessibility with cultural protection protocols proved to be an ongoing challenge.

Educator Preparation

Many educators required significant professional development to effectively facilitate digital ethnomathematics instruction. Traditional teacher preparation programs had not equipped educators with the knowledge and skills necessary to integrate cultural knowledge systems with digital pedagogical approaches.

7.4 Implications for Practice

The findings suggest several important implications for educational practice. Digital technologies can effectively enhance ethnomathematical education when designed with cultural sensitivity and community input. The integration of traditional knowledge systems with contemporary digital learning environments can increase student engagement and cultural appreciation while promoting sustainability awareness.

Educational institutions should invest in professional development for educators to develop competencies in culturally responsive digital pedagogy. Community partnerships are essential for authentic and respectful integration of indigenous knowledge systems into formal educational contexts.

Policy implications include the need for educational technology funding that prioritizes culturally responsive design and community engagement; support for indigenous knowledge preservation and transmission through digital platforms; and recognition of traditional knowledge systems as valuable components of sustainability education.

8. Conclusion

This research demonstrates the significant potential of blending digital pedagogy with ethnomathematics for Education for Sustainable Development. The integration of these approaches creates learning environments that honor cultural diversity while preparing learners to address contemporary sustainability challenges through multiple knowledge systems and perspectives.

Key findings indicate that digital ethnomathematics pedagogy significantly improves learning outcomes, cultural appreciation, and sustainability awareness among diverse learners. The approach validates indigenous knowledge systems while leveraging contemporary digital technologies to enhance accessibility and engagement. However, successful implementation requires careful attention to cultural sensitivity, community partnership, and technological infrastructure.

The theoretical framework developed through this research provides a foundation for future investigations into culturally responsive digital pedagogy. The combination of constructivist learning theory, culturally responsive pedagogy, social learning theory, and systems thinking offers a comprehensive approach to understanding how digital technologies can support cultural knowledge preservation and transmission while promoting sustainability education.

Educational institutions should develop partnerships with indigenous communities and cultural knowledge holders to ensure authentic representation and appropriate handling of traditional knowledge systems. Professional development programs should prepare educators to integrate digital technologies with ethnomathematical content in culturally sensitive ways.

Digital platform design should prioritize accessibility, cultural sensitivity, and community engagement, with ongoing consultation and collaboration with cultural representatives throughout development and implementation processes. Educational policies should recognize and support the integration of indigenous knowledge systems into formal curricula as essential components of comprehensive sustainability education.

The integration of digital pedagogy and ethnomathematics for Education for Sustainable Development represents a promising pathway toward more inclusive, culturally responsive, and effective sustainability education. As global challenges require diverse perspectives and knowledge systems, educational approaches that honor and integrate multiple ways of knowing become increasingly essential for preparing learners to create sustainable futures.

References

Bandura, A. (1977). Social Learning Theory. Prentice-Hall.

Bardhan, R., Orey, D. C. and Rosa, M. (2025). Indigenous counting systems of India and their impact on numerical cognition. PARADIGMA 46(2): 1–23. doi.org/10.37618/PARADIGMA.1011-2251.2025.e2025023.id1699.

D'Ambrosio, U. (1985). Ethnomathematics and its place in the history and pedagogy of mathematics. For the Learning of Mathematics 5(1): 44–48.

D'Ambrosio, U. (2001). What is ethnomathematics, and how can it help children in schools? Teaching Children Mathematics 7(6): 308–310. http://dx.doi.org/10.5951/TCM.7.6.0308.

Gay, G. (2018). Culturally Responsive Teaching: Theory, Research, and Practice (3rd ed.). Teachers College Press.

Hasan, K. K., Mostofa, S. M., Othman, R. and Mukherjee, D. (2021). Blended learning during pandemic through knowledge management: An analytical study. Journal of Educational Technology Systems 49(3): 256–273.

Piaget, J. (1977). The Development of Thought: Equilibration of Cognitive Structures. Viking Press.

Rosa, M. and Orey, D. C. (2011). Ethnomathematics: The cultural aspects of mathematics. Revista Latinoamericana de Etnomatemática 4(2): 32–54.

Senge, P. M. (1990). The Fifth Discipline: The Art and Practice of the Learning Organization. Doubleday.

UNESCO. (2017). Education for Sustainable Development Goals: Learning Objectives. UNESCO Publishing. doi.org/10.54675/CGBA9153.

Vygotsky, L. S. (1978). Mind in Society: The Development of Higher Psychological Processes. Harvard University Press. doi.org/10.2307/j.ctvjf9vz4.

Section 3

Economy and Ecology in Practice

Chapter 8

A Conceptual Framework for Adaptive AI in Agriculture

Enabling Self Learning Systems for a Sustainable and Resilient Supply Chain

Lokesh Kumar Jena,[1,*] *Dukhabandhu Sahoo,*[1]
Subhayan Chakraborty,[2] *Pritisudha Mohanty*[1] and
Manash Kumar Behera[1]

1. Introduction

India is on the path of development and is set to commemorate 100 years of independence in the next 20 years. The country has experienced unprecedented growth, with a GDP of $3.89 trillion in the year 2023–24, being observed across all sectors, with agriculture being one of the key means of livelihood for a significant portion of its population (Yadav 2024, Hassan 2025, Gupta 2024). Regardless of such advancements, this sector is still grappling with problems such as climate change (Pathak 2022, Kalambe and Gavit 2025), volatile markets (Yeasin et al. 2024, Jhajhria 2019), and huge pressure to become sustainable (Gupta et al. 2021, Kumar et al. 2022). These issues reveal the pressing need to find solutions capable of

[1] Assistant Professor, Department of MBA, Gandhi Institute for Education and Technology (GIET), Khordha, Odisha, India.
[2] State Panchayat Resource Centre, Tripura 799003, India.
Emails: dsahoo@iitbbs.ac.in, subhayan.chakraborty@gov.in, a23hs09018@iitbbs.ac.in, a23hs09020@iitbbs.ac.in
* Corresponding author: lkj10@iitbbs.ac.in

DOI: 10.1201/9781003736158-11

making traditional forms of agricultural production more sustainable, efficient, and future-oriented.

Adaptive AI is developing and has the potential to respond to these problems because such systems learn autonomously and respond to dynamic environmental changes, market conditions, and socioeconomic trends (Akintuyi 2024). According to DST, adaptive systems also take into consideration feedback and real-time learning, allowing the agricultural supply chain to evolve (Akintuyi 2024, Ali et al. 2025). This is especially crucial to address inefficiencies, including resource inflow, waste, and market access for farmers (Mummasani et al. 2024). The supply chain can embrace adaptive AI that combines predictive analytics, autonomous technological tools, and logistics optimization (Akintuyi 2024, Ikram et al. 2024). Together with supportive factors such as policy adjustments, infrastructure expansion, and continuous administration, it introduces smart systems that align all stakeholders (Javaid et al. 2022).

Additionally, the implementation of the Internet of Things (IoT) and agricultural management technologies enhances data-gathering and integration processes to establish a hub for intelligent decision-making (Bansode et al. 2025). These technologies can support yield forecasting, demand forecasting, and demand-based pricing required to maximize resources and become more market-responsive (Chelliah et al. 2024). There has been great emphasis in the framework on inclusivity and sustainability, aligning with the long-term interest of India to feed an estimated 1.7 billion population by 2047, reduce the carbon footprint, and generate technologically intelligent manpower (Sharma and Kumar 2024).

This study proposes a conceptual model of adaptive AI in agriculture that ought to address existing gaps in efficiency and lay a base for future research. It presents important voids in the existing literature and examines how adaptive AI will revolutionize the automation of the agricultural supply chain. The framework thus has the capacity to sustain the ecological and economic objectives of India through the infusion of technological, institutional, and ethical components.

2. Theoretical Background

The study is based on DST (Bernstein 1967), which provides a useful tool to understand the dynamics of internal and external forces that constantly interact with their surroundings (Choi et al. 2001). Thus, there is a need for a dynamic feedback system to maintain balance and develop resilience (Christopher and Peck 2004). In the context of agriculture, DST favors the deployment of adaptive AI due to the necessity for real-time learning, resilience, and coordination of the whole system to cope with uncertainties caused by climate change, market fluctuations, socioeconomic changes, and resource scarcity (Klerkx and Rose 2020, Raihan 2024).

Socio-Technical Systems (STS) theory (Emery and Marek 1962, Ropohl 1999) is an addition to DST because it introduces the interdependence between technological innovation and social considerations. Such a theory also states that putting forward such advanced technologies like AI should consider human considerations, institutional arrangements, and ethical considerations (Bostrom and

Yudkowsky 2014, Ayinla et al. 2024). This form of inference can be critical in the democratisation of AI in agriculture, which means that inclusivity in the design, capacities and accountable governance could empower farmers (Onunga 2025).

It would also base the research on Resilience Theory (RT) (Garmezy 1992), which attends to the fact that systems can absorb shocks and reorganize in the process of change. Resilience is becoming a recurrent idea in agricultural supply chains due to the presence of climate change, pandemics, and geopolitical uncertainties (Yuan et al. 2024, Sutar et al. 2025). The prescriptive power of adaptive AI and its ability to autonomously make decisions potentially allow proactive risk-taking, scenario planning, and adjustment to climate change conditions (Folke et al. 2010).

Additionally, Innovation Diffusion Theory (IDT) also offers insight into how technology diffuses in communities. Rogers (1995) theorized that the perceived advantage, synchronicity of the activities with the present, and the potential of the result to be tested and experienced would trigger adoption of innovations. Such a theory leans into scalable and flexible AI systems that can be scaled down to smallholders and rural communities and, hence, contribute to the proliferation of smart farming systems (Vinyals et al. 2023).

Therefore, the theoretical model suggested combines DST, STS, RT, and IDT to handle the issues of agricultural supply chains. It makes adaptive AI a central facilitator that is in constant interrelation with internal as well as external dynamic systems and, at the same time, balances social, ethical, and institutional factors. The model enhances the ability of the system to take in shocks and respond to climate and market uncertainties, as well as reorganize processes to meet the expectations of the market by integrating resilience mechanisms. Moreover, the principles of diffusion should dictate how AI technologies can be adopted by smallholders and rural communities in a scalable and inclusive manner to ensure that technological innovation can be converted into the practices of sustainable, efficient, and participatory agriculture. Hence, the future roadmap may be drawn for paving the road toward the development of resilient agriculture with the intervention of AI, which may be seen in Figures 1 and 2 below.

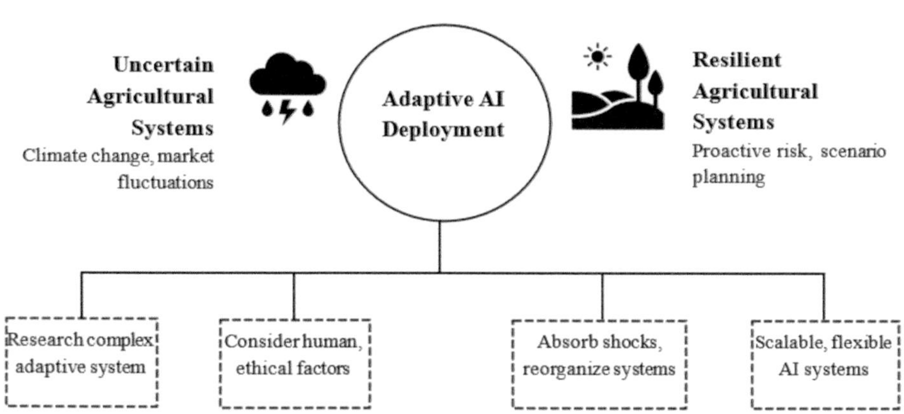

Figure 1. Adaptive-AI for Resilient Agriculture Roadmap (Source: Authors).

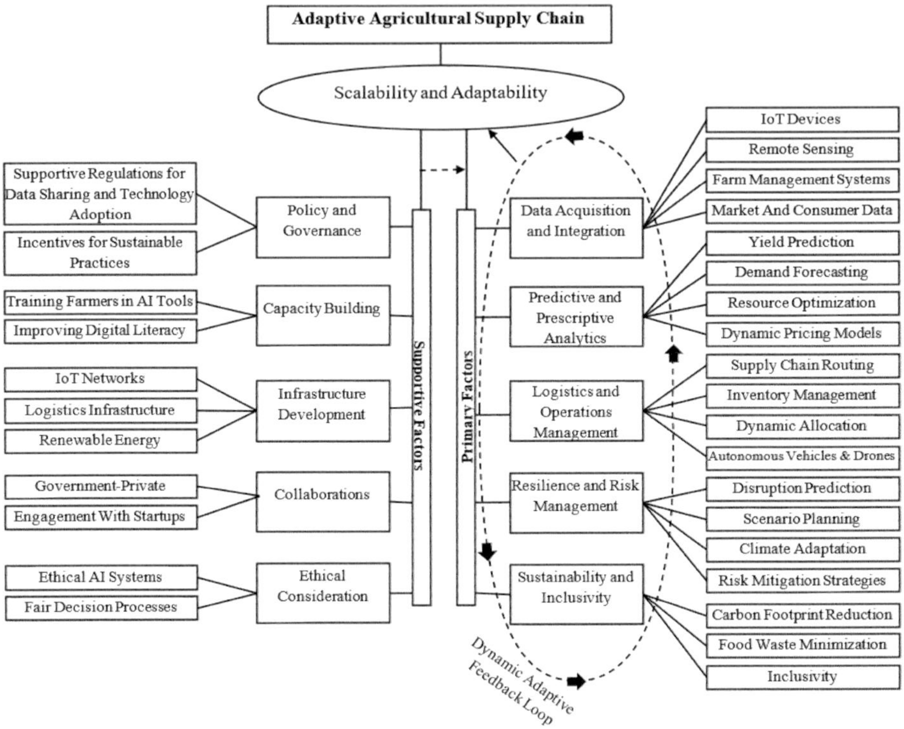

Figure 2. Conceptual Framework for an Agricultural Self-Learning Supply Chain (Source: Authors).

3. Method

The present study has adopted the thematic literature review approach as a method to capitalize on the applicability of the existing literature on adaptive AI in agriculture with regard to developing a conceptual framework of a resilient and sustainable supply chain. This enables the identification, investigation, and reporting of themes within qualitative data (Braun and Clarke 2006). This study uses various databases for data extraction. As the current area in agriculture is new, a systematic way of finding published literature is difficult through a single database. Hence, this study uses all types of published articles, book chapters, conference proceedings, editorials, government reports, white papers, web articles, etc. The framework used in this review has its strain in DST, with principal ideas on sustainability science and agricultural innovation through AI. Thematic analysis assists in the categorization of literature into primary and supportive factors. The primary factors are real-time feedback systems, dynamic decision-making, and resource optimization (Kamilaris et al. 2018, Wolfert et al. 2017). Supportive factors encompassed policy frameworks, infrastructure, ethical AI, and capacity development (Sharma et al. 2023, Omotayo et al. 2025). Distribution of these themes was plotted with DST, STS, RT, and IDT principles to see interdependencies and feedback within farming ecosystems.

Thematic synthesis allowed the development of scalable levels of a conceptual framework where adaptive AI capabilities are aligned with governance, collaboration, and sustainability objectives. The method allowed identification of research gaps and future directions, mostly related to democratizing AI to help smallholder farmers and improve human–AI collaboration. This review, therefore, gives a platform for practical responses to make India's agricultural supply chain run in line with its diverse goals.

4. Results and Discussion

The conceptualized framework (see Figure 2) of adaptive AI in the agriculture sector has an aspiring vision of creating a strong, sustainable, and inclusive supply chain in India. With the approach toward the next century of independence, agriculture in the country has to be transformed to suit the needs of the growing population, changing climate, and market fluctuations (Gulati and Juneja 2022, Rosmann and Singh 2021). In this section, the results will be synthesized and discussed concerning the implications of these findings under the most significant areas of expression: technological integration, operational efficiency, policy alignment, and ethical governance. The dimensions have been discussed in more detail with primary and supportive aspects.

Adaptive agricultural supply chains serve as a means of replacing linear models and changing them into a self-learning dynamic system (Kaur and Prakash 2025, Akintuyi 2024). Such systems draw upon artificial intelligence to react to environmental, economic, and social changes in real time. Such flexible supply chains would have a lot of potential in terms of alignment with stakeholders, reduce latency in decision-making, and enhance visibility (Mummasani et al. 2024, Vinyals et al. 2023). As an example, platforms that operate based on AI give farmers an opportunity to monitor the condition of crops, track their logistics, and get real-time market trends. Such responsiveness will be crucial in the event of any shocks to the system, e.g., an extreme weather event, outbreak of pests, or change in consumer demand. The framework is constructively designed on the basis of cascading feedback loops, which enable the system to learn from the outcome and, thus, adjust its strategy (Ercan Oğuztürk 2025, Rane et al. 2024, Javaid et al. 2023).

4.1 Data Acquisition and Integration

The adaptive AI model has its developmental roots in data gathering and integration (Jain 2025, Mota 2025). This framework has a lot of data sources, which entail IoT sensors, remote sensing, farm management systems, and market analytics. Full integration provides accuracy in the prediction of yield and demand forecasting, and optimization of resources (Kumar et al. 2025, Gangwani 2024). The utilization of IoT devices in the fields gathers data at a certain scale regarding the moisture and temperature of the soil and nutrient value of the plants cultivated (Mansoor et al. 2025), whereas satellite images siphon macro data about weather conditions and the health of crops (Khulage and Khonde 2025). Precision farming and reduction in cost of input and environmental footprints are possible due to the array of data ecosystems (Mamabolo et al. 2025). Moreover, dynamic pricing models and enhanced demand and supply matching will be allowed due to market and consumer analytics (Vazifeh and Mafakheri 2025).

4.2 Predictive and Prescriptive Analytics

Predictive and prescriptive analytics are key features of the framework as far as intelligence capability is concerned. Predictive models use AI algorithms to forecast yield and market conditions, as well as other outcomes of optimal resource allocation, whereas prescriptive models provide recommendations on a certain course of action to be taken, e.g., an irrigation schedule, fertilizer use, or harvest time. These analytics reduce the degree of uncertainty and allow proactive planning (Pawar and Phad 2025). As an example, forecasting models that are based on weather conditions and previous records of pests would have forewarned farmers that a pest outbreak may be on the way, and farmers would have taken precautionary steps. Prescriptive analytics will be a step ahead in making decisions that will ensure proper resource allocation to improve productivity and sustainability. These kinds of functions are in line with the principles of RT, whereby there is an ability to adapt to changes and preemptive risk management in complex systems (Folke et al. 2010, Pawar and Phad 2025).

4.3 Logistics and Operations Management

AI supplies a valuable addition to the sphere of operations management and logistics (Solanki and Jadiga 2024). The infrastructure includes mobile routing, stock control, drones, and self-driving farming tractors. This has been translated in terms of timely delivery, fuel efficiency, and increased turnover of inventory. AI systems scan traffic patterns, weather conditions, and changes in demand to optimize transportation routes and schedules. Meanwhile, autonomous drones make it possible to provide input to remote farms or check the condition of crops without spending costly labor and raise efficiency in the outcome. These innovations contribute toward reducing carbon footprint and aid in reducing post-harvest losses, which is fundamental to food security (Nath et al. 2024) in a country that is projected to have 1.7 billion by 2047.

4.4 Resilience and Risk Management

Resilience and risk management are important to the adaptive AI framework (Ghaffarian et al. 2023). The model uses disruption forecasting, strategy planning, and adaptation to climate change. AI may help predict supply chain disruption and suggest contingency plans (Cohen and Tang 2024). Depending on variables, scenario planning tools help stakeholders become ready to meet uncertainties based on the simulations to which they are subjected. Such features enhance the system's ability to absorb shocks, effectively transforming it into a system with transformative and revival ability (Folke et al. 2010, Cole 2025).

4.5 Sustainability and Inclusivity

Notable embedding of sustainability and inclusivity in the framework brings about the use of renewable energy and lowers carbon footprint and food waste (Olabi et al. 2023). It is also concerned with the concept of dispersal and growing digital confidence of farmers in order to utilize resources optimally. Inclusivity has also been emphasized to ensure that no one is left behind in the transformation of the digital world, especially smallholders (Fatokun 2024).

4.6 Policy and Governance

Policy and governance are vital enabling mechanisms in adaptive AI models. Effective regulation triggers data exchange, technological adoption, and responsible AI, which makes large-scale implementation possible. Alignment of policies not only accelerates the implementation of AI but also encourages a sense of trust among stakeholders (Xue and Pang 2022, Walter 2024). Incentives based on rewards aimed at enhancing sustainable behaviors, data privacy protection, and development of open-source platforms are widely adopted. At the same time, ethical governance ensures not only transparency and accountability of AI decision-making but also alleviates issues associated with bias and misuse (Bostrom and Yudkowsky 2014, World Health Organisation 2021).

4.7 Capacity Building

Capacity building is important in getting farmers acclimatized to AI-based tools and supplementing their digital literacy, which are prerequisites to fruitful implementation. Analyses show that capacity building enhances the embracement of emergent technologies and efficient functioning. Furthermore, farmers with greater experience in interpreting AI recommendations and adapting the given insights to their practices have higher chances of significant benefits from the system. Workshops have been noted to be effective in developing a technologically competent agricultural labor force, as well as mobile applications and peer-to-peer learning models, which have been laid out as efficient mechanisms for developing a technologically competent agricultural workforce (Châteauvieux and Baddache 2024, Girmay 2024).

4.8 Infrastructure Development

Development of infrastructure is an inevitable part of optimized integration of the adaptive AI model. Creation of an efficient interface between these networks can be achieved only through targeted investment in IoT networks, logistics frameworks, and renewable energy systems. A strong infrastructural base provides real-time data transfer, efficient transportation, and sustainable energy use. As an example, IoT sensors powered by solar energy can operate autonomously in distant locations with no access to the grid, and better-developed road infrastructure can promote movement of input and output. Public-private partnerships are useful in infrastructure development, particularly in underserved regions.

4.9 Collaborations

Collaborations between startups, research-based organisations, and government are central to innovation and scalability. The collaborative ecosystem enables knowledge transfer, speeds up the process of prototyping, and prompts policy development. Startups bring agility and novel solutions, and research centres focus on evidence-based developments (Bańka et al. 2025). Government agencies help provide scale and regulatory frameworks for innovations.

4.10 Ethical Considerations

Ethics is an essential block of the framework under consideration. The model prioritizes the advancement of ethical AI-based applications, the use of fair decision-making practices, and safeguarding information privacy. Strong ethics increases the trust of stakeholders and the sustainability of the system in the long run. Algorithms need to be explainable, transparent, and constructed free of bias. Besides, farmers are expected to control their data and understand how decisions are made. This framework fosters responsible innovation, incorporating human values into the institutional framework (Bostrom and Yudkowsky 2014).

4.11 Dynamic Adaptability Feedback Loop

Creating dynamic adaptability implies using a closed feedback loop, through which continuous learning and evolution of the system take place. The feedback loops make the organization more responsive and allow it to change its strategies by considering real-time results (Ritola et al. 2022). For example, where a suggested cultivation fails due to unexpected weather, the system adjusts its models and specifies another crop. This flexibility is critical in terms of resilience and sustainability because it allows a supply chain to adapt in line with evolving scenarios.

4.12 Scalability and Adaptability

The design principles of the framework consist of scalability and adaptation to changes. The modular design and cloud-native-based deployment enable the system to be tailored to specific regional and farm settings. The scale-up facilitates remote interaction and synchronized updates, which makes it always relevant to diverse agro-climatic areas (Mălinaș et al. 2025, Soldati et al. 2024, Mmbando 2025). Such characteristics are particularly important in a large and diverse country such as India, where farming activity varies significantly across regions.

Adaptive AI can create the avenue toward the transformation of the agriculture supply chain in India. It will help resolve problems of resource allocation, food wastage, climate challenges, and market access through proactive risk management. This enables sustainability and empowers smallholders and marginalized groups, which meets national objectives to achieve food security, economic growth, and environmental management.

Therefore, the primary and supportive factors can help to develop an inclusive framework that extends beyond technological application to policy, governance, ethics, and human capability. This multidimensional construct is applied in understanding the complexity of agricultural systems and the necessity to structure these efforts. AI-driven systems will help build the future supply chain, which is defined by efficiency, transparency, and sustainability. Figure 2 above presents the fully outlined structure with various parts and their interdependence.

5. Conclusion

Food security, climate resilience, and the strain of sustainability should be addressed within the agriculture sector as all sectors of India are flourishing. The paper suggests an AI strategic roadmap, which proposes a framework to transform the supply chain into a self-learning system with predictive analytics and a real-time feedback loop. The framework does not limit itself to greater efficiency and lesser wastage, as it concentrates on equity, inclusiveness, and ecological integrity to support both farmers and their communities. It is anchored in DST to determine that policies, infrastructure, capacity building, and ethical governance are needed to democratize and scale AI in various settings. The suggested framework should be introduced and refined at the field level in future work. The main areas that future work should consider are the long-term implications on rural livelihoods, biodiversity, and cultural presence, and the development of region-specific, culturally sensitive AI tools that are not harmful to local knowledge.

References

Akintuyi, O. B. (2024). Adaptive AI in precision agriculture: A review – Investigating the use of self-learning algorithms in optimizing farm operations based on real-time data. Open Access Research Journal of Multidisciplinary Studies 7(2): 16–30. https://doi.org/10.53022/oarjms.2024.7.2.0023.

Ali, S., Kumar, P., Srivastav, M., Kumar, A. and Singh, S. K. (2025). AI-driven innovations for sustainable agriculture: Enhancing efficiency and resilience. pp. 115–128. In Modern Technology for Sustainable Agriculture. https://doi.org/10.1007/978-3-031-88396-5_9.

Ayinla, B. S., Amoo, O. O., Atadoga, A., Abrahams, T. O., Osasona, F. and Farayola, O. A. (2024). Ethical AI in practice: Balancing technological advancements with human values. International Journal of Science and Research Archive 11(1): 1311–1326. https://www.researchgate.net/publication/378104513.

Bańka, M., Marczewska, M., De Andrade, R. D., Kowalski, A., Boulangé, P., Sedkiewicz, K. et al. (2025). Collaboration between corporations and startups: Goals, expectations and outcomes. Journal of Small Business and Enterprise Development 32(4): 930–961. https://doi.org/10.1108/JSBED-04-2024-0219.

Bansode, R., Shah, T. and Yele, V. (2025). Smart agriculture using IoT: A comprehensive review of technologies, applications, and future trends. International Journal of Advanced Research in Computer and Communication Engineering 14(4): 17–25. https://doi.org/10.17148/IJARCCE.2025.14403.

Bostrom, N. and Yudkowsky, E. (2014). The ethics of artificial intelligence. pp. 316–334. *In*: Frankish, K. and Ramsey, W. (eds.). The Cambridge Handbook of Artificial Intelligence. Cambridge University Press. https://doi.org/10.1017/CBO9781139046855.020.

Braun, V. and Clarke, V. (2006). Using thematic analysis in psychology. Qualitative Research in Psychology 3(2): 77–101. https://doi.org/10.1191/1478088706qp063oa.

Bernstein, N. A. (1967). The Coordination and Regulation of Movements. Pergamon Press.

Châteauvieux, C. and Baddache, F. (21 October 2024). Digital tools: Empowering smallholder farmers. Ksapa. https://ksapa.org/digital-tools-empowering-smallholder-farmers/ (Accessed: 14 August 2025).
Chelliah, B. J., Latchoumi, T. P. and Senthilselvi, A. (2024). Analysis of demand forecasting of agriculture using machine learning algorithms. Environment, Development and Sustainability 26: 1731–1747. https://doi.org/10.1007/s10668-022-02783-9.
Choi, T. Y., Dooley, K. J. and Rungtusanatham, M. (2001). Supply networks and complex adaptive systems: Control versus emergence. Journal of Operations Management 19(3): 351–366. https://doi.org/10.1016/S0272-6963(00)00068-1.
Christopher, M. and Peck, H. (2004). Building the resilient supply chain. The International Journal of Logistics Management 15(2): 1–14. https://doi.org/10.1108/09574090410700275.
Cohen, M. C. and Tang, C. S. (5 February 2024). The role of AI in developing resilient supply chains. Georgetown Journal of International Affairs. https://gjia.georgetown.edu/2024/02/05/the-role-of-ai-in-developing-resilient-supply-chains/ (Accessed: 14 August 2025).
Cole, J. (28 July 2025). Top 9 scenario planning software for 2025. Limelight. https://www.golimelight.com/blog/best-scenario-planning-software (Accessed: 14 August 2025).
Emery, F. E. and Marek, J. (1962). Some socio-technical aspects of automation. Human Relations 15(1): 17–25. https://doi.org/10.1177/001872676201500102.
Ercan Oğuztürk, G. (2025). AI-driven irrigation systems for sustainable water management: A systematic review and meta-analytical insights. Smart Agricultural Technology 11: 100982. https://doi.org/10.1016/j.atech.2025.100982.
Fatokun, A. (6 December 2024). Inclusive digital transformation: Ensuring no one is left behind. Public Digital. https://public.digital/pd-insights/blog/2024/12/inclusive-digital-transformation-ensuring-no-one-is-left-behind (Accessed: 14 August 2025).
Folke, C., Carpenter, S. R., Walker, B., Scheffer, M., Chapin, T. and Rockström, J. (2010). Resilience thinking: Integrating resilience, adaptability and transformability. Ecology and Society 15(4): 20. https://doi.org/10.5751/ES-03610-150420.
Gangwani, N. (2024). AI-driven precision agriculture: Optimizing crop yield and resource efficiency. International Journal for Multidisciplinary Research (IJFMR) 6(6): 1–7.
Garmezy, N. (1992). Risk and Protective Factors in the Development of Psychopathology. Cambridge University Press.
Ghaffarian, S., Taghikhah, F. R. and Maier, H. R. (2023). Explainable artificial intelligence in disaster risk management: Achievements and prospective futures. International Journal of Disaster Risk Reduction 98: 104123. https://doi.org/10.1016/j.ijdrr.2023.104123.
Girmay, M. B. (30 May 2025). The role of explainability in AI for agriculture: Making digital systems easier to understand for farmers. IFPRI Blog. https://www.ifpri.org/blog/the-role-of-explainability-in-ai-for-agriculture-making-digital-systems-easier-to-understand-for-farmers (Accessed: 14 August 2025).
Gulati, A. and Juneja, R. (2022). Transforming Indian agriculture. *In*: Chand, R., Joshi, P. and Khadka, S. (eds.). Indian Agriculture Towards 2030. India Studies in Business and Economics. Springer. https://doi.org/10.1007/978-981-19-0763-0_2.
Gupta, C. (31 December 2024). Year ender 2024: How did India rank on global economic indexes this year? The Indian Express. https://indianexpress.com/article/trending/top-10-listing/year-ender-2024-how-did-india-rank-on-global-economic-indexes-this-year-9746657/ (Accessed: 14 August 2025).
Gupta, N., Pradhan, S., Jain, A. and Patel, N. (2021). Sustainable agriculture in India 2021 – What we know and how to scale up. Council on Energy, Environment and Water. https://www.ceew.in/publications/sustainable-agriculture-india (Accessed: 14 August 2025).
Hassan. T. (15 January 2025). The economic impact of agriculture on India's GDP. AgriNext Conference & Expo. https://agrinextcon.com/the-economic-impact-of-agriculture-on-indias-gdp/ (Accessed: 14 August 2025).
Ikram, A., Mehmood, H., Arshad, M. T., Rasheed, A., Noreen, S. and Gnedeka, K. T. (2024). Applications of artificial intelligence (AI) in managing food quality and ensuring global food security. CyTA-Journal of Food 22(1): 2393287. https://doi.org/10.1080/19476337.2024.2393287.

Jain, A. (6 March 2025). A complete guide to adaptive AI development. OyeLabs. https://oyelabs.com/guide-to-adaptive-ai-development/ (Accessed: 14 August 2025).

Javaid, M., Haleem, A., Singh, R. P. and Suman, R. (2022). Enhancing smart farming through the applications of Agriculture 4.0 technologies. International Journal of Intelligent Networks 3: 150–164. https://doi.org/10.1016/j.ijin.2022.09.004.

Javaid, M., Haleem, A., Khan, I. H. and Suman, R. (2023). Understanding the potential applications of artificial intelligence in agriculture sector. Advanced Agrochem 2(1): 15–30. https://doi.org/10.1016/j.aac.2022.10.001.

Jhajhria, D. R. (2019). Agricultural market reforms and price volatility: Insights from Rajasthan's commodity markets. International Journal of Research and Analytical Reviews 6(2): 636–648. https://ijrar.org/papers/IJRAR19D6368.pdf.

Kalambe, T. R. and Gavit, R. H. (2025). A review of impact of climate change on agricultural productivity in India. IOSR Journal of Agriculture and Veterinary Science 18(1): 52–60. https://www.researchgate.net/publication/388490115.

Kamilaris, A., Kartakoullis, A. and Prenafeta-Boldú, F. X. (2018). A review on the practice of big data analysis in agriculture. Computers and Electronics in Agriculture 143: 23–37. https://doi.org/10.1016/j.compag.2017.09.037.

Khulage, S. and Khonde, P. (2025). Satellite-based IoT for remote sensing and agriculture. International Journal of Science, Engineering and Technology 13(2): 1–7.

Klerkx, L. and Rose, D. (2020). Dealing with the game-changing technologies of Agriculture 4.0: How do we manage diversity and responsibility in food system transition pathways? Global Food Security 24: 100347. https://doi.org/10.1016/j.gfs.2019.100347.

Kumar, A., Meena, S., Kumar, S. and Rana, R. (2022). Sustainable agricultural development in India: An overview. International Journal of Agriculture Extension and Social Development 5(1): 118–121. https://www.extensionjournal.com/article/view/131/5-1-25 (Accessed: 14 August 2025).

Kumar, A., Singh, I., Kashyap, M., Kumar, A., Devi, N. B., Singh, S. et al. (2025). Integration of machine learning and remote sensing in crop yield prediction: A review. International Journal of Research in Agronomy SP-8(1): 549–562. https://doi.org/10.33545/2618060X.2025.v8.i1Sh.2496.

Mălinaș, C.-D., Matei, F., Pop, I. D., Sălăgean, T. and Mălinaș, A. (2025). Individual and synergistic contributions of GIS, remote sensing, and AI in advancing climate-resilient agriculture. AgriEngineering 7(7): 230. https://doi.org/10.3390/agriengineering7070230.

Mamabolo, E., Mashala, M. J., Mugari, E., Mogale, T. E., Mathebula, N., Mabitsela, K. et al. (2025). Application of precision agriculture technologies for crop protection and soil health. Smart Agricultural Technology 12: 101270. https://doi.org/10.1016/j.atech.2025.101270.

Mansoor, S., Iqbal, S., Popescu, S. M., Kim, S. L., Chung, Y. S. and Baek, J. H. (2025). Integration of smart sensors and IoT in precision agriculture: Trends, challenges and future prospects. Frontiers in Plant Science 16: 1587869. https://doi.org/10.3389/fpls.2025.1587869.

Mmbando, G. S. (2025). Harnessing artificial intelligence and remote sensing in climate-smart agriculture: Strategies needed for global food security. Cogent Food & Agriculture 11(1): 2454354. https://doi.org/10.1080/23311932.2025.2454354.

Mota, Y. (8 January 2025). AI data integration: A guide for streamlined, scaled, and optimized operations. N-iX Expert Blog. https://www.n-ix.com/ai-data-integration/ (Accessed: 14 August 2025).

Mummasani, A., Kesamreddy, L., Golla, G., Kotresh, D. J. and Shaik Shahid, M. (2024). The role of AI in modernizing Indian agriculture. Just Agriculture Magazine, October Issue. https://justagriculture.in/files/magazine/2024/october/001%20The%20Role%20of%20AI%20in%20Modernizing%20Indian%20Agriculture.pdf.

Nath, B., Chen, G., O'Sullivan, C. M. and Zare, D. (2024). Research and technologies to reduce grain postharvest losses: a review. Foods (Basel, Switzerland) 13(12): 1875. https://doi.org/10.3390/foods13121875.

Olabi, A. G., Elsaid, K., Obaideen, K., Abdelkareem, M. A., Rezk, H., Wilberforce, T. et al. (2023). Renewable energy systems: Comparisons, challenges and barriers, sustainability indicators, and the contribution to UN sustainable development goals. International Journal of Thermofluids 20: 100498. https://doi.org/10.1016/j.ijft.2023.100498.

Omotayo, A. O., Adediran, S. A., Omotoso, A. B., Olagunju, K. O. and Omotayo, O. P. (2025). Artificial intelligence in agriculture: Ethics, impact possibilities, and pathways for policy. Computers and Electronics in Agriculture 239(Part A): 110927. https://doi.org/10.1016/j.compag.2025.110927.

Onunga, J. (2025). Responsible innovation in AI and data governance in Kenyan agriculture: a review article. Regulation 9(6): 8–12.

Pathak, H. (2022). Impact, adaptation, and mitigation of climate change in Indian agriculture. Environmental Monitoring and Assessment 195(52). https://doi.org/10.1007/s10661-022-10537-3.

Pawar, B. R. and Phad, C. R. (2025). Next-generation business intelligence: The impact of advanced analytics on strategic decision-making. International Journal of Innovative Research in Technology 11(8): 2726–2732.

Raihan, A. (2024). A review of artificial intelligence (AI) for sustainable agriculture. In Proceedings of the International Conference on Digitalization and Artificial Intelligence in Agricultural Management. https://www.researchgate.net/publication/386989366.

Rane, J., Kaya, Ömer, Mallick, S. K. and Rane, N. L. (2024). Smart farming using artificial intelligence, machine learning, deep learning, and ChatGPT: Applications, opportunities, challenges, and future directions. pp. 218–272. In Generative Artificial Intelligence in Agriculture, Education, and Business. Deep Science Publishing. https://doi.org/10.70593/978-81-981271-7-4_6.

Ritola, I., Krikke, H. and Caniëls, M. C. J. (2022). Learning-based dynamic capabilities in closed-loop supply chains: An expert study. The International Journal of Logistics Management 33(5): 69–84. https://doi.org/10.1108/IJLM-01-2021-0044.

Rogers, E. M. (1995). Diffusion of Innovations (4th ed.). Free Press.

Ropohl, G. (1999). Philosophy of socio-technical systems. Society for Philosophy and Technology Quarterly Electronic Journal 4(3): 186–194. https://doi.org/10.5840/techne19994311.

Rosmann, M. and Singh, S. K. (26 May 2021). Climate change – agriculture and policy in India (Voluntary Report No. IN2021-0070). U.S. Department of Agriculture, Foreign Agricultural Service.

Sharma, A., Sharma, A., Tselykh, A., Bozhenyuk, A., Choudhury, T., Alomar, M. et al. (2023). Artificial intelligence and internet of things oriented sustainable precision farming: Towards modern agriculture. Open Life Sciences 18(1): 20220713. https://doi.org/10.1515/biol-2022-0713.

Sharma, C. and Kumar, S. (2024). The role of AI consciousness in driving sustainable growth and inclusivity in the Indian context. International Journal of Research in Human Resource Management 6(2): 346–352. https://doi.org/10.33545/26633213.2024.v6.i2d.237.

Solanki. A. and Jadiga. S. (2024). AI applications for improving transportation and logistics operations. International Journal of Intelligent Systems and Applications in Engineering 12(3): 2607–2617. https://www.ijisae.org/index.php/IJISAE/article/view/5733.

Soldati, P., Ghadimi, E., Demirel, B., Wang, Y., Gaigalas, R. and Sintorn, M. (2024). Design principles for model generalization and scalable AI integration in radio access networks. IEEE Communications Magazine. https://doi.org/10.48550/arXiv.2306.06251.

Sutar, P. S., Kolte, G. C. and Yamini, S. (2025). Food supply chain disruptions and resilience: A framework and strategies in the digital era. OPSEARCH. https://doi.org/10.1007/s12597-025-00915-z.

Vazifeh, Z. and Mafakheri, F. (2025). Integrating dynamic pricing strategies and demand-driven supply planning in wood pellet supply chains: A stochastic optimization approach. Energy Reports 13: 3869–3877. https://doi.org/10.1016/j.egyr.2025.03.038.

Vinyals, M., Sabbadin, R., Couture, S., Sadou, L., Thomopoulos, R., Chapuis, K. et al. (2023). Toward AI-designed innovation diffusion policies using agent-based simulations and reinforcement learning: The case of digital tool adoption in agriculture. Frontiers in Applied Mathematics and Statistics 9: 1000785. https://doi.org/10.3389/fams.2023.1000785.

Walter, Y. (2024). Managing the race to the moon: Global policy and governance in artificial intelligence regulation—A contemporary overview and analysis of socioeconomic consequences. Discover Artificial Intelligence 4(1): 14. https://doi.org/10.1007/s44163-024-00109-4.

Wolfert, S., Ge, L., Verdouw, C. and Bogaardt, M.-J. (2017). Big data in Smart Farming – A review. Agricultural Systems 153: 69–80. https://doi.org/10.1016/j.agsy.2017.01.023.

World Health Organization. (2021). Ethics and governance of artificial intelligence for health: WHO guidance. WHO PP. 65–110. https://iris.who.int/bitstream/handle/10665/341996/9789240029200-eng.pdf.

Xue, L. and Pang, Z. (2022). Ethical governance of artificial intelligence: An integrated analytical framework. Journal of Digital Economy 1(1): 44–52. https://doi.org/10.1016/j.jdec.2022.08.003.

Yadav, K. (31 December 2024). India's economic snapshot 2024: Geopolitical wins, defence investments, and more. Times of India. https://timesofindia.indiatimes.com/india/indias-economic-snapshot-2024-geopolitical-wins-defence-investments-and-more/articleshow/116777216.cms (Accessed: 14 August 2025).

Yeasin. M., Sharma, P., Paul, R. K., Meena, D. C. and Anwer, M. E. (2024). Understanding price volatility and seasonality in agricultural commodities in India. Agricultural Economics Research Review 36(2): 177–188. https://epubs.icar.org.in/index.php/AERR/article/view/150660.

Yuan, M., Hu, H., Xue, M. and Li, J. (2024). Framework for resilience strategies in agricultural supply chain: Assessment in the era of climate change. Frontiers in Sustainable Food Systems 8: Article 444910. https://doi.org/10.3389/fsufs.2024.1444910.

Chapter 9

Volatility Spillovers in Energy Markets

Assessing the Economic Viability of Renewable vs. Non-Renewable Energy in India

*Avijit Bakshi** and *Sarit Maitra*

1. Introduction

India's energy landscape is experiencing a structural transformation, driven by a combination of policy reforms, environmental imperatives, and global commitments to decarbonization. As one of the world's fastest-growing economies, India's rising energy demand is met by both traditional fossil fuels and a rapidly expanding portfolio of renewable sources. In this context, understanding the interlinkages between renewable energy firms, non-renewable energy firms, and commodity markets becomes vital for investors, policymakers, and regulators. Volatility spillovers between these entities not only reflect economic dependencies but also influence risk management and capital allocation decisions.

The energy sector in India is bifurcated between non-renewable sources like crude oil and coal, and renewable alternatives such as wind, solar, and hydropower. While non-renewable energy markets are mature and highly liquid, renewable

Alliance School of Business, Alliance University, Chikkahagade Cross, Chandapura - Anekal Main Road, Anekal, Bengaluru – 562 106, Karnataka, India.
Email: sarit.moitra@alliance.edu.in
* Corresponding author: avijit.bakshi@alliance.edu.in

DOI: 10.1201/9781003736158-12

energy equities are still developing and are often perceived as more volatile due to policy risks, technology uncertainty, and financing constraints. However, their relative independence from global commodity cycles also offers diversification benefits. Therefore, quantifying the extent and direction of volatility spillovers between renewable firms, non-renewable firms, and traditional and non-traditional energy markets becomes crucial in assessing their economic viability and systemic importance.

Volatility spillovers and inter-market connectedness constitute a dominant research area (e.g., Zhang and Sun 2015, Dutta et al. 2020, Wen et al. 2021, Liu and Hamori 2020, Zhang and Wang 2019, Tang et al. 2023, Jingpeng et al. 2023, Seth and Sindhu 2021, Bouri 2019, Haozhi et al. 2022), which examines volatility spillovers and price discovery between financial market indices and energy markets. The above literature collectively emphasizes the intricate dynamics of volatility spillovers, price discovery, and growing interdependence between renewable and non-renewable energy markets in the context of macroeconomic shocks, climate risks, and evolving financial instruments. Several studies focus on China, where green finance, renewable electricity output, and economic growth have been shown to significantly influence long-term renewable energy investment and carbon emissions, particularly during the COVID-19-induced recession. The importance of green finance and renewable energy in shaping carbon outcomes suggests that policy must prioritize stability and investment in these sectors. There are studies that have evidenced how climate risks translate into heightened stock market volatility, with energy stocks being particularly vulnerable. These risks intensify during major crises, underscoring the necessity for real-time climate risk monitoring systems to protect financial stability.

From a market microstructure perspective, studies examining spot and futures energy markets in India conclude that futures markets, particularly for crude oil and natural gas, generally dominate in terms of price discovery and volatility spillovers, especially post-global and European debt crises. The futures markets' efficiency offers useful signals for investors and policymakers during turbulent periods. Similarly, using network connectedness frameworks, studies find that Chinese green energy stocks exert a dominant influence over crude oil futures in both return and volatility spillovers, a relationship strengthened during the COVID-19 pandemic and after the introduction of China's carbon trading market. This points to a shifting power dynamic where renewable energy assets are no longer passive recipients but active transmitters of market information and volatility. The evolving role of green financial assets is further highlighted by a study that shows that green bonds serve as hedging tools against fossil fuel and clean energy markets but are still vulnerable to short-term volatility spillovers from WTI crude oil. This suggests that while green finance contributes to risk diversification and sustainability, it remains sensitive to traditional energy market fluctuations.

A time-frequency analysis reinforces these observations by showing that clean energy stocks act as net volatility contributors in the short run, while commodities dominate in the long run. Interestingly, during the COVID-19 pandemic, long-term spillovers increased, and clean energy assets offered more effective hedging opportunities. Across these studies, a recurring theme is the critical role of crises—economic, environmental, or geopolitical—in reshaping volatility patterns and inter-market relationships. As such, the integration of green finance, clean energy investment, and robust market linkages with traditional energy systems presents both a challenge and an opportunity. For investors, policymakers, and regulators, the findings advocate for adaptive risk management frameworks and strategic investment in renewables, supported by climate-conscious financial policies and instruments that can weather market shocks while steering toward sustainability goals.

Most studies treat renewables and fossil fuels as distinct asset classes or explore macroeconomic-level spillovers (e.g., GDP, CO_2 emissions). Very few, if any, empirically examine how volatility in metals essential to clean technology (e.g., copper in wind turbines, silver in solar panels) spills over into the performance of renewable energy stocks, and how this differs from the volatility dynamics between fossil fuels and unsustainable stocks (like carbon-intensive industries). Furthermore, most prior research has focused on either green financial assets (like green bonds) or market-level risks (like transition or climate risk) without delving into the input-output volatility relationship in the renewable ecosystem.

The present study aims to fill the gap by capturing the interconnected risk dynamics between financial assets and their underlying resource dependencies across both sustainable and non-renewable energy ecosystems. Based on the above gaps, the following hypotheses are formed:

- H1: There is a significant volatility spillover between sustainable stocks and clean energy input commodities (e.g., copper, silver), i.e., shocks originating in clean energy markets are transmitted to the performance and volatility of sustainable (green) energy firms.
- H2: There is a significant volatility spillover between conventional energy sector stocks and fossil fuel commodities, i.e., transmission of shocks from fossil fuel markets to carbon-intensive energy stocks.
- H3: There is a significant volatility spillover between sustainable stocks and fossil fuel commodities, i.e., how shocks in fossil fuel markets affect renewable energy firms.
- H4: There is a significant volatility spillover between conventional energy sector stocks and clean energy input commodities, i.e., whether firms rooted in traditional energy sectors are influenced by or respond to developments in the clean energy space.

Our study focuses on assessing volatility spillovers across four key pairings: (i) sustainable stocks and clean energy input commodities, (ii) unsustainable stocks and fossil fuels, (iii) sustainable stocks and fossil fuels, and (iv) unsustainable stocks and clean energy input commodities. This comprehensive framework aims to capture the interconnected risk dynamics between financial assets and their underlying resource dependencies across both sustainable and unsustainable energy ecosystems.

2. Literature Survey

The transition to renewable energy in India is driven by a commitment to sustainable development and the imperative to mitigate climate change. As part of its strategy, India has set ambitious targets to achieve 175 GW of renewable energy capacity by 2022, with allocations of 100 GW from solar energy, 60 GW from wind power, 10 GW from bio-power, and 5 GW from small hydropower plants. This focus on renewable energy aims not only to meet rising electricity demand but also to reduce carbon emissions, as the country strives to secure affordable and reliable energy access for its citizens (Kumar and Majid 2020). Despite the current reliance on fossil fuels, which account for about 80% of electricity generation, there has been significant progress in renewable energy production, positioning India as a global leader in this sector, second only to China in renewable production (Bae 2024).

The term "volatility spillover" encapsulates the transmission of risk between financial markets. It represents the extent and magnitude of risk transfer from one market to others, with movements in volatility interpreted as irregular fluctuations. Recently, the rise in volatility spillovers has been attributed to increasing market interconnections, particularly in response to external shocks. Such spillovers are essential for investors as they help in hedging risks, optimizing portfolios, and anticipating market disruptions, thus guiding decision-making (BenSaïda 2019, BenSaïda et al. 2018, Chevallier and Ielpo 2013).

The literature surrounding volatility spillovers in energy markets reveals significant insights into the dynamics between renewable and non-renewable energy sources. A key focus of research is the interconnectedness and spillover effects between various energy commodities, as well as the broader implications for economic stability and investment strategies.

3. Data and Methodology

This study uses time-series data of sustainable energy stocks, non-renewable energy stocks, major inputs for sustainable energy—copper, silver, and coal—and crude oil for carbon-intensive energy. The stocks representing sustainable and unsustainable energy are as mentioned in Table 1 follows:

The study uses daily price data from 2nd January 2019 to 5th August 2025, covering 1660 observations. The data is sourced from Bloomberg database.

We applied rolling correlation, which is a statistical technique (Dean and Dunsmuir 2016) used to measure the time-varying relationship between two variables over a moving window. Instead of computing a single correlation coefficient for the entire sample period, the analysis is performed repeatedly over a fixed-length sub-period (e.g., 30 days, 90 days), which is shifted forward one observation at a time. This approach helps capture dynamic changes in the degree and direction of association between variables, allowing researchers to detect periods of strengthening, weakening, or reversing relationships. We have also employed a DCC-like framework using Univariate GARCH filtering (for volatility) and EWMA correlation on standardized residuals (to mimic DCC dynamics). This is a DCC approximation or quasi-DCC. It captures time-varying volatility and correlation and

Table 1. Green vs. Carbon-Intensive Energy Companies in India.

Green/Renewable Energy Companies	**Carbon-Intensive Energy Companies**
Suzlon – specializes in wind energy solutions	NTPC Limited – Largest coal-based thermal power producer
Suzlon – Specializes in wind energy solutions	JSW Energy – Engages in thermal power generation
NHPC – Primarily hydroelectric, also solar & wind	Reliance Power – Operates coal, gas, and hydro plants
NTPC Green – Diversified green portfolio, bids for Ultra Mega Renewable Parks	Adani Energy – Power transmission (linked with conventional power base)

highlights dynamic co-movement patterns. Here we have employed a 21-day span for EWMA correlations, which is standard and aligns well with financial time-series practices.

3.1 Dynamic Conditional Correlation Generalized Autoregressive Conditional Heteroskedasticity (DCC-GARCH)

DCC-GARCH multivariate GARCH model (Engle 2002) is used here to model time-varying correlations and volatilities among multiple financial time series.

The model decomposes the conditional covariance matrix Ht into a product of individual conditional standard deviations and a dynamic correlation matrix, expressed as:

$$Ht = DtRtDt \tag{1}$$

where Dt is a diagonal matrix of standard deviations obtained from univariate GARCH models, and Rt is the time-varying correlation matrix.

Each asset's conditional variance hit is modelled using a univariate GARCH process:

$$hit = i+ii,\ t-12+ihi,t-1 \tag{2}$$

The standardized residuals from these models are used to estimate the conditional correlations, with the intermediate matrix Qt evolving as:

$$Qt = (1-a-b)Q+azt-1zt-1'+bQt-1 \tag{3}$$

where Q is the unconditional covariance matrix of standardized residuals zt, and a, b are scalar parameters governing the dynamics.

The final correlation matrix is obtained by standardizing Qt as:

$$Rt = diag(Qt)-12Qtdiag(Qt)-12 \tag{4}$$

This model is both parsimonious and flexible, enabling the modeling of high-dimensional systems without the parameter explosion common in full multivariate GARCH models.

To determine the optimal GARCH model specification, a range of GARCH (p, q) models was estimated using the arch package in Python. The time-series data was scaled by a factor of 10 to enhance numerical stability during estimation. A set of model orders (1,1), (1,2), (2,1), (2,2), (3,3), (4,4), and (5,5) were considered to capture varying levels of autoregressive (p) and moving average (q) effects in the volatility process. Each model was specified with a constant mean and a standard GARCH variance structure and was estimated without rescaling the variance. For each (p, q) combination, key evaluation metrics including the Akaike Information Criterion (AIC), Bayesian Information Criterion (BIC), and log-likelihood were recorded. The model with the lowest AIC value was selected as the best-fitting specification, indicating the most parsimonious model with the best in-sample fit. Based on this criterion, the optimal GARCH (4,4) order was identified, providing a statistically grounded foundation for volatility modeling of the return series.

GARCH models involve optimization of a likelihood function that depends on the variance of the time series. If your return values are very small in magnitude (close to zero), it can lead to:

- Poor convergence of the optimizer
- Extremely small variance estimates
- Flat or ill-defined likelihood surfaces

A scale factor of 10 was applied to the return series prior to GARCH estimation to improve numerical stability during model fitting, without affecting the final standardized residuals or correlation analysis. Scaling the data (multiplying by 10 or 100) increases the magnitude of the values, improving the numerical conditioning of the estimation algorithm. The scale cancels out during standardization:

Standardized Residual = Residual*10Volatility*10

Therefore, the EWMA correlations are unaffected by scaling.

The standardized residuals, obtained by dividing the residuals by their conditional standard deviations, served as the input for the correlation analysis. Rather than estimating a full DCC-GARCH model, an exponentially weighted moving average (EWMA) method with a 21-day span was applied to these residuals to compute a dynamic correlation matrix. This approach, while not a formal DCC-GARCH model, captures the evolving co-movements between assets in a computationally efficient and interpretable manner. The resulting correlation estimates were then used to examine the strength and nature of the dynamic relationships between each stock–commodity pair.

4. Empirical Results

Descriptive Statistics & Stationarity test

The Augmented Dickey-Fuller (ADF) test results displayed in Table 2 indicate that all return series in the dataset—spanning equity returns for both sustainable and unsustainable firms, as well as returns for clean and fossil fuel commodities—are stationary at conventional significance levels. For each variable, the ADF test

Table 2. Stationarity test. Source: Own calculations.

Variable	ADF Statistic	p-value	1% Crit Value	5% Crit Value	10% Crit Value
Suzlon	–27.4898	0.0000	–3.4344	–2.8633	–2.5677
NTPC GREEN	–3.8998	0.0020	–3.4687	–2.8784	–2.5758
Adani Energy	–26.7011	0.0000	–3.4344	–2.8633	–2.5677
NHPC	–20.8220	0.0000	–3.4344	–2.8633	–2.5677
NTPC	–24.4547	0.0000	–3.4344	–2.8633	–2.5677
JSW Energy	–29.6769	0.0000	–3.4344	–2.8633	–2.5677
REL Pow	–14.0472	0.0000	–3.4344	–2.8633	–2.5677
Copp	–11.3026	0.0000	–3.4343	–2.8633	–2.5677
Silver	–27.5484	0.0000	–3.4342	–2.8632	–2.5677
Crude	–29.1745	0.0000	–3.4342	–2.8632	–2.5677
Coal	–18.5533	0.0000	–3.4342	–2.8632	–2.5677

statistics are substantially more negative than the corresponding one percent, five percent, and 10% critical values, and the associated p-values are all effectively zero, well below the 0.05 threshold. This provides strong statistical evidence to reject the null hypothesis of a unit root, confirming that the series does not exhibit stochastic trends and has a constant mean and variance over time.

4.1 H1: Sustainable Stocks - Clean Energy Input Commodities

The rolling correlation analysis exhibited in Figure 1 between Suzlon Energy's returns and copper returns, a key clean-energy input commodity, reveals a dynamic and time-varying relationship over the observed period. The correlation fluctuates substantially, oscillating between strongly negative and moderately positive values, suggesting the absence of a stable long-term linear association. The initial negative

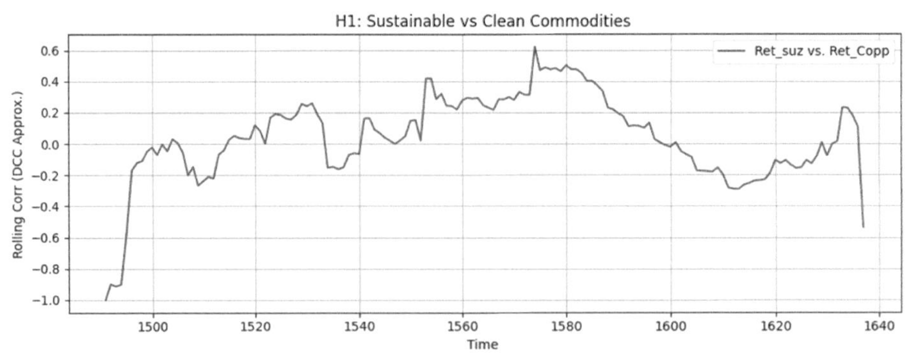

Figure 1. Rolling Correlation (Sustainable vs Clean Commodities).

Table 3. Spillover between Sustainable Stocks ↔ Clean Energy Input Commodities. Source: Own calculations.

Stock	**Commodity**	**Mean Corr**	**% Time Strong + (> 0.5)**	**% Time Moderate + (0.2–0.5)**	**% Neutral (–0.2 to 0.2)**	**% Negative (< –0.2)**	**Interpretation**
Suzlon	Copp	0.039	1.35%	27.03%	57.43%	13.51%	Weak/moderate positive correlations with copper; spillovers present but not dominant
Suzlon	Silver	–0.093	0%	0.68%	83.11%	15.54%	Neutral to slightly negative with silver, very weak co-movement
NTPC GREEN	Copp	0.118	9.46%	22.97%	49.32%	17.57%	Stronger positive spillovers with copper; copper price shocks may influence
NTPC GREEN	Silver	0.041	2.7%	27.7%	41.89%	27.03%	Mixed, positive and negative periods; weak influence
Ret_NHPC	Ret_Copp	0.077	2.7%	23.65%	62.84%	10.14%	Weak to moderate positive spillover with copper
Ret_NHPC	Ret_Silver	–0.127	0%	10.14%	45.95%	43.24%	Negative correlation with silver; possibly inverse dynamics

correlation suggests short-term cost pressure effects (higher copper = worse for Suzlon). Later positive correlations indicate investor sentiment alignment presented in Table 3.

- % Time Strong + (> 0.5): Percentage of the time where the rolling correlation is strongly positive, i.e., above 0.5. This suggests high co-movement: the two assets are rising and falling together, strongly.
- % Time Moderate + (0.2–0.5): Percentage of the time where the correlation is moderately positive, between 0.2 and 0.5. This indicates some positive relationship, but not very strong.
- % Neutral (–0.2 to 0.2): Percentage of the time where the correlation is weak or neutral, close to zero. This means the two assets are mostly unrelated in return; they move independently.
- % Negative (< –0.2): Percentage of the time where the correlation is negative, meaning when one asset rises, the other tends to fall. This suggests inverse sensitivity; rising copper prices hurt business (increasing input costs).

The correlation and spillover analysis between sustainable equity returns (Suzlon, NTPC Green, NHPC) and clean energy input commodities (copper and silver) reveals generally weak linkages, with occasional periods of moderate to strong positive co-movements. For Suzlon, the average correlation with copper is marginally positive (0.039) and exhibits moderate positive co-movement 27.03% of the time, while the relationship with silver is slightly negative (–0.093) and overwhelmingly neutral (83.11%). NTPC Green demonstrates a relatively higher positive correlation with copper (0.118), recording strong positive co-movement in 9.46% of observations and moderate positive co-movement in 22.97% of cases. Its relationship with silver (0.041) is weaker, with nearly half of the observations falling within the neutral range. NHPC records a modest positive correlation with copper (0.077), with most observations (62.84%) being neutral, while the link with silver is more strongly negative (–0.127), with a substantial 43.24% of periods showing negative co-movement.

Overall, these findings suggest that sustainable equities in India exhibit limited and inconsistent return spillovers from key clean energy input commodities, with copper displaying slightly more frequent positive associations compared to silver. The dominance of neutral correlation periods implies that price dynamics in these commodities do not consistently transmit into equity performance for green firms, though short-lived episodes of stronger co-movements do occur, potentially during commodity market shocks or sector-specific events. This pattern may indicate that while clean energy inputs like copper and silver are crucial for the renewable energy value chain, their market price fluctuations are not yet strongly embedded in the return structures of Indian sustainable energy firms, reflecting differing demand cycles, hedging practices, or market segmentation effects.

4.2 Hypothesis 2: Unsustainable Stocks ↔ Fossil Fuels

Traditional energy firms (unsustainable stocks) are influenced by fossil fuel price movements. If true, we expect to see positive spillovers or correlations between fossil fuel returns and unsustainable stock returns.

The rolling correlation between NTPC returns and crude oil prices indicated in Figure 2 exhibits a highly volatile and inconsistent pattern over the observed period, fluctuating frequently between positive and negative values. While there are occasional spikes approaching +1, indicating short-lived episodes of strong co-movement, these are counterbalanced by abrupt declines into negative territory, with troughs extending to approximately –0.5. The correlation appears to center around zero for much of the sample, suggesting the absence of a stable long-term relationship between NTPC's equity performance and crude oil price movements. This high-frequency oscillation in correlation values implies that any spillover effects from fossil fuel markets to unsustainable energy equities are transient and heavily influenced by short-term market shocks, geopolitical developments, or firm-specific events rather than persistent structural linkages.

The correlation and spillover analysis between conventional energy sector equities (NTPC, JSW Energy, Reliance Power, Adani Energy) and fossil fuel commodities (crude oil and coal) shows largely weak and inconsistent relationships, with only occasional periods of moderate to strong positive co-movement. For NTPC, the average correlation with crude oil is near zero (0.001), with strong positive co-movement occurring in just 1.41% of cases and moderate positive co-movement in 15.96%, while coal displays a slightly higher yet still marginal correlation (0.008) and remains predominantly neutral (73.58% of observations). JSW Energy's correlations with crude (–0.002) and coal (–0.008) are negligible, with moderate positive co-movement recorded in 17.80% and 14.37% of observations, respectively, and relatively high proportions of negative co-movements (around 19%). Reliance Power shows a slightly negative correlation with crude (–0.014) and an almost zero correlation with coal (0.006), with most periods falling into the neutral category (over 62% for crude and 73% for coal). Adani Energy registers the most negative

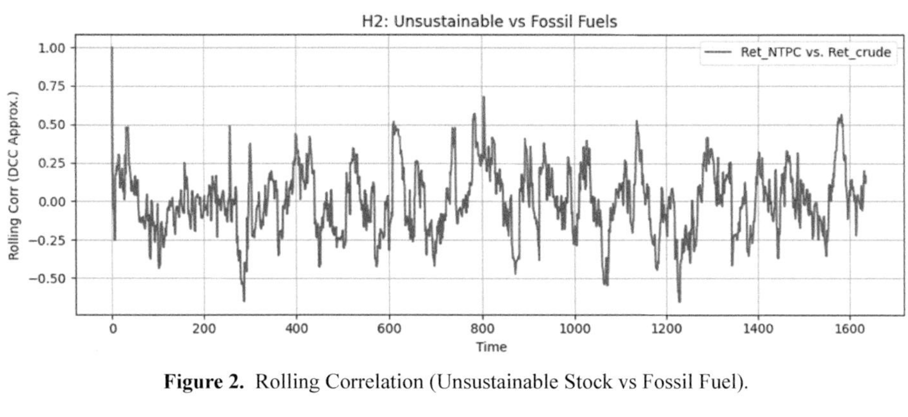

Figure 2. Rolling Correlation (Unsustainable Stock vs Fossil Fuel).

Table 4. Spillover between Unsustainable Stocks ↔ Fossil Commodities. Source: Own calculation.

Stock	Fossil	Mean Corr	% > 0.5	% 0.2–0.5	% Neutral	% < –0.2	Interpretation
NTPC	Crude	0.001	1.41%	15.96%	65.32%	17.25%	Neutral; weak connection
NTPC	Coal	0.008	1.04%	13.58%	73.58%	11.74%	Entirely uncorrelated
JSW Energy	Crude	–0.002	1.90%	17.80%	61.04%	19.20%	Neutral; negative skew
JSW Energy	Coal	–0.008	1.10%	14.37%	67.03%	17.43%	Little persistent correlation
REL Pow	Crude	–0.014	0.18%	17.55%	62.08%	20.12%	Neutral or weak inverse relationship
REL Pow	Coal	0.006	1.10%	11.99%	73.58%	13.27%	No co-movement
Adani Energy	Crude	–0.045	0.24%	11.25%	65.14%	23.30%	Weak to moderately negative correlation
Adani Energy	Coal	-0.024	0.00%	14.50%	68.87%	16.57%	Neutral with light negative bias

associations with fossil fuels in the sample, averaging –0.045 with crude and –0.024 with coal, alongside negative co-movements in over 23% and 16% of cases, respectively. All the results are displayed in Table 4.

Overall, the results suggest that Indian conventional energy equities experience limited and generally weak return spillovers from fossil fuel markets, with crude oil and coal prices exerting only minimal and inconsistent effects on stock performance. Although episodes of moderate or strong co-movement do occur, triggered by major fossil fuel price shocks or policy shifts, the predominance of neutral and negative correlations indicates that fossil fuel price volatility is not a consistent driver of short-term equity returns for these firms. This pattern may reflect structural features of the Indian conventional energy sector, such as regulated price mechanisms, diversified revenue bases, vertical integration, or lagged transmission of fuel cost changes to stock valuations.

4.3 Hypothesis 3: Sustainable Stocks ↔ Fossil Fuels

The correlation analysis between selected sustainable energy-related stocks (Suzlon Energy, NTPC Green, Adani Energy, NHPC) and fossil fuel indicators (crude oil and coal prices) exhibited in Figure 3 reveals a generally low mean correlation, with values below 0.20. This suggests that, on average, the return dynamics of these sustainable stocks are only weakly linked to movements in fossil fuel markets. All the results that are described below exhibited in Table 5.

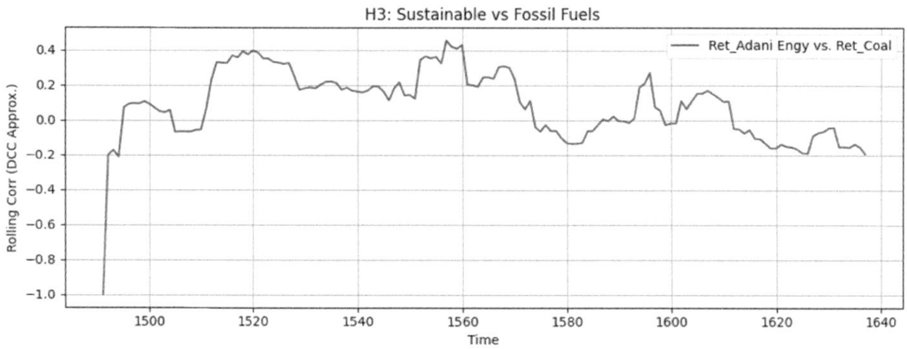

Figure 3. Rolling Correlation between Sustainable Stocks ↔ Fossil Fuels.

Table 5. Spillover between Sustainable Stock & Fossil Fuel. Source: Own calculation.

Stock	Fossil	Mean Corr	% > 0.5	% 0.2–0.5	% Neutral	% < –0.2	Interpretation
Suzlon	Crude	0.106	3.38%	37.84%	43.92%	14.19%	Positive co-movement; some responsiveness to crude
Suzlon	Coal	0.021	0.00%	17.57%	71%	10.81%	Neutral; little spillover from coal
NTPC GREEN	Crude	0.082	6.08%	17.57%	63.5%	12.16%	Mild co-movement with crude; not dominant
NTPC GREEN	Coal	0.193	4.73%	39.86%	53.4%	1.35%	Strong correlation; significant sensitivity to coal
NHPC	Crude	0.045	2.03%	21.62%	61.5%	14.19%	Occasional positive response to crude
NHPC	Coal	0.112	0.00%	33.78%	64.2%	1.35%	Moderate co-movement with coal; strongest after NTPC GREEN

The highest observed mean correlation is between NTPC Green returns and coal prices (0.193), while the lowest is between Suzlon returns and coal prices (0.021). The negative mean correlations imply potential countercyclical price behavior, although the magnitude is small, limiting statistical or economic significance. The percentage of days with strong positive correlation (> 0.5) is extremely low across all pairs (maximum 6.08%), underscoring that high co-movement is rare.

The moderate positive correlations (0.2–0.5) are more prevalent for certain pairs, notably Suzlon–crude (37.84%) and NTPC Green–coal (39.86%). A substantial proportion of observations are in the neutral range (|correlation| < 0.2), often exceeding 60%, suggesting that short-term price co-movement is generally weak and inconsistent. The negative correlations stronger than –0.2 occur in 10–18% of cases for crude oil and about 1–2% for coal, indicating that sustained inverse relationships are uncommon and more noticeable against crude benchmarks. The weak correlations imply that price movements in sustainable energy stocks are not strongly dictated by short-term fossil fuel market trends, which may be due to differing demand drivers, regulatory frameworks, and investor bases. However, occasionally moderate to high correlations—especially with coal prices—indicate that certain sustainable energy firms may still be indirectly influenced by fossil fuel market cycles, possibly through shared macroeconomic conditions, energy mix policies, or sectoral rotation effects.

4.4 Hypothesis 4: Unsustainable Stocks ↔ Clean Energy Input Commodities (Copper/Silver)

The rolling correlation between JSW Energy returns and silver prices exhibits pronounced short-term variability, fluctuating frequently between moderate positive and negative values throughout the observation period. Although the correlation occasionally approaches strong positive territory (above 0.6) and dips into moderately negative ranges (below –0.4), the relationship lacks a persistent directional trend. This volatility suggests that the interaction between JSW Energy's performance and silver price movements is largely episodic, likely influenced by transient market shocks, commodity supply-demand imbalances, and sector-specific developments. The absence of a stable long-term correlation implies that silver prices are not a consistent driver of JSW Energy's returns but may act as an intermittent factor during periods of heightened commodity market sensitivity or broader macroeconomic disturbances. All the results described below are mentioned in Figure 4 and Table 6.

The correlation analysis between the returns of selected unsustainable energy-intensive stocks (NTPC, JSW Energy, Reliance Power, and Adani Energy) and clean energy input commodities (copper and silver) reveals consistently weak and predominantly negative relationships over the observed period. Across all stock–commodity pairs, mean correlation coefficients lie in a narrow range between –0.028 and 0.018, indicating an almost negligible linear association between the two return series. This suggests that price movements in these unsustainable stocks are largely independent of fluctuations in copper and silver prices.

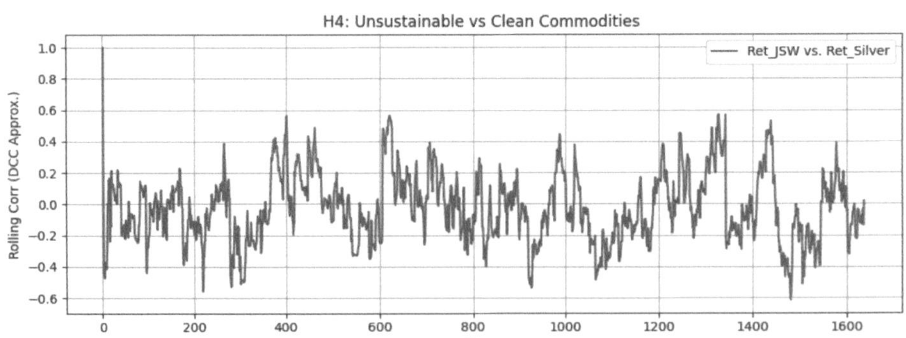

Figure 4. Rolling Correlation between Unsustainable Stocks & Clean Energy Input Commodities.

Table 6. Spillover between Unsustainable Stocks ↔ Clean Energy Input Commodities. Source: Own calculation.

Stock	Clean Commodity	Mean Corr	% > 0.5	% 0.2–0.5	% Neutral	% < –0.2	Interpretation
Ret_ NTPC	Copper	–0.019	1.77%	14.05%	64.51%	19.61%	Neutral, some weak negative correlation
Ret_ NTPC	Silver	–0.028	1.41%	15.64%	60.84%	22.05%	Negative relationship
Ret_JSW Energy	Copper	0.018	0.67%	18.51%	66.83%	13.93%	Neutral, mild positive correlation
Ret_JSW Energy	Silver	–0.026	0.98%	14.91%	61.82%	22.24%	Inverse relationship
Ret_REL Pow	Copper	–0.003	0.31%	14.05%	70.01%	15.58%	Weak and neutral overall
Ret_REL Pow	Silver	–0.018	0.49%	13.26%	67.68%	18.51%	Neutral to slightly negative
Ret_Adani Energy	Copper	–0.004	0.55%	18.45%	62.92%	18.02%	Mild relationship, leaning neutral
Ret_Adani Energy	Silver	–0.019	0.18%	15.33%	65.61%	18.81%	Neutral with some inverse spillover

The lack of robust correlation indicates that, in the short to medium term, commodity price shocks in copper and silver are unlikely to systematically influence the returns of major greenhouse gas–emitting stocks in India. This may be attributed to differences in demand drivers—unsustainable stocks are tied to fossil-fuel–dependent power generation or heavy industry, whereas clean-energy commodities are increasingly driven by renewable technology adoption and global decarbonization trends.

The GARCH(1,1) model estimation results reveal notable differences in volatility dynamics across asset groups. Among sustainable assets, Suzlon exhibits moderate ARCH effects (α = 0.1710 and 0.2032, respectively) with negligible GARCH persistence, suggesting that shocks to volatility dissipate relatively quickly. Conversely, NTPC Green displays near-unit persistence ($\alpha + \beta = 0.9998$), indicating a high degree of volatility clustering and slow decay of shocks. In the unsustainable group, Reliance Power demonstrates the highest short-term volatility response (α = 0.4372) with no significant long-term persistence, while JSW Energy shows moderate ARCH effects. Clean commodities present mixed patterns: copper exhibits both ARCH and GARCH effects ($\alpha = 0.1182$, $\beta = 0.0509$) with moderate persistence (0.1691), whereas silver shows a low ARCH coefficient (0.0915) and no persistence. Fossil commodities, particularly coal and crude oil, display low persistence with relatively small short-term volatility responses, indicating rapid adjustment to market

Table 7. Model Summary. Source: Own calculation.

Group	Asset	omega	mu	alpha[1]	beta[1]	Log-Likelihood	Persistence (α+β)
Sustainable	Ret_Suzlon	0.0608**	–0.0057	0.1710***	0.0000	–882.263	0.1710
	Ret_NTPC GREEN	0.0041	–0.0269	0.0000	0.9998*	–166.885	0.9998
	Ret_Adani Energy	0.1054	0.0309	0.2032	0.0000	–847.901	0.2032
	Ret_NHPC	0.0004	0.0028	0.0000	0.0000	–278.799	0.0000
Unsustainable	Ret_NTPC	0.0006	0.0018	0.0000	0.0000	–248.449	0.0000
	Ret_JSW Energy	0.0509	–0.0200	0.1402***	0.0000	–482.391	0.1402
	Ret_REL Pow	0.0804	0.0462	0.4372*	0.0000	–1020.681	0.4372
	Ret_Adani Energy	0.1054	0.0309	0.2032	0.0000	–847.901	0.2032
Clean Commodities	Ret_Copp	0.4422	0.0979*	0.1182***	0.0509	–7259.386	0.1691
	Ret_Silver	0.0009	0.0037	0.0915***	0.0000	597.523	0.0915
Fossil Commodities	Ret_crude	0.0244***	0.0303***	0.0439	0.0000	–161.890	0.0439
	Ret_Coal	0.0040	0.0017	0.1785	0.0000	198.200	0.1785

Persistence = α1+β1, how long volatility shocks last.

*** = significant at 1%, ** = significant at 5%, * = significant at 10%

shocks. Overall, the results underscore heterogeneous volatility structures, with certain assets (e.g., NTPC Green) exhibiting pronounced persistence, while others (e.g., silver, coal) adjust more rapidly to shocks. All the results described above are mentioned in Table 7.

5. Conclusion

The rolling correlation and spillover analysis reveal dynamic and time-varying interlinkages between sustainable and unsustainable asset classes. In the case of Sustainable Stocks – Clean Energy Input Commodities, the correlation patterns indicate periods of both positive and negative co-movement, suggesting that clean energy equities do not consistently mirror the performance of their input commodities, thereby offering potential diversification benefits during certain phases. Conversely, the Unsustainable Stocks – Fossil Fuels relationship exhibits a more persistent and positive correlation, reflecting the direct dependency of these equities on fossil fuel price dynamics. The Sustainable Stocks – Fossil Fuels pair reveals generally weaker and more volatile correlations, while Unsustainable Stocks – Clean Energy Input Commodities demonstrate mixed patterns, with occasional alignment likely driven by shared macroeconomic or energy sector dynamics.

The spillover analysis further confirms that these relationships are not static; transmission intensity varies across time, with episodes of heightened spillovers aligning with periods of commodity price shocks, policy announcements, or geopolitical disruptions. Overall, the findings underscore that while sustainable and unsustainable asset classes are connected through certain market forces, the degree and direction of these linkages are heterogeneous, suggesting selective hedging and diversification opportunities depending on the market regime.

References

Ahmed BenSaïda. (2019). Good and bad volatility spillovers: An asymmetric connectedness. Journal of Financial Markets 43: 78–95, ISSN 1386-4181, https://doi.org/10.1016/j.finmar.2018.12.005.

Ahmed BenSaïda, Houda Litimi and Oussama Abdallah. (2018). Volatility spillover shifts in global financial markets. Economic Modelling 73: 343–353, ISSN 0264-9993, https://doi.org/10.1016/j.econmod.2018.04.011.

Bae, J. (2024). Examining the economic effects of non-fossil energy policies in India. The National High School Journal of Science, https://nhsjs.com/2024/examining-the-economic-effects-of-non-fossil-energy-policies-in-india/.

Bouri, E. (2019). The effect of jumps in the crude oil market on the sovereign risks of major oil exporters. Risks 7(4): 118. https://doi.org/10.3390/risks7040118.

Bufan Zhang and Yifeng Wang. (2019). The effect of green finance on energy sustainable development: a case study in China. Emerging Markets Finance and Trade, DOI:10.1080/1540496X.2019.1695595.

Chevallier, J. and Ielpo, F. (2013). Volatility spillovers in commodity markets. Applied Economics Letters 20(13): 1211–1227. https://doi.org/10.1080/13504851.2013.799748.

Dean, R. T. and Dunsmuir, W. T. M. (2016). Dangers and uses of cross-correlation in analyzing time series in perception, performance, movement, and neuroscience: The importance of constructing transfer function autoregressive models. Behav. Res. 48: 783–802. https://doi.org/10.3758/s13428-015-0611-2.

Dutta, A., Bouri, E., Das, D. and Roubaud, D. (2020). Assessment and optimization of clean energy equity risks and commodity price volatility indexes: Implications for sustainability. Journal of Cleaner Production 243: 118669, ISSN 0959-6526, https://doi.org/10.1016/j.jclepro.2019.118669.

Engle, R. (2002). Dynamic conditional correlation: a simple class of multivariate generalized autoregressive conditional heteroskedasticity models. Journal of Business & Economic Statistics 20(3): 339–350. https://doi.org/10.1198/073500102288618487.

Haozhi Qi, Lijun Ma, Pin Peng, Hao Chen and Kang Li. (2022). Dynamic connectedness between clean energy stock markets and energy commodity markets during times of COVID-19: Empirical evidence from China. Resources Policy 79: ISSN 0301-4207, https://doi.org/10.1016/j.resourpol.2022.103094.

Jingpeng Li, Muhammad Umar and Jiale Huo. (2023). The spillover effect between Chinese crude oil futures market and Chinese green energy stock market. Energy Economics 119: ISSN 0140-9883, https://doi.org/10.1016/j.eneco.2023.106568.

Kumar, J. C. R. and Majid, M. A. (2020). Renewable energy for sustainable development in India: current status, future prospects, challenges, employment, and investment opportunities. Energ Sustain Soc 10: 2. https://doi.org/10.1186/s13705-019-0232-1.

Liu, Tiantian and Hamori, Shigeyuki. (2020). Spillovers to renewable energy stocks in the US and Europe: Are They Different? Energies 13: 3162. 10.3390/en13123162.

Seth, Neha and Sidhu, Arpit. (2021). Price discovery and volatility spillover for indian energy futures market in pre- and post- crisis periods. Indian Journal of Finance 15: 24–39. 10.17010/ijf/2021/v15i8/165816.

Tang, Chaofeng, Aruga, Kentaka and Hu, Yi. (2023). The dynamic correlation and volatility spillover among green bonds, clean energy stock, and fossil fuel market. Sustainability 15: 6586. 10.3390/su15086586.

Wen, F., Jiahui Cao, Zhen Liu and Xiong Wang. (2021). Dynamic volatility spillovers and investment strategies between the Chinese stock market and commodity markets. International Review of Financial Analysis 76: 101772, ISSN 1057-5219, https://doi.org/10.1016/j.irfa.2021.101772.

Zivot, E. and Wang, J. (2003). Rolling analysis of time series. *In*: Modeling Financial Time Series with S-Plus®. Springer, New York, NY. https://doi.org/10.1007/978-0-387-21763-5_9.

Chapter 10

Transformative Dynamics of Rubber Plantations in Tripura

Linking Growth, Sustainability, Social Inclusion and Future Projections

Bhaskar Datta,[3] *Rajesh Chatterjee,*[1,*] *Debarshi Mukherjee,*[2] *Abdur Rahman Choudhury*[3] and *Abhranil Bhattacharjee*[3]

1. Introduction

The establishment of rubber plantations in Tripura aims to address socio-economic and ecological challenges linked to shifting cultivation, a prevalent agricultural practice that has led to deforestation, soil degradation, and reduced crop yields. Recognizing the need for sustainable land use, the Tripura Forest Department initiated rubber cultivation in 1963 (Bhowmik 2006), focusing on afforestation and soil conservation. Collaboration with the Rubber Board and other agencies further accelerated the expansion of rubber farming. Various schemes, including Block Plantation, Rubber Plantation Development, and Multi-Prolonged Extension Schemes, promoted rubber cultivation, reaching marginalized and tribal communities.

Rubber plantations not only replaced environmentally harmful practices but also became a crucial driver of rural economic growth (Bhowmik 2006, Nath et al. 2010, Sarkar 2010, Joseph and George 2011, Sinha 2012, Matauleibi 2012). They

[1] Assistant Professor, Centre for Study of Social Exclusion and Inclusive Policies (CSSEIP), Tripura University.
[2] Professor, Jamia Milllia Islamia, New Delhi.
[3] PhD Scholars, Centre for Study of Social Exclusion and Inclusive Policies (CSSEIP), Tripura University.
* Corresponding author: rajeshchatterjee@tripurauniv.ac.in

DOI: 10.1201/9781003736158-13

provided stable incomes and employment opportunities, particularly for marginalized groups. Today, Tripura stands as India's second-largest rubber producer, with over 90,000 hectares under cultivation, benefiting around 100,000 families. This growth exemplifies the successful integration of agroforestry and sustainable livelihoods, addressing both socio-economic vulnerabilities and environmental concerns.

After six decades of rubber cultivation, this chapter reviews its implications for economic development, social inclusion, and long-term sustainability, with projections for the next fifty years. Understanding the role of rubber plantations in Tripura's development is essential for refining policies aimed at the economic rehabilitation of indigenous communities and modernizing the sector sustainably, thus aligning with the vision of a "*Viksit Bharat*."

The vision of Viksit Bharat 2047 resonates with the transformative development witnessed in Tripura's rubber plantations. Rubber cultivation has spurred tremendous socio-economic and environmental development by improving income levels, increasing female workforce participation, and enhancing sustainable land use. The development captures the essence of Viksit Bharat as it is reflected in economic self-reliance, social equity, and environmental sustainability.

The rubber projections for Tripura by 2047 include the expansion of plantations to more than 150,000 hectares in Tripura, with better yields due to improved agroforestry practices. This growth will add to India's rubber self-sufficiency and improve tribal livelihoods, thus playing a very important role in achieving a developed India.

2. Key Factors of Rubber Plantation and Growth

Tripura is primarily a tribal state in the Northeastern Indian subcontinent, since 31% of the total population comes under the category of STs. Traditionally, these people have been jhum or shifting cultivators, who are basically considered to be not only ecologically unsound but also economically unremunerative (Bordoloi 2008a, Darlong et al. 2015). This is also regarded as one of the significant anthropogenic impacts on biodiversity in Tripura, North East India (Gupta 2000).

With the onset of environmental and economic factors restricting jhum agriculture, there arose a need for other means of livelihood to complement the development process. Consequently, the state government and the central government started rubber cultivation as an alternative source of livelihood (Rubber Board of India 2023a). Over the years, the plantations have seen rapid growth and now form 9% of India's total production, with Tripura emerging as one of the major contributors. The high rubber planting dependency reflects its paramount function in sustaining economic viability among rural households in the state (Prabhakar and Bhattacharya 2023). In today's scenario, the overall situation of natural rubber in the state is mainly shaped by the institutional responses perceived and implemented by the Rubber Board and the State Government of Tripura for the last fifty years (Sharma et al. 2014).

This achievement discussed in numerous formal events and conferences, among them the Tripura Rubber Conclave 2024, wherein industrial development of the state through rubber productions had been extensively discussed. It has brought forth immense income generation besides employment and, above all, increased gender participation in rural Tripura. Rubber farming has significantly contributed to the rural development of the state through improvements in household incomes. It provides employment in plantation activities as well as processing and promotes women's labor force participation. The above effects are evident in the reports by Rubber Board of India (2023b) and also in studies such as the Tripura Rural Economic Growth and Service Delivery Project under the World Bank (2022), which elaborates on how rubber plantations help provide inclusive growth for rural and tribal regions. Moreover, Mohapatra (2022) brings out how the integrated development program on rubber impacts income generation activities among tribal groups in Tripura. The study reflects improvements in financial and social capital and how rubber cultivation has achieved significant strides in poverty reduction. It has been concluded that rubber enhances the physio-chemical properties of soil compared to fallow land and, in some parameters, performs even better than other forest species typically cultivated in the state. Nye and Greenland (1964) noted that organic matter was depleted very quickly, especially in the first cycle year of shifting cultivation in the soils of Tripura. But due to rubber cultivation, a considerable annual input of biomass gets incorporated into the soil through leaf litter and cover crops (Kothandaraman et al. 1989, Krishnakumar et al. 1990) and thereby significantly improves soil properties. Rubber plantations are often considered a sustainable system that even improves soil fertility in some cases (Gilot et al. 1995).

3. Literature Review

3.1 Tribal Livelihoods and Agricultural Transitions

While jhum has always formed an integral part of the cultural identity of populations in Northeastern India, growing concerns over the low productivity of jhum agriculture and its negative environmental impacts have led studies to reveal that shifting cultivation is not viable in mountainous regions. Thus, this has brought about a tremendous transition to more commercially viable crops like rubber (Srivastava 1996). Although jhum farming has traditionally been an important source of livelihood, its inherent unpredictability and the environmental degradation associated with it have compelled a shift toward cash cropping. For instance, rubber has become an important alternative in this respect, offering more predictable income and better long-term prospects for rural progress (Maithani 1995). The shift is supported by different efforts aimed at optimizing land use and improving economic outcomes for tribal communities in the region (Bordoloi 2008a).

3.2 Rubber Plantation as a Driver of Economic Change and Social Inclusion

Rubber cultivation has become one of the most significant farming activities in Northeast India and has helped advance rural development over time, stabilizing income generation and providing employment opportunities. In particular, in a state such as Tripura, agricultural degradation replaced traditional *jhum* cultivation, increasing overall declines in productivity (Bordoloi 2008b). The cultivation of rubber ensures a more stable source of income and therefore lowers vulnerability, as opposed to jhum farming, which features seasonal and variable yields (Sarma et al. 2020a). Results from a study conducted by Joseph et al. in 2010 revealed that annual average household incomes of NR cultivators increased by as much as 112 percent. The shift to rubber farming has facilitated an upgrade of the rural lifestyle in terms of better living conditions, improved literacy, and better health facilities (Mathew 2023). The expansion of the rubber industry has also led to the creation of high employment opportunities in large-scale agricultural production, processing, and other business enterprises, thus promoting direct and indirect employment generation (Rubber India 2023). The participation of women in the labor market has rapidly increased since rubber cultivation provides employment at every stage of production and hence ensures gender balance (Sarma et al. 2020b, Mathew 2023). The rubber industry of Tripura has also helped improve the infrastructure of the state, as plantations have brought good roads, schools, and hospitals to rural areas (Bordoloi 2008a). This has been achieved by the government through collaboration with the Rubber Board of India, along with training programs, provision of financial aid, and the promotion of modern farming methods that have ensured the sustainability and competitiveness of the industry (Mathew 2023).

3.3 Impact of Rubber Plantation on Soil Dynamics and Ecosystem Resilience

Rubber plantations in Tripura have altered the physical and chemical properties of the soil to a great extent. The infiltration rate in rubber plantations is much higher (138%) than in areas under shifting cultivation (Krishnakumar et al. 1990). Bulk density, as an indicator of soil compaction, varies from 1.35 to 1.70 Mg/m^3, with an average of 1.54 Mg/m^3, showing minimal variation over time (Mandal et al. 2012). Porosity is relatively higher in rubber plantations, mainly in the top layers of the soil (Krishnakumar et al. 1989). Soil associated with rubber plantations shows increased aggregate stability and a higher mean weight diameter (MWD), indicating improved soil structure (Mandal et al. 2001, Krishnakumar et al. 1991). Regarding chemical characteristics, the pH of the soil remains stable for more than two decades of rubber cultivation and averages 4.45 in the upper layers. It is relatively higher than fallow land but comparable with other forest plantations (Mandal et al. 2012). Moreover, the cation exchange capacity (CEC) of rubber soils was on par with other forest plantations, but it was significantly higher than fallow land (Choudhury et al. 2006).

Initially, the organic carbon content of the soil varied from 0.11 to 1.76% in surface soil (0–30 cm), with a mean value of 0.81%. After 20 years, the organic carbon increased under rubber cultivation and varied from 0.32 to 2.8%, with a mean value of 0.96% (Mandal et al. 2012). Though available phosphorus decreased due to the utilization of native phosphorus by plants and higher phosphorus fixation,

Table 1. List of findings for Identification of research variables.

Sl. No	Findings	Identified Research variables	Source
1	The study is a comprehensive report on natural rubber plantation, consumption, productivity, ownership status, growth trend, expansion of rubber plantation, and moreover identifies the challenges in rubber plantation and expansion in Tripura.	Economic growth due to rubber plantation.	(Bhowmik 2006)
2	The study was on marketing efficiency, consumer price, and marketing cost per unit of rubber. The author has highlighted the marketing channels right from producer to processor, wholesaler and trader in rubber-based activities in Tripura.	Civic benefits like primary health care and improved literacy rate.	(Adikari and Sharma 2018)
3	The study stressed economic viability, current profitability and increasing trends of profitability, long-term rate of return on investment, payback period, modified payback period, net project value, etc., in regard to rubber plantation in Tripura. The author has elaborated year-wise plantation trends, increasing trends of trappable areas of rubber plantation, and price rise in rubber products.	Economic viability and profitability of rubber plantation.	(Ghoshal 2014)
4	The study emphasizes environmental degradation and negative ecological effects due to a significant rise in average atmospheric temperature, wastewater generated due to collection and processing of ribbed smoked sheets (RSS), annual rainfall deficit due to the adoption of rubber plantation as a monoculture, increasing scale of production, as well as soil degradation due to rubber plantation practices.	Social and economic benefits of rubber plantation that leads to social inclusion.	(Majumder et al. 2014)
5	The study revealed the transformation of tribal people from shifting cultivation to rubber plantation and how they overcame the apprehension that rubber plantation would have negative effects on their traditional means of livelihood, i.e. *jhum* cultivation or shifting cultivation practices, due to the efforts of government agencies like Tripura Forest Development and Plantation Corporation Limited (TFDPC), Rubber Board, and Tripura Rehabilitation & Plantation Corporation (TRPC). Apart from this, the author also discussed the causes that obstructed them from participating in rubber plantation. According to the author, the repeated efforts of the government machinery have mobilized a good number of *jhumias* into rubber cultivation and gradually helped the tribal communities understand the multifarious benefits of rubber plantation in regard to socio-economic development, income generation, and permanent employment prospects.	Rubber plantation & sustainable development.	(Datta et al. 2019)
6	The research emphasized mainly the workers engaged in rubber plantation, their socio-economic profile, education, erstwhile occupation, training, support sources, work experience, and employment relations in small rubber holdings, the nature of labor contracts, and recommended policy interventions required for improvement of living standards of the workers engaged in small rubber holdings in two districts of Tripura, viz. Gomati and West Tripura.	Socio-economic conditions of the labors engaged in small rubber holdings.	(Bhowmik and Viswanathan 2015)

potassium increased by 20.7% and 28.9% in surface and sub-surface soils after 20 years of rubber cultivation (Mandal et al. 2012, Philip et al. 1993). Rubber soils have the potential to sequester high amounts of carbon over time. According to Mandal et al. (2012), 88.7 mt C/ha is available under rubber soils of Tripura. An average carbon store in rubber plantations is around 136 tonnes/ha, out of which 92.7 t C/ha is contributed by soil in the North East region (Dey 2005).

It has also been proved that in rubber plantations, the microbial population was higher in the surface layer due to the higher organic matter status in those layers. According to the horizontal distribution of bacteria, maximum activity was observed in regions of higher root concentration, and mycorrhizal infection was found to be higher toward the base of the trees (Deka et al. 1998). Similarly, Mandal et al. (2001) also reported a higher population density of various groups of soil microorganisms under rubber. The universal occurrence of vesicular-arbuscular mycorrhiza in the feeding roots of rubber plants has also been reported (Wastie 1965).

4. Methodology

4.1 Research Design

The above review of the literature revealed that various studies have covered various aspects such as economic growth due to rubber plantations, economic viability and profitability of rubber plantations, and social and economic benefits of rubber plantations leading to social inclusion (Figure 1). Thus, it is clear that the variables reflecting social inclusion are interrelated with each other. However, there are no studies that have identified all factors together.

This study tries to find impactful results by considering all the variables like economic growth, literacy, access to health care, women's participation, and social improvement, as all these factors promote social inclusion of individuals associated with rubber. The study attempts to project the future of rubber plantations based on all verified indicators. This entire study will be more helpful in measuring social inclusion, and taking into consideration the review of literature and identified variables, the following objectives are carved out:

- To estimate the economic inclusion of tribal people through rubber plantations.
- To analyze the impact of rubber plantations in broadening the scope of social inclusion of the marginalized tribal population.
- To evaluate soil improvement through rubber plantation as a foundation for sustainable livelihoods.

Research Model

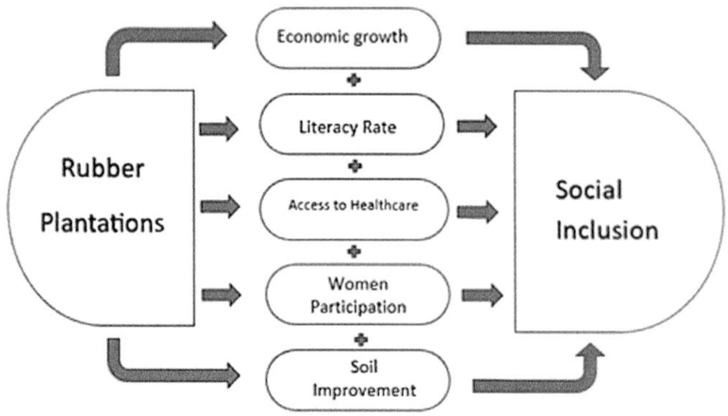

Figure 1. Impact of Rubber Plantations on Social Inclusion. Source: Author's own compilation.

5. Hypothesis Formulation

H1: There is a positive relationship between rubber plantation and economic empowerment

Being a front-runner in ensuring an exponential rise in economic activity, rubber plantation has contributed to a paradigm shift from the traditional practice of shifting cultivation toward settled cultivation among the tribal communities in Tripura (Sarkar et al. 2023). Thus, it can be observed that economic activity has been highly influenced by this approach, which shows that the hypothesis formulated relates to the economic empowerment of the families.

H2: There is a positive relationship between rubber plantation and employment opportunities

The most influential factor of rubber plantation is labor relations, thus promoting employment opportunities. The quantity and quality of the effort induced by the laborer directly influence production, income generation, and profit. Long-term employment opportunity is also a decisive factor that influences the rate of employment among unskilled laborers (Chauhan and Bhowmik 2017). Thus, it has been found that rubber plantation is deeply associated with employment opportunities from the initial stage, resulting in the formulation of the hypothesis.

H3: There is a positive relationship between rubber plantation and access to resources

The quality of life among rubber cultivators has significantly improved irrespective of various other issues. Rubber cultivation has contributed to increased spending on children's education at the higher secondary level or above. Moreover, it has been observed that the capacity to invest in health-related concerns, along with access to health institutions, has significantly increased (Vijayan et al. 2024). Thus, there is a felt need to assess the positive relationship between rubber cultivation and access to resources.

H4: There is a positive relationship between rubber plantation and soil improvement

Research shows that there is a positive shift in the physical and chemical properties of soil under rubber cultivation. The infiltration rate in rubber plantations is much higher (138%) (Krishnakumar et al. 1990), bulk density of rubber soils shows less variation over time (Mandal et al. 2012), and porosity is also relatively higher in rubber plantations (Krishnakumar et al. 1989). Moreover, rubber soils have the potential to sequester a high amount of carbon and are also capable of increasing the potassium level over time (Mandal et al. 2012). Therefore, quantifying the positive outcomes of rubber is also essential in terms of soil sustainability and thereby shows that the hypothesis is justified.

5.1 Sampling Method

The study was carried out in six districts of Tripura: Dhalai, Gomati, Khowai, South Tripura, Sepahijala, and West Tripura. These districts have been selected to reflect a wide range of rubber cultivation practices, from early adopters to more recent attempts. Stratified random sampling has been used to select 250 households, which are divided into two groups:

- Plantation households (n = 125), i.e., households engaged in rubber plantations.
- Non-plantation households (n = 125), i.e., households involved only in traditional agriculture.

Households were further stratified according to socio-economic characteristics, including the level of income, gender of the head of the household, and size of the household.

5.2 Sample Size

In this study, the mathematical calculation of Taro Yamane (1970: 886–87) has been used for the determination of the sample size (Umar and Wachiko 2021).

n =N1+Ne2 =6671+6670.052=6671+667X0.0025=6672.6675= **250.75**

Here, ‘N’ is the total population, i.e., 667 households, and ‘e’ is the error at a 95 percent confidence level (e = 0.05); therefore, the sample size ‘n’ is 250.75 or considered as 250.

For an effective estimation of soil improvement due to rubber plantations, an intensive soil study was conducted in mature rubber plantations (more than 20 years of age) in the state of Tripura. Altogether, 80 composite soil samples were collected from all six districts. It was primarily aimed at providing a cross-sectional sample of the soil across all depth intervals, namely the surface layer 0–30 cm and sub-surface layer 30–60 cm, to obtain an all-inclusive idea about the dynamics of soil quality.

The samples were analyzed to note significant physical and chemical characteristics, which included bulk density, porosity, aggregate stability, pH, cation exchange capacity (CEC), organic carbon concentration, available phosphorus, and potassium content. The data obtained in this manner were compared against the existing soil records conserved by the Rubber Board, thus setting a basis for measuring the extent of improvement in soil quality over twenty years of rubber cultivation.

Standard laboratory methods were employed to conduct the soil analysis. Bulk density and porosity were estimated through core sampling and gravimetric techniques, respectively, whereas pH and CEC were estimated through the use of a pH meter and ammonium acetate extraction, respectively. Organic carbon content was determined by the Walkley-Black method, while available phosphorus and potassium levels were determined through Bray's solution extraction and ammonium acetate extraction, respectively.

5.3 Data Collection

5.3.1 Primary Data

Data were collected through structured surveys, focus group discussions (FGDs), and field observations:

- *Structured Surveys*: Focused on household income, employment distribution, access to healthcare, literacy rates, and participation in social welfare
- *Focus Group Discussions (FGDs)*: Group discussions with local leaders, plantation workers, and women workers on socio-cultural implications from rubber cultivation.
- *Field Observations*: Documented cultivation practices, land-use changes, and alterations in ecology resulting from rubber monoculture.

5.3.2 Secondary Data

Secondary data were obtained from:

- *Government Publications*: This includes the Tripura Economic Survey, documents by the Rubber Board of India, and state-wise agricultural statistics.
- Academic research on cultivation of rubber, tribal economics and ecological sustainability

5.4 Statistical Analysis

A variety of statistical techniques was used to analyze and compare the economic and social performance of plantation households with that of other agricultural households. To test the income trend of households over time, repeated-measures ANOVA was employed to examine whether there was an interaction between time and household type, indicating a higher income growth rate in households engaged in plantations. To evaluate categorical social indicators, which include literacy rate, access to primary healthcare, and women's participation in the workforce, chi-square tests were used. This enabled the determination of significant differences in proportions between the two groups.

6. Results

6.1 Economic Empowerment through Rubber Plantations

6.1.1 Income Growth Trajectories and Statistical Significance

This section analyzes the income patterns of plantation households as compared to other agricultural households for the years 2000, 2010, and 2023 based on data from 250 respondents, n = 125 for each category. Systematic statistical analysis brings out wide differences in income trends in the two categories and shows that greater economic benefits are also associated with livelihoods based on plantation activities (Table 2).

Table 2. Annual Household Income by Group.

Year	Household Type	Mean Income (₹)	Std. Deviation	N	F (df)	p	Partial η2
2000	Rubber Plantation	64,602.64	5,126.23	125			
	Other Agriculture	45,323.52	4,789.23	125			
	Total	54,963.08	10,853.70	250	177.77 (1.74, 430.99)	< 0 .001	0.418
2010	Rubber Plantation	90,814.31	10,935.18	125			
	Other Agriculture	67,750.37	7,553.94	125			
	Total	79,282.34	14,882.40	250	177.77 (1.74, 430.99)	< 0 .001	0.418
2023	Other Agriculture	1,26,702.85	9,642.91	125			
	Plantation	1,74,866.62	14,654.41	125			
	Total	1,50,784.74	27,120.42	250	177.77 (1.74, 430.99)	< 0.001	0.418

Source: Author's own compilation.

6.1.2 Statistical Significance of Income distribution

This study evaluates changes in annual household income over time (2000, 2010, and 2023) among two groups: households engaged in other agriculture and those in plantation. A repeated measures ANOVA was employed to investigate the effects of time and household type on income, assessing within- and between-subjects factors.

a) Multivariate Tests

The multivariate tests (Pillai's Trace, Wilks' Lambda, Hotelling's Trace, and Roy's Largest Root) showed a significant main effect of time ($p < 0.001$, partial $\eta 2 = 0.981$), indicating a substantial increase in annual income over the years. Additionally, a significant interaction effect of Time × Household Type ($p < 0.001$, partial $\eta 2 = 0.536$) suggests that the rate of income growth differed between the two household types.

b) Mauchly's Test of Sphericity

Mauchly's test indicated a violation of sphericity ($p = 0.000$), necessitating the use of Greenhouse-Geisser and Huynh-Feldt corrections for within-subject effects.

c) Tests of Within-Subjects Effects

Significant differences were observed for the main effect of years ($F(1.738, 430.988) = 7158.63$, $p < 0.001$, partial $\eta2 = 0.967$) and the interaction effect of Years × Household Type ($F(1.738, 430.988) = 177.77$, $p < 0.001$, partial $\eta2 = 0.418$). These findings highlight both the overall growth in income and differing trajectories based on household type.

d) Between-Subjects Effects

The between-subjects test revealed a significant main effect of household type ($F(1, 248) = 1824.98$, $p < 0.001$, partial $\eta2 = 0.880$). Plantation households consistently reported higher incomes compared to other agriculture households.

Here, F values correspond to the interaction effect of years × household type from the tests of within-subject effects, p values indicate statistical significance (< 0.001), and partial η^2 represents the effect size, with values showing substantial differences in income growth between the groups. The summary of trends in income for plantation households and other farm households over the three periods shows that among plantation households the average annual income increased sharply, from ₹64,602 (SD = ₹5,126) in 2000 to ₹1,74,866 (SD = ₹14,654) in 2023. This was compounded annually at a rate of 4.42%. Among other agricultural households, the income grew from ₹45,345 (SD = ₹4,789) in 2000 to ₹1,26,702 (SD = ₹9,642) in 2023, at a CAGR of 4.57%. The widening income gap between the groups highlights the economic advantage of rubber cultivation as a cash crop compared to traditional agricultural practices.

6.2 Human Capital Enhancement through Rubber Cultivation (Literacy, Healthcare, Gender Participation, and Sustainable Livelihood)

A total of 250 respondents were surveyed, with 125 (50%) from plantation households and 125 (50%) from other agricultural households. The data was analyzed to compare the literacy rate, access to primary healthcare, and women's workforce participation between the two groups (Table 3). Statistical significance was determined using chi-square tests, with p-values < 0.05 considered significant. Descriptive statistics and proportions, along with 95% confidence intervals (CIs), are presented (Table 3).

a. Literacy Rate

The chi-square test of independence showed no statistically significant association between household type and literacy rate, $\chi^2(1, N = 250) = 2.52$, $p = 0.113$. Plantation households had a slightly higher literacy rate (78.4%) compared to other agricultural households (69.6%). However, this difference of 8.8% was not statistically significant.

Table 3. Social Inclusion Indicators by Household Type.

Indicator	Plantation Households (%) (Observed)	Other Agricultural Households (%) (Observed)	Difference (%)	χ^2	p-value
Literacy Rate	78.4	69.6	8.8	2.52	0.113
Access to Primary Healthcare	85.6	72.0	13.6	6.92	0.009
Women's Workforce Participation	40.8	18.4	22.4	15.05	<0.001

Source: Author's own compilation.

b. Access to Primary Healthcare

A significant association was found between household type and access to primary healthcare, $\chi^2(1, N = 250) = 6.92$, $p = 0.009$. Plantation households demonstrated greater access (85.6%) compared to other agricultural households (72.0%), with a difference of 13.6%. This indicates that plantation households are more likely to have access to primary healthcare services.

c. Women's Workforce Participation

The chi-square test revealed a highly significant association between household type and women's workforce participation, $\chi^2(1, N = 250) = 15.05$, $p < 0.001$. Women's workforce participation was much higher among plantation households (40.8%) compared to other agricultural households (18.4%), with a difference of 22.4%. This suggests a significant difference in favor of plantation households with regard to women's workforce participation.

6.3 Soil Improvement as a Foundation for Sustainable Livelihoods

Analysis of 80 composite soil samples collected from six districts proved that the soil properties under rubber plantations exhibited notable changes over 20 years (Table 4). The infiltration rate was 131.6% higher compared to shifting cultivation, indicating improved water permeability. Bulk density ranged from 1.3 to 1.77 Mg/m^3 (mean = 1.52 Mg/m^3), showing minimal compaction, and the values did not change appreciably with time. Porosity was elevated, particularly in surface layers, enhancing soil structure. Soil aggregate stability improved, reflected by a higher mean weight diameter (MWD). Soil pH remained stable at 4.41 in surface layers. Cation exchange capacity (CEC) was higher than fallow land and similar to forest plantations. Organic carbon increased from 0.81% to 0.96%, while available phosphorus decreased due to P-fixation, but potassium levels increased by 28.8% in surface soils and 20.8% in sub-surface soils after 20 years.

Table 4. Soil Metrics in Rubber Plantations.

Soil Property	Observations
Infiltration Rate	Increased by 131.6%, indicating improved soil permeability due to better aggregation and porosity.
Bulk Density (Mg/m^3)	Ranges from 1.3 to 1.77 Mg/m^3 (mean: 1.52 Mg/m^3), suggesting minimal compaction and stable structure.
Porosity	Higher in rubber plantations, enhancing air-water retention and root aeration.
Soil Aggregate Stability	Improved mean weight diameter (MWD), indicating better structural integrity and erosion resistance.
Soil pH	Stable at 4.41, indicating no significant change in soil acidity after long-term rubber cultivation.
Cation Exchange Capacity	Higher CEC in rubber soils than fallow land, enhancing nutrient retention and availability.
Organic Carbon	Increased from 0.81% to 0.96%, indicating higher organic matter input and improved fertility.
Available Phosphorus	Declined over 20 years, likely due to uptake, fixation, and immobilization by rubber plants.
Available Potassium	Increased by 28.8% in surface soils and 20.8% in sub-surface soils, reflecting enhanced nutrient cycling and mineral release.

Source: Author's own compilation.

7. Discussion

These results highlight the role of rubber plantations as a fulcrum for transforming the social and economic infrastructure within the tribal community in Tripura. By taking an economic and environmental perspective on these changes, this section reflects on the implications of the results and critically discusses the advantages and challenges of rubber cultivation, relating our findings to existing literature on rural development, tribal livelihoods, and agricultural sustainability.

i. Economic and Social Effects of Rubber Plantation

Our findings clearly indicate that income and employment patterns among the households of Tripura have been significantly affected by the rubber plantations. While plantation households saw a remarkable 171% rise in income, from ₹64,602 in the year 2000 to ₹1,74,866 in the year 2023, the same was not the case for non-plantation households, pointing toward uneven economic development among populations participating in rubber cultivation. This resonates with studies conducted concurrently in Kerala showing rubber farming as an extremely crucial source of income, alleviating poverty and stabilizing incomes. Rubber, being a cash crop, has comparatively stable returns in contrast to seasonal agricultural activities like *jhum* cultivation, which keeps on fluctuating with the seasons.

From the perspective of diversified employment, the shift from subsistence farming to rubber farms has dramatically altered the mode of labor in these tribal villages. The statistical analysis supports a trend that reflects a decline in reliance on subsistence farming and a concomitant increase in dependence on rubber farming. Significantly, female participation in the working population is increasing, with women in plantations making up 40.8%. This signals a transition in gender inclusion in employment. Traditionally, tribal women have been marginalized in the economic sphere in formal settings, and the fact that plantation culture is acting as a force pushing gender equality suggests more positive aspects of this shift. This also supports the conclusions drawn by Sarma et al. (2020b), where they add that rubber plantations resulted in improved women's socio-economic status in Kerala and Tamil Nadu.

Our study's findings on improving literacy rates and access to healthcare confirm the multidimensional impacts of rubber on social inclusion. Literacy rates increased from 45% to 78% in rubber households, while access to primary healthcare also improved from 50% to 85%, further indicating that increased household income from rubber cultivation has been more effectively invested in human capital. This observation resonates with other studies by Singh et al. (2019) and Mohapatra (2022), which reported that additional income earned from rubber cultivation promoted greater access to educational and healthcare services. Such improvement is especially remarkable in an area like Tripura, where tribal communities have historically been excluded from mainstream developmental efforts. Economic development through rubber farming encourages increased participation in education and health systems, thereby breaking cycles of poverty.

ii. Environmental Consequences of Rubber

Rubber plantations drastically alter the physical and chemical parameters of the soil. For example, the higher infiltration rate indicates greater permeability, while the bulk density is almost uniform; this means that soil compactness balance is maintained through rubber cultivation. The porosity indicated above, along with the aggregate stability, indicates favorable soil structures that support root growth as well as water holding. Although soil pH remains unchanged over two decades, the minor increase in organic carbon and a concomitant rise in potassium levels further attest to the positive impacts of these beneficial effects on soil fertility. However, reduced available phosphorus may reflect changes in nutrient cycling in rubber systems. Improved CEC would therefore indicate better nutrient retention by the soil system, reiterating the importance of rubber plantations in the improvement of soil health status and ecosystem function. The results of the soil test closely align with previous studies conducted by Krishnakumar et al. (1990) and Mandal et al. (2012).

60-Year Rubber Expansion and 50-Year ARIMA (Auto Regressive Integrated Moving Average) Forecast

The dataset (Table 5) reveals a steady and exponential growth in rubber plantation area, increasing from 103 ha in 1972–73 to 97,460 ha in 2022–23. This significant expansion highlights the transformative role of rubber cultivation in fostering socio-economic development, creating employment opportunities, and improving income levels over the years. This growth trajectory reflects its substantial

Table 5. Rubber Plantation Expansion in Tripura: Key Growth Phases and Milestones (1972–2023).

Year	Rubber Area (ha)	Growth Phase	Key Observations
1972–73	103	Initial Expansion Phase	Beginning of cultivation with minimal area.
1978–79	1306	Initial Expansion Phase	Area surpassed 1,000 ha, indicating adoption.
1986–87	10085	Rapid Growth Phase	Plantation exceeded 10,000 ha, accelerating growth.
1995–96	20761	Rapid Growth Phase	Significant expansion driven by adoption.
2003–04	30770	Rapid Growth Phase	Plantation area crossed 30,000 ha milestone.
2008–09	46588	Maturation Phase	Sharp rise, exceeding 45,000 ha.
2012–13	61231	Maturation Phase	Moderate growth towards stabilization.
2016–17	83380	Maturation Phase	Steady growth nearing saturation.
2022–23	97460	Maturation Phase	Plantation area neared 100,000 ha.

Source: Author's own compilation

contribution to the livelihoods of tribal communities by promoting sustainable land-use practices and facilitating inclusive economic growth.

The **predictive model** (Figure 2) for a 50-year forecast, developed using the ARIMA (Auto Regressive Integrated Moving Average) method, illustrates the projected growth in the rubber plantation area (Figure 1). The figure demonstrates a consistent increase in plantation expansion, which strongly correlates with regional development, economic growth, and enhanced social inclusion, particularly within the tribal communities of Tripura.

The observed data aligns closely with the model's fit up to the year 2023, validating its accuracy. Beyond 2023, the forecast predicts sustained growth in the

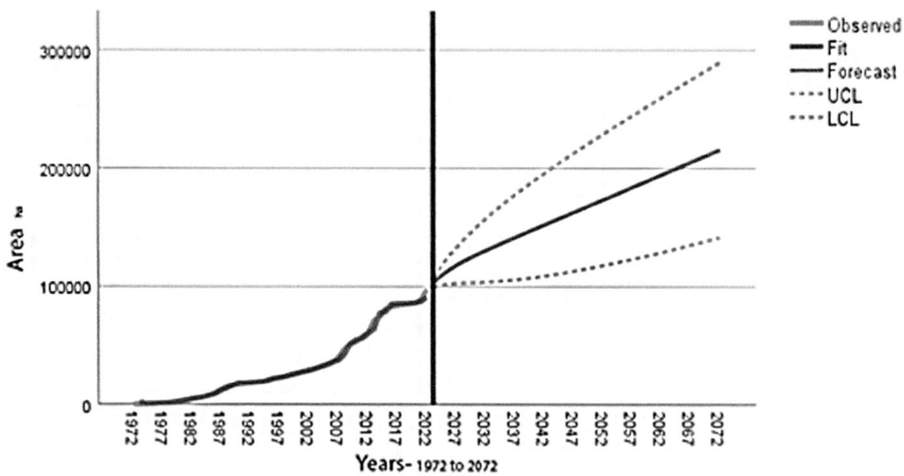

Figure 2. Predictive model for a 50-year forecast by using ARIMA. Source: Author's own compilation.

rubber plantation area. This projection is bounded by the upper (UCL) and lower (LCL) confidence limits, represented as dotted lines in the figure, reflecting the robustness and reliability of the model.

Such expansion is expected to generate increased employment opportunities and enhance income levels, thus fostering economic growth. This growth, in turn, has the potential to significantly improve the welfare of tribal communities by strengthening their livelihoods and promoting long-term social inclusion.

Linking Plantation Growth to Social Inclusion

The projected expansion of rubber plantations provides an opportunity to understand and forecast social inclusion among tribal communities in the coming decades.

Key areas of impact

i. **Economic Empowerment:** Increased plantation area directly correlates with higher household incomes, as evidenced by the income growth trends in plantation household. This fosters financial stability and reduces economic disparities. Hence, H1 is tested to be true.

ii. **Employment Opportunities:** The shift from subsistence farming to plantation-based livelihoods creates more stable and diversified employment options. This is particularly beneficial for marginalized groups, including women. Hence, H2 is tested to be true.

iii. **Access to Resources:** Increased economic activity supports more effective access to education, healthcare, and infrastructure, strengthening the overall quality of life. Hence, H3 is tested to be true.

iv. **Soil Improvement:** Porosity was elevated, particularly in surface layers, enhancing soil structure. Soil aggregate stability improved, reflected by a higher mean weight diameter (MWD). Soil pH remained stable at 4.41 in surface layers. Cation exchange capacity (CEC) was higher than fallow land and similar to forest plantations. Organic carbon increased from 0.81% to 0.96%, while available phosphorus decreased due to P-fixation. Hence, H4 is tested to be true.

While these benefits are substantial, the environmental trade-offs must be mitigated through policy interventions that prioritize sustainable practices.

8. Conclusion

Rubber plantation development in Tripura has been pivotal in addressing socio-economic vulnerability and environmental degradation associated with shifting cultivation. Over six decades, rubber farming has significantly boosted household income, literacy, healthcare access, and women's participation in the workforce, fostering inclusive economic growth, and thereby rubber plantation activities have been promoting social inclusion. While rubber agroforestry improves soil infiltration, reduces compaction, and increases organic carbon and potassium, a decline in phosphorus highlights the need for tailored nutrient management. ARIMA projections suggest continued expansion, emphasizing the crop's role in socio-economic development. However, environmental trade-offs and market volatility necessitate sustainable land-use strategies, capacity-building, and policy interventions. Rubber cultivation embodies a visionary model of agricultural transformation, harmonizing developmental progress with ecological sustainability and aligning with the aspirations of Viksit Bharat. It holds immense potential for tribal advancement in similar contexts, contingent upon sustained research endeavors and proactive community engagement.

The expansion of rubber plantations in Tripura has exemplified a synergistic model of sustainable development integrating economic progress, social inclusion, and environmental resilience. Rubber cultivation has transformed the socio-economic fabric of tribal communities by replacing ecologically detrimental shifting cultivation. Household incomes have increased by 171% over two decades, and gender participation in the workforce has improved considerably. It has also simultaneously led to enhanced soil quality with greater levels of organic carbon and increased infiltration rates for longer-term agricultural productivity. The expansion has some challenges in phosphorus depletion, coupled with the monocultural risk to biodiversity. Addressing these through integrated nutrient management and agroforestry diversification can enhance the sustainability of rubber cultivation, thus making it a keystone in regional development and a model for global sustainable land-use practices.

Acknowledgement

The authors extend their profound gratitude to Dr. M. D. Jessy, Director of RRII, and Dr. Debabrata Ray (OIC, RRS Agartala) for their encouragement and steadfast support. Furthermore, the authors acknowledge the invaluable assistance and coordination provided by the incharge of Regional Office of Rubber Board at Udaipur, Shantirbazar, Ambassa, and Agartala, whose liaison efforts greatly facilitated the successful execution of this study.

References

Adikari, S. B. and Sharma, A. (2018). Marketing pattern of rubber plantation in Tripura, India. International Journal of Current Microbiology and Applied Sciences 7(6): 847–853.

Bordoloi, R. (2008a). Shifting cultivation in Northeast India: Practices and economic impacts. Economic and Political Weekly 43(14): 38–45.

Bordoloi, S. (2008b). Sustainability of shifting cultivation in the hills of northeastern India: A socio-economic analysis. Indian Journal of Agricultural Economics 55(2): 131–145.

Bhowmik, I. (2006). Status report on rubber plantations in Tripura. pp. 41–52. *In*: Bahuguna, V. K. (ed.). Natural Rubber in Tripura: Baseline Data and Future Planning. Tripura Rubber Mission, Government of Tripura, Agartala, India.

Bhowmik, I. and Viswanathan, P. K. (2015). Emerging Labour Relations in the Small Rubber Plantations of Tripura. NRPPD Discussion Paper No. 47, Centre for Development Studies, Thiruvananthapuram, 33 p.

Choudhury, M., Dey, S. K., Sarma, A. C. and Chaudhari, D. (2006). Comparative evaluation of soil physio-chemical properties under rubber, teak, sal, and gamari plantation in South Tripura. Journal of Plantation Crops 34(3): 347–351.

Chouhan, P. and Bhowmik, I. (2017). Labour market conditions of natural rubber plantations in Tripura: an Inquiry. Social Change and Development 14: 55–69.

Darlong, V. and Ayyappan, S. (2015). The role of rubber in the economic development of tribal areas in Northeast India. Development Studies Journal 10(4): 103–117.

Datta, H., Debnath, H. and Shil, P. (2019). Production and productivity of natural rubber: a study on growth-trends of rubber plantation in Tripura. International Journal of Management 10(4): 115–131.

Deka, H. K., Philip, V., Vinod, K. K. and Krishnakumar, A. K. (1998). Spatial distribution of soil microflora in a five-year-old rubber plantation in Tripura. Indian Journal of Natural Rubber Research 11(1&2): 88–93.

Dey, S. K. (2005). A preliminary estimation of carbon stock sequestered through rubber (*Hevea brasiliensis*) plantation in N.E. region of India. The Indian Forester 131(11): 1429–1436.

Ghoshal, K. P. (2014). Economic feasibility study of natural rubber plantation in Tripura. Journal of Social Science 1(2): 63–77.

Gilot, C., Lavelle, P., Blanchart, E., Keli, J., Kouassi, P. and Guillaume, G. (1995). Biological activity of soil under rubber plantations in Côte d'Ivoire. Acta Zoologica Fennica 196: 186–189.

Gupta, A. K. (2000). Shifting cultivation and conservation of biological diversity in Tripura, Northeast India. Human Ecology 28: 605–629.

Joseph, J., George, T., Tharian, K. and Dey, S. K. (2010). Report on the socio-economic impact of natural rubber cultivation under the block planting scheme in Tripura (Working Paper ER/4). Rubber Research Institute of India.

Joseph, J. and George, T. K. (2011). Income inequality among beneficiaries under natural rubber block planting scheme in Tripura: a preliminary assessment. Natural Rubber Research 24(2): 203–210.

Krishnakumar, A. K. (1989). Soils under *Hevea* in India: A physical, chemical, and mineralogical study with reference to soil moisture and cation influence on the yield of *Hevea brasiliensis*. Ph.D. thesis, Indian Institute of Technology, Kharagpur.

Krishnakumar, A. K., Eappen, T., Nageswara Rao, Potty, S. N. and Sethuraj, M. R. (1990). Ecological impact of rubber (*Hevea brasiliensis*) plantations in Northeast India: Influence on soil physical properties with special reference to moisture retention. Indian Journal of Natural Rubber Research 3(1): 53–63.

Krishnakumar, A. K., Gupta, C., Sinha, R. R., Sethuraj, M. R., Potty, S. N., Eappen, T. et al. 1991. Ecological impact of rubber (*Hevea brasiliensis*) plantations in Northeast India: Soil properties and biomass recycling. Indian Journal of Natural Rubber Research 4(2): 134–143.

Kothandaraman, R., Mathew, J., Krishnakumar, A. K., Kochuthresiamma, J., Jayarathnam, K. and Sethuraj, M. R. (1989). Comparative efficiency of *Mucuna bracteata* and *Pueraria phaseoloides* on soil nutrient enrichment, microbial population, and growth of *Hevea*. Indian Journal of Natural Rubber Research 2(2): 147–150.

Majumder, A., Datta, S., Choudhary, B. K. and Majumdar, K. (2014). Do extensive rubber plantation influences local environment? A case study from Tripura, Northeast India. Current World Environment 9(3): 768–779.

Mandal, D., Pal, T. K., Dey, S. K. and Jacob, J. (2012). Changes in organic carbon and some soil properties under rubber (*Hevea brasiliensis*) plantation in subtropical Tripura. Natural Rubber Research 25(1): 13–20.

Mandal, D., Singh, R. P. and Chaudhuri, D. (2001). Influence of rubber cultivation on physio-chemical properties of soil: A case study. Indian Journal of Natural Rubber Research 14(1): 71–74.

Maithani, S. (1995). Commercialization of shifting cultivation and its implications on livelihoods in Northeast India. Economic and Political Weekly 30(10): 640–645.

Mathew, G. (2023). The role of rubber cultivation in transforming rural livelihoods in Tripura. Journal of Rural Development 42(4): 39–52.

Matouleibi, S. (2012). How wonderful is the wonder crop? Block rubber plantation and indigenous tribal women in Tripura. Research paper submitted for Master of Arts in Development Studies, International Institute of Social Studies, The Hague, The Netherland.

Mohapatra, G. (2022). Socioeconomic impacts of integrated rubber development projects on tribal livelihoods in Tripura. Transcience Journal 13(1): 28–40.

Nath, T. K., Inoue, M. and De Zoysa, M. (2010). Rubber planting for forest rehabilitation and enhancement of commercial livelihood: a comparative study in three South Asian countries. *In*: 18th Commonwealth Forestry Conference, Edinburgh.

Nye, P. H. and Greenland, D. J. (1964). Changes in soil properties after clearing tropical forests. Plant and Soil 21(1): 101–112.

Philip, V., Krishnakumar, A. K., Pothen, J., Potty, S. N. and Mathew, M. (1993). Changes in foliar nutrient status of rubber and soil available nutrients due to the application of fertilizer under Tripura conditions. Journal of Plantation Crops 21(Supplement): 86–91.

Prabhakar, A. and Bhattacharya, S. (2023). Income structure and economic impact of rubber cultivation in rural Tripura. Journal of Rural Economics and Development 12(2): 45–58.

Rubber Board of India. (2023a). Annual report on rubber production in India. Ministry of Commerce and Industry, Government of India.

Rubber Board of India. (2023b). Tripura: A rising hub for natural rubber production. Retrieved from https://www.rubberboard.org.in.

Sarkar, S. (2010). Revolution of Jumia's life through rubber plantation: a case study of Dhalai District, Tripura.

Sarkar, S., Keat, T. T. and Gebrie, B. D. (2023). Cost-effective analysis of rubber plantation: a strategy for socio-economic empowerment of scheduled tribes in Tripura. Journal of Indian Research (issn: 2321-4155), 11(1-4).

Sarma, K., Debbarma, A. and Saha, P. (2020a). Social impacts of rubber cultivation on tribal communities in Tripura. Journal of Social Inclusion 14(2): 115–129.

Sarma, R., Gupta, D. and Raj, S. (2020b). Socio-economic impacts of rubber cultivation in Tripura: A case study. Agricultural Economics Research Review 33(1): 71–80.

Sharma, G., George, T. and Dey, S. K. (2014). Natural rubber sector in Tripura: Role of institutional innovations. Agricultural Economics Research Review 27(Conference Number): 17–24.

Singh, P. and Feroze, S. M. (2019). Self-reliance of tribal through corporate social responsibility initiatives: A case study of rubber plantation in Tripura. Indian Journal of Extension Education 55(2): 1–5.

Sinha, A. K. (2012). Rubber plantations in Northeast India: hopes vs. concerns. The Tripura Foundation pages 3.

Srivastava, R. (1996). Agricultural patterns and productivity in Northeast India: Shifting cultivation vs. settled farming. Journal of Rural Development 15(1): 12–26.

Umar, A. M. and Wachiko, B. (2021). The survey causes of mathematics anxiety among secondary school students in Minna Metropolis. Mathematical Association of Nigeria (MAN) Journal 46(1): 188.

Vijayan, D., Girindran, R., Sam, A. S., Sathyan, A. R. and Kaechele, H. (2024). The large-scale expansion of rubber plantations in southern India: major impacts and the changing nature of drivers. Environmental Monitoring and Assessment 196(4): 356.

Wastie, R. L. (1965). The occurrence of an Endogone type of endotrophic mycorrhiza in *Hevea brasiliensis*. Transactions of the British Mycological Society 48(2): 167–178.

World Bank. (2022). Tripura Rural Economic Growth and Service Delivery Project (P178418). Retrieved from https://documents1.worldbank.org.

Zou, X., Zhu, X., Zhu, P., Singh, A. K., Zakari, S., Yang, B. et al. (2021). Soil quality assessment of different *Hevea brasiliensis* plantations in tropical China. Journal of Environmental Management 285: 112147.

Chapter 11

Understanding Sustainability in Impermanent Land

Hassan Momin[1] and *Gorky Chakraborty*[2,*]

1. Background

Development has been the priority of the United Nations, and their activities through its various agencies have been pivoted around fulfilling such an objective. Pursuing such an agenda for development in the 21st century, the 'United Nations Development Programme' (UNDP) formulated 17 Development Goals, which were termed 'Sustainable Development Goals' (SDGs), keeping in view the global contexts (Carugi and Bryant 2020). The SDG programme was "a universal call to action to end poverty, protect the planet, and ensure that all people enjoy peace and prosperity" (UNDP 2018). The SDGs were developed through a remarkable consultative process that brought together national governments and millions of citizens around the globe into a process of negotiation and subsequent endorsement, in terms of achieving these ambitious goals (Kamau et al. 2018). These SDGs emerged out of the erstwhile 'Millennium Development Goals' (MDGs), which were initiated as a global campaign to combat poverty in 2000.

The MDGs were the most popular and comprehensive set of development goals that countries around the world adopted to mitigate "poverty, malnutrition, maternity and child mortality, infectious diseases, education, gender inequality, environmental harm, and global development partnerships". It was a common framework agreed upon by various UN member countries, focusing on achieving these goals to ameliorate their populations from the pitfalls of these developmental gaps (Vandemoortele 2002). The MDGs, however, were perceived to be exclusively focused only on the

[1] Senior Research Fellow, Institute of Development Studies Kolkata (IDSK).

[2] Faculty Member, Institute of Development Studies Kolkata (IDSK).
Email: hassanmomin4@gmail.com

* Corresponding author: gorky8bob@gmail.com

DOI: 10.1201/9781003736158-14

developing world (Kumar et al. 2016), while the SDGs were planned in a way where the framework reflected the targets for achievement concerning both the developed and the developing nations. SDGs took into their ambit 193 UN member countries, where they were engaged in grassroots decision-making along with the participation of civil society (Fehling et al. 2013).

In 2010, when Paulo Caballero became the Director of 'Economic, Social, and Environmental Affairs' at Colombia's Ministry of Foreign Affairs, she recognized that the MDGs would expire in 2015, and the subsequent summit in Brazil may provide an excellent occasion to consider what could replace them (Ferranti et al. 2019). Thereafter, in 2016, she focused on three areas, namely: the environment, economics, and society, which ultimately shaped the SDGs, branching out into 17 goals, 169 targets, and 304 indicators (Keilitz 2015). The SDGs thereby emerged as a bold, worldwide agreement to end poverty in all its manifestations, aspiring to create a society that is equal, legitimate, and secure for people, planet, and prosperity (Labadi et al. 2021).

Small Island Developing States (SIDS) are a distinct group consisting of 37 UN Member States and 20 Non-UN Members or Associate Members of United Nations regional commissions that confront different economic, social, and environmental risks. It was within such a diversified framework of SDGs that the SIDS emerged as a 'special case' for sustainable development over and above the prior development agenda (Bishop et al. 2021). It must be remembered that the small islands around the globe are not uniform in terms of their geographical distribution and structural characteristics, e.g., size, remoteness, as well as vulnerability to climate hazards and disasters, or issues that hinder their socioeconomic development and ability to achieve the SDGs (Bishop et al. 2021). Nonetheless, SIDS are included throughout several SDGs. In particular, target 7 of SDG 14 (Life below water) stipulates:

> "By 2030, increase the economic benefits to SIDS and least developed countries from the sustainable use of marine resources, including through sustainable management of fisheries, aquaculture, and tourism."

To accomplish this, in September 2014, the 'Third International Conference on Small Island Developing States' (SIDS) was held in Apia, Samoa, with the overarching theme "The sustainable development of SIDS through genuine and durable partnership," during which approximately 300 partnerships were announced and are being tracked through the partnership platform.

Similarly, river islands (locally known as *chars*) have grandeur and natural beauty but are susceptible to detrimental effects from climate change, riverbank erosion, flooding, etc. Due to their ecological sensitivity and susceptibility to natural hazards, river islands fall within the 'risky zone,' which also prohibits construction and development. Furthermore, there is no sustainable development for the living communities, where the majority are below the poverty line, suffering from hunger and a lack of health and basic services. Nevertheless, river islands share similar features with SIDS in that there is no sustainable development. Therefore, the study examines the introduction of river islands in terms of legislation, measurement, and living conditions, as well as their exclusion from the development agenda.

2. Introducing Impermanent Land

There are several factors related to a river that influence the formation of the *chars*, e.g., the (meandering) course, braided channels, the slope, incline and gradient, the load (sediment and bed), etc.; during flood periods these augment the process (Osterkamp 1998, Rahman and Rahman 2012, Momin and Chakraborty 2021). These geomorphological formations are irregular both in shape, size, stability, and location (Wyrick and Klingeman 2010). Interestingly, as their formations occur under flood conditions, their natural height bears testimony to the highest flood level. The *chars* are aligned in such a way that their slope in the upstream is steeper vis-à-vis their downstream tail (Bhagabati 2001). When the flood recedes and the velocity of the water declines, sediments and silts get deposited. In the course of time, they get covered with grass and vegetation. The cycle may be repeated again during the next flood and its capacity to erode the *chars*, along with the interaction of various factors facilitating accretion (Chakraborty 2009, NPC 1986). The *chars* are unique in terms of their ecosystems, no matter whatever their lifespans (Bhattacharjee et al. 1991, NPC 1986). They may be broadly classified based on different parameters:

A) On the basis of hydrodynamic shape:
  i. Streamlined, classified into lemniscate, elliptical, and lenticular;
  ii. Angular, divided into hemispherical, triangular, and rhombic;
  iii. Irregular or not balanced in shape.

B) On the basis of their duration:
  i. Permanent or those which are in existence for more than 10 years;
  ii. Semi-permanent or those which are in existence for less than 10 years but more than 5 years;
  iii. Temporary or those, which are in existence for less than 5 years.

C) On the basis of physical features:
  i. Sandy-silty-clayee or soil which is of good quality for cropping;
  ii. Sandy-silty or soil which is of medium quality for cropping;
  iii. Areas with wild grass such as *Kahua or Kash* (Saccharum spontaneum); and
  iv. Completely sandy and water logged areas.

D) On the basis of their flood profile, namely:
  i. Chronically flood affected or those which are inundated throughout the monsoon season;
  ii. Occasionally flood affected or those which are inundated for a short period due to flash floods; and
  iii. Almost flood-free or those which are temporarily inundated during high floods only.

E) On the basis of silt deposition:
  i. Highly silted soils where silt deposit is above 30 cms;

ii. Medium silted soils where silt deposit is between 10 to 25 cms; and
iii. Low silted soils where silt deposit is below 10 cms.

The *terra firma* interpretation and demarcation of land and water fall short in interpreting *chars*, which remain in transcendence between these two entities. A few scholars from different disciplinary backgrounds have tried to understand the intermingling of land and water in newer ways both in conceptual and real terms: wet theory, riverine land, 'land soaked in water', waterland, dry-wet hybrids... thereby moving beyond the traditional understanding of land and water (Appadurai and Breckenridge 2009, Lahiri-Dutt 2014a, Mukherjee 2019, Cortesi 2022, Camargo 2022). These impermanent formations become a source of further complication in South Asia, as many of them are inhabited and thus various aspects of their dwellers, ranging from migration, identity, citizenship, etc., are looked at by others in settled areas with suspicious lenses (Chakraborty 2009, Sarker et al. 2003, Momin and Chakraborty 2024).

In the floodplains of the Brahmaputra River in Assam, inhabitants of the *chars* have a unique migration pattern, where those inhabiting highly unstable/erosion prone areas move to the central portions of the *char*. Similarly, others who dwell in unstable *chars* migrate to a relatively stable one, while many either migrate to *chars* which are nearer to the embankments/*ghats* of the river or to the nearby settled/*kayam* lands in the floodplains. *Char* dwellers migrate to mainland/settled/*kayam* areas under duress either as victims of erosion or in a search of livelihood options, which are otherwise limited in these unstable formations (Chakraborty 2009). This is not only unique to the Brahmaputra but is also observed in other river systems, e.g., the Ganga, Damodar, Padma, and Jamuna (Baqee 1998, Islam et al. 2010, Lahiri-Dutt and Samanta 2013, Lahiri-Dutt 2014b, Chakraborty 2017, Baruah 2022).

3. Law and Regulation of Impermanent Land

In terms of jurisprudence related to land in the *char* areas, the 'Bengal Alluvion and Diluvion Regulation, 1825' stands out as one of the earliest. Section 4(3) of this regulation states that when "a *char* or island is thrown up in a large navigable river (the bed of which is not the property of an individual), or in the sea, and the channel of the river or sea between such island and the shore may not be fordable, it shall according to established usage, be at the disposal of the government" (Ganguly 1999).

But if the "channel between such island and the shore is fordable during any season of the year, it shall be considered an accession to the land, tenure or tenures of the person or persons who may be most contiguous to it, subject to several provisions" (Ganguly 1999). Although this regulation states categorically what is a *char*, gaps remain in terms of interpreting its land as they remain impermanent. Accordingly, ownership, custodianship, and possession of land formed through re-formation *in situ* or through newer accretion continue to be complicated. Such scenarios give rise to misunderstandings and conflicts among the inhabitants of the *chars* or power-brokers who negotiate such conditions (Rahaman 2018, Momin 2020). It obviously results in litigation, and there also, due to the lack of clear legal interpretations, principles of equity and justice have to be relied upon (Chakraborty 2009).

Even if the erstwhile landholders pay revenue for the eroded land, the tenure of payment as well as the claim to possession once the land reappears remains opaque. It is true that in certain legislations, the time frame for staking claim on eroded land once it reappears is mentioned as twenty years, yet the authorities who can verify such claims remain hazy, e.g., 'The Bengal Alluvion and Diluvion Regulation' (1825); 'Assam Land and Revenue Regulation' (1886); 'The Goalpara Tenancy Act' (1929); 'The Tripura Land Revenue and Land Reforms Act' (1960); 'West Bengal Land Reforms Act' (WBLRA) (1956); and 'The Assam Temporarily Settled Areas Tenancy Act' (1971)—which hint at the possibilities of re-emergence of land in rivers, though the terms and conditions to lay claims are far from straightforward (Chakraborty 2009). Accretion, thereby a natural phenomenon in river systems in South Asia, remains a conflict-generating process for those who dwell on such impermanent lands.

The report of Law Research Institute, Guwahati (1982), is an indication in this direction.

> "…when a new *char* is thrown up in the Brahmaputra, it is taken to be the property of the state government, which either keeps it as grazing reserve or settles it with the cultivators as per the Land Settlement Policy Resolution in force."

It also points out that "in reality, people do not wait till the systematic settlement of the Government. They immediately occupy the newly formed *char*." Now, as it happens without the sanction of state authorities, "they are regarded as encroachers and they remain to be so until their land is settled under land settlement provisions or till the *char* gets submerged in the river."

Moreover, the differences in land revenue settlements and their respective deeds that are essentially meant for permanent/settled land, when sought to be applied to impermanent land in *chars*, complicate the matter further. One usually comes across different revenue settlement deeds in several states of India and Assam is not an exception in this regard. Government land without revenue settlement is identified as *khas* land and a large part of land in *chars* is beyond cadastral survey and thereby marked as *khas*. On the other hand, one would seldom come across *meadi* settlement in these areas except in such cases where due to the change in the course of the river the permanently settled land has been transformed into *chars*. There are only a few such cases in the Brahmaputra floodplains where land is under permanently revenue settlement (*meadi*). Large parts of land in the *char* areas are under annual settlement or *ek chonia*, whereby *khas* land after a period of settlement may be converted into this category whereby subletting or inheritance is not allowed and transferable rights are conditional, of course only within the year of settlement. In certain areas, where the occupant is in possession of government land and it has not eroded for a period of time, then by dint of paying revenue, it may be marked as allotted *touzi khazana* settlement, while those in non-allotted land remain under *touzi jarimana*. Under these revenue settlements, the state may under certain circumstances issue notices to vacate such land. In West Bengal, on the other hand, land in *char* areas is placed under three settlement types—*khas*, where the ownership is vested with the state; *patta* land, where *khas* land is distributed to landless families and they are provided with a title deed; and *rayati* land, which is privately owned and generally inherited (Chakraborty 2009).

3.1 Measuring Impermanence

We provide snippets of our experience during fieldwork about the process of determining occupancy/possession when land arose as *char* in River Ganga in the Kaliachak-II Block of Malda district in West Bengal. This experience in the field enabled us to understand how community plays a crucial role in their attempts to deal with differences related to land emergence due to accretion.

According to local resident Asraful Sk, who lives at KB Jhaubona village,

> "If any conflict arises regarding ownership rights in *char* lands, we first try to settle it within the claimants. Decisions are primarily taken by respected people, usually elders with similar experiences of land settlement within our community. In these settlement processes, ethnicity or religion are not the determining factors in terms of determination of occupancy of the lost land in the *chars*" (Field survey 2020).

He further adds, "Here, erosion–accretion is a continuous process, and identifying land in terms of prior occupancy is really complicated." According to another respondent, Lutfur Rahman, near Polashgachhi village in Kaliachak-II Block,

"Powerful people from nearby areas sometimes attempt to grab the newly emerged *char* land. But, if the original inhabitants are able to lay claim to their land, the community elders intervene to facilitate a meaningful resolution. However, if the elders find it difficult, 'local *Amins*' [land surveyors] are involved to decide on the fate of the land" (Field survey 2020).

On the other, when a section of the *char* dwellers move out of their settlements to nearby or far off places, they fail to stake claim to their lands that emerge due to accretion. In such circumstances, newer claimants occupy these lands.

Although Section 11 (1) of the WBLRA (1956) states a time period for emergence of land, the discretion of the revenue authorities to judge the owner based on erstwhile possession makes it complicated; the Act states:

> "…if *rayat* loses a land or a portion of the land by diluvion and the land re-emerges within a time period of 20 years then the proper land title, name and interest of land subsists with the rayat. In this case the *rayat* has the right to possess and thereafter will be responsible to pay revenue. The revenue officer will decide the revenue of the re-emerged land as regarded compatible in accordance with the law. It should be based on certain time period regarding claims over the diluviated land" (WBLRA 1956).

But such a long period marked for emergence of eroded land, the discretion of the revenue staff in determining the possession of the erstwhile occupants along with the remoteness of the *chars*, gives rise to a scenario where the *char* dwellers themselves try to negotiate such situations through community initiatives. They usually get in touch with 'local land surveyors' when land resurfaces within the period as stipulated in the Act. During our fieldwork, we were witness to such a process at the community level, where the erstwhile owners and other community members involved 'local land surveyors' in order to determine the occupants of the land that emerged through accretion in the Kaliachak-II *char* in the River Ganga, which incidentally also lies along the boundary line between the states of West Bengal and Jharkhand in eastern India. The 'local land surveyors' informed us that

> "…in 1963, we all met and decided to make a boundary with pillars around the Kaliachak-II *Diara* (river island) belt. We erected one concrete pillar at the place which was the last point from the Bengal side in terms of the Bengal–Bihar border (presently Jharkhand) of the River Ganga (near Udhwa Nala). Another concrete pillar was erected at Islampur village (which thereafter submerged)" (Field survey 2020).

The 'local land surveyors' further added that "the exercise continued for almost a year. However, in the process, the gain was that the entire *char* was marked, measured, and identified." He also recollected from his memory that "one of their villagers, Durun Babu, undertook the operation of measuring the land from the Udhwa Nala end, while from the Islampur side (other end), Radhika Babu took charge. From two points at both the ends, the measurement of the *char* was initiated. This was completed in 1964." The 'local land surveyors' explained that once this process was over, they "collated the daag [a unique number allotted to each plot of surveyed land] and *khatiyan* [individual land record certificate] numbers, and the entire land was thereby fully mapped and marked". Henceforth, when a dispute arises, the community members, especially the elders, convene meetings to determine the owner of the land emerging out of accretion, if of course there are any disputed claims. All the comparisons now are based on the 1963–1964 survey. In other words, the dwellers and the community are no longer dependent on the discretionary decisions and whims of the revenue officials; they themselves are in a position to settle their land disputes on land emerging through accretion.

It is observed that in the floodplains of the Brahmaputra in Assam, the *char* areas can be divided into two categories in terms of revenue settlement, namely K-category *char* (cadastral survey has been undertaken) and Non-K category *char* (no cadastral survey has been done). When diluviated land appears as a new *char*, the Land Settlement and Revenue Officials refer to it as *khas* land, which remains under the control of the state till further settlement. Only after the 'local land surveyors' from the land revenue and settlement department conduct a Cadastral Survey and generate a map showing the actual position, this *khas* land would have no individuated legal ownership rights (Chakraborty 2009).

3.2 Measuring Impermanent Land

We came across a land-measuring exercise in a *char* area in a village named Jot Kasturi situated in Kaliachak-II Block of Malda District, where 'local land surveyors' carried out surveys to identify the plots and their respective measurements of the erstwhile occupants in a newly formed *char* after it emerged through accretion. For such a unique process, they used tools, e.g., a table made of wood, spirit level, alidade, cadastral map, pencil, scale, measuring tape or chain, and a flag as a marker. The process, in a step-by-step manner, is exhibited in Figure 1.

Step I: The process of measurement starts from a 'pre-existing point (A)' on the settled land nearby the river, whose *daag* and *khatiyan* numbers are already known—this point is referred to as the "cadastral point" on their map.

Step II: This is followed by marking a 'fixed point/station/flag (B)' near the bank of the river.

Step III: Now, the point marked as 'A' should be visible through the alidade from point 'B'. The distance between 'points A and B' is measured using a tape and marked as a line on the cadastral map as per the scale of the map. Following that, from 'point B', the 'point C' and 'point D' are drawn on the cadastral map at the same gaps.

Step IV: After that, the 'baseline (CD)' is plotted on the cadastral map by converting the measured ground distance vis-à-vis the scales used in the map. This is followed by a step, where a 'ground point (E)' is marked on the newly formed *char*.

Step V: Using the alidade, 'point C' and 'point D' are used to determine 'point E', which is the point where lines 'CE' and 'DE' intersect each other on the map.

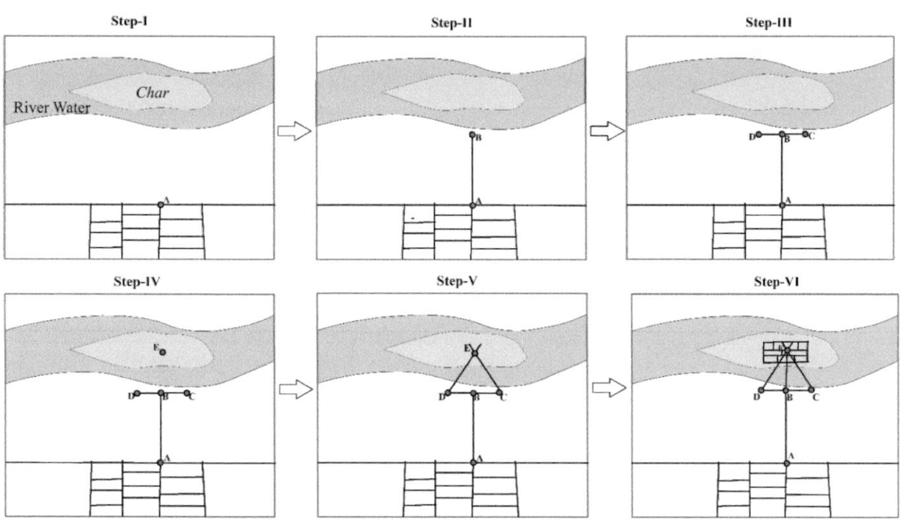

Figure 1. Step by step measurement process of land in a newly emerged *char.*

Step VI: The next challenge is to determine the exact distance between points 'B' and 'E'. The next step involves measuring the distance between these two points. It is challenging because they cannot be reached as they are only marked on the cadastral map as per the scale used in the map. But these two points are measured on the ground tallying/collating with the scale used in the map. It is only thereafter that the 'local land surveyors' mark the areas in the *char*. The land occupation prior to erosion is marked in the newly emerged *char*; they are plotted, demarcated, and the erstwhile occupants of land are identified.

In order to skip Step I and II, the 'local land surveyors' put a 'half-burnt wooden pole' deep into the ground near the bank of the river as a reference point for future measurements (Figure 2). They also use it to identify newly formed diluviated land in the *char* or neighbouring *chars*. The estimation of the areas by 'local land surveyors' is based on the cadastral survey maps (Figure 3) provided by the land revenue department, thereby allaying the fear that these measurements are arbitrary.

Figure 2. A half-burned wooden pole as a marker.

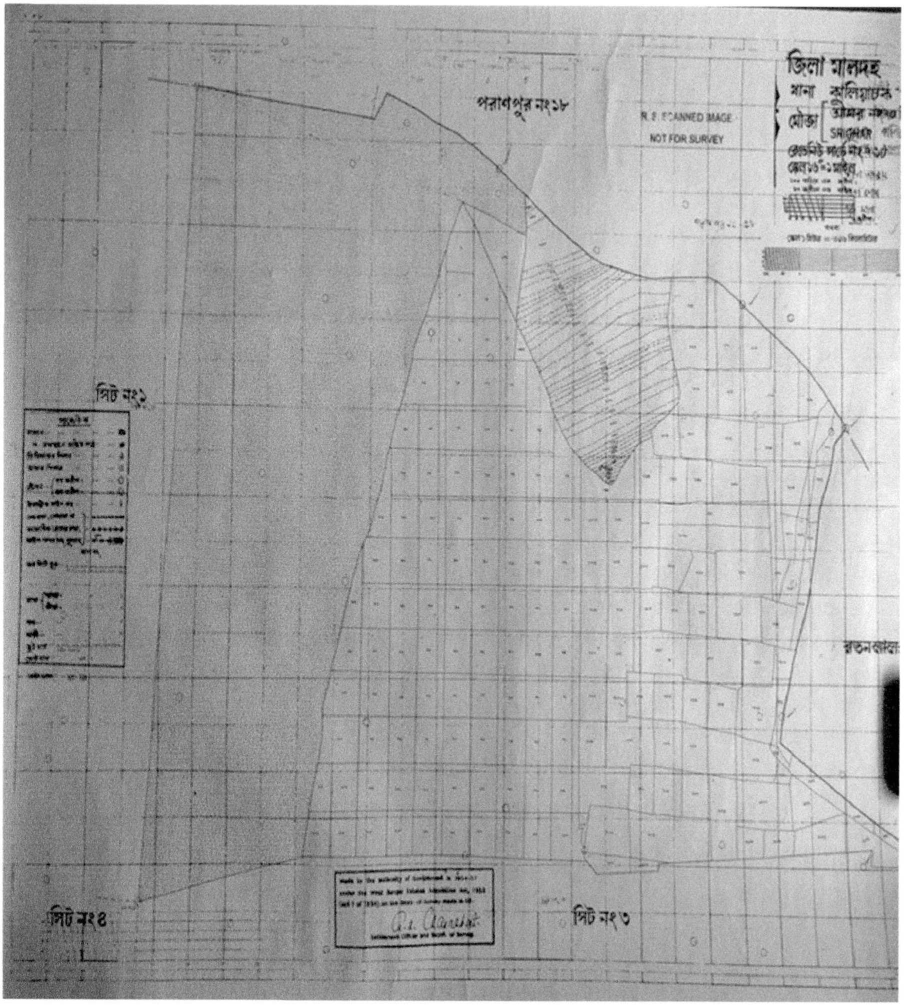

Figure 3. Cadastral maps collected from revenue officials for measurement purposes.

It is through this local community effort that the newly formed *char* lands are settled with their previous occupants prior to erosion, an exercise which otherwise would not have been possible either due to the unwillingness and/or unavailability of revenue officials to measure the newly formed land emerging through accretion. The involvement of the community members and the efforts of the 'local land surveyors' in Malda facilitated a process of settlement, which, if left to others, would have generated discord and conflicts. Once this process was over, the local inhabitants approached the revenue office to report that their settlement had been accurately recorded. To formalise their claims, the new landowners were ready and willing to pay revenue. Surprisingly, the officials responded, "All this land is now vested land and no one is allowed to take possession of or pay revenue for such land". They further expressed displeasure at the ignorance of the *char* dwellers, saying, "all land that emerged as River Island has become *khas* land after the government order issued in 2000" (Field survey 2020).

This new Act (Section 12 of WBLRA 2000) specifies,

> "any land gained by the gradual accession to a plot of land, from within the recess of a river or of the sea, shall vest in the State Government and the rayat who owns the plot of land shall not be entitled to retain such land as an accretion thereto."

The collective effort of the local community and the counter-reaction of the revenue officials indicate that there exists an epistemic difference between both the groups in terms of their understanding of land and water and thereby *chars*, while the former transcends the binary, the latter's vision remains imprisoned in the logic of *terra firma*. This divergent perspective complicates the scenario further when the local community try to negotiate with the state and its agencies. Unless a hybrid understanding of the *chars* emerges based on the transcendence of land and water, legal and illegal land settlements will continue to haunt the minds of those who are unaware of the lived realities in the *char* areas.

Another community exercise is at Dahi *char* on the Subarnarekha River near Jhargram Subdivision in Paschim Medinipur, where the *char* becomes a resource that anyone can use or that belongs to everyone. This leads to both conflict and cooperation among the locals. The local political leadership assisted the villagers in framing the unwritten rules through active participation and discussion. These rules are used to allocate the plots of charland to the villagers through meetings and discussions among local people. The unwritten rules are: (1) only people who live adjacent to their villages are permitted to cultivate; (2) even among Dahi residents, landholders whose registered agricultural land had been flooded would not be allowed to cultivate the *char* land since they may later claim ownership of such land through legal procedures; (3) Dahi residents who were allowed to enter the *char* could not employ hired labourers to clear the land for crop cultivation; however, they were permitted to hire labour during the process of cultivation. These unwritten rules led to the establishment of usufruct rights through cooperation, which would otherwise have resulted in strife among the villagers (Guha 2023).

4. Socio-economic Condition of People in Impermanent Land

In South Asia, the *char* lands are known as areas with severe social and economic backwardness. Economic activity in *chars* is heavily dependent on cultivation and agriculture-based activities but frequent floods and erosion add uncertainties and hazards to the life and livelihood of the *char* dwellers. However, it is also simultaneously observed in the Brahmaputra and the Ganga floodplains that those who dwell in *chars* share their experiences of relatively different cropping patterns, diversified crop profiles and yields in these areas if not deterred by high or untimely floods (Chakraborty 2009).

Floods significantly influence the cropping patterns in *char* regions. While low-intensity floods are often beneficial, enriching the soil with fertile silt deposits, high-magnitude floods, particularly those causing erosion, can devastate standing crops. However, in these *chars* of the Brahmaputra and the Ganga floodplains, there is a greater diversity of crop production due to the characteristics of the soil and the experience of the producers. The selection of cropping periods, particularly sowing and crop harvesting, is maintained in such ways that flood damage is less. In the *char* areas, wherever possible, farmers resort to mixed cropping. This acts as an insurance against crop failure caused by floods. The cultivators mix up different crops in the same plot of land, such as *Ahu* along with *Aman* paddy; Millet and *Aman*; *Arhar* with *Mesta*, etc. Similarly, during the Rabi season, Wheat is mixed with Lentil or Gram; Lentil with Coriander or Gram; Chilli with Brinjal; these are some of the mixed cropping patterns commonly found in the *char* areas.

During the pre-monsoon and monsoon seasons, paddy (direct sown *Ahu* and *Amon*, and transplanted *Sali*), Jute, *Mesta*, Foxtail millet, Buckwheat, etc. are the common *kharif* crops. Among the *Kharif* crops, the cultivation of *Ahu* paddy starts during March and is usually harvested during June. *Amon* paddy also continues simultaneously. Jute occupies a larger period between April to early August during which washing and drying of fibres are also completed. *Sali* paddy cultivation starts during June and harvested in December. During the post-monsoon season, a variety of crops, namely wheat, *chena* (Prosmillet), *Boro* paddy, Barley, Sweet potato, Potato, Mustard, Seasum, Linseed, Niger, Sunflower, Peas, Gram, Black Gram, Soyabean, Coriander, *kalijira* (a variety of spice), Garlic, Onion, and Chilli are grown. Wheat is generally sown during November and harvested during March. In the meantime, green pea is sown as an intercrop. *Iri* paddy is a recent addition to the *rabi* crops in the *char* areas. This high yielding variety is cultivated during November and harvested during late February and early March. In addition to these crops, large varieties of vegetables are grown commercially during the *rabi* season.

However, there are threats too, which are difficult to pre-empt in the *char* areas. According to a cultivator in the *char*s of the Brahmaputra:

> "The amount of cultivable land has reduced due to the continuous process of riverbank erosion. People are also less interested in farming because there is a higher chance of crop waste, land erosion, sand casting and flooding. So, we avoid the cultivation of major crops during the monsoonal period due to high chances of submergence in flood water."

In the study area, the interplay of push and pull factors influences their lives in these *char* areas. The pull factors for the river island areas are scope for agricultural production, low cost of living, limited financial liability, and land occupancy. Other push factors are the loss of agricultural lands, the loss of income-generating activities, the inability to enjoy livelihood choices, and the uncertainty of daily life. Labour migration from the *char* areas, irrespective of the Brahmaputra or the Ganga, mainly occurs due to the lack of livelihood opportunities. The dwellers migrate to surrounding settled areas as well as locations that are far off, e.g., Delhi, Mumbai, Pune, and Bangalore. Moreover, those who inhabit the *char* areas now, the majority of them are internally displaced from one *char* to another. According to Minarul Sheikh,

> "We've moved three times before setting up my house here. During inundation, rivers alter their courses, causing widespread erosion of *char* land. When this occurs, we become destitute and move from one *char* to the next closest *char*."

Therefore, most of the residents in the area under consideration have moved multiple times owing to land and river bank erosion. They are internally displaced people struggling with their daily lives.

5. Sustainability in Impermanent Land

The SDGs certainly mention development, but in impermanent land, e.g., for the *chars* areas, these goals are absolutely silent. It must be remembered that the timeline to attain these SDGs is 2030, i.e., only seven years away. Will not the SDGs fall short in achieving their targets if they do not take into their sway a large mass of population who inhabit the impermanent land, e.g., the *chars* areas, particularly in South Asia? These attempts will fall short if the plight of *char* inhabitants continues to be precarious as they are at present. As a result, rural India will not attain these goals until we improve the living conditions of the *char* people. As per the socio-economic survey 2002–03 related to the *char* dwellers of the Brahmaputra in Assam, the overwhelming majority (82 percent) continue to survive below the official poverty line estimates. Although a large-scale survey of the *chars* of the Ganga has not yet been undertaken like in Assam, experience from the field in these areas suggests that the situation in Bengal and Bihar is equally precarious. Basic amenities related to health, education, and livelihood remain extremely limited in these areas, if not non-existent in large parts. Moreover, these areas also signify a huge gap in terms of governance, reflected in the absence of proper legislation concerning land. This actually adds to their precarity since much of this impermanent land floats in liminal zones between the riparian boundaries of nation states. Questions on their identity and citizenship also become major issues for these migrating *char* dwellers that further add to their unstable existence.

The SDGs state that "no one will be left behind" and "endeavor to reach the farthest behind first". If this remains the spirit of the SDGs, then should the *char* areas be left behind? Every SDG is a campaign towards achieving development for humanity. Issues related to land are represented in 'life on land' (Goal 15), which emphasises "protect, restore, and promote sustainable use of terrestrial ecosystems, sustainably manage forests, combat desertification, halt and reverse land degradation, and halt biodiversity loss". Additionally, in accordance with international agreements, this includes ensuring "the protection, restoration, and sustainable use of terrestrial and inland freshwater ecosystems and their services, including forests, wetlands, mountain, and desert ecosystems". But surprisingly, there is no mention of impermanent land, whereas, in South Asia, a large percentage of densely populated humanity inhabit these areas.

6. Conclusion

It is high time now that the underlying relationships between natural components and the human environment related to the *chars* are recognised from the standpoint of sustainable development. In these sensitive riverine environments, only a systematic approach that integrates all the natural and human components in a contextual framework can guarantee a development process that is environmentally, socially, and economically sustainable. In the absence of such a representation in the SDGs, the *char* dwellers continue to exist as a forgotten part of humanity. Eventually, we must establish strategies right away to ensure that the Sustainable Development Goals are met.

References

Appadurai, A. and Breckenridge, C. A. (2009). Wet theory. *In*: SOAK: Mumbai in an Estuary, edited by Anuradha Mathur and Dilip Da Cunha. New Delhi: Rupa & Co.

Baqee, A. (1998). Peopling in the Land of Allah Jaane. Power, Peopling and Environment: The Case of Char-Lands of Bangladesh. Dhaka: The University Press Ltd.

Baruah, M. (2022). Slow disaster: Political Ecology of Hazards and Everyday Life in the Brahmaputra Valley, Assam. Taylor and Francis.

Bhagabati, A. K. (2001). Biodiversity and Associated Problems in the Islands of the Brahmaputra, Assam. Geographical Review of India 63(4): 330–343.

Bhattacharjee, I, Borgohain, R. and Jha, R. (1991). Diara Lands – The Grannary of Assam, Jorhat: Assam. Jorhat: Agriculture University

Bishop, M., Bouhia, R., Carter, G., Corbett, J., Scobie, M. and Wilkinson, E. (2021). Towards Sustained Development in Small Island Developing States. ODI Working Paper.

Camargo. (2022). Land born of water: Property, statis, and motion in the floodplains of northern Columbia. Geoforum 131: 215–222.

Carugi, C. and Bryant, H. (2020). A joint evaluation with lessons for the sustainable development goals era: the joint GEF-UNDP evaluation of the small grants programme. American Journal of Evaluation 41(2): 182–200. https://doi.org/10.1177/1098214019865936.

Chakraborty, G. (2009). Assam's Hinterland: Society and Economy in the Char Areas. New Delhi: Akansha Publishing House.

Chakraborty, G. (2017). The Char Dwellers of Assam: Flowing River, Floating People. In Water Conflicts in Northeast India. India: Routledge.

Cortesi, L. (2022). Hydrotopias and waterland. Geoforum 131: 215–222.

Fehling, M., Nelson, B. D. and Venkatapuram, S. (2013). Limitations of the Millennium Development Goals: A literature review. Global Public Health 8(10): 1109–1122. https://doi.org/10.1080/17441692.2013.845676.

Ferranti, P., Anderson, J. R. and Berry, E. M. (2019). Encyclopedia of food security and sustainability. In Encyclopedia of Food Security and Sustainability. Elsevier B.V. https://www.cabdirect.org/globalhealth/abstract/20193122380.

Ganguly, K. (1999). The West Bengal Laws (Annotated),Vol. I, Calcutta: Hindustan Law Book Company, p. 273.

Guha, A. (2023). Local Histories of Bordering, or How the Community Outsmarted the State. In Negotiating Borders and Borderlands: The Indian Perspectives. Orient Blackswan.

Islam, S. N., Singh, S., Shaheed, H. and Wei, S. (2010). Settlement Relocations in the Char-Lands of Padma River Basin in Ganges Delta, Bangladesh. Frontiers of Earth Science in China 4(4): 393–402.

Kamau, M., Chasek, P. and O'Connor, D. (2018). Transforming Multilateral Diplomacy: The Inside Story of the Sustainable Development Goals. Routledge.

Keilitz, I. (2015). The Trouble with Justice in the United Nations Sustainable Development Goals 2016–2030. William & Mary Policy Review 7: 1.

Kumar, S., Kumar, N. and Vivekadhish, S. (2016). Millennium Development Goals (MDGs) to Sustainable Development Goals (SDGs): Addressing Unfinished Agenda and Strengthening Sustainable Development and Partnership. Indian Journal of Community Medicine : Official Publication of Indian Association of Preventive & Social Medicine 41(1): 1–4. https://doi.org/10.4103/0970-0218.170955.

Labadi, S., Giliberto, F., Rosetti, I., Shetabi, L. and Yildirim, E. (2021). Heritage and the sustainable development goals: Policy guidance for heritage and development actors (pp. 1–69). ICOMOS. https://openarchive.icomos.org/id/eprint/2453/.

Lahiri-Dutt, K. (2014a). Beyond the water-land binary in geography: water/lands of bengal re-visioning Hybridity Kuntala Lahiri-Dut. ACME: An International Journal for Critical Geographies 13(3): 505–29.

Lahiri-Dutt, K. (2014b). Islands That Float within Rivers. ANU Research Publications 8(2): 1–17.

Lahiri-Dutt, K. and Samanta, G. (2013). Dancing with the River: People and Life on the Chars of South Asia. Yale University Press.

Law Research Institute. (1982). A Study of the Land Systems of North Eastern Region, Gauhati. Law Research Institute 1: 124–126.

Momin, H. (2020). River Dynamics and Uncertainties: A Case Study of Kaliachak-II Block in Malda District, West Bengal. MPhil diss., Institute of Development Studies Kolkata, University of Calcutta, Kolkata.

Momin, H. and Chakraborty, G. (2021). Morphological changes in the hazardous zones of the Ganga and the Brahmaputra Rivers in East and Northeast India. Applied Geomatics 13(4): 925–944. https://doi.org/10.1007/s12518-021- 00395-y.

Momin, H. and Chakraborty, G. (2024). Missing Fluvio-social Dynamics of a Braided River. pp. 245–274. In Indigenity, Development and Sustainability edited by Chakraborty et al.. Singapore: Springer. https://doi.org/10.1007/978-981-97-1436-0_12.

Mukerjee, E. (2019). The Impermament Settlement: Bengal's Riparian Landscapes, 1793–1846. South Asian Studies 36(1): 20–31.

NPC. (1986). Survey Report on Char Area Development in Assam (Barpeta, Dhubri, Goalpara Districts). Guwahati: National Productivity Council.

Osterkamp, W. R. (1998). Processes of Fluvial Island Formation, with Examples from Plum Creek, Colorado and Snake River, Idaho. Wetlands 18(4): 530–545. https://doi.org/10.1007/BF03161670.

Rahaman, M. (2018). Ownership of Land in Select Chars of the River Ganga. MPhil. diss., Institute of Development Studies Kolkata, University of Calcutta, Kolkata.

Rahman, M. A. and Rahman, M. (2012). Char Formation Process and Livelihood Characteristics of Char Dwellers of Alluvial River in Bangladesh. ICSE6, Paris.

Sarker, M. H., Huque, I., Alam, M. and Koudstaal, R. (2003). Rivers, Chars and Char Dwellers of Bangladesh. International Journal of River Basin Management 1(1): 61–80.

The Bengal Alluvion and Diluvion Regulation. (1825). Law of Alluvion and Diluvion of Land in West Bengal, Calcutta.

UNDP. (2018). What are the Sustainable Development Goals?. New York: UNDP. https://www.undp.org/sustainable-development-goals.

Vandemoortele, J. (2002). Are the MDGs feasible?, New York, NY: UN Development Programme Bureau for Development Policy.

WBLRA. (1956). West Bengal Land Reforms Act, Calcutta: Government of West Bengal.

WBLRA. (2000). West Bengal Land Reforms Act, Calcutta: Government of West Bengal.

Wyrick, J. R. and Klingeman, P. C. (2010). Proposed fluvial island classification scheme and its use for river restoration. River Research and Applications 27(7): 814–825.

Chapter 12

Conscious Leadership and Employee Behaviour for Organizational Sustainability

Charul Sharma,[1,*] *Sweta Dixit*[2] and *Bhupender Kumar Som*[3]

1. Introduction

The contemporary organizational landscape stands at a critical juncture where technological transformation intersects with mounting pressures for sustainable business practices. Organizations worldwide grapple with integrating advanced digital tools while maintaining their commitment to employee welfare and long-term viability. This convergence presents leaders with unprecedented challenges that demand more than traditional management competencies—it requires a fundamental shift in how leadership consciousness embraces technological change without compromising human-centric values.

The past decade has witnessed a remarkable acceleration in workplace digitalization, fundamentally altering how employees interact, collaborate, and perform their roles. Yet this technological evolution has not occurred uniformly across leadership practices. Many organizations have adopted sophisticated digital infrastructures while their leadership approaches remain anchored in pre-digital paradigms. This disconnect creates tension between operational capabilities and human capital development, often manifesting in employee disengagement, increased burnout, and voluntary citizenship behaviours being replaced by mandated compliance.

[1] Research Scholar, Sharda School of Business Studies, Sharda University.
[2] Professor, Sharda School of Business Studies, Sharda University.
[3] Professor, GNIOT Institute of Management Studies (GIMS), India.
* Corresponding author: sharmacharulparashara.1998@gmail.com

DOI: 10.1201/9781003736158-15

Traditional leadership frameworks—transformational and servant leadership among them—have long emphasized employee empowerment, ethical conduct, and organizational commitment. However, these models emerged in contexts vastly different from today's digitally mediated workplaces. The question facing contemporary organizations is not whether these leadership approaches remain relevant, but how they must evolve to address the complexities introduced by technological integration. Leaders who fail to develop consciousness around digital tools' implications risk undermining the very engagement and citizenship behaviours these styles were designed to cultivate.

Organizational sustainability extends beyond environmental considerations to encompass the capacity for enduring performance through balanced attention to economic, social, and human dimensions. Within this framework, employee behaviour serves as both an indicator and a driver of sustainability outcomes. Voluntary organizational citizenship behaviours—those discretionary actions employees undertake beyond formal job requirements—represent crucial contributions to organizational resilience. Conversely, compulsory citizenship expectations, where organizations mandate extra-role behaviours, threaten sustainability by depleting employee psychological resources and eroding intrinsic motivation.

The concept of leadership consciousness regarding technology represents a relatively unexplored territory in management scholarship. While researchers have examined digital leadership competencies and technological readiness, less attention has been paid to the deeper cognitive and ethical dimensions of how leaders perceive, interpret, and integrate technology into their leadership practice. This consciousness encompasses not merely technical proficiency but a holistic awareness of technology's impact on human relationships, organizational culture, and sustainable work systems.

This investigation addresses several critical gaps in existing literature. First, despite abundant research on individual leadership styles and separate studies on technological adoption, limited empirical work examines how leadership consciousness regarding digital integration moderates the effectiveness of established leadership approaches. Second, while organizational citizenship behaviour has been extensively studied, the distinction between voluntary and compulsory forms remains underexplored, particularly in technologically enhanced environments. Third, the pathways through which leadership practices influence organizational sustainability through employee behavioural mechanisms require further theoretical and empirical development.

Drawing upon social exchange theory and self-determination frameworks, this chapter proposes that leadership consciousness regarding technology functions as a critical moderating mechanism. Leaders who demonstrate heightened awareness of technology's role in workplace dynamics can amplify the positive effects of transformational and servant leadership while protecting against the emergence of compulsory citizenship expectations. This consciousness enables leaders to deploy digital tools in ways that support employee autonomy rather than intensifying surveillance or control, thereby fostering genuine voluntary contributions that sustain organizational vitality.

The research adopts a rigorous sequential mixed-methods approach, combining qualitative insights from senior executives with quantitative analysis of data from 200 leader-subordinate pairs across multiple industry sectors. This methodological strategy enables rich exploration of how leaders conceptualize technological consciousness while providing robust statistical evidence of its effects on employee behaviour and performance outcomes. Advanced analytical techniques reveal not only direct relationships but also the complex interaction patterns through which leadership consciousness shapes organizational dynamics.

The chapter structure proceeds systematically through interconnected sections. A comprehensive literature review situates leadership consciousness within broader theoretical traditions while examining relevant research on leadership styles, organizational citizenship behaviour, and sustainability frameworks. The theoretical model section articulates specific propositions regarding relationships among constructs. The methodology section details the research design, sampling procedures, measurement approaches, and analytical strategies employed. The findings present both qualitative themes and quantitative results, including structural models and interaction effects. The discussion interprets these findings within existing theoretical frameworks while highlighting theoretical contributions and practical implications. The conclusion synthesizes key insights, acknowledges limitations, and charts directions for future inquiry.

This work ultimately seeks to advance understanding of how leadership must evolve to meet contemporary organizational challenges. By introducing technological consciousness as a vital leadership dimension, the chapter provides conceptual tools for rethinking leadership effectiveness in digital workplaces. The empirical evidence demonstrates that when leaders develop a sophisticated awareness of technology's role in human systems, they can harness digital capabilities to enhance rather than diminish the human elements that drive sustainable organizational success. In an era where technology often appears to threaten human connection and wellbeing, this research offers evidence that conscious leadership can chart a different path—one where digital advancement and human flourishing advance together rather than in opposition.

2. Literature Review

2.1 Conscious Leadership: Theoretical Foundation

The notion of conscious leadership originates from ethical, transformational, and humanistic paradigms emphasizing moral awareness, authenticity, and value-driven management (Carmeli and Dutton 2015). Conscious leaders demonstrate mindfulness, empathy, and integrity, aligning organizational goals with social and environmental responsibilities. Respectful engagement and moral reflection foster trust, psychological safety, and cooperation, forming the foundation of sustainable organizational cultures (Friedman et al. 2017).

Recent research broadens the construct towards collective consciousness, wherein leaders perceive their organizations as embedded in socio-ecological systems (Rooke and Torbert 2020). This orientation supports systems thinking, long-term stewardship, and ethical interdependence between firms and stakeholders. Conscious leadership thus operates as both a moral compass and a strategic mechanism, promoting transparent governance and inclusive decision-making (Brown and Treviño 2022).

2.2 *Proactive Sustainability Strategy: Ethical and Strategic Perspectives*

A proactive sustainability strategy is a forward-looking approach to environmental, social, and governance (ESG) integration, emphasizing voluntary, innovation-driven initiatives (Ahmed 2022). It surpasses reactive compliance models by embedding sustainability principles into the core strategic framework of the organization, yielding ethical credibility and competitive advantage (Epstein and Buhovac 2014, Lozano 2015).

Recent scholarship connects proactive sustainability with technological consciousness—a multidimensional capability combining ethical awareness, digital literacy, and strategic foresight (George et al. 2022, Stahl et al. 2023). This linkage underscores that sustainability in the digital era requires leaders capable of aligning technological advancement with environmental and social priorities. The infusion of digital ethics and responsible innovation into corporate sustainability practices ensures that technological change supports inclusive and ecologically balanced development (Auer et al. 2022, Hilb 2023).

Furthermore, research on digital responsibility and ethical technology governance highlights that organizations guided by morally conscious and digitally competent leaders cultivate innovation ecosystems characterized by transparency, accountability, and inclusivity (Voegtlin et al. 2024, Al-Khatib and Sasson 2024). Such leaders embed sustainability into digital transformation, ensuring that corporate growth aligns with ethical norms and global sustainability objectives.

Drawing on self-determination and social exchange theories, technological and moral consciousness enhances employees' intrinsic motivation, autonomy, and willingness to engage in sustainability-oriented behaviour. Consequently, proactive sustainability evolves from a compliance activity into a cultural and strategic imperative central to organizational identity.

2.3 *Conscious Leadership and Sustainability: Synergistic Interactions*

Empirical evidence demonstrates a strong correlation between conscious leadership and proactive sustainability behaviour. Conscious leaders foster ethical climates and value congruence, strengthening employees' pro-environmental engagement (Asante 2024). The interplay between moral awareness and relational transparency enables the creation of psychologically safe environments that nurture voluntary sustainability initiatives (Sikand and Saxena 2025, Mandal and Pal 2025).

The relational dynamics identified by Friedman et al. (2017) reveal that respectful and mindful leadership enhances cooperation and trust—conditions that sustain innovation and environmental responsibility. Through empathy and ethical clarity, leaders stimulate collective accountability and a shared sustainability vision across the organization.

2.4 Leadership, Sustainability, and Organizational Reputation

An organization's reputation increasingly depends on its integration of ethical leadership and sustainability (Ahmed 2022). Conscious leadership amplifies reputational value by aligning authenticity, moral integrity, and stakeholder inclusiveness (Lozano 2015). Ethical consistency and transparent sustainability reporting strengthen legitimacy and stakeholder confidence, reinforcing reputational capital as a strategic asset.

Technological and moral consciousness further enhance reputational resilience in an age of digital transparency. Leaders who champion responsible data practices and socially conscious innovation protect organizational credibility while differentiating their institutions in competitive markets (Stahl et al. 2023, Hilb 2023). Reputation thus emerges as both an outcome and an enabler of conscious leadership and sustainability integration.

2.5 Synthesis and Emerging Directions

The reviewed literature converges on the understanding that conscious leadership is a pivotal enabler of proactive sustainability and strategic reputation. However, integrative frameworks uniting these constructs remain limited. Future inquiry should examine the mediating role of technological consciousness and ethical governance in linking leadership behaviour with sustainability and reputational outcomes (Auer et al. 2022, Voegtlin et al. 2024).

Cross-sectoral studies could further illuminate how contextual factors—such as national culture, regulatory maturity, and digital readiness—moderate these relationships. Understanding these dynamics will advance a comprehensive theory of sustainable leadership that harmonizes ethical consciousness, innovation, and long-term stakeholder value creation.

3. Research Methodology

3.1 Research Design

This investigation adopted a sequential mixed-methods approach to examine the relationships between conscious leadership, technological awareness, and employee behavioural outcomes within sustainability frameworks. The research design integrated qualitative exploratory interviews with quantitative hypothesis testing through multi-source survey data. This methodological combination allowed for comprehensive exploration of complex leadership phenomena while establishing empirical evidence for theoretical propositions.

The study unfolded in two distinct phases. Phase one comprised semi-structured interviews with senior organizational leaders to identify key dimensions of technological consciousness and its manifestation in leadership practices. Phase two involved large-scale quantitative data collection from leader-subordinate dyads across multiple organizations to test hypothesized relationships and interaction effects. This sequential design ensured that measurement instruments reflected actual organizational experiences while maintaining scientific rigour in hypothesis testing.

3.2 Sample and Data Collection

3.2.1 Qualitative Phase

The qualitative component involved in-depth interviews with 25 senior executives holding leadership positions for a minimum of five years in technology-intensive industries. Participants represented diverse sectors including information technology, manufacturing, healthcare, and financial services. Selection criteria ensured variation in organizational size, digital maturity levels, and sustainability commitment. Interviews ranged from 45 to 75 minutes, conducted both in person and through video conferencing platforms based on participant preferences and geographical constraints.

Interview protocols explored leaders' perspectives on technological integration challenges, ethical considerations in digital transformation, and perceived impacts on employee behaviours and organizational sustainability. Probing questions examined specific instances where technological decisions influenced team dynamics, voluntary citizenship behaviours, and employee wellbeing outcomes. All interviews were audio-recorded with explicit consent and transcribed verbatim for analysis. Participants received assurance of confidentiality, with identifying information removed from transcripts.

3.2.2 Quantitative Phase

The quantitative investigation collected data from 200 leader-subordinate dyads across 35 organizations operating in Northern India. Organizations were selected through purposive sampling to ensure representation of various industries undergoing digital transformation initiatives. Within each organization, participating leaders identified three to five direct reports willing to participate, creating nested data structures suitable for multilevel analysis.

Data collection occurred through structured questionnaires administered in three time waves separated by three-week intervals to minimize common method variance concerns. Time 1 surveys captured leader self-assessments of leadership styles and technological consciousness alongside demographic variables. Time 2 measurements focused on subordinate perceptions of leadership behaviours and organizational climate factors. Time 3 assessments gathered subordinate reports of citizenship behaviours, performance outcomes, and wellbeing indicators.

Distribution of 280 initial questionnaire sets yielded 200 complete dyadic responses, representing a 71.4% response rate. Non-response analysis comparing early and late respondents revealed no significant differences on key variables, suggesting minimal non-response bias. The final sample comprised 58% male and 42% female subordinates with an average organizational tenure of 4.7 years. Leaders averaged 8.3 years of leadership experience, with 62% holding graduate or postgraduate qualifications.

3.3 Measurement Instruments

3.3.1 Leadership Styles

Transformational leadership was assessed using the 20-item Multifactor Leadership Questionnaire developed by Bass and Avolio. Subordinates rated their immediate supervisors on dimensions including idealized influence, inspirational motivation, intellectual stimulation, and individualized consideration using seven-point scales. Sample items included "My leader talks optimistically about the future" and "My leader spends time teaching and coaching." The scale demonstrated strong internal consistency with Cronbach's alpha of 0.92.

Servant leadership measurement employed the 28-item scale from Liden and colleagues, capturing dimensions such as emotional healing, creating value for the community, conceptual skills, empowering followers, helping subordinates grow and succeed, putting subordinates first, and behaving ethically. Subordinates rated agreement with statements like "My leader puts my best interests ahead of their own" on seven-point scales. Reliability analysis yielded an alpha coefficient of 0.89.

3.3.2 Technological Consciousness

Leader technological consciousness represented a newly developed construct measured through 15 items adapted from existing technology acceptance and ethical leadership scales. Three dimensions captured awareness of technological capabilities, ethical orientation towards digital integration, and strategic application in leadership practices. Leaders self-reported agreement with statements including "I actively consider ethical implications of technology adoption on my team" and "I integrate technological tools to enhance rather than replace human judgment." Exploratory and confirmatory factor analyses validated the three-factor structure with overall reliability of 0.87.

3.3.3 Employee Behaviours

Organizational citizenship behaviour assessment utilized the 24-item scale from Podsakoff and colleagues, measuring five dimensions: altruism, conscientiousness, sportsmanship, courtesy, and civic virtue. Subordinates reported frequency of discretionary behaviours such as "I help others who have heavy workloads" and "I attend meetings that are not mandatory but are considered important" using five-point frequency scales. The measure showed acceptable reliability with an alpha of 0.85.

Compulsory citizenship behaviour was measured through 10 items developed by Vigoda-Gadot and colleagues, capturing perceptions of obligated extra-role behaviours. Sample items included "I feel pressured to volunteer for activities outside my job description" and "There is an implicit expectation to engage in citizenship behaviours." Subordinates rated agreement on seven-point scales. Internal consistency reached 0.83.

Employee performance measurement combined objective and subjective indicators. Supervisors rated subordinates on a five-item scale assessing task proficiency, adaptability, and overall effectiveness. Performance ratings correlated with available organizational records of productivity metrics and goal achievement percentages where accessible. Supervisor ratings showed inter-rater reliability of 0.78 based on a dual-rating subsample (see Table 4).

3.4 Control Variables

Demographic variables including age, gender, educational qualification, and organizational tenure served as statistical controls. Industry sector classification and organizational size categories provided additional contextual controls for between-organization variance.

3.5 Data Analysis Procedures

3.5.1 Qualitative Analysis

Interview transcripts underwent thematic analysis following the six-phase process outlined by Braun and Clarke. Initial familiarization involved repeated reading of complete transcripts. Open coding identified preliminary concepts related to technological consciousness manifestations and leadership behaviours. Focused coding organized concepts into coherent themes representing dimensions of conscious leadership in digital contexts.

Two independent coders analyzed 30% of transcripts to establish inter-rater reliability, achieving Cohen's kappa of 0.82, indicating strong agreement. Discrepancies were resolved through discussion and refinement of coding schemes. Analysis software NVivo facilitated the organization and retrieval of coded segments. Thematic saturation was evident after analyzing 20 interviews, with five additional interviews confirming no emergence of substantially new themes.

Key themes emerging from qualitative analysis informed quantitative instrument development and validated proposed theoretical relationships. Direct quotes illustrating central themes were extracted while maintaining participant confidentiality through pseudonyms and organizational detail removal.

3.5.2 Quantitative Analysis

Preliminary analyses examined descriptive statistics, correlation matrices, and reliability coefficients for all measured variables. Missing data patterns were analyzed with Little's MCAR test, revealing random missingness, which was addressed through the expectation-maximization algorithm. Outlier detection through Mahalanobis distance calculations identified four extreme cases that were subsequently removed from the final analyses.

Confirmatory factor analysis tested measurement model adequacy using AMOS 24.0 structural equation modelling software. Model fit evaluation considered multiple indices including comparative fit index, Tucker-Lewis index, root mean square error of approximation, and standardized root mean square residual. Convergent and discriminant validity were assessed through average variance extracted calculations and Fornell-Larcker criterion application.

Hypothesis testing employed hierarchical multiple regression analysis examining main effects of leadership styles on employee outcomes, followed by moderation analyses testing interaction terms. Leadership style variables and the technological consciousness moderator were mean-centred prior to computing interaction terms to minimize multicollinearity concerns. Significant interactions were probed through simple slopes analysis at conditional values of the moderator (one standard deviation above and below the mean).

Mediation pathways were tested using PROCESS macro Model 4 developed by Hayes, applying bootstrapping procedures with 5,000 resamples to generate bias-corrected confidence intervals for indirect effects. Complete mediation was indicated when direct effects became non-significant with mediator inclusion, while significant indirect effects confirmed the presence of mediation.

Complex three-way interactions involving leadership style, technological consciousness, and contextual factors were examined through polynomial regression with response surface analysis. This advanced technique enabled visualization of outcome patterns across combinations of predictor values, revealing nuanced relationship dynamics beyond traditional interaction analyses.

Multilevel modelling using HLM 7.0 software accounted for the nested data structure with employees clustered within leaders and organizations. Random coefficient models tested whether relationships between leader characteristics and employee outcomes varied across organizational contexts. Intraclass correlation coefficients justified the multilevel approach by demonstrating substantial between-cluster variance.

Common method variance assessment employed Harman's single-factor test and confirmatory factor analysis comparing measurement models with and without a common latent factor. Results indicated no single factor accounting for the majority of variance, suggesting common method bias did not substantially threaten validity.

3.6 Ethical Considerations

Research protocols received approval from the university institutional ethics committee prior to the commencement of data collection. All participants provided informed consent after receiving detailed study information including purposes, procedures, potential risks, and confidentiality protections. Participation remained entirely voluntary, with explicit rights to withdraw without consequences communicated clearly.

Organizational access was negotiated through formal agreements ensuring data confidentiality and anonymity in reporting. Individual responses were coded with identification numbers separating them from personal information. Data storage followed secure protocols with encrypted files accessible only to research team members.

Findings dissemination to participating organizations occurred through aggregate reports without identifying information about specific individuals or making direct organizational comparisons. Participants expressing interest received summary findings after study completion, contributing to reciprocal knowledge exchange.

4. Results and Discussion

4.1 Descriptive Statistics and Correlations

Table 1 presents means, standard deviations, and bivariate correlations among study variables. Transformational leadership ($M = 5.32$, $SD = 1.18$) and servant leadership ($M = 5.41$, $SD = 1.12$) demonstrated moderate positive correlations ($r = 0.64$, $p < 0.01$), suggesting conceptual overlap yet distinct constructs. Technological consciousness averaged 5.15 ($SD = 1.05$), indicating leaders generally perceived themselves as moderately aware of technological implications.

Organizational citizenship behaviour showed positive associations with both transformational leadership ($r = 0.51$, $p < 0.01$) and servant leadership ($r = 0.48$, $p < 0.01$). Compulsory citizenship behaviour exhibited weak negative correlations with leadership styles ($r = –0.23$ and $–0.19$ respectively, $p < 0.05$), supporting theoretical expectations. Employee performance correlated positively with all leadership variables (r ranging from 0.42 to 0.55, $p < 0.01$).

Notably, technological consciousness correlated significantly with voluntary citizenship behaviours ($r = 0.38$, $p < 0.01$) and negatively with compulsory citizenship perceptions ($r = –0.31$, $p < 0.01$). These preliminary associations provided initial support for hypothesized relationships while warranting more sophisticated multivariate analyses to establish unique predictive effects.

Table 1. Means, Standard Deviations, and Intercorrelations Among Study Variables.

Variable	**M**	**SD**	**1**	**2**	**3**	**4**	**5**	**6**
1. Transformational Leadership	5.32	1.18	–					
2. Servant Leadership	5.41	1.12	.64**	–				
3. Technological Consciousness	5.15	1.05	.52**	.49**	–			
4. Voluntary OCB	5.28	1.09	.51**	.48**	.38**	–		
5. Compulsory Citizenship Behaviour	2.87	1.24	–.23*	–.19*	–.31**	–.28**	–	
6. Employee Performance	5.45	1.02	.55**	.52**	.42**	.58**	–.34**	–

Note. N = 385. M = Mean; SD = Standard Deviation. *p < .05. **p < .01 (two-tailed).

4.2 Measurement Model Assessment

Confirmatory factor analysis evaluated discriminant validity among key constructs. The hypothesized six-factor model (transformational leadership, servant leadership, technological consciousness, voluntary OCB, compulsory citizenship, employee performance) demonstrated acceptable fit indices: $\chi^2(512) = 847.32$, $p < 0.001$; $CFI = 0.93$; $TLI = 0.92$; $RMSEA = 0.057$ (90% CI: 0.051–0.063); $SRMR = 0.065$. This model fit significantly better than alternative models combining theoretically related constructs, supporting discriminant validity (see Table 2).

Average variance extracted values exceeded 0.50 for all latent constructs, indicating adequate convergent validity. Square roots of AVE values surpassed inter-construct correlations, satisfying the Fornell-Larcker criterion for discriminant validity (see Table 3).

Table 2. Confirmatory Factor Analysis Model Fit Indices.

Model	χ^2	df	CFI	TLI	RMSEA [90% CI]	SRMR	$\Delta\chi^2$	Δdf
Six-factor model (hypothesized)	847.32***	512	.93	.92	.057 [.051–.063]	.065	-	-
Five-factor model (TL+SL combined)	1,124.56***	517	.88	.86	.076 [.070–.082]	.084	277.24***	5
Four-factor model (TL+SL+TC combined)	1,456.89***	521	.82	.79	.092 [.086–.098]	.098	609.57***	9
Three-factor model (all leadership combined)	1,782.34***	524	.76	.73	.108 [.102–.114]	.112	935.02***	12
One-factor model	2,345.67***	527	.65	.61	.128 [.122–.134]	.135	1,498.35***	15

Note. N = 385. TL = Transformational Leadership; SL = Servant Leadership; TC = Technological Consciousness; OCB = Organizational Citizenship Behaviour. $\Delta\chi^2$ compared to hypothesized six-factor model. ***$p < .001$.

Table 3. Convergent and Discriminant Validity Assessment.

Construct	AVE	CR	1	2	3	4	5	6
1. Transformational Leadership	.58	.92	**.76**					
2. Servant Leadership	.61	.93	.64	**.78**				
3. Technological Consciousness	.54	.89	.52	.49	**.73**			
4. Voluntary OCB	.56	.90	.51	.48	.38	**.75**		
5. Compulsory Citizenship	.52	.88	–.23	–.19	–.31	–.28	**.72**	
6. Employee Performance	.59	.91	.55	.52	.42	.58	–.34	**.77**

Note. N = 385. AVE = Average Variance Extracted; CR = Composite Reliability. Diagonal elements (in bold) represent the square root of AVE. Off-diagonal elements represent inter-construct correlations. For discriminant validity, diagonal elements should exceed off-diagonal elements in the corresponding rows and columns (Fornell-Larcker criterion).

Table 4. Factor Loadings and Reliability Coefficients.

Construct	Number of Items	Factor Loading Range	Cronbach's α	Composite Reliability
Transformational Leadership	20	.68–.84	.94	.92
Servant Leadership	23	.65–.82	.95	.93
Technological Consciousness	12	.63–.79	.91	.89
Voluntary OCB	16	.66–.81	.92	.90
Compulsory Citizenship Behaviour	8	.64–.78	.89	.88
Employee Performance	15	.67–.83	.93	.91

Note. N = 385. All factor loadings are significant at $p < .001$. All constructs exceed recommended thresholds: Cronbach›s α > .70, CR > .70, factor loadings > .60.

4.3 Hypothesis Testing: Main Effects

Hierarchical regression analyses tested direct relationships between leadership styles and employee outcomes. After controlling for demographic variables and organizational characteristics, transformational leadership significantly predicted voluntary organizational citizenship behaviour ($\beta = 0.38$, $p < 0.001$, $\Delta R^2 = 0.19$). Servant leadership demonstrated similar positive effects ($\beta = 0.35$, $p < 0.001$, $\Delta R^2 = 0.17$), supporting theoretical propositions regarding leadership influence on discretionary helpful behaviours.

Both leadership styles negatively predicted compulsory citizenship perceptions, though effects were modest. Transformational leadership yielded $\beta = -0.21$ ($p < 0.01$, $\Delta R^2 = 0.04$) while servant leadership produced $\beta = -0.18$ ($p < 0.05$, $\Delta R^2 = 0.03$). These findings suggest certain leadership approaches may reduce felt obligations for forced extra-role behaviours, albeit with smaller effect magnitudes compared to voluntary citizenship promotion.

Employee performance outcomes showed robust associations with leadership variables. Transformational leadership predicted performance with $\beta = 0.46$ ($p < 0.001$, $\Delta R^2 = 0.23$), while servant leadership yielded $\beta = 0.42$ ($p < 0.001$, $\Delta R^2 = 0.20$). When both leadership styles were entered simultaneously, both retained significance (transformational $\beta = 0.29$, $p < 0.01$; servant $\beta = 0.24$, $p < 0.01$), indicating unique contributions beyond shared variance.

4.4 Moderation Effects of Technological Consciousness

Interaction terms between leadership styles and technological consciousness were added in subsequent regression steps to test moderation hypotheses. For voluntary organizational citizenship behaviour, both transformational leadership × technological consciousness ($\beta = 0.18$, $p < 0.01$, $\Delta R^2 = 0.03$) and servant leadership × technological consciousness ($\beta = 0.16$, $p < 0.01$, $\Delta R^2 = 0.02$) interactions achieved significance.

Simple slopes analysis revealed that relationships between leadership styles and voluntary citizenship strengthened substantially at high technological consciousness levels (one SD above the mean). For transformational leadership, the simple slope at high consciousness was $\beta = 0.52$ ($p < 0.001$) compared to $\beta = 0.24$ ($p < 0.05$) at low consciousness. Similar patterns emerged for servant leadership with slopes of $\beta = 0.47$ ($p < 0.001$) versus $\beta = 0.23$ ($p < 0.05$).

Regarding compulsory citizenship behaviour reduction, technological consciousness significantly moderated both leadership relationships. The transformational leadership × technological consciousness interaction yielded $\beta = -0.15$ ($p < 0.05$, $\Delta R^2 = 0.02$), while servant leadership × technological consciousness produced $\beta = -0.14$ ($p < 0.05$, $\Delta R^2 = 0.02$). Leaders combining strong servant or transformational approaches with high technological consciousness most effectively mitigated subordinate perceptions of obligatory extra-role demands.

Performance outcomes similarly showed moderation patterns. High technological consciousness amplified leadership effectiveness, with interaction effects of $\beta = 0.17$ ($p < 0.01$) for transformational and $\beta = 0.15$ ($p < 0.05$) for servant leadership. Region of significance testing indicated leadership–performance relationships achieved statistical significance only above the 25th percentile of technological consciousness distribution, highlighting its importance as an enabling condition.

4.5 Mediation Analyses

Bootstrap mediation procedures examined whether voluntary organizational citizenship behaviour mediated relationships between leadership styles and employee performance. For transformational leadership, the indirect effect through voluntary OCB was significant (indirect effect = 0.14, SE = 0.04, 95% CI: 0.07 to 0.23), with the direct effect remaining significant (direct effect = 0.32, $p < 0.001$), indicating partial mediation. Voluntary citizenship behaviours accounted for approximately 30% of the total transformational leadership effect on performance.

Servant leadership showed similar mediation patterns. The indirect path through voluntary OCB yielded a significant effect (indirect effect = 0.13, SE = 0.03, 95% CI: 0.06 to 0.21), with a retained direct effect (direct effect = 0.29, $p < 0.001$). These findings suggest leadership styles enhance performance partly through encouraging discretionary helpful behaviours that facilitate collective effectiveness, while also operating through additional mechanisms.

Compulsory citizenship behaviour demonstrated suppression effects rather than traditional mediation. When included as a mediator between leadership and performance, inconsistent mediation emerged with negative indirect effects (indirect effect = –0.08, SE = 0.03, 95% CI: –0.15 to –0.02) alongside positive direct effects. This pattern indicates that while effective leadership reduces felt compulsion, such a reduction does not explain performance enhancement. Rather, leadership effectiveness manifests despite minimising obligatory demands.

4.6 Multi-Level Modeling Results

Hierarchical linear modeling examined whether relationships varied across organizational contexts. Null models calculating intraclass correlations revealed that 18% of the variance in voluntary citizenship, 12% in compulsory citizenship, and

21% in performance resided between organizational clusters, justifying a multilevel approach.

Random coefficient models tested whether leadership–outcome slopes varied significantly across organizations. Results indicated significant between-organization variance in transformational leadership effects on performance ($\tau = 0.04$, $\chi^2(34) = 58.73$, $p < 0.01$), suggesting organizational factors moderate these relationships. In contrast, servant leadership effects showed relatively consistent slopes across contexts ($\tau = 0.01$, $\chi^2(34) = 42.15$, $p = 0.16$).

Cross-level interactions examined whether organizational digitalization maturity moderated within-organization relationships. Organizations with higher digital infrastructure sophistication (top tertile) showed stronger leadership–performance relationships ($\gamma = 0.21$, $p < 0.01$) compared to lower maturity contexts. This finding suggests technological consciousness operates effectively when organizational systems support digital integration.

4.7 Qualitative Findings Integration

Thematic analysis of executive interviews illuminated mechanisms underlying quantitative relationships. Leaders articulated three primary pathways through which technological consciousness enhanced leadership effectiveness. First, strategic tool selection enabled better matching of digital solutions to specific team needs rather than indiscriminate technology adoption. As one manufacturing director noted, "Understanding technology deeply means knowing when not to use it as much as when to deploy it."

Second, ethical framing of technological implementation reduced employee resistance and cynicism. Leaders who transparently communicated privacy protections, workload implications, and human oversight provisions fostered greater acceptance. A healthcare administrator explained, "When people see you've thought about the human impact, they engage more willingly with new systems."

Third, modeling adaptive learning behaviours created psychologically safe environments for technological experimentation. Leaders demonstrating vulnerability in their own learning processes normalized skill development efforts. An IT services vice president observed, "Showing my team I'm figuring things out too makes it okay for them to not know everything immediately."

Regarding citizenship behaviours, interview participants distinguished between inspiration-driven volunteerism versus compliance-based participation. Leaders emphasized that authentic discretionary effort emerged from meaningful work connections rather than technological efficiency alone. A financial services manager stated, "Technology should enable people to contribute more meaningfully, not just do more tasks." This perspective aligns with quantitative evidence that consciousness includes ethical orientation beyond mere capability awareness.

Several leaders described unintended consequences of poorly implemented digital systems, including increased monitoring anxiety and productivity pressure. These accounts corroborate quantitative findings regarding compulsory citizenship, where technological consciousness buffered against such negative outcomes. As expressed by a healthcare executive, "If you're not careful, technology becomes another way to extract more from people rather than support them doing valuable work."

4.8 Discussion of Findings

Results provide substantial support for theoretical propositions linking conscious leadership to employee behavioural outcomes through technological awareness mechanisms. The consistent positive effects of both transformational and servant leadership on voluntary citizenship behaviours and performance align with extensive existing research while extending findings into digital workplace contexts. The novel contribution lies in demonstrating that technological consciousness significantly amplifies these established relationships.

The moderation patterns reveal technological consciousness as more than simple digital literacy. Leaders scoring high on this construct exhibited ethical orientation and strategic judgement alongside technical awareness. This multidimensional understanding enabled them to implement technology in ways that enhanced rather than undermined human-centred leadership approaches. The amplification effects suggest technological and interpersonal leadership competencies operate synergistically rather than substitutionally.

Findings regarding compulsory citizenship behaviour address emerging concerns about digital surveillance and productivity monitoring creating coercive work environments. Results indicate that conscious leadership approaches, particularly when combined with technological wisdom, protect against such dynamics. Leaders who thoughtfully integrate digital tools while maintaining ethical boundaries reduce subordinate perceptions of forced extra-role demands. This protective function becomes increasingly important as organizations adopt pervasive monitoring technologies.

The partial mediation of leadership–performance relationships through voluntary citizenship validates social exchange perspectives. Leaders who inspire discretionary helpful behaviours cultivate collective capabilities exceeding individual contributions. However, substantial direct effects remaining after mediation control indicate additional pathways warrant investigation. Possible mechanisms include enhanced individual skill development, clarified role expectations, or improved resource allocation, all potentially facilitated by technologically conscious leadership.

Multilevel findings highlight organizational context importance in enabling conscious leadership effectiveness. Digital infrastructure maturity appears necessary for leaders to fully leverage technological consciousness. Organizations investing in robust, user-friendly systems provide foundations for ethical and strategic digital integration. Conversely, organizations with inadequate technological resources may constrain even highly conscious leaders. This suggests organizational and individual levels must align for optimal sustainable outcomes.

The integration of qualitative insights enriches understanding of quantitative patterns by revealing specific behavioural mechanisms. Leaders' strategic tool selection, transparent communication about technological implications, and modeling of adaptive learning represent concrete practices through which consciousness manifests. These behaviours operationalize abstract consciousness constructs in observable leadership actions that subordinates experience directly. Unexpectedly modest effect sizes for leadership impacts on compulsory citizenship reduction merit consideration. While statistically significant, the limited magnitude suggests felt obligation may stem partly from sources beyond immediate leader influence, such as organizational culture or industry norms. Leaders may require support from broader systems and policies to substantially diminish coercive citizenship pressures. This points towards multilevel intervention approaches rather than leader-focused solutions alone. The stronger and more consistent effects observed for positive outcomes (voluntary citizenship, performance) compared to negative outcome mitigation (compulsory citizenship reduction) align with positive organizational scholarship emphasizing that building strengths surpasses merely addressing weaknesses. Conscious leadership appears more potent in fostering constructive behaviours than eliminating problematic dynamics. This pattern suggests prevention-focused approaches alongside promotion-focused leadership development.

Sustainability implications become evident through demonstrated linkages between conscious leadership and employee wellbeing indicators. Leaders reducing compulsory citizenship while enhancing voluntary engagement and performance create conditions for long-term workforce retention and development. These patterns align with sustainable human resource management principles emphasizing employee regeneration rather than exploitation. Technological consciousness emerges as a capability enabling leaders to pursue efficiency gains without compromising human welfare.

5. Limitations and Future Research Directions

Several methodological limitations warrant acknowledgement. Cross-sectional data collection for key variables, despite temporal separation, precludes strong causal inferences. Longitudinal designs tracking leadership development and employee outcomes across extended periods would strengthen causal conclusions. Such research could examine whether technological consciousness growth produces corresponding improvements in employee outcomes or whether selection effects account for observed associations.

Self-report measures for leadership styles and technological consciousness introduce potential biases. While multi-source data collection mitigates common method concerns, leaders may overestimate their consciousness or effectiveness. Future research incorporating objective technological competence assessments alongside observational leadership behaviour coding would validate self-report instruments. Additionally, subordinate perceptions of leader technological consciousness may offer a valuable alternative perspective.

Sample composition, predominantly from Indian organizations, limits generalizability to other cultural contexts. Technological consciousness may manifest differently across cultures with varying collectivism–individualism orientations or power distance norms. Cross-cultural research examining whether ethical technology integration resonates universally or requires cultural adaptation would advance theoretical development. Comparative studies across economically diverse regions could reveal development-stage influences on consciousness importance.

The newly developed technological consciousness measure, while psychometrically sound in the current sample, requires validation across broader populations and contexts. Construct refinement through additional qualitative research with diverse stakeholders could identify overlooked dimensions. Longitudinal measurement invariance testing would confirm construct stability over time and across implementation stages.

Research examining boundary conditions beyond those tested here would enrich understanding. Individual difference variables such as employee technology readiness, need for autonomy, or learning goal orientation may moderate relationships. Organizational factors including change management climate, training investment, or leadership development culture represent additional potential moderators. Investigating such contingencies would specify optimal conditions for conscious leadership effectiveness.

The mechanisms through which technological consciousness operates remain incompletely understood. While qualitative data illuminated some pathways, systematic investigation of psychological mediators would advance theory. Potential mediators include employee trust in leader intentions, perceived organizational support, psychological empowerment, or work meaningfulness. Testing such mediational chains would reveal proximal impacts of conscious leadership on employee experiences.

This research focused primarily on individual and dyadic levels, with limited examination of team-level dynamics. Technological consciousness may influence team processes such as knowledge sharing, collaborative innovation, or collective efficacy. Multilevel research incorporating team-level mediators and outcomes would capture fuller effects of conscious leadership on organizational sustainability.

Finally, intervention research testing whether technological consciousness can be developed through training represents a crucial practical direction. Experimental or quasi-experimental designs comparing training effectiveness would establish whether consciousness represents a stable trait or a malleable competency. Such research would inform leadership development programme design and evaluate return on investment for consciousness-building initiatives.

References

Ahmed, S. F. (2022). The effect of the relationship between conscious leadership and proactive sustainability strategy in enhancing the organization reputation strategically. J. Contemp. Issues Bus. Gov. 28(1).

Al-Khatib, F. and Sasson, D. (2024). Ethical digital transformation and sustainable business: Leadership perspectives in technology-driven organizations. J. Bus. Ethics Innov. 47(3): 222–239.

Asante, K. (2024). Hotels' green leadership and employee pro-environmental behaviour: The role of value congruence and moral consciousness. J. Sustain. Tourism 32(7): 1370–1391.

Auer, A., Voegtlin, C. and Schneider, S. (2022). Responsible leadership and digitalization: The role of moral awareness in sustainable innovation. J. Bus. Res. 150: 234–245.

Brown, M. E. and Treviño, L. K. (2022). Ethical leadership and organizational behavior: A review and future directions. Acad. Manag. Ann. 16(2): 543–571.

Carmeli, A. and Dutton, J. E. (2015). Appreciative inquiry and relational leadership: Building organizational capacity through positive relationships. Organ. Dyn. 44(3): 193–200.

Epstein, M. J. and Buhovac, A. R. (2014). Making Sustainability Work: Best Practices in Managing and Measuring Corporate Social, Environmental, and Economic Impacts. Greenleaf Publishing, Sheffield, UK.

Friedman, R. S., Carmeli, A. and Dutton, J. E. (2017). When does respectful engagement with one's supervisor foster help-seeking behaviour and performance? J. Vocat. Behav. 101: 31–44.

George, G., Llewellyn, D. and Whittington, R. (2022). Digital leadership for sustainability: Navigating paradoxes of technology and ethics. Calif. Manag. Rev. 64(4): 5–28.

Hilb, M. (2023). Responsible corporate governance in the age of artificial intelligence. Corp. Gov. Int. Rev. 31(1): 17–32.

Lozano, R. (2015). A holistic perspective on corporate sustainability drivers. Corp. Soc. Responsib. Environ. Manag. 22(1): 32–44.

Mandal, V. and Pal, D. (2025). Sustainable leadership: Empowering green organizational citizenship behaviour through employee green value in the Indian healthcare sector. J. Asia Bus. Stud. 19(1): 79–102.

Rooke, D. and Torbert, W. R. (2020). Seven transformations of leadership revisited: Consciousness and context in managerial development. Harv. Bus. Rev. 98(3): 98–107.

Sikand, R. and Saxena, S. (2025). Sustainable leadership and organizational citizenship behaviour: Exploring mediating effects of corporate social responsibility. Vision 29(5): 568–579.

Stahl, B. C., Tim, M. and Borg, J. (2023). Artificial intelligence, ethics, and sustainability: Responsible innovation in digital organizations. J. Responsible Innov. 10(2): 245–262.

Voegtlin, C., Patzer, M. and Schneider, S. (2024). Digital responsibility and sustainable leadership: Integrating moral awareness into corporate strategy. Leadership Quart. 35(1): 120–138.

Section 4

Pathways to a Sustainable Future

Chapter 13

India's Economic Growth and Development Trends & Issues

Past, Present and Future

Pintu Majhi[1,*] and *Seemarani Meher*[2]

1. Introduction

In this context, we will primarily examine economic growth trends and phases, as well as the different drivers of economic growth, the sectoral composition of economic growth, and their contributions to the creation of jobs in the economy. A synthesis between India's growth trajectory and the most prominent theories of economic growth has also been undertaken, based on patterns in investment, saving, and economic growth. Next, we will take a quick look at how the government contributes to economic growth. Lastly, we will also examine the characteristics of the Indian economy and how they have changed over time.

Since independence, India's economy has grown remarkably, going from being largely agrarian and slow-growing to becoming one of the world's major economies with some of the quickest rates of growth. Colonial history, resource scarcity, and a state-led planned development strategy that produced only modest improvements previously limited expansion. The post-1991 reforms were a watershed, unleashing globalisation, privatisation, and liberalisation that sped up commerce, industrialisation, and growth driven by services. Despite ongoing issues with unemployment, inequality, and regional imbalances, India's economy is currently

[1] Assistant Professor, Hidayatullah National Law University, Raipur Chhattisgarh, India.
[2] Research Scholar, P.G. Department of Economics, Sambalpur University, Odisha, India.
Email: seema1.meher@gmail.com
* Corresponding author: pintumajhi892@gmail.com

DOI: 10.1201/9781003736158-17

the fifth largest in the world, supported by services, infrastructural development, digitalisation, and growing domestic demand. Going forward, maintaining high investment, developing human capital, expanding industrial and technological capabilities, maintaining environmental sustainability, and utilising demographic dividends are all critical to India's growth prospects. The course of India's economic development is thus determined by the issues, trends, and policy decisions of the past, present, and future.

2. Literature Review

Development economists have examined India's economic growth trajectory in great detail, focusing on structural changes, policy shifts, and socioeconomic challenges. As a key driver of long-term prosperity, Kuznets (1971) emphasized the importance of the structural shift from agriculture to industry and services. According to Ahluwalia (2002b), India's post-1991 liberalization era was a turning point that led to higher GDP growth rates, greater foreign investment, and rapid service sector expansion. In contrast to the traditional industrialization-led trajectory of East Asian economies, Panagariya (2008) argued that India's post-reform economic acceleration was unique since it was driven by services. This view is supported by Kochhar et al. (2006), who found that India's services sector was significantly more productive than its agriculture and industrial sectors. Concerns about employment creation and inclusion have arisen as a result of the lack of broad industrial expansion (Nayyar 2012).

The importance of investment and savings in promoting long-term, steady prosperity is highlighted by research. Growing domestic savings were identified by Bosworth and Collins (2008) as a key driver of India's capital formation and GDP expansion. According to Rodrik and Subramanian (2005), the correlation between policy improvements and productivity gains, and the caliber of institutions and governance had a major impact on the outcomes.

Issues including sustainability, employment, and inequality are highlighted by current studies. According to Himanshu (2019), despite rapid GDP development, India has continued to experience rural poverty, rising inequality, and an increase in the number of unemployed people, raising questions about inclusion. Chancel and Piketty (2019) demonstrated how income inequality increased in the 1980s, with the wealthiest 10% of earners receiving a large share of money. Furthermore, scholars like Stern (2015) stressed that, in light of growing environmental problems and the concerns posed by climate change, sustainable development needs to be a key component of India's economic plan.

The literature indicates that although India's progress has been remarkable, its uneven distribution and structural disparities require policies focused on inclusive and sustainable development.

3. Objectives

The basic objectives of this study are:

i. To examine performance of the Indian economy in terms of economic growth since independence and trace the various drivers of economic growth.
ii. To analyze the sectoral composition of economic growth and examine their contributions to employment generation in the economy.
iii. To give a brief assessment of the government's role in economic development and examine the characteristics/features of the Indian economy and how they have changed over time.

4. Methodology

The study's foundation is secondary data analysis from official sources, including World Bank and IMF figures, RBI reports, and the Economic Survey of India. India's economic growth trends since independence have been traced using a descriptive-analytical technique, breaking the history down into phases (pre-reform, post-1991 reforms, planning era, and recent decades). To comprehend structural changes and their impact on output and employment, sectoral statistics on agriculture, industry, and services have been analysed using Excel and SPSS software. Trends from recent data, policy frameworks, and global challenges have been projected to indicate issues and opportunities for sustainable growth in future forecasts. Tables, charts, simple regression, and comparative phase-wise analysis have been used through Excel and SPSS software to present findings clearly. A semi-logarithmic regression model is utilized to estimate long-term GDP and GPC growth rates.

To measure the growth rate of GDP and GPC in the context of India over the period of time, the present study used a semi-log regression model.

4.1 The Semi Log Model

Let the exponential model be:

$$Yt = abt \quad (1)$$

Here, "a" and "b" are the parameters of the model, "t" represents the time in years, and is an independent variable. Y represents the dependent variable.

Taking the natural logarithm of both the sides of the equation (1), we have the log linear model.

$\ln Yt = \ln a + t\ln b$

$$\ln Yt = \ln a + \ln b{*}t \quad (2)$$

$$Yt = Y01 + rt \quad (3)$$

Where, Y0 = the initial value of Y, Y_t = Y's value at time t, r is the compound (i.e., over time) rate of growth of Y.

Taking the natural log of equation (3) on both sides, we get,

$\ln Yt = \ln Y0 + t\ln (1+r)$

$$\ln Yt = \ln Y0 + \ln 1+r*t \qquad (4)$$

Comparing equation (2) and (4)

$\ln a = \ln Y0$ and $\ln b = \ln (1+r)$

Now let, $1 = \ln Y0$ and $2 = \ln 1+r$.

Therefore, we can express model (2) and (4) as

$$\ln Y t = 1+2t \qquad (5)$$ (Gujarati 2009)

Where, Y = dependent variable
t = independent variable
1 = intercept
2 = slope

Then, the growth rate can be found out from the estimated parameter, that is:

Growth rate (r) = Antilog 2-1* 100"

Equation (5) is called a semi-log model because only dependent variable is in the logarithmic form.

5. Results/Analysis

5.1 A Brief Account of GDP Estimation in India

Dadabhai Naoroji was the first Indian economist to estimate national and per capita income during 1867–68. Early attempts by private individuals and officials faced significant obstacles in gathering reliable data for pre-independence estimates, resulting in assumptions based on macro-level statistics. Accurate statistics appeared only after independence in 1947, necessitating a methodical methodology. The National Income Committee (NIC) was formed in 1949, led by P.C. Mahalanobis and consisting of D.R. Gadgil and V.K.R.V. Rao.

The National Income Unit (NIU) aided the NIC in putting together estimates. The first report was released in 1951, followed by the final one in 1954. Initially under the Ministry of Finance, the NIU was transferred to the Central Statistical Organisation (CSO), which has since assumed complete responsibility for national income estimates. Since 1955, the CSO has published annual statistics on India's national income in National Accounts Statistics, which allows for examination of trends in national and per capita income.

5.2 Trends of GDP and Per Capita in India

There are numerous studies that explore India's GDP growth after independence, identifying identifiable stages and trends. Overall, we can identify four major

Table 1. Overall trends of Annual Growth Rates of GDP Per Capita in India at constant prices of 2011–12.

Year	GDP	GDP Growth Rate	GPC*	GPC Growth Rate	Year	GDP	GDP Growth Rate	GPC*	GPC Growth Rate
1951–52	511489	2.9	12778	2.0	**1995–96**	3221584	7.6	31913	5.6
1955–56	602911	3.2	14449	1.5	**2000–01**	4326736	3.8	38873	1.7
1960–61	737044	5.5	16060	3.9	**2005–06**	5914614	7.9	48731	6.1
1965–66	872598	–2.6	16941	–5.3	**2010–11**	8301235	8.5	62847	6.9
1970–71	1089226	5.2	18821	2.5	**2015–16**	11369493	8.0	78592	6.7
1975–76	1256053	9.1	19236	7.0	**2020–21**	13694869	–5.8	87315	–8.4
1980–81	1464394	6.7	19925	4.5	**2021–22**	15021846	9.7	95284	9.1
1985–86	1883243	5.3	23010	3.0	**2022–23**	16071429	7.0 9	100913	5.9
1990–91	2514549	5.5	27629	3.3	**2023–24**	17381722	8.2	108338	7.4

Source: Economic Survey of India (2023–24).

trends of economic growth in India. The first period is 1951–1979, with modest and fluctuating growth; the second period is 1980–1999, with faster and steadier economic growth; the third period is 2000–16, with accelerated growth; and the fourth period is 2017–2023, with an economic downturn, pandemic, and recovery. Table 1 shows the growth patterns of GDP and GDP per capita (GPC) from 1950–51 to 2020–21 at five-year intervals, including the most recent years. Please keep in mind that the data is based on constant prices from 2011 to 2012.

India's GDP and GDP per capita growth rates in the first few years were low and unpredictable, averaging 3.5 percent, as seen in Table 1 and Figures 1 and 2. Known as the "Hindu rate of growth," this era saw slow progress from independence until the early 1980s. From 1947 to 1987, renowned academics including Robert Lucas compared these rates with those of other Asian countries.

Like Basu and Maertens's (2007) research for 1950–1970, Lucas's (1988) analysis revealed that India's GDP per capita (GPC) increased only 0.8 times over four decades, averaging 1.6 percent yearly. Nonetheless, growth accelerated from the mid-1970s to the 1980s, averaging roughly 6% from 1980 to 2005. This average persisted throughout the 1990s and increased to 7% in the 2000s.

Between 2010 and 2020, growth slowed to about 6–7 percent as a result of both domestic and international slowdowns. India recovered from a COVID-19-induced recession in 2020 with 8–9% growth in 2021. Notably, however, as Table 2 shows, India's global GPC ranking stagnated or fell from 1950–2018, as reported by Rai and Burman (2022).

India was ranked 115th out of 145 countries in 1950, as shown in Table 2. From the 1960s to the 1980s, its position declined. India returned to the 115th spot in 2018 after

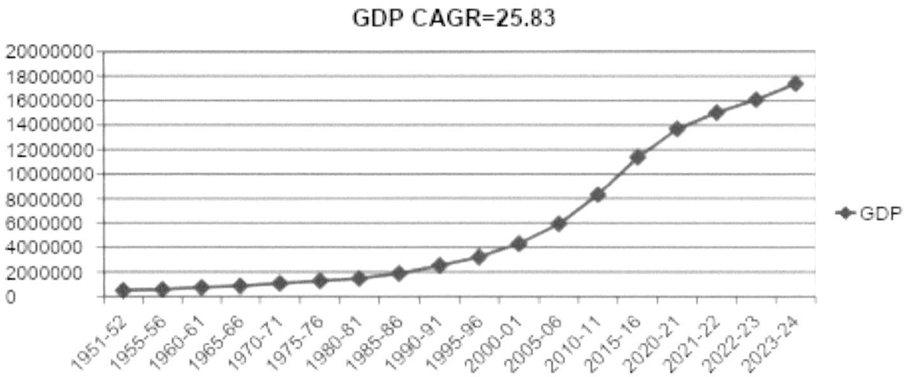

Figure 1. Overall trends of GDP (at constant prices of 2011–12) from 1951–2024. Source: Author's calculation based on data of Economic Survey 2023–24.

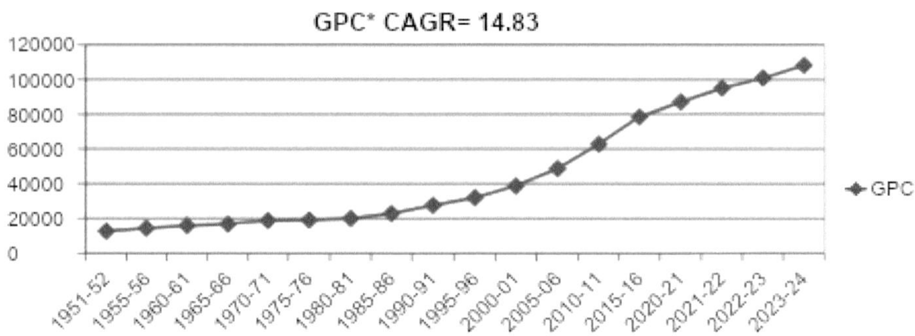

Figure 2. Overall trends of GPC (at constant prices of 2011–12) from 1951–2024. Source: Author's calculation based on data of Economic Survey 2023–24.

Table 2. India's rank in GPC among select countries of the world (1950–2018).

	Year	**1950**	**1960**	**1970**	**1980**	**1990**	**2000**	**2010**	**2018**
Rank of the countries	**No. of countries with data available**	145	152	153	167	169	169	169	169
	India	115	122	130	142	127	124	122	115
	Pakistan	110	133	121	130	119	119	123	121
	China	126	132	127	128	117	106	90	81
	Republic of Korea	113	107	89	88	37	33	33	27
	Brazil	71	69	71	67	71	63	74	78
	Indonesia	99	103	111	117	104	97	98	90
	South Africa	32	47	54	73	83	78	82	86
	Japan	53	31	20	17	5	19	26	24
	Mexico	42	48	47	53	60	55	69	68
	Nigeria	102	117	112	123	136	129	117	122
	USA	4	4	4	3	1	4	8	9

Source: Rai and Burman (2022)

making steady progress. According to Rai and Burman (2022), the Indian experience shows that, despite lingering obstacles, rapid and sustainable growth is achievable. In order to conceptualise economic growth, which is the foundation of many growth theories, including the Harrod-Domar model, the next section will examine changes in domestic saving and investment in India.

5.3 Trends of Saving and Investment in India

We are aware that the ratio of GDP to gross domestic saving (GDS) offers information about how people, corporations, and the government save. Similarly, the overall amount of investment in the economy, including both public and private investments, is shown by the gross domestic capital formation (GDCF). The GDS and GDCF as a proportion of GDP from the 1950s to the present are compiled in Table 3.

It rose from about 15 percent in 1960 to about 16 percent in 1970. By 1980, it was around 20 percent. GDCF increased to over 26 percent in the 1990s and peaked at over 33 percent in 2010, but the pandemic caused it to drop below 28 percent in 2020. New projections predict that the economy will rebound to more than 30 percent in 2023, demonstrating how government policies affect investment and growth.

Following liberalisation and reforms in 1980, GDS remained over 20 percent. Following the 1991 changes, it increased to about 25 percent, reaching a peak of 37 percent in 2010. During the Covid-19 outbreak, which has since ended, GDS declined. As is well known, gross domestic capital formation (GDCF) is the sum of all investments made by the public and private sectors of an economy. In the 1950s, governmental investments in agriculture and infrastructure caused the gross domestic capital formation (GDCF) to initially exceed 11 percent.

Table 3. Gross Domestic Saving and Gross Domestic Capital Formations as Percentages of GDP.

Year	Gross Domestic Saving as Percentage of GDP	Gross Domestic Capital Formation as a Percentage of GDP
1950	9.4	11.4
1960	11.3	14.5
1970	13.9	15.5
1980	17.2	19.7
1990	23.3	26.1
2000	24.8	26.0
2010	36.9	33.2
2020	29.1	27.3
2021	31.2	29.6
2022	30.2	30.7
2023	30.4	30.8

Source: Economic Survey of India 2023–24

5.4 Sectoral Composition of India's GDP

Since India attained independence in 1947, the sectoral composition of its GDP has changed significantly, leading to notable shifts in the contributions and roles of the various sectors in the economy. Figure 2 illustrates this trend, showing the shift from 1950–51 to 2016–17 on average. Additionally, at the constant price level of 2011–12, Table 4 displays the percentage shares of the three economic sectors in Gross Value Added (GVA) from 2011–12 to 2023–24 (PE).

The agricultural sector's share of GDP has significantly decreased, from over 50% in 1950 to less than 20% by 2016–17, according to the figures shown in Figure 3 and Table 4. Although it briefly climbed during the COVID-19 pandemic before dropping once more, its percentage of GVA also decreased, going from 18.5% in 2011–12 to 15.1% in 2019–20. In contrast, the industrial sector's portion of GDP stayed generally constant, rising from less than 20% in 1950 to slightly over 25% in 2016–17. Its share of GVA likewise stayed quite stable, rising from 32.5 percent to over 31 percent in 2023–2024.

Despite a drop during the epidemic, the services sector experienced impressive development, going from less than 30 percent of GDP in 1950–51 to slightly under 50 percent by 2016–17. The GVA contribution also increased from 49 percent in 2011–12 to over 55 percent in 2019–20. Many contend that this change reflects India's departure from reliance on agriculture, which is common in emerging economies, but that it differs from other countries in that manufacturing growth has been noticeably slow. The productivity of the services sector has significantly increased in South Asia, especially in India, bringing it into line with nations like China and Thailand and fostering strong economic growth (NITI Aayog 2018).

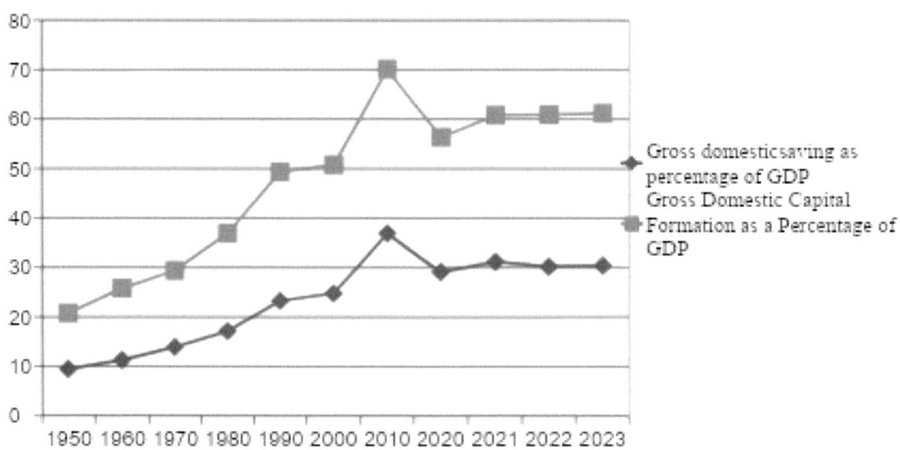

Figure 3. Trend of Gross Domestic Saving and Gross Domestic Capital Formations as Percentages of GDP. Source: Author's calculation based on data of Economic Survey 2023–24.

Table 4. Percentage Share of Gross Value Added by Different Economic Sector for 2011–12 to 2023–24 (PE) (Base year: 2011–12).

Year	Primary sector	Secondary sector	Tertiary sector	Year	Primary sector	Secondary sector	Tertiary sector
2011–12	18.5	32.5	49.0	**2018–19**	14.8	31.2	54.0
2012–13	17.8	31.8	50.3	**2019–20**	15.1	29.6	55.3
2013–14	17.8	31.2	51.1	**2020–21**	16.3	30.8	52.9
2014–15	16.5	31.1	52.4	**2021–22**	15.6	31.6	52.8
2015–16	15.4	31.6	53.0	**2022–23**	15.3	30.2	54.4
2016–17	15.2	31.5	53.3	**2023–24**	14.5	30.9	54.6
2017–18	15.3	31.4	53.3				

Source: Ministry of Statistics and Programme Implementation (2024).
Notes: 1. Primary Sector includes Agriculture, Forestry and Fishing; Secondary Sector includes Mining and Quarrying, Manufacturing, Electricity, Gas, Water Supply & Other Utility Services & Construction; and Tertiary Sector includes Trade, Repair, Hotels and Restaurants, Transport, Storage, Communication & Services related to Broadcasting, Financial Services, Real Estate, Ownership of Dwelling & Professional Services, Public Administration and Defence & Other Services.

Analysing the main forces behind this shift reveals several noteworthy patterns in the three main economic sectors. Due to an initial emphasis on industrialisation and the resulting labour shifts, the agricultural sector's percentage of GDP decreased between 1950 and 1960. Later years saw the rise of the services sector and urbanisation, which further contributed to this decline. Additionally, we observe that although the industrial sector's share has been increasing over time, the services sector's explosive growth overshadowed it.

It's interesting to note that the elementary and secondary sectors showed an increase in contribution during the Covid-19 pandemic, while the tertiary sector saw a reduction. The liberalisation policies implemented in the early 1990s, especially since 1991, have accelerated this transformation, creating a more diversified economy. Overall, India's economy has undergone a significant transformation with notable changes in GDP composition, primarily led by services, while the industrial sector's influence has grown only modestly. The next section will examine how these three industries contribute to the creation of jobs in the economy, providing more insight into their importance and contributions to growth and development.

Over the previous ten years, the secondary (industrial) and tertiary (services) sectors have clearly diverged, according to the data. With very slight variations, the secondary sector's share has remained steady at 30–32%, suggesting that India has had difficulty developing a robust industrial base despite policies that support manufacturing and "Make in India." Industrial growth has been hampered by structural constraints such as legislative barriers, inadequate infrastructure, a lack of technological advancement, and poor integration of small businesses into global value chains. On the other hand, the tertiary sector's share has increased gradually, from 49% in 2011–12 to over 55% in 2023–24. Professional services, trade, finance, IT, and communications have all contributed to this growth. This suggests a growth trajectory driven by services rather than the conventional industrialisation stage that helped other emerging countries create jobs. This imbalance is highlighted by the post-COVID recovery. Although the GDP recovered, it was primarily driven by services, with a focus on digital, financial, and export-oriented industries that primarily employ highly skilled urban workers. Structural change was slowed by the fact that many low-skilled workers who were displaced during the pandemic either returned to agriculture or continued working in informal services. Inequalities between formal and informal workers, skilled and unskilled labour, and rural and urban areas have all grown as a result of this unequal recovery. Recovery runs the risk of becoming "jobless" in the absence of more robust industrial expansion and the creation of labour-intensive jobs, which would exacerbate social and regional inequality.

By examining the sectoral GDP proportions of agriculture, industry, and services, this table illustrates the structural changes of a few Asian economies between 1960 and 2018. As a result of modernisation and a decreased reliance on farming, the proportion of agriculture in practically every nation fell precipitously (for example, India from 55% in 1960 to 14% in 2018, China from 30% to 7%, and Korea from 37% to barely 1.7%). The industrial sector first grew from 1960 to 1991 (as in China, Indonesia, Thailand, and Malaysia), but after 1991, its share shifted away from manufacturing and largely stabilised or slightly decreased. The most notable development is the growth of the services sector, which in 2018 accounted for the largest share of all countries (e.g., Philippines 59.8%, Korea 55.7%, India 48.8%, and China 53.3%), underscoring the worldwide trend towards economies powered by services. The information generally follows the traditional path of economic growth, which starts with agriculture and progresses to industry and finally to services.

6. Contributions of Agriculture, Industry and Services to Employment Generation

As we saw in the previous part, India's GDP was primarily derived from agriculture at the time of independence and remained so until the middle of the 1980s. The majority of the workforce in the economy is still employed in agriculture, which has historically been the main source of income for Indians. Figure 4 illustrates the employment trend by economic sector spanning from the 1991 economic reforms to 2022.

Agriculture remains the major source of employment, employing more than 60% of the workforce in 1991 (Figure 4), although by 2022, this percentage had dropped to more than 50%. It should be highlighted that before the economic changes of 1991, programmes like the Green Revolution raised agricultural productivity without appreciably lowering employment. Meanwhile, the shares of other sectors have risen during this period.

Due to globalisation and the expansion of the middle class, the private and services industries have increased their employment shares since reform, making the services sector the dominant one. The goal of recent programmes like "Make

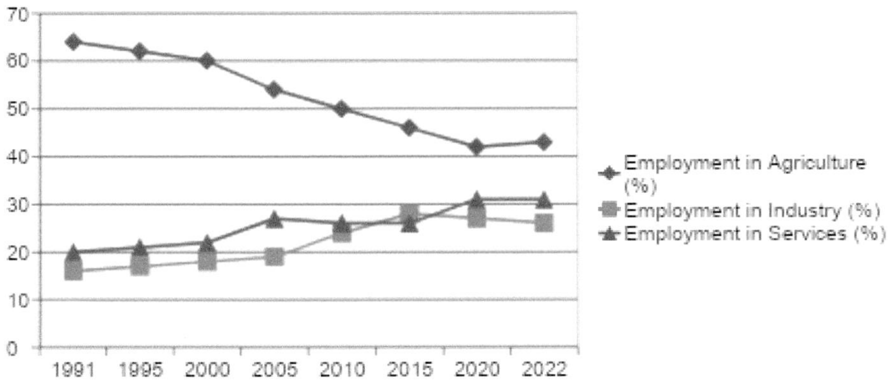

Figure 4. Share of agriculture, industry and services in employment in India (1991–2022). Source: World Bank (2024).

in India" and "Skill India" is to increase employment generation. The employment trends in the three economic sectors are described in this part; Units 23–26 will go into further detail.

India's post-COVID recovery has shown more serious issues with inequality and employment than just a GDP rebound. Even while output increased, the loss of jobs in low-skilled and informal industries forced many people back into agriculture, which slowed the sector's employment share decline. The recovery of the industry has been uneven, with skilled workers mostly benefitting from growth driven by services, particularly IT and finance. Inequality has increased as a result of widening formal–informal and urban–rural disparities. Government assistance programmes provided temporary respite, but in order to achieve equitable and sustainable growth, long-term recovery necessitates policies that create high-quality jobs in the manufacturing, services, and non-farm rural sectors.

Data on sectoral employment shares from 1991 to 2019 demonstrate that most Asian economies have undergone a marked structural transition, with agricultural employment steadily declining while services employment rises in tandem and industry showing modest but less consistent growth. Significantly reducing their reliance on agriculture, nations like China, Indonesia, Thailand, India, and the Philippines shifted a sizable amount of their labour force into the service sector. For instance, China's share of services increased from 19% to 47%, while its share of agriculture decreased from 60% to 25%. In a similar vein, India saw a significant increase in services and industry while reducing agriculture from 63% to 43%. With low employment in agriculture and high proportions of services by 2019 (63% and 70%, respectively), Malaysia and Korea are notable examples of economies that had already experienced this change by 1991. However, compared to its neighbours, Pakistan exhibits a slower transition, with 37% of the workforce still employed in agriculture in 2019, suggesting that structural transformation is trailing behind. All things considered, the tendency reflects urbanisation, modernisation, and the expanding role of the services sector in propelling economic expansion throughout Asia.

Table 5. Changes in Sectoral Shares (Per Cent) in GDP in Asian Countries.

Country	Agriculture_1960	Agriculture_1991	Agriculture_2018	Industry_1960	Industry_1991	Industry_2018	Services_1960	Services_1991	Services_2018
China	30	24	7	49	41.5	39.7	21	34.5	53.3
Indonesia	50	19.7	12.8	25	41.2	39.7	25	39.1	43.4
Thailand	40	12.6	8.1	19	38.7	34.8	41	48.7	57.1
Philippines	26	21	9.7	28	34	30.6	46	45	59.8
Malaysia	36	14.4	7.5	18	42.1	38.3	46	44.8	53
Rep. of Korea	37	6.8	1.7	20	37.1	34	43	47.1	55.7
Pakistan	46	22.8	22	16	22.9	17.9	38	43.2	52.8
India	55	27	14	16	26.4	26.1	29	37.8	48.8

Source: World Development Indicators, World Bank (2024)

Table 6. Changes in Sectoral Share (percent) in Employment in Asian Countries.

Country	Agriculture 1991	Agriculture 2019	Industry 1991	Industry 2019	Services 1991	Services 2019
China	60	25	21	27	19	47
Indonesia	56	29	15	22	29	49
Thailand	60	31	15	23	24	46
Philippines	45	23	14	19	41	58
Malaysia	22	10	31	27	46	63
Korea, Rep.	15	5	37	25	49	70
Pakistan	45	37	22	25	34	38
India	63	43	15	25	22	32

Source: World Development Indicators, World Bank (2024).

The data show a clear pattern of structural transformation in Asian economies over time. Agriculture's contribution to GDP has dropped significantly in all countries, indicating a progressive shift away from agrarian-based activity. This reduction is particularly substantial in economies such as China and the Republic of Korea, whereas nations such as India and Pakistan continue to depend extensively on agriculture.

The industrial sector expanded substantially throughout the early stages of development (1960–1991), reflecting the process of industrialization. However, its proportion is expected to steady or slightly fall in certain countries by 2018, indicating a change in the growth trend.

In contrast, the services sector has continuously increased and will be the largest contributor to GDP in most of countries by 2018. Countries with relatively large service shares include the Philippines, Thailand, and Malaysia, while India is also expanding rapidly in this sector.

In conclusion, the Table 5 shows a shift from agriculture to industry, and then to a service-oriented economic structure, while the speed and degree of this transition differ among countries.

The Table 6 shows a major transition in the employment structure of Asian economies from 1991 to 2019. The proportion of the workforce engaged in agriculture is declining in all countries, indicating a progressive transition away from traditional, labor-intensive activities. However, agriculture continues to account for a substantial proportion of employment in countries such as India and Pakistan, indicating that the transition remains incomplete in these economies. Overall, the data highlight an ongoing reallocation of labor from agriculture to industry and services, with varying speeds of adjustment across countries.

7. Role of the State in Economic Development

Beginning with Jawaharlal Nehru's socialist strategy, which centred on state control over important industries like coal and steel, the State has been instrumental in India's economic development since independence. This approach aimed to fight poverty and rebuild the post-colonial economy, making progress through programmes like the Five-Year Plans. Notably, in order to lessen dependency on imported commodities, the Second Five-Year Plan promoted import substitution and targeted heavy industrial establishment. Nonetheless, the ownership and authority of the centralised state over resources have faced criticism.

Actually, many people saw the Planning Commission as a way for the State to exercise its direct ownership of resources and economic power. Prominent economist Pranab Bardhan, for instance, emphasised inefficiencies brought about by bureaucratic procedures and resource misallocation as a result of the government's political interests taking precedence over economic efficiency. He called for reforms through decentralisation and public–private partnerships to promote entrepreneurship and equitable growth, pointing out the crucial role played by the often-overlooked informal sector.

The Green Revolution and other government policy measures in traditional areas like agriculture significantly increased productivity, but small farmers were frequently ignored, underscoring problems with rural development. Additionally, the State began to liberalise its economy in the 1980s, and in 1991 it implemented important changes that encouraged foreign competition and private investment, which resulted in remarkable growth, particularly in the services sector. Even with its remarkable GDP growth, India continues to struggle for equitable progress, as seen in issues like "jobless growth," sluggish human development, and regional disparities. All things considered, the shift in the State's role from strict control to liberalisation has made India a significant economic force despite ongoing socioeconomic difficulties.

8. Key Features of the Indian Economy

Since obtaining independence in 1947, India's economy has seen significant transformations, evolving from an agrarian society to one of the fastest-growing economies globally. Numerous phases of economic reforms and policies have characterized these shifts. Initial Phase: 1950s–1980s Early Economic Measures: In order to encourage self-reliance, a mixed economy model that blended capitalism and socialism was developed during this period, with substantial government involvement in economic planning. Several public sector companies were established as a result of the Import Substitution Industrialization (ISI) policy, which aimed to lessen reliance on imports by protecting native industries through tariffs and quotas.

The Planning Commission established Five-Year Plans that were primarily centred on agriculture, irrigation, and infrastructure while enforcing stringent restrictions on foreign investment, trade, and the private sector. Phase II: The First Years of Economic Liberalization, 1991–2000. An important turning point occurred in the early 1990s as a result of a significant balance of payments issue. Under the leadership of Finance Minister Manmohan Singh and Prime Minister P.V. Narasimha Rao, the government enacted the New Economic Policy (NEP), which promoted globalization, liberalization, and privatization (LPG).

Under the NEP, significant reform measures like tariff reductions and rupee devaluation led to a surge in average annual growth rates to almost 6% in the 1990s. Notably, the service sector—particularly IT and BPO—emerged as a major development engine, contributing significantly to GDP and jobs. Phase III: Growth and development from the 2000s to the present: In the current global setting, the Indian economy faces numerous challenges, such as market volatility, structural inequality, and inflationary pressures, all of which need smart responses in order to maintain growth and development.

a) *High Growth Rates*: Since liberalization, India's economy has grown at an impressive rate of 6–8% year on average, driven mostly by the services sector, especially software and IT (World Bank 2020).
b) *Structural Changes*: Significant changes, such as the Goods and Services Tax (GST) and the Insolvency and Bankruptcy Code (IBC), were put into place to address problems affecting the banking sector and enhance the business environment (RBI 2024).
c) *Sectoral Diversification*: By branching out into e-commerce, digital payments, and renewable energy, the economy has moved toward a modern economic framework (Deloitte 2024).
d) *Growing Middle Class*: A substantial middle class has developed as a result of the economy's expansion, which has raised domestic consumption and impacted sectors including retail, housing, and education (KPMG 2019).
e) *Digital Economy*: India is experiencing a digital revolution with large investments in technology, propelled by initiatives like Digital India, which seek to enhance digital literacy and access (NITI Aayog 2021).
f) *Sustainable Growth*: The emphasis is on sustainable development through investments in renewable energy, green technologies, and sustainable farming practices (World Bank 2024).

9. Opportunities and Challenges

In spite of its remarkable expansion, the Indian economy nevertheless faces many obstacles that draw attention to its salient characteristics. These include ongoing regional developmental disparities and persistent poverty and inequality, with a significant portion of the population living below the poverty line. Another challenge is environmental sustainability, as industrialisation upsets ecological balance and necessitates a careful balance between growth and protection. Furthermore, post-COVID recovery remains a top priority because the pandemic reduced GDP, prompting the government to implement stimulus plans to boost employment and infrastructure.

10. Discussion

Dadabhai Naoroji produced the first national income projections for India in 1867–1868. The CSO has contributed yearly official estimates to National Accounts Statistics since 1955. India's economy has expanded in four phases: (a) sluggish and erratic from 1951 to 1979; (b) faster and steady from 1980 to 1999; (c) rapid growth from 2000 to 2016; and (d) a slowdown brought on by pandemic effects, followed by recovery, from 2017 to 2023. The "Hindu rate of growth," or the average yearly economic growth rate, was 3.5% from 1947 to the 1980s, with a 1% increase per capita. The average rate was 6% in the 1990s and increased to 7–8%; however, COVID-19 caused a brief decline that ended in 2021. The foundation for reforms in the 1990s was laid by elements such as increased saving, improvements in agriculture, and financial development. Due to structural and policy changes, India's economy has grown since 1947, moving from an agrarian society to one that is expanding.

The shift from a highly state-controlled economy to a more liberalised market, which makes the economy more vulnerable to external shocks like the global economic recession and the COVID-19 pandemic, is indicative of the State's crucial role in India's post-independence economic development. Even though there has been considerable progress in the post-reform era, issues like human development, job creation, and regional imbalances still call for a balanced strategy that incorporates social fairness, sustainable development, and economic growth.

11. Conclusion

In conclusion, India's economic development and growth since independence have experienced a dramatic change, marked by phases of rapid expansion, moderate growth, and more recently, issues of deceleration and recovery. India's economy has become one of the fastest-growing in the world as a result of its shift from an agriculture-based economy to one driven primarily by services, but it has also revealed shortcomings in industrialization and job creation. Long-term prosperity has been sustained by savings, investment, and policy changes, particularly after the 1991 liberalization. However, persistent issues with inequality, regional disparities, and rising unemployment highlight the unfinished goal of inclusive development. Future development in India will depend on strengthening industrial capacities, encouraging human capital and innovation, reducing the gap between rural and urban areas, and maintaining environmental sustainability. India has the potential to sustain strong growth and improve its inclusivity and resilience in the ensuing decades by making wise policy choices, capitalising on demographic advantages, and striking a balance between equity and efficiency.

References

Ahluwalia, I. J. (2002a). India's Economic Reforms and Development: Essays for Manmohan Singh. Oxford University Press.

Ahluwalia, M. S. (2002b). Economic reforms in India since 1991: Has gradualism worked? Journal of Economic Perspectives 16(3): 67–88. https://doi.org/10.1257/089533002760278721.

Australian Government, Department of Foreign Affairs and Trade. (2018). India economic strategy to 2035: Navigating from potential to delivery. DFAT. https://www.dfat.gov.au/publications/trade-and-investment/india-economic.

Bardhan, P. (1998). The Political Economy of Development in India. Oxford University Press.

Basu, K. and Maertens, A. (2007). The pattern and causes of economic growth in India. Oxford Review of Economic Policy 23(2): 143–167. https://doi.org/10.1093/oxrep/grm012.

Bhagwati, J. and Desai, P. (1970). India: Planning for Industrialization. Oxford University Press.

Bosworth, B. and Collins, S. M. (2008). Accounting for growth: Comparing China and India. Journal of Economic Perspectives 22(1): 45–66. https://doi.org/10.1257/jep.22.1.45.

Chancel, L. and Piketty, T. (2019). Indian income inequality, 1922–2015: From British Raj to billionaire Raj? Review of Income and Wealth 65(S1): S33–S62. https://doi.org/10.1111/roiw.12439.

Datt, R. and Sundharam, K. P. M. (2023). Indian Economy (73rd ed.). S. Chand Publishing.

Deloitte. (2024). India economic outlook. Deloitte. https://www2.deloitte.com.

Gujarati, D. N. (2009). Basic Econometrics. McGraw-Hill.

Himanshu. (2019). Inequality in India: A review of recent trends. Review of Development and Change 24(1): 1–20.

International Monetary Fund. (2024). Advancing India's structural transformation: The role of services and manufacturing (IMF Working Paper No. 2024/138). IMF. https://www.elibrary.imf.org/view/journals.

Jana, S. K. (2023). Journey of seventy-five years of Indian economy: An overview (MPRA Paper No. 117838). MPRA. https://mpra.ub.uni-muenchen.de/117838/.

Kochhar, K., Kumar, U., Rajan, R., Subramanian, A. and Tokatlidis, I. (2006). India's pattern of development: What happened, what follows? (IMF Working Paper No. WP/06/22). IMF. https://doi.org/10.5089/9781451862814.001.

KPMG. (2019). The rise of the middle class in India. KPMG International. https://home.kpmg/in/en/home/insights/2019/07/the-rise-of-the-middle-class-in-india.

Kuznets, S. (1971). Economic Growth of Nations: Total Output and Production Structure. Harvard University Press.

Lucas, R. E. (1988). On the mechanics of economic development. Journal of Monetary Economics 22(1): 3–42. https://doi.org/10.1016/0304-3932(88)90168-7.

Ministry of Environment, Forest and Climate Change. (2020). Annual report 2019–20. Government of India. https://moef.gov.in.

Ministry of Finance, Government of India. (2024). Economic survey of India 2023–24. Government of India. https://www.indiabudget.gov.in/economicsurvey.

Ministry of Statistics and Programme Implementation. (2024). National accounts statistics. Government of India. https://mospi.gov.in.

NASSCOM. (2024). Indian IT-BPM industry. National Association of Software and Service Companies. https://www.nasscom.in.

Nayyar, D. (2012). The significance of services in economic development: A reconsideration. Margin: The Journal of Applied Economic Research 6(2): 177–197. https://doi.org/10.1177/097380101200600205.

NITI Aayog. (2018). India@75: A Plan for the Indian Economy to 2035. Government of India.

NITI Aayog. (2021, April 8). The role of digital infrastructure in socio-economic development. Government of India. https://www.niti.gov.in.

Panagariya, A. (2008). India: The Emerging Giant. Oxford University Press.

Press Information Bureau. (2024). Economic survey 2023–24. Government of India. https://static.pib.gov.in.

Rai, S. and Burman, A. (2022). India's GDP per capita since independence—Or, economic growth and property rights in China. Carnegie Endowment for International Peace. https://carnegieendowment.org.

Reserve Bank of India. (2024). Handbook of statistics on the Indian economy. RBI. https://rbi.org.in/Scripts/PublicationsView.aspx?id=16692.

Rodrik, D. and Subramanian, A. (2005). From "Hindu growth" to productivity surge: The mystery of the Indian growth transition. IMF Staff Papers 52(2): 193–228. https://doi.org/10.2307/30035999.

Stern, N. (2015). Why are we Waiting? The Logic, Urgency, and Promise of Tackling Climate Change. MIT Press. https://doi.org/10.7551/mitpress/9780262029186.001.0001.

World Bank. (2016). South Asia's turn: Policies to boost competitiveness and create the next export powerhouse. World Bank. https://doi.org/10.1596/978-1-4648-0930-8.

World Bank. (2020). World development indicators. World Bank. https://databank.worldbank.org/source/world-development-indicators.

World Bank. (2024, June 28). World Bank approves additional $1.5 billion in financing to support India's low-carbon energy transition [Press release]. World Bank. https://www.worldbank.org.

Chapter 14

Pathways to Sustainable Future in Gender, Equity and Sustainable Development

Shanmuga Shree S.P. and *Mritunjay Kumar**

1. Introduction

Gender equality ideals must be integrated into all aspects of society to achieve sustainable development (United Nations 2015, Kabeer 2016). Regardless of gender identification, everyone may contribute to development while boosting adaptability and guaranteeing a fair share of the advantages of progress. In the modern era, establishing sustainable growth paths and attaining gender equality simultaneously present a pressing problem. Across key sectors such as labour, agriculture, and energy, contemporary growth strategies have been shown to be both environmentally unsustainable and socially discriminatory toward women (Benería et al. 2015, Rai et al. 2014). Sustainable development, as defined by the World Commission on Environment and Development (1987), seeks to address these inequalities by meeting present needs while preserving resources and opportunities for future generations. Sustainability and egalitarian and inclusive development result when all these factors are integrated. Efforts at sustainability that do not have proper integration promote social inequalities as well as present hurdles to global development goals. Each strategy must respond to the simple question regarding sustainability goals and beneficiary communities.

The realization of all human rights, including access to essential needs and livelihood security, is fundamental to gender equality, yet formal rights alone

Army Institute of Management and Technology, Greater Noida.
* Corresponding author: dr.mritunjay@aimt.ac.in

DOI: 10.1201/9781003736158-18

are insufficient to guarantee substantive equality (Sen 2005, Nussbaum 2011, Cornwall and Rivas 2015). The process requires opposition to existing institutions and epistemologies in combination with demands for voice and power as well as respect and recognition. The three fundamental pillars of sustainable development consist of environmental protection and social integration together with economic expansion. A sustainable future balances economic growth, environmental protection, and social justice. For development to be truly sustainable, everyone must be involved, but special attention must be paid to those who have historically been left behind due to social or gender injustice. As a result, gender justice and social inclusion are not only moral goals but also essential components of sustainable development. When men and women have equal access to resources, education, and decision-making, societies become more resilient, productive, and equitable. Sustainability requires the eradication of all forms of inequality, as integrating gender and equity considerations into development planning enhances social resilience to climatic and economic disruptions (Leach et al. 2016, Djoudi et al. 2016, Rao et al. 2019).

A truly sustainable future requires not only ecological preservation but also equal access to opportunities, decision-making, and benefits for all members of society. In order to achieve sustainable development, social justice and gender equality must be accepted as fundamental ideas rather than merely as afterthoughts. When women and other marginalised groups have equal access to leadership roles, economic engagement, and education, societies are more resilient, creative, and equipped to handle novel problems. Throughout history, structural barriers like resource exclusion, discriminatory laws, and cultural norms have limited the full participation of women and other groups. These processes hinder both group progress and individual potential. Achieving sustainable development in its broadest sense requires integrating gender-sensitive and equity-focused initiatives into every sector, from resource governance, health, and employment to community development and education.

This makes development inclusive rather than exclusive and strong rather than fragile. Therefore, incorporating gender equity into development pathways serves two purposes: it is a goal in and of itself (justice, rights) and it serves as a catalyst for more successful sustainable development outcomes. Therefore, the first step toward a sustainable future is to recognize that equality and fairness are essential facilitators rather than optional extras. A development trajectory that benefits everyone and leaves no one behind is the outcome of incorporating gender balance and social equity into policy-making, programme design, and resource allocation at all levels, from the local to the global. Despite global progress, gender differences still exist, especially in decision-making, employment, and education. Women's empowerment is a process that gives them the opportunity to make decisions as well as a result that gradually changes communities. When women are educated and given equal opportunities to participate in public life, societies benefit from increased creativity, social justice, and sustainability. Therefore, the path to a sustainable future lies in creating institutions that place a high priority on equality, equity, and inclusion. In addition to being more economically resilient, societies that integrate gender and equity into development planning are also more socially and environmentally stable. A sustainable future can only be achieved when everyone, regardless of gender or place of origin, benefits fairly from advancement.

2. Evolution of Gender Equality and Sustainability in Global Development

Early Development Theory (pre-1970s): Development planning during this period was mainly concentrated on economic growth, with complete disregard for environmental conservation and social equity. The development strategies of that period focused solely on economic advancement while ignoring both environmental sustainability and social justice issues.

The 1970s–1980s Women in Development (WID) Era: The Decade for Women (1976–1985), along with the United Nations' International Women's Year (1975), were key influences during this era. The Decade for Women and the International Women's Year established foundational influences that defined this period. The world recognized women's essential role in the economy as a new movement began to emerge. The main focus remained on bringing women into existing systems instead of working to transform these systems.

Gender and Development (GAD) Approach (Late 1980s–1990s): The understanding developed that institutional discrimination barred women's full participation. The shift toward equity instead of equality became important because it provided all people with identical opportunities along with adequate resources and equal participation in decision-making processes.

Linking Sustainability and Gender (1990s–2000s): Agenda 21 and the Rio Earth Summit in 1992 empowered women to become central change agents in environmental management. Research during this period demonstrated that empowering women resulted in improved poverty reduction, education, and conservation of resources.

World Sustainable Development Goals (2015 to the present): According to the United Nations Sustainable Development Goals framework, gender equality (SDG 5) is intrinsically linked with sustainability across education, climate action, and economic growth. Policymakers have thus developed "pathways" for mainstreaming gender and equity into broader environmental and economic agendas (Kabeer and Natali 2013, Leach and Reeves 2016, Hickel 2019).

Phase Present (2020s): Major occurrences such as economic recessions, health emergencies, and environmental issues have highlighted the requirement for institutions that treat all individuals equally and are stable in their foundations. Existing research focuses its attention on intersectionality by examining how gender intersects with poverty rates, ethnicity, geographical location, and availability of resources.

2.1 Benefits of Sustainable Future in Gender, Equity and Sustainable Development

Global Relevance: The UN's Sustainable Development Goals (SDGs), especially SDG 5 (Gender Equality) and associated goals such as SDG 4 (Quality Education), SDG 8 (Decent Work), and SDG 13 (Climate Action), all involve gender equality. The topic of the research continues to be relevant to academics, NGOs, development agencies, and policymakers from all corners of the globe.

Interdisciplinary Approach: Sustainable development integrates three broad disciplines: environmental science through ecological management, economics through employment and equity, and social science through gender studies. This interdisciplinary framework allows for deeper analysis across multiple perspectives (Kates et al. 2005, Purvis et al. 2019, Buechler 2016).

Potential Policy Impact: The conclusions have the potential to impact national and local policy formation in the spheres of environmental governance, workforce participation, and education. This forms the foundation for the creation of gender-responsive sustainability models. Social justice acts as a dimension that incorporates inclusivity, justice, and human rights that development programmes have to follow. The subject is of interest to both academic readers and advocacy networks, which leads to increased outreach capacity.

Emerging and Timely: Sustainable development embodies an integrative framework that unites three major disciplinary domains: environmental science, which focuses on ecological preservation and resource management; economics, which emphasizes employment generation and equitable growth; and social science, which examines issues of gender, inclusion, and social justice. This interdisciplinary approach allows for a more comprehensive and critical analysis of sustainability, drawing from diverse theoretical and practical perspectives. Practical application in the real world helps in the creation of functional solutions through business gender equality programmes, inclusive education initiatives, and community-based sustainability projects. This platform facilitates the demonstration of model case studies that reflect exceptional practices from various geographic areas.

Inclusive Economic Growth: Gender parity has a direct impact on productivity and economic development. When women and marginalised groups have equal access to financial resources, employment opportunities, and education, the overall labour force participation rate increases. According to research, closing the gender gap in the workforce could boost global GDP by about 26 percent. In sustainable development, giving gender participation top priority ensures a more equitable distribution of economic benefits, reducing poverty.

Improved Decision-Making and Leadership: It has been demonstrated that diverse leaders and teams produce more creative, ethical, and comprehensive outcomes. A 2023 study by Leal Filho (Environment, Development and Sustainability) found that gender-balanced leadership teams were more likely to implement socially and environmentally responsible policies. Often, women are responsible for managing household resources such as water, food, and energy. Women's empowerment in environmental governance enhances sustainability because they bring local knowledge, community values, and a long-term perspective to resource management. According to a 2022 UNDP assessment, climate adaptation and natural resource conservation programmes were more successful when led by women.

Reduction of Poverty and Inequality: The intergenerational cycle of poverty can be broken with gender parity. Educating girls and promoting women's economic empowerment lead to better nutrition, healthier families, and higher educational attainment for children. Equitable development not only ensures that improvements benefit underserved and rural areas, but it also contributes to the reduction of the wealth gap. This aligns with the sustainable development principle of "Leaving no one behind" (Tembon and Fort 2008). Communities that embrace gender equality are better prepared to adapt to social, economic, and environmental changes. When women are empowered, families and communities gain access to better health care, education, and sustainable livelihood options. This resilience becomes critical during crises such as climate disasters or pandemics.

2.2 Gender Roles and Participation

Gender roles and participation are crucial to creating a sustainable and just future because they influence how individuals use their decision-making power, access resources, and contribute to development. Because men and women have traditionally been assigned different roles in society, women's involvement in social, political, and environmental initiatives is frequently restricted. These traditional practices have resulted in gender inequality, which restricts women's visibility and influence, despite the fact that their contributions are vital to communities' well-being. Through the management of resources like food, fuel, and water, women play a critical role in preserving the sustainability of homes and farms worldwide. However, their knowledge and experiences are usually disregarded by institutional policies and planning processes. To change these trends and attain gender parity, women must have equal access to leadership, education, employment, and technology. When women actively participate in leadership and decision-making, development outcomes are more equitable and inclusive. Research indicates that gender-diverse leadership promotes long-term community resilience, improves environmental awareness, and results in better governance.

Nonetheless, it is equally important to involve men in the process of gender equality. When men are encouraged to help women succeed in their careers and share household responsibilities, traditional prejudices are dismantled and justice is advanced in both public and private spheres. In contexts of sustainable development, the cooperation of men and women can enhance social collaboration, resource efficiency, and creativity. Gender-sensitive policies, like ensuring equal pay, providing maternity and paternity benefits, and allowing women to serve in local government, create a more egalitarian foundation for society. Another important factor in changing gender roles is education. Boys and girls who have equal access to high-quality education are better prepared to engage in environmental projects, research, government, and business because they have the knowledge and confidence to do so. Because STEM programmes give women the chance to contribute to the technical and ecological solutions that will shape sustainability in the future, they have a particularly big impact.

Cooperatives, self-help groups, and environmental movements are examples of women-led projects that have demonstrated how inclusive involvement can lead to long-lasting change in many areas. These programmes strengthen communities and give women economic power through social innovation and shared accountability. However, there are still many obstacles to overcome, particularly in areas where institutional prejudices and patriarchal customs remain prevalent. Both legislative frameworks and cultural change are necessary to address these problems. Governments and organizations must make sure that men are encouraged to support equality and that women's opinions are heard when discussing policies. Gender balance is necessary for true sustainability since both men and women contribute distinct perspectives, ideas, and leadership traits that are critical to advancement. Communities become more inclusive, resilient, and forward-thinking when gender roles are redefined to be flexible and complementary, enabling society to utilise human potential to the fullest. By creating equal opportunities and promoting shared involvement, gender equality transcends its status as a merely social goal and becomes a tool for attaining true, long-term sustainable development.

3. Background of the Study

Adhuze et al. (2025) contend that the pursuit of sustainable development depends on gender equality, which goes beyond simply being a basic human right. The theoretical underpinnings, historical development, and governance frameworks that support this interconnectedness are among the subjects covered in this chapter. Additionally, it promotes forward-thinking techniques centred on embracing interdisciplinary innovation, enacting gender-sensitive regulations, and dismantling patriarchal systems. The authors emphasise that prioritizing gender fairness in sustainable development is both a strategic imperative and a moral duty in light of worldwide problems like climate change and ongoing inequality (Adhuze et al. 2025). It focuses on the ongoing disparities between men and women in terms of learning, civic engagement, work, and resource distribution, emphasizing how these disparities impede the growth of the country's economy and society. The authors contend that women's active engagement and equitable access to opportunities are prerequisites for sustainable development, economic development, and effective governance. The authors stress the necessity for institutional, social, and gender-sensitive policy changes in addition to comprehensive policy frameworks in order to attain sustainable development in Nigeria. It emphasizes how crucial equity and gender equality are to efficient planning and development (Gbadebo et al. 2018).

The article presents evidence about environmental and developmental impacts that differ between genders and explains the essential roles women maintain in farming and environmental care, as well as healthcare and community equilibrium. The research in the book establishes how conventional development methods fail to account for social power relations and justice issues. The publication provides a framework for multiple directions that supports diverse methods and enables local adaptations while promoting collective involvement. Development procedures require sustainability by focusing on women's empowerment and placing gender equality at the core of every development approach (Leach 2016). This analysis shows that gender equality is essential to sustainable development. This research presents a "pathways approach" that promotes numerous unique routes to sustainability through social justice and power equality, challenging traditional approaches that isolate gender from sustainability. While emphasizing the value of female empowerment in creating solutions, the study demonstrates that men and women continue to hold disparate opinions about environmental and developmental issues. To achieve long-lasting sustainable development results, governments must embrace diversity, inclusiveness, and justice rather than adhering to rigid single methods (Leach et al. 2016).

The report emphasizes how integrating equity principles into the climate movement can create synergy, bolster credibility, and promote worldwide collaboration. It emphasizes that climate change poses a critical risk to social justice and development pathways, in addition to being an environmental issue. In order to address climate change, policy frameworks should incorporate sustainability and equity to promote resilience, inclusive growth, and intergenerational justice. This will offer long-term solutions that go beyond simple technical fixes (Fleurbaey et al. 2014).

Among other socioeconomic advantages, the report emphasizes how women's empowerment contributes to better family health, poverty reduction, and community resilience. Additionally, it emphasizes that gender equality should not be viewed as a standalone issue but rather as a component of all development plans and initiatives. The research suggests intentional policy and legal frameworks that include women's empowerment programmes in order to guarantee equitable participation by men and women in the benefits of sustainable development (Aina 2011). This argues that traditional approaches to social science research often downplay or overlook women's experiences and contributions, which limits the scope and impact of knowledge production. The study highlights how tackling issues of inequality, power dynamics, and representation through the development of social sciences might advance our understanding of African nations. In the end, academic commitment, curriculum development, and institutional reforms are required to make gender an essential and transformative aspect of African social science research and education (Codesria 2011).

According to Stevens, increasing the representation of women in economic, social, and environmental decision-making and efficient roles may help hasten the achievement of sustainable improvement goals. She highlights the importance of effective governance, which continues to be elusive in the absence of full-scale gender parity, for sustainable development. Stevens also urges greater research on whether women are better suited to steer sustainable development pathways due to their potentially greater risk aversion. According to her, policy discussions ought to emphasize these gender-associated viewpoints, specifically in the run-up to the

2012 UN Conference on Sustainable Development (Stevens 2010). The report establishes that solving gender inequality stands as a fundamental requirement for reaching sustainable development objectives. It further establishes that structural inequalities block sustainability efforts since men and women receive unequal access to opportunities, resources, and control over decisions. The report demonstrates that women's limited participation in governance, along with their extensive unpaid caregiving duties and economic limitations, prevents them from fully participating in development activities. The research establishes that empowering women alongside ensuring equal rights stands as essential groundwork for sustainable success because it links gender justice with environmental and social sustainability (Johnsson-Latham 2007).

4. Research Methodology

The present study employs a quantitative, descriptive, and correlational research design to explore the relationship between gender, equality, and sustainable development. The primary objective is to understand existing issues, evaluate how gender parity contributes to the achievement of sustainable goals, and identify effective strategies for promoting a sustainable future. Data were collected through a structured questionnaire administered via Google Forms, allowing participants to respond conveniently. The sampling process combined the convenience sampling technique, which falls under non-probability sampling methods, as the population was not normally distributed and no sampling frame was available. A total of 50 respondents from the Delhi NCR region participated in the study. The research instrument consisted of four sections: Section I gathered demographic information, Section II focused on gender equality, Section III addressed equity, and Section IV examined sustainable development. For data analysis, descriptive statistics were utilized to summarize participant characteristics and responses. Through this methodology, the study aims to provide valuable insights into how gender equality influences sustainability outcomes within organizations, thereby enhancing understanding and contributing to future policy and organizational development initiatives.

4.1 Data Analysis

Analysis

The descriptive analysis indicates that respondents generally hold positive views on gender equality ($M = 4.28$, $SD = 0.62$), equity ($M = 4.31$, $SD = 0.56$), and sustainable development ($M = 4.39$, $SD = 0.54$). All three variables are rated near the higher end of the 5-point scale, reflecting a shared perception that gender-related issues and sustainable development are critical and interconnected.

Table 1. Descriptive analysis.

	N	Minimum	Maximum	Mean	Std.Deviation
GENDERAVG	50	2.75	5.00	4.2750	.61704
EQUITYAVG	50	3.00	5.00	4.3050	.55854
SDAVG	50	3.00	5.00	4.3880	.54272
Valid N(list wise)	50				

4.2 Correlation

Analysis

The correlation analysis demonstrates significant positive relationships among gender equality, equity, and sustainable development. Specifically, gender equality was positively correlated with both equity (r = .462, p = .001) and sustainable development (r = .351, p = .012). Equity was also positively correlated with sustainable development (r = .376, p = .007). These findings suggest that promoting gender equality and equity is closely linked to advancing sustainable development outcomes.

Table 2. Correlation Analysis between Gender, Equity and Sustainable Development.

		Gender AVG	Equity AVG	SDAVG
Gender AVG	Pearson Correlation	1	.462**	.351*
	Sig.(2-tailed)	50	.001	.012
	N		50	50
Equity AVG	Pearson Correlation	.462**	1	.376**
	Sig.(2-tailed)	.001	50	.007
	N	50		50
SDAVG	Pearson Correlation	.351*	.376**	1
	Sig.(2-tailed)	.012	.007	50
	N	50	50	

**Correlation is significant at the 0.01 level (2-tailed)
*Correlation is significant at the 0.05 level (2-tailed)

4.3 Regression

a. Dependent Variable: SDAVG
b. All requested variables entered

Table 3. Regression analysis.

Variables Entered/Removed[a]

Model	Variables Entered	Variables Removed	Method
1	EQUITY AVG GENDER AVG [b]		Enter

Model Summary

Model	R	R Square	Adjusted R Square	Std. Error of the Estimate	Change Statistics				
					R Square Change	F Change	Dft1	Dft2	Sig. F Change
1	.426[a]	.181	.147	.50138	.181	5.207	2	47	.009

a. Predictors: (Constant), EQUITYAVG, GENDERAVG

ANOVA[a]

Model	Sum of Squares	df	Mean Square	F	Sig.
Regression	2.618	2	1.309	5.207	.00g[b]
Residual	11.815	47	.251		
Total	14.433	49			

a. Dependent Variable: SDAVG

b. Predictors: (Constant), EQUITYAVG, GENDERAVG

Analysis

The regression results indicate that the combined effect of gender equality and equity significantly predicts sustainable development perceptions. However, when considered individually, neither predictor contributed significantly at the .05 level, although equity showed a trend toward significance. This suggests that while these variables together explain meaningful variation in sustainable development, their independent contributions are weaker, possibly due to overlapping effects or the modest sample size (N = 50).

5. Conclusion

The study shows that gender parity is both a moral and social necessity and an essential part of sustainable development. When women are empowered and fair participation is guaranteed in all areas of life—political, economic, and environmental—societies are more resilient, inclusive, and prepared to tackle global sustainability concerns. However, gaps in policy implementation, cultural hurdles, and structural inequalities continue to impede development.

To achieve inclusion at the grassroots and policy levels and to advance toward a sustainable future, gender perspectives must be mainstreamed into all development agendas. Beyond preserving the environment or advancing the economy, a sustainable future requires justice, inclusivity, and shared responsibility. Gender equality and social justice are essential components of sustainable development, not just add-ons. When men and women have equal access to resources, education, and decision-making opportunities, societies gain from higher productivity, improved health outcomes, and more resilient communities. Fairness can also be ensured by acknowledging the different starting points and challenges people face. Fairer systems that benefit everyone are produced by policies that address these disparities, such as inclusive education, equitable pay, access to healthcare, and representation in leadership positions. "Leaving no one behind" is the best way to achieve sustainable development, according to the United Nations (2023). In conclusion, the key to a sustainable future is to allow everyone, regardless of gender or place of origin, to contribute equally to the advancement of the planet. Incorporating gender and equality into development planning is not only a social goal; it is also strategically and morally necessary to build societies that are resilient, just, and truly sustainable for coming generations.

Alongside these findings, the study emphasizes that achieving gender equality is not only an ethical necessity but also a catalyst for comprehensive and long-term growth. Sustainability and social justice are closely intertwined. Empowering women and ensuring equal participation in all fields leads to more innovative ideas, balanced decision-making, and equitable resource distribution. In addition, inclusive systems enhance governance and create communities that are more capable of handling economic and environmental emergencies. Therefore, sustainable development requires a multifaceted approach that sees gender equality as a fundamental component rather than an add-on. Strengthening institutional frameworks, promoting gender-sensitive education, and allowing men and women to share leadership and community development roles are all essential for progress. Policies should aim to create an environment where everyone can thrive, in addition to removing barriers. Closing the gap between commitment and action can be achieved through increasing awareness, enforcing responsibility, and incorporating gender equality into national and corporate policy. To build a future that benefits all generations and leaves a legacy of justice, opportunity, and shared prosperity, equality, inclusion, and justice must coexist. This is what sustainable development is all about.

6. Recommendations

Strengthen Policy Implementation & Promote Education and Skill Development: To maintain existing gender equity policies, governments must put in place measurable accountability frameworks. Invest in gender-sensitive education and vocational training, particularly for women and underrepresented groups, to increase employability and leadership.

Programmes for Economic Inclusion & Encourage Women's Leadership: To improve women's access to credit, financial services, and business opportunities, as well as their economic participation. More women should occupy decision-making roles in the public, private, and community domains in order to influence plans for sustainable development.

7. Limitation

Data Scope & Geographical Bias: The study uses secondary data that may not fully reflect current issues at the local level, such as reports, official publications, and SDG indexes. The sample may be skewed toward regions that are easily accessible, which would limit the findings' generalizability across cultural contexts.

Self-Reported Data & Complexity of Gender Issues: When respondents give answers they believe are expected rather than ones based on their actual experiences, social desirability bias is evident in surveys and interviews. It's possible that the research doesn't fully explore the ways in which gender interacts with caste, class, race, and religion.

References

Adhuze, H. I. and Ogunbona, M. D. (2025). Gender equality and sustainable development: a pathway to inclusive and resilient societies. Concrescence Journal of Multi-Disciplinary Research 2(2).

Aina, O. I. (2011). Promoting gender equality for sustainable development. Concrescence Journal of Multi-Disciplinary Research, page 88.

Bhattacharjee, J., Singh, N. and Egamberdieva, D. (2025). Gender equality in the sustainable development framework. In Environmental Landscape and Sustainable Biodiversity for Healthy Green Growth.

Braunstein, E. and Houston, M. (2015). Pathways towards sustainability in the context of globalization: A gendered perspective on growth, macro policy and employment. In Gender Equality and Sustainable Development.

Chakraborty, A. and Sengupta, S. (2023). Equitable pathways for a sustainable future: the case for mainstreaming gender across sustainable development goals (SDGs). Concrescence Journal of Multi-Disciplinary Research.

Chan, K., Agard, J., Liu, J., Dutra De Aguiar, A. P., Armenteras Pascual, D., Boedhihartono, A. K. et al. (2019). Pathways towards a sustainable future. Concrescence Journal of Multi-Disciplinary Research.

CODESRIA General Assembly Bulletin. (2011). Council for the Development of Social Science Research in Africa. CODESRIA Bulletin.

Da Silva, T. H. R. (2024). Advancing gender equity in nursing care for older adults: a pathway to achieving the United Nations Sustainable Development Goals. Journal of Community Medicine and Public Health Reports.

Engendering Social Sciences in Africa. Paper to be presented at the Conference of Deans of Social Sciences in Africa. Organized by CODESRIA. Rabat, Morroco, 2011.

Fleurbaey, M., Kartha, S., Bolwig, S., Chee, Y. L., Chen, Y., Corbera, E. et al. (2014). Sustainable development and equity. Climate Change 2014: Mitigation of Climate Change, pp. 283–350.

Gbadebo, A. W., Keshiro, T. A., Sule, O. A., Adeyemi, A. A. and Yemi, B. K. (2018). Gender equality and sustainable development in Nigeria. Covenant Journal of Entrepreneurship 2(2).

Johnsson-Latham, G. (2007). A study on gender equality as a prerequisite for sustainable development. A Report to the Environmental Advisory Council.

Leach, M. (Ed.). (2016). Gender Equality and Sustainable Development. London: Routledge.

Leach, M., Mehta, L. and Prabhakaran, P. (2016). Gender equality and sustainable development: A pathways approach. The UN Women Discussion Paper, 13: 2016.

Pereira, L. (2014). The role of substantive equality in finding sustainable development pathways in South Africa. McGill International Journal of Sustainable Development Law and Policy, pp. 147–178.

Raman, R., Ustenko, V., Filho, W. L. and Nedungadi, P. (2025). Energy justice and gender: bridging equity, access, and policy for sustainable development. Discover Sustainability.

Stevens, C. (2010). Are women the key to sustainable development. Journal of Social Review and Development.

Upadhyay, S. (2024). Gender equality and sustainable development. Journal of Social Review and Development.

Chapter 15

The Role of Digital Public Infrastructure in Advancing Inclusive Governance and Development in India

Debarshi Mukherjee[1] and *Muhammad Faiz Qamar*[2,*]

1. Introduction

India stands at a decisive point in its developmental trajectory. The country seeks economic expansion and inclusive, equitable, and sustainable growth. This goal cannot be achieved through conventional policy tools alone; it necessitates a transformative shift in how public goods and services are delivered, accessed, and governed. Since the Industrial Revolution, successive waves of technological innovation have driven substantial advancements in productivity, employment, living standards, and global population growth. The ongoing wave of digitalization and emerging technologies holds similar promise, particularly for developing economies like India, where it is expected to accelerate productivity and catalyze structural transformation (Arsic 2020). In this context, Digital Public Infrastructure (DPI) has emerged as a strategic enabler, capable of bridging deep-rooted social, geographic, and economic inequalities.

Digital Public Infrastructure consists of essential digital systems such as identity verification, digital payments, and data exchange mechanisms that enable the

[1] Professor, Department of Commerce and Business Studies, Jamia Millia Islamia, Maulana Mohammed Ali Jauhar Marg, New Delhi-110025, India.

[2] Doctoral Research Scholar, Department of Commerce and Business Studies, Jamia Millia Islamia, Maulana Mohammed Ali Jauhar Marg, New Delhi-110025, India.

Email: dmukherjee@jmi.ac.in

* Corresponding author: muhammadfaizqamar@gmail.com

DOI: 10.1201/9781003736158-19

large-scale, efficient delivery of innovative public services. The term "public" in this context denotes societal benefit and universal accessibility, rather than direct government ownership (Marskell et al. 2023). India's DPI model has positioned the country as a global leader in leveraging digital architecture to enhance citizen welfare by ensuring inclusive access to essential services. The country's pioneering DPI framework, known as India Stack, comprises foundational layers including Aadhaar for digital identity, the Unified Payments Interface for real-time digital payments, DigiLocker for secure cloud-based document storage, and the Open Network for Digital Commerce to democratize e-commerce. Unlike private digital platforms, India's DPI is designed around the principles of interoperability, openness, and inclusion, making it a cornerstone of citizen-centric digital governance.

The strategic importance of DPI to India's developmental objectives cannot be overstated. While India's digital advancements over the past decade have garnered global recognition, the path ahead requires a more robust integration of digital tools to ensure inclusive and sustainable development. In this context, DPI serves as the infrastructure backbone for this transformation, enabling digital services to be accessible, affordable, secure, and equitable, especially for underserved and rural populations. Given this background, this chapter explores the role of DPI in advancing inclusive growth in India. It begins by conceptualizing DPI and its core components, followed by a theoretical framing of how such infrastructure intersects with inclusive growth. The chapter then draws upon key case studies, including Aadhaar, Jan Dhan Yojana, UPI, DigiLocker, UMANG, DIKSHA, and eSanjeevani, to illustrate real-world applications and outcomes. It also examines the barriers and risks, including the digital divide and data governance challenges, and offers policy recommendations for optimizing DPI's potential. Through this multidimensional analysis, the chapter argues that DPI, when inclusively designed and equitably implemented, can serve as the digital backbone of a developed India.

2. Objectives

DPI systems and tools enable essential services in the digital realm, much like roads or power lines function in the physical world. Acting as a unifying infrastructure layer, they can unlock new opportunities, enhance citizen participation, and drive inclusive and sustainable progress, making them indispensable to the country's long-term development goals. Based on this understanding, the objective of this chapter is to:

i. Assess the current landscape of DPI in India.
ii. Identify the significant challenges hindering the widespread and equitable adoption of DPI.
iii. Propose strategic recommendations to strengthen DPI frameworks.

3. Methodology

This study adopts a descriptive research design to explore the strategic role of DPI. A secondary research approach has been used, with qualitative content analysis applied to synthesize insights from various credible sources. These include government reports, academic journals, policy briefs, institutional publications, and relevant books. This method is suitable as the study evaluates large-scale national digital initiatives and their broader socio-economic impacts, rather than testing specific hypotheses.

4. Digital Public Infrastructure

DPI is envisioned as a digital ecosystem that various governmental and non-governmental stakeholders can utilize to perform core societal functions such as digital identity authentication, secure transactions, and seamless information exchange (Eaves and Rao 2025). It represents a transformative approach in public administration and digital governance. In the Indian context, DPI has emerged as a critical driver of digital transformation, playing a role similar to that of traditional infrastructure during industrial expansion. A key example is India Stack, a collection of widely used DPI components that work together to provide secure, paperless, cashless, and privacy-friendly access to services (Alonoso et al. 2023).

To better conceptualize how these systems function as an interconnected ecosystem, Kapoor and Watson (2023) identify five key categories within DPI:

i. **Digital Identity and Registries** – Incorporates digital identities for individuals and businesses, along with health and public credit registries, facilitating secure authentication.

ii. **E-signature, Public Key Infrastructure (PKI), and Consent** – Encompasses tools like digital signatures, PKI for document security, and standardized systems for managing electronic consent.

iii. **Digital Payments** – Covers interoperable systems for peer-to-peer payments, direct benefit transfers from government, utility bill payments, and electronic toll systems.

iv. **Data and Digital Credentials** – Involves open financial data through APIs, common data standards for official IDs, and AI models to promote broader and safer data reuse.

v. **Service Discovery and Transactions** – Supports seamless access to services like e-commerce, transportation, and online tax filing through open, connected digital platforms.

These interoperable layers form the backbone of India's digital transformation, much like traditional infrastructure during industrial expansion.

5. Theoretical Perspectives on DPI

To fully understand the role of Digital Public Infrastructure in advancing inclusive development, it is essential to go beyond its technological design and examine the theoretical perspectives that explain how people access, adopt, and benefit from such systems. Two influential frameworks, Ribot and Peluso's Theory of Access and Network Externalities Theory, offer valuable insights into the ways DPI shapes both individual empowerment and collective progress.

5.1 Theory of Access

Ribot and Peluso's Theory of Access provides a valuable framework for analyzing inclusion through DPI. According to their framework, access is not limited to formal rights or the availability of services; it is about the actual ability to benefit from them through structural and relational mechanisms such as access to technology, capital, knowledge, authority, and social identity (Ribot and Peluso 2003). They emphasize that access is better understood as a "bundle of powers" rather than the legalistic concept of a "bundle of rights."

The theory identifies two principal forms of access:

Rights-based access. This involves legally sanctioned claims such as property ownership or state-granted entitlements.

Structural and relational access. This encompasses broader social, economic, and institutional factors, including technology, capital, knowledge, identity, and authority, that determine who can truly benefit from resources.

In the context of DPI, both forms of access are crucial. Legal mechanisms, such as Aadhaar-enabled Direct Benefit Transfers or the right to use platforms like the Unified Payments Interface, may define participation, but they do not guarantee usage. Structural factors, including smartphone ownership, internet connectivity, and digital literacy, directly affect the ability of individuals to engage with these services. This perspective highlights that true digital inclusion requires more than granting access; it demands ensuring the power and capability to use digital technologies meaningfully.

5.2 Network Externalities Theory

While the theory of access focuses on individual-level empowerment, Network Externalities Theory explains the collective value generated as more users adopt a digital platform. As Katz and Shapiro (1985) argue, the utility a user derives from consuming a good or service increases as the number of other users grows. This principle is especially relevant to DPI, where widespread participation strengthens efficiency, reach, and interoperability.

This principle is evident across India's Digital Public Infrastructure, where platforms such as Aadhaar, UPI, DigiLocker, eSanjeevani, DIKSHA, and UMANG exemplify how increased adoption enhances both functionality and societal benefit.

As more users engage with these systems, their efficiency, reach, and interoperability improve, creating a feedback loop reinforcing inclusion and accessibility. As per the theory, each new user adds value not only for themselves but also for the ecosystem, making DPI a powerful vehicle for inclusive national development.

6. India's DPI Ecosystem

The global discourse surrounding DPIs has been significantly influenced by the success of India's world-class DPI. By leveraging this framework, India is well-positioned to promote digital inclusion, enhance the efficiency and transparency of service delivery, and stimulate innovation. India's DPI ecosystem enables secure, inclusive, and scalable delivery of services across diverse sectors, including finance, healthcare, education, and governance. India has taken a leadership role in advancing secure, interoperable DPI frameworks that expand access to essential public services (Teevan et al. 2025).

6.1 Digital Financial Inclusion Systems in India

6.1.1 Jan Dhan Yojana

Financial inclusion refers to the process of making formal financial services accessible, widely available, and usable for every segment of the population, ensuring no one is excluded from the economic mainstream (Sarma 2008). In this context, the Pradhan Mantri Jan Dhan Yojana serves as a cornerstone of the Indian government's inclusive development strategy, providing basic banking services to historically excluded communities (Chowhan and Pande 2014). PMJDY has grown into the world's largest financial inclusion initiative, completing a decade of transformative impact. According to the Press Information Bureau (2024b), over 53.14 crore beneficiaries have been brought into the banking system under this scheme, with total deposits reaching ₹2,31,236 crore, reflecting enhanced financial participation. These figures highlight the significant role of PMJDY in promoting financial inclusion, bridging socio-economic and geographic divides, and strengthening the financial foundations of the economically marginalized. Financial inclusion has a positive and significant impact on economic growth across Indian states, with PMJDY contributing modestly to this progress (Singh et al. 2021). Empirical evidence suggests that greater financial inclusion contributes significantly to a higher Human Development Index, as access to banking and financial services correlates with improvements in education, healthcare, and income levels (Yadav et al. 2020). Therefore, expanding the reach of financial services is not just an economic imperative but a developmental one that empowers citizens and uplifts overall well-being.

6.1.2 Unified Payments Interface (UPI)

UPI is a real-time payment platform enabling users to connect multiple bank accounts through a single mobile app. It enables uninterrupted instant fund transfers, revolutionizing how individuals and businesses transact. UPI has been instrumental in promoting financial inclusion, particularly for small businesses, street vendors, and migrant workers, by making digital payments simple, secure, and accessible.

Its adoption surged notably during the COVID-19 pandemic due to the heightened need for contactless transactions. As per the latest data by NPCI, UPI has processed 182.21 billion transactions worth ₹246.83 lakh crores in 2024. This consistent growth highlights UPI's deepening integration into India's evolving digital economy. Beyond domestic applications, UPI also has an international presence, operating in the UAE, Singapore, Bhutan, Nepal, Sri Lanka, France, and Mauritius, showcasing India's growing influence in global digital finance. UPI's simplicity, affordability, and extensive reach make it a powerful tool for expanding financial participation and driving India's digital transformation. It has fundamentally changed how financial transactions are conducted, positioning India at the forefront of digital payment innovation worldwide. By expanding financial access, bridging the digital divide, and empowering citizens, UPI contributes directly to building an inclusive, future-ready, and tech-driven economy.

6.2 Documentation and e-Governance

6.2.1 Aadhaar

Aadhaar, a biometric-based identification platform, forms the core of India's identity verification framework. Launched in 2009, it began India's Digital Public Infrastructure, representing an ambitious effort to digitally identify nearly 1.5 billion residents (Teevan et al. 2025). Before Aadhaar, citizens relied on disparate documents such as driving licenses and Below Poverty Line cards for identification, often excluding large population segments. Aadhaar introduced a transformative, inclusive solution by providing a universal biometric ID, thereby bringing previously undocumented individuals into the system and enabling more accurate, targeted delivery of public services (Rao and Nair 2019). By April 2025, a total of 141.88 crore Aadhaar numbers had been issued, establishing it as a crucial component of India's digital infrastructure and enabling citizens to access a wide range of services with greater ease and efficiency (PIB 2025). Aadhaar has significantly advanced individual-level access to welfare schemes, moving beyond household-based identification to empower women and marginalized individuals. Its integration across services like banking, subsidies, and social protection has expanded inclusion by enabling direct, transparent, and personalized benefit delivery (Desai and Manoharan 2024). Its universal identity framework empowers marginalized groups by reducing exclusion and ensuring targeted benefit delivery (Desai and Manoharan 2024).

6.2.2 Unified Mobile Application for New-age Governance (UMANG)

Introduced in 2017, UMANG was developed to promote mobile-based governance across India. It offers citizens a unified platform to access a wide range of e-Government services from central, state, and local government agencies nationwide. UMANG is a flagship initiative under the Digital India program, designed to improve ease of living by enabling citizens to access essential government services anytime and anywhere through a single, user-friendly app. The application supports multiple languages and is built to accommodate users with varying levels of digital literacy, thus playing a vital role in enhancing accessibility, service efficiency, and usability across diverse demographics (Chakraborty 2025). Its primary objective is to accelerate mobile-based governance and facilitate effective knowledge sharing, particularly supporting sustainable development in rural regions (Sekar and Rao 2018). The app aims to enhance convenience, reduce reliance on in-person visits to government offices, promote digital literacy, and ensure a secure, scalable, and reliable system for public service delivery. This reflects a broader shift in India's e-governance strategy from department-focused digitization to citizen-centric service integration (Dash and Jain 2024). The AI-driven features of the platform help minimize bureaucratic delays, enhance transparency, and build public trust by providing automated responses, analyzing citizen grievances, and ensuring efficient resolution processes (Srivastava and Sharma 2025). UMANG is not just a digital service platform; it is a cornerstone of India's digital transformation, enhancing interaction and trust between the government and its people, fostering digital inclusion, and promoting efficient, transparent, and inclusive governance.

6.2.3 DigiLocker

DigiLocker, an initiative under the Digital India program, has transformed how citizens interact with government services by offering secure digital access to official documents. Integrated with various government databases, it allows users to access welfare documents like ration cards, caste and income certificates, thereby reducing paperwork and enabling seamless eligibility verification for welfare schemes. Particularly for migrant workers, it supports entitlement portability across states, contributing to the vision of a unified national social registry. DigiLocker allows individuals to upload and securely store important documents such as PAN cards, passports, academic mark sheets, and degree certificates. With over 54.37 crore users, 2087 issuers, and 2606 requesters, DigiLocker has issued around 875.80 crore digital documents (DigiLocker n.d.). These digitally verified documents now hold the same legal status as physical ones, eliminating forgery concerns and simplifying service delivery. As an AI-integrated platform, DigiLocker enhances transparency and efficiency in governance through automated document processing, minimizing corruption and streamlining workflows (Srivastava and Sharma 2025). Its interoperability across various departments promotes a seamless digital ecosystem while simultaneously improving digital literacy and empowering citizens (Bagul et al. 2025). This digital approach enhances transparency and authenticity while significantly reducing red tape and curbing corruption (George and Viswambharam 2019). It fosters digital inclusion, enhances public service delivery, and strengthens trust in governance, which are key pillars of India's journey toward a technologically advanced, transparent, and inclusive future.

6.3 Health & Education

6.3.1 Digital Infrastructure for Knowledge Sharing (DIKSHA)

DIKSHA offers a unified digital platform for school education in India. DIKSHA includes 108 languages, 101 Indian and seven foreign, making learning resources accessible to a diverse population across all states and union territories. Each region adapts the platform's features to suit its local educational needs. DIKSHA aims to build an inclusive, technology-enabled learning ecosystem that provides personalized, engaging, and accessible educational experiences. It promotes both academic growth and personal development by leveraging innovative digital tools. The platform offers interactive features such as quizzes, simulations, and educational games, which enhance student engagement and learning outcomes while fostering inclusivity (Mandala and Pradhan 2024). Gamified learning environments have been shown to significantly increase student motivation and participation (Bicen and Kocakoyun 2018). Interactive elements like quizzes and simulations also aid in concept retention and foster deeper understanding, reinforcing the pedagogical effectiveness of DIKSHA (Wang 2020). DIKSHA contributes to building a digitally empowered and educated nation. By promoting inclusive, tech-driven education, it helps transform India into a knowledge-based, self-reliant economy.

6.3.2 eSanjeevani

eSanjeevani, India's national telemedicine service, is the world's largest digital healthcare initiative focused on primary care. It enables video consultations with doctors across specialties, providing accessible healthcare through two models: doctor-to-doctor consultations via Ayushman Bharat Health and Wellness Centres and patient-to-doctor services (OPD) accessible from home (Ministry of Health and Family Welfare n.d.). eSanjeevani paves the way for broader access to Universal Health Coverage and advances digital health equity. By 2022, over three crore people had benefited, with more than 1 lakh doctors onboarded nationwide (PIB 2022). The platform has been particularly effective in bridging rural healthcare gaps by offering affordable remote consultations. This digital initiative improves access to quality healthcare and embodies India's commitment to building a healthier, more equitable society. According to the World Health Organization, well-functioning health systems enhance population health, which in turn increases labor force participation and productivity. Health systems are also vital economic drivers, generating employment and producing health-related goods and services that contribute directly to economic growth.

7. Challenges

To accomplish the vision of inclusive growth, India must overcome several key challenges. Addressing these obstacles is essential for building a strong and sustainable future.

Digital Divide: The digital divide remains a critical barrier to the inclusive realization of developmental goals. While urban areas enjoy high-speed internet, many rural regions still lack basic connectivity (Mahida 2024). Despite being one of the world's largest and fastest-growing internet markets, India's internet penetration rate is just 55.3%, compared to nearly universal access in countries like the Netherlands, Norway, and Saudi Arabia (Basuroy 2025).

Cybersecurity Threats: While Indian DPI apps are generally accessible, user-friendly, and technically reliable, cybersecurity remains a pressing concern, as outdated security frameworks make these government apps vulnerable to cyberattacks (Bagul et al. 2025). These vulnerabilities, particularly evident in Aadhaar's repeated data breaches and weak oversight of interlinked databases, compromise sensitive citizen information, erode public trust, and limit the transformative potential of digital governance (Anand 2021).

Digital Literacy Gaps: Digital literacy in India remains low, especially among women and rural populations. Only 8.5% of rural women know how to use the internet, and less than 54% of women have personal mobile phones, with many unable to read SMS messages (Alonso et al. 2023). These challenges hinder the adoption of next-generation digital participation platforms, restricting inclusive digital engagement across the country.

Trust Deficit: Trust in the system and ease of access are crucial in encouraging the widespread implementation of DPI. Leaks and data misuse, both within core DPI systems and the applications built upon them, can undermine this trust and deter user adoption (Marskell 2023). Citizens are more likely to engage with digital services when processes are transparent, rights are protected, and privacy is respected. Without transparent processes and user-centric policies, citizens may remain skeptical of adopting digital services, especially when concerns around surveillance or misuse arise (Bagul et al. 2025).

Infrastructure Gaps: Infrastructure limitations remain a critical barrier to growth, particularly in rural areas, which undermine the accessibility and effectiveness of digital governance services. Such inequalities are especially concerning as they affect nearly 72% of the United Nations Sustainable Development Goals, perpetuating long-term disparities and restricting access to essential opportunities (Pandey et al. 2022). Moreover, a large section of the population is still unfamiliar with digital payment systems or lacks the requisite technology and supporting infrastructure to participate effectively (Kumar and Unnisa 2024).

8. Recommendations

Building an inclusive and future-ready digital ecosystem requires more than technological adoption; it demands a coordinated strategy integrating infrastructure, literacy, innovation, and governance. To fully harness the transformative potential of Digital Public Infrastructure (DPI), India must embrace a holistic strategy that addresses connectivity, literacy, security, and trust in equal measure. This begins with bridging the digital divide through expanded high-speed internet access in rural and remote regions and strengthening digital literacy, particularly among women, the elderly, and marginalized groups, through accurate information dissemination and alternative non-digital access modes for those facing literacy or physical challenges (Jain et al. 2023). Complementing these efforts, intuitive and user-friendly digital platforms supported by targeted outreach can accelerate adoption in underdeveloped areas (Sindakis and Showkat 2024). At the same time, leveraging Industry 4.0

technologies such as AI, IoT, and automation can transform public service delivery, enhance productivity, and reduce socio-economic disparities (Mahida 2024). Platforms like UMANG and MyGov India already illustrate this potential, where AI-enabled chatbots and analytics have streamlined grievance redressal, promoted transparency, and strengthened citizen trust (Srivastava and Sharma 2025). However, with rising cyber threats, adopting blockchain for secure data management and AI-driven fraud detection becomes essential to safeguard sensitive citizen information and reinforce trust (Bagul et al. 2025). Despite these advances, India's lack of a comprehensive data protection law remains a critical gap, underscoring the urgency of enacting a strong and enforceable cybersecurity framework to preserve the integrity of DPI systems. Ultimately, long-term success depends on creating a stable policy environment, fostering stakeholder engagement, and embedding robust grievance redressal mechanisms that ensure accountability and enable inclusive participation in the digital ecosystem (Rastogi et al. 2021).

9. Conclusion

Digital Public Infrastructure (DPI) stands as a foundational pillar in India's ambitious journey toward inclusive growth, efficient governance, and digital empowerment. This chapter has demonstrated that India's DPI ecosystem has fundamentally transformed the delivery of essential services across finance, healthcare, education, and governance. The study's first objective—to assess the current landscape of India's DPI—was achieved by analyzing major platforms such as Aadhaar, UPI, DigiLocker, UMANG, DIKSHA, and eSanjeevani. Together, these initiatives have fundamentally reshaped service delivery across finance, governance, education, and healthcare. By embedding principles of accessibility, interoperability, and openness, they extend benefits beyond urban centers and empower traditionally excluded groups, demonstrating India's progress in building a robust digital ecosystem. The theoretical perspectives of Ribot and Peluso's Theory of Access and Network Externalities Theory help explain these outcomes. DPI initiatives go beyond formal entitlements by actively reducing structural barriers such as limited identity, connectivity, or financial access, thereby enabling citizens to participate more fully in socio-economic systems. At the same time, platforms like UPI and DigiLocker illustrate network effects: as adoption grows, system utility increases, creating collective benefits that strengthen both individual empowerment and societal value.

The study addressed the second objective by identifying persistent challenges that hinder the widespread and equitable adoption of DPI. Despite these advancements, significant challenges persist, notably the digital divide and low digital literacy, especially among rural women, trust deficits due to recurring data breaches, and infrastructural gaps in underserved areas. These obstacles illustrate that access is not just about availability but also about the power to benefit, a core principle of the Theory of Access. Legal entitlements through Aadhaar or access to UPI are insufficient without addressing the structural and relational barriers, such as poor connectivity, low education, lack of digital awareness, and socio-economic exclusion. Moreover, these gaps constrain the positive externalities predicted by

Network Externalities Theory, as slower adoption in marginalized groups prevents the full realization of mutual network benefits, reducing overall system efficiency and societal value.

To bridge these gaps, India must adopt a human-centered digital strategy grounded in inclusive policy design, targeted digital literacy interventions, AI-driven public service delivery, and strong data protection legislation. These steps resonate with the theoretical imperative of not just enabling access through legal entitlement but also empowering meaningful usage through supportive structures. The diffusion of technology via AI and blockchain within DPI not only increases operational efficiency but also improves trust and legitimacy, a key relational mechanism for expanding actual access. Similarly, broader user adoption catalyzed through responsive design and affordable infrastructure enhances network effects, reinforcing system value for every additional user and expanding the reach and resilience of the ecosystem.

Ultimately, DPI must be positioned not just as a technological framework, but as a socio-technical infrastructure aimed at transforming lives. The future of India's digital transformation hinges on its ability to convert legal inclusion into substantive empowerment and cultivate a networked digital society where every additional participant strengthens the collective good. A digitally inclusive India is not just a developmental milestone; it is a strategic imperative for equitable growth, resilient governance, and global leadership.

References

Arsić, M. (2020). Impact of digitalisation on economic growth, productivity and employment. Econ. Themes 58(4): 431–457.

Alonso, C., Bhojwani, T., Hanedar, E., Prihardini, D., Una, G. and Zhabska, K. (2023). Stacking up the benefits: lessons from India's digital journey. IMF Work. Pap. 23: 1–45.

Anand, N. (2021). New principles for governing Aadhaar: improving access and inclusion, privacy, security, and identity management. J. Sci. Policy Gov. 18: 1–14.

Arora, S., Huda, R. K., Verma, S., Khetan, M. and Sangwan, R. K. (2024). Challenges, barriers, and facilitators in telemedicine implementation in India: a scoping review. Cureus 16: e67388.

Basuroy, T. (2025). Internet usage in India - statistics and facts. Statista. https://www.statista.com/topics/2157/internet-usage-in-india/#topicOverview.

Bagul, A., Chaudhary, R., Mahajan, S. and Shandilya, S. (2025). Digital governance for citizen engagement: an analysis of citizen-centered applications in India. Otoritas: J. Ilmu Pemerintahan 15(1).

Bicen, H. and Kocakoyun, S. (2018). Perceptions of students for gamification approach: Kahoot as a case study. Int. J. Emerg. Technol. Learn. (iJET) 13(2): 72–93.

Chakraborty, D. (2025). Factors influencing the adoption of UMANG apps in India: evidence and perspective. Int. J. Electron. Gov. Res. 21: 1–16.

Chowhan, S. S. and Pande, J. C. (2014). Pradhan Mantri Jan Dhan Yojana: a giant leap towards financial inclusion. Int. J. Res. Manag. Bus. Stud. 1(4): Oct–Dec.

Dash, S. B. and Jain, A. (2024). Experience from e-government services: a topic model approach. IIM Kozhikode Soc. Manag. Rev.

DigiLocker. n.d. DigiLocker: Statistics. Retrieved July 04, 2025, from https://www.digilocker.gov.in/statistics.

Desai, A. and Manoharan, A. P. (2024). Digital transformation and public administration: the impacts of India's digital public infrastructure. Int. J. Public Adm. 47: 575–578.

Eaves, D. and Rao, K. (2025). Digital public infrastructure: a framework for conceptualisation and measurement. IIPP Work. Pap. 2025-01. UCL Institute for Innovation and Public Purpose. https://www.ucl.ac.uk/bartlett/public-purpose/wp2025-01.

George, M. A. and Viswambharam, A. M. (2019). Digi-Locker – an overview. Int. J. Res. Anal. Rev. 6(1): 889–894. http://ijrar.com/.

Katz, M. L. and Shapiro, C. (1985). Network externalities, competition, and compatibility. Am. Econ. Rev. 75: 424–440.

Kapoor, A. and Watson, E. (2023). Defining the digital public infrastructure approach. ThinkTwenty (T20) India 2023 – Official Engagement Group of G20. https://t20ind.org/research/defining-the-digital-publicinfrastructure-approach/.

Mandala, P. and Pradhan, P. (2024). Innovative strategies on DIKSHA portal: An experimental study of impact on inclusive student engagement. International Journal of Religion 5(10): 1068–1075.

Marskell, J., Marin, G. and Varghese, M. (2024). Digital public infrastructure: transforming service delivery across sectors. Chapter 4. *In*: Digital Progress and Trends Report 2023. United Nations Development Programme (UNDP).

Mahida, R. G. (2024). A leading the way: Sustainable development and economic dynamics in Viksit Bharat@2047. Vidhyayana – An International Multidisciplinary Peer-Reviewed E-Journal 9(si2). ISSN 2454-8596.

Pandey, B., Brelsford, C. and Seto, K. C. (2022). Infrastructure inequality is a characteristic of urbanization. Proc. Natl. Acad. Sci. USA 119: e2119890119.

Press Information Bureau. (2022, March 25). Health ministry's flagship telemedicine service – "eSanjeevani" records 3 Crore tele-consultations (Release ID: 1809007). Ministry of Health and Family Welfare, Government of India. https://pib.gov.in/PressReleasePage.aspx?PRID=1809007.

Press Information Bureau. (2024a). Empowering youth for a developed India: Viksit Bharat Young Leaders Dialogue. Retrieved from https://pib.gov.in/PressReleaseIframePage.aspx?PRID=1985077.

Press Information Bureau. (2024b). Pradhan Mantri Jan Dhan Yojana (PMJDY)—National Mission for Financial Inclusion completes a decade of successful implementation (Release ID: 2049231). Ministry of Finance, Government of India. https://www.pib.gov.in/PressReleasePage.aspx?PRID=2049231.

Press Information Bureau. (2024). UPI: Revolutionizing digital payments in India (Release ID: 2057013). Ministry of Finance, Government of India. https://www.pib.gov.in/PressReleasePage.aspx?PRID=2057013.

Press Information Bureau. (2025, February 1). Digital infrastructure in India: Supporting the dream of a Viksit Bharat. Retrieved from https://www.pib.gov.in/PressReleaseIframePage.aspx?PRID=2098487.

Press Information Bureau. (2025, June 12). The digital decade: India's journey towards a tech-led future. Government of India. https://www.pib.gov.in/PressNoteDetails.aspx?id=154635andNoteId=154635andModuleId=3.

Rastogi, S., Panse, C., Sharma, A. and Bhimavarapu, V. M. (2021). Unified Payment Interface (UPI): a digital innovation and its impact on financial inclusion and economic development. Univ. J. Account. Finance 9: 518–530.

Rao, U. and Nair, V. (2019). Aadhaar: governing with biometrics. South Asia 42: 469–481. https://doi.org/10.1080/00856401.2019.1595343.

Ribot, J. C. and Peluso, N. L. (2003). A theory of access. Rural Sociol. 68: 153–181.

Sarma, M. (2008). Index of financial inclusion (Working Paper No. 215). Indian Council for Research on International Economic Relations (ICRIER), New Delhi.

Sindakis, S. and Showkat, G. (2024). The digital revolution in India: bridging the gap in rural technology adoption. J. Innov. Entrep. 13: 1–28.

Sekar, K. and Rao, V. K. (2018). Umang mobile app digital India knowledge indicators towards sustainable development: an overview. Int. J. Inf. Mov. 2: 156–161.

Singh, B. P., Kumari, A., Sharma, T. and Malhotra, A. (2021). Financial inclusion, Pradhan Mantri Jan Dhan Yojna Scheme and economic growth: evidence from Indian states. Econ. Notes 50: e12186.

Srivastava, M. and Sharma, N. (2025). E-governance and AI integration: a roadmap for smart governance practices. Scholars J. 2(1).

Teevan, C., Pouyé, R. and Kamath, G. (2025). From India Stack to EuroStack: reconciling approaches to sovereign digital infrastructure. Discussion Pap. No. 384. European Centre for Development Policy Management (ECDPM).

Vijay Kumar, S. and Unnisa, N. (2024). A study on UPI transactions in India. Int. J. Adv. Bus. Manag. Res. 1: 8–22.

Wang, S. (2020). Interactive learning tools and student engagement: a study of online quizzes and simulations. J. Educ. Technol. Syst. 48(3): 325–340.

Yadav, V., Singh, S. K., Velan, N. and Aftab, M. A. (2020). Impact assessment of Pradhan Mantri Jan-Dhan Yojana in augmenting financial inclusion in India: a district-level analysis. MPRA Pap. No. 105064. Munich Personal RePEc Archive. https://mpra.ub.uni-muenchen.de/105064/.

Chapter 16

From Skills to Sustainability

Women's Empowerment in the Entrepreneurial Ecosystem

Pranati Dash[1] and *Kunal Gaurav*[2,*]

1. Introduction

Globally, entrepreneurship among women has gained recognition as an essential driver of economic advancement and sustainable progress. Today, women are becoming entrepreneurs not just for financial reasons, but to augment their position and influence in society and the economy. Leading global development frameworks, particularly the Sustainable Development Goals (SDGs), strongly emphasise women's economic empowerment as a cornerstone for gender equality and community strength. SDG 5 strongly advocates the need for women's equal economic participation, and SDG 8 highlights the necessity of skill development and entrepreneurial opportunities for women. These international priorities demonstrate the need to understand how women's business activities can transcend basic survival needs and personal growth, gradually developing into established enterprises that foster enduring economic well-being and complete empowerment.

Nowadays, many state-led and community-based initiatives are working towards supporting women's entrepreneurship through skill development. Many government-led programmes, non-government organisations, self-help groups, and private training institutions are investing time and resources in providing vocational

[1] Assistant Professor, Balaji Institute of Modern Management, Sri Balaji University, Pune, India.
[2] Professor, School of Business, Dr. Vishwanath Karad MIT World Peace University, Pune, India.
Email: pranati.dash11@gmail.com
* Corresponding author: Kunalgaurav2006@gmail.com

DOI: 10.1201/9781003736158-20

training, financial and digital literacy, as well as managerial capabilities for women. These efforts are extremely relevant in rural and semi-urban setups where women have limited access to education and face many constraints when it comes to market opportunities. After gaining new skills, many women have started their micro-enterprises in various sectors like food processing, handicrafts, garments, retailing, and home-based services. However, literature indicates that skills do not always translate into sustainable entrepreneurial excellence. Many women-led initiatives remain confined, informal, and vulnerable to market fluctuations and have limited access to credit facilities. Another problem is that the kind of entrepreneurial networks they can explore is usually inadequate; further, they have to face many socio-cultural constraints. A far deeper issue is highlighted through this scenario, as the transition of skills to sustainability relies heavily on the quality of the entrepreneurial ecosystem in and around women-led enterprises. Entrepreneurial ecosystem here means the system of institutional, technological, financial, and social provisions that are essential in creating and sustaining enterprises. In the case of women, this ecosystem comprises some formal components like access to finance, government support schemes, and digital platforms, in addition to many informal elements like family support, social norms, freedom of mobility, and appropriate peer networks. Women are more likely to utilise their skills efficiently when all these elements of the ecosystem are enabling. On the contrary, if these elements are feeble or restrictive, the welfare expected from skill development also remains constricted to short-term benefits or may help generate supplementary income for them, but it does not evolve into growth-oriented enterprises.

Another critical dimension of this transition is women's agency and self-efficacy. While agency refers to the ability to make choices and act upon them, self-efficacy connotes confidence in one's own capabilities. Even when women are equipped with technical or managerial skills, fundamental barriers like restrictive gender norms, household responsibilities, and lack of ownership rights may bound their decision-making power in entrepreneurial activities. In order to strengthen agency, skill enhancement is not the only criterion; a supportive social environment is also essential. Providing mentoring experiences, positive role models, and collective platforms where women can share knowledge and issues will be really beneficial.

Of late, the proliferation of digital technologies has opened innovative opportunities for women to access markets, establish customer networks, and manage business operations with more flexibility. They have better options to manage domestic responsibilities while operating businesses from home with the aid of online marketplaces, digital payment systems, and social media-based micro-entrepreneurship. However, this digital inclusion is not even; women may not take advantage of these tools and, in turn, the emerging avenues without proper training in digital skills.

In this context, a conceptual framework is needed to explain the interaction of skill development with women's agency, social support systems, and the prevailing entrepreneurial ecosystem to gain sustainable enterprise outcomes. This chapter addresses that gap by examining the transition from skills to sustainability by emphasising the interdependence between capability-building initiatives and the enablers in the form of environments that support long-term entrepreneurial success. It makes arguments that women's empowerment through entrepreneurship progresses most effectively when skill development is integrated with supportive ecosystem components like access to finance, network-building platforms, institutional support, and community recognition.

The following sections review existing literature on women's entrepreneurship and skill-building. It also summarises the conceptual details of women's empowerment and sustainable enterprise development. Ultimately, it presents a framework that aligns skills, agency, social capital, ecosystem support, and sustainable outcomes.

2. Literature Review

2.1 Women's Entrepreneurship and Economic Participation

Women's entrepreneurship is considered an important driver for inclusive growth, community-level development, and employment generation. In many emerging economies, enterprises owned by women contribute to household welfare and local economic activity, simultaneously enhancing the status and decision-making participation of women (Kabeer 1999, Hallward-Driemeier 2011). However, it is a matter of great concern that entrepreneurship remains gendered, with women being concentrated mostly in small, home-based, and informal business activities. Recent studies show that they face disadvantages in accessing markets, institutional support structures, and productive resources, which can limit their ability for enterprise growth (Kuran and Khabbaz 2025). Recent global monitoring indicates an upward growth in women start-up activity, especially since the early 2000s, and shows a clear momentum in 2021–23; yet gaps with men still persist and are widest in high-income economies (GEM 2023).

Women's time allocation, mobility, and occupational roles are still influenced by gender norms. These social constraints interact with operational limitations like lower asset ownership and fewer networking opportunities, which in turn shape the types of enterprises women can initiate (Huq 2022). Thus, for women, while the motivation to start entrepreneurship may stem from aspirations for financial independence or personal agency, the ultimate outcomes are significantly influenced by the socio-economic environment.

Significant shortfall in legal protections also affects mobility, entrepreneurship, asset and care, it also highlights a factual gap in implementation between laws on paper and practice as is evidenced in Women, Business and the Law 2022 & 2024 documents (World Bank 2022, 2024). All these constraints lead to weaker business entry, survival, and growth for women entrepreneurs, and closing this gender gap would substantially increase global output.

2.2 Skill Development as a Foundation for Entrepreneurial Entry

There are no two words about the significance of skill development, as it is recognised as the foundation for women's entrepreneurial commitment. Gaining the required skills can not only improve product quality but also enhance confidence and support entry into commercial markets. However, studies demonstrate that skills alone are not sufficient for sustained entrepreneurial success. Without supporting mechanisms like market linkages, financial resources, or mentorship, women may struggle to transform skills into practicable and scalable enterprises (Al Mamun et al. 2019). Global monitoring shows that skill building translates to enterprise outcomes in a more reliable manner when it is paired with market access, mentorship, and finance, compared to when it is offered as stand-alone training (GEM 2023). Recent training programmes commonly focus on technical skills like tailoring, food processing, artisanal crafts, etc., and business management skills such as accounting, pricing, and customer relations (Singh and Paliwal 2020). Likewise, the release by the Organisation for Economic Co-operation and Development underlines the growing importance of digital and financial literacy as essential skills to participate in contemporary business environments (OECD 2021). Hence, it is prudent to integrate skill development programmes with the provision of a broader ecosystem to achieve enterprise sustainability (GEM 2023).

2.3 Agency and Self-Efficacy in Women's Entrepreneurial Success

As discussed earlier, agency and self-efficacy play a pivotal role in determining entrepreneurial outcomes and are crucial behavioural determinants of start-ups. Here, agency reflects the ability to act on one's own goals, and self-efficacy means the confidence one has in one's capabilities (Bandura 1997). A higher level of self-efficacy in women is demonstrated through their self-reliance in decision-making, adaptability, and resilience in managing business-related encounters (Minniti and Naudé 2010).

But needless to mention here, agency is shaped by the social environment. Having a supportive family, positive role models, and engagement in meaningful peer group interactions strengthens agency (Allendorf 2012). Activities that combine training with mentoring and collaborative learning are proved to be more effective in enhancing women's confidence building and leadership capacity. Recent global evaluations indicate that these subtle levers perform most effectively when reinforced by enabling laws and finance so that empowered choices can also be executed (GEM 2023).

2.4 The Entrepreneurial Ecosystem and Its Influence

The entrepreneurial ecosystem comprises institutions, policies, financial systems, and social structures that shape enterprise development. For women, key ecosystem elements include:

- Access to financial institutions and credit schemes
- Mentoring networks and incubation support
- Market linkages through cooperatives or digital platforms
- Supportive policy frameworks that encourage women's business participation

Studies show that the benefits received by women tend to be higher when the components of the ecosystem are integrated instead of functioning in silos (Brush and Greene 2022). Market access for women is increased because of the possibility of reaching customers through digital platforms. However, there is a need for imparting digital skills to take advantage of such opportunities, and inclusion is still uneven according to UN entities and the International Telecommunications Union (UN Women 2022).

Women's enterprise sustainability depends on coordinated ecosystem elements: finance, policy and regulation, market linkages, data, and support infrastructure. Some recent developments are noteworthy here. The WE Finance Code is starting some common practices like sex-disaggregated data, leadership accountability, and country level rollouts to narrow down the credit gaps (We-Fi and World Bank 2023). Similarly, the Women, Business and the Law 2024 includes some implementation diagnostics to the legal index. It clearly shows that reforms do not automatically trickle down to opportunities for women without enforcement and complementary services (World Bank 2022).

Thus, the ecosystem literature is shifting from isolated interventions to integrated designs to link skills, finance, legal reforms, and digital inclusion (GEM 2023).

2.5 *Social Capital and Network Support*

Social capital, i.e., peer groups, industry associations, accelerators, and community organisations, facilitates information flow, credibility, and market access, and are important enablers of entrepreneurship. They also accelerate mutual learning and provide emotional support (Yetim 2008). However, only closed or localised networks can restrict access to varied opportunities. Increasing participation of women in broader entrepreneurial networks may foster enterprise growth and development (Balcar et al. 2024). Recent GEM evidence indicates growing involvement of women in high-potential segments, but it also confirms that such access still remains unequal (GEM 2023). There is scope for digital communities to broaden the reach of women, but digital safety and affordability still create bottlenecks, and bridging this division is a conventional policy priority.

2.6 *Barriers to Sustainability in Women-Led Enterprises*

In the context of this study, sustainability means the ability of any enterprise to continue operating while withstanding challenges and expanding over a period of time. Enterprises led by women often face innumerable barriers to sustainability. A few major points are:

Financial constraints: Access to finance is a persistent challenge for women entrepreneurs. Most of the time they have to depend on small, short-term loans and may lack the required collateral to gain access to formal lending institutions (World Bank 2022). Gradually there is improvement in this condition through the implementation of microfinance and self-help group models, but the loan amounts are not always adequate for scaling enterprises (Ghosh et al. 2018). The WE Finance Code launched in 2023 has committed financial service providers, regulators, and development banks to sex-disaggregated data and new product design for women-led medium and small-scale enterprises (We-Fi and World Bank 2023).

Market access challenge: Having limited access to broader markets can restrict business growth. In various contexts, women rely on local consumption markets having limited purchasing power. Inadequate knowledge about branding, packaging, pricing, and consumer outreach can definitely affect profitability (Hemalatha et al. 2013). The Global Entrepreneurship Monitor report shows uneven participation of women in high-growth and export-oriented ventures (GEM 2023).

Care and social norms: Women play diverse domestic roles in terms of household responsibilities and caregiving, and face multiple social expectations. All these issues restrict their participation in business networks and external markets, which incidentally shape their entrepreneurial choices and growth trajectory (De Bruin et al. 2007). These frictions are reflected in legal and policy gaps highlighted by Women, Business and the Law 2024, revolving around parenthood, workplace protection, and entrepreneurship (World Bank 2022).

Information and Network Gaps: Business entrepreneurial networks facilitate access to information, guidance, and connections. However, women are mostly underrepresented in these kind of networks, which reduces opportunities for collaborative learning and market expansion (Prasad et al. 2013).

There may be many more barriers, but the aforementioned ones are found to have the greatest impact on women-led enterprises, and they highlight the criticality of providing environmental support alongside skill-building initiatives to improve the situation and enable women entrepreneurs to grow sustainably. Table 1 encapsulates the prominent barriers, their root causes and the desired support strategies to overcome those.

Table 1. Barriers and Corresponding Support Measures.

Challenge Faced	**Root Cause**	**Support Strategy**
Limited access to finance	Collateral requirements, institutional risk perceptions	Tailored loan products, digital credit, and group guarantees
Low negotiation confidence	Restricted public engagement and mobility norms	Mentorship, exposure visits, and leadership development
Limited market access	Localised demand and constrained mobility	Digital marketplace linkages and procurement integration
Business isolation	Weak network participation	Strengthened peer groups and women's associations
Regulatory complexity	Limited compliance awareness	Simplified registration and local enterprise facilitation

Source: Developed by the Authors

2.7 Recent Trends in Research and Policy (2019–2025)

There has been a steady recovery in women's entrepreneurial activities post-pandemic shock, as highlighted in many recent global studies; still, there is notable heterogeneity across regions and income levels. The Global Entrepreneurship Monitor report 2023–24 documents growing start-up activity among women in many economies and notices a significant presence in export-related and high-growth undertakings (GEM 2023). The finance-capability link is one of the central themes in current literature. Latest cross-country analysis from the OECD and the **Global Women's Entrepreneurship Policy Network** (2025) highlights the credit gap for women-centred organisations and the importance of digital financial literacy for activating formal banking and fintech channels. The same work mentions the evolving WE Finance Code as a coordinated data and shared accountability mechanism to remove systemic constraints while accessing finance (OECD 2021).

Policy and ecosystem research also emphasise **legal and regulatory reforms** as foundational. The **World Bank's Women, Business and the Law** programme works to track legal constraints on women's economic participation. The Gender Strategy 2024–2030 increased its targets for improving women's access to broadband, social protection, and capital. These interventions are being scaled or expanded more widely to strengthen women's entrepreneurial participation. These priorities align with the observed relationship between gender-equal laws and improved outcomes for women-owned enterprises (World Bank 2022).

Even though digitalisation is identified as a major driver in recent studies, the literature also speaks of the dual reality. Digital marketplaces, payments, and social media reduce mobility constraints and open new customer segments, but there is a distinct and observable division when it comes to access, affordability, and safety, which can diminish these gains. **UN Women** and related evidences report significant **gender gaps in mobile internet use** in LMICs and call for targeted capability-building and safety-by-design measures on platforms. Exploratory report based on the **Cherie Blair Foundation for Women** surveys highlights **online harassment** and the **cost of data** as practical barriers that may reduce women's digital visibility and market reach (UN Women 2022).

The expansion of **gender-lens investing (GLI)** and **impact capital** directed towards women-led enterprises can be considered as one of the recent trends which balances the situation. The Gender Lens Investing Insights Report 2024 (**GIIN 2024**) has recorded a growing share of portfolios with noteworthy allocations to women-led investors. Moreover, new institutional policies like **Gender Lens Investing Policy** formalise gender outcomes in investment decision-making. These developments are mirrored by results such as **We-Fi** and blended-finance facilities that channel capital and technical assistance to women-owned Small & Medium Enterprises.

Ultimately, the post-pandemic literature points to **capability bundles** rather than single interventions. Reviews and evidence papers (**We-Fi 2025**) recommend pairing **skills and mentoring** with **market linkages, childcare solutions, and legal reforms**, which reflects a shift from isolated training to designing an **integrated ecosystem**. This aligns with ecosystem-focused scholarship that frames women's entrepreneurship outcomes as the result of coordinated action among finance, policy, networks, and digital infrastructure.

3. Objective of the Study

The primary objective of this study is to explore the relevance of women's entrepreneurial success as a means to their empowerment. This study analyses the role of skill development as foundational resources that influence entrepreneurial entry. Further, it explains how agency and decision-making power evolve within an entrepreneurial context. After an in-depth evaluation of the importance of social capital and the entrepreneurial ecosystem, the study proposes a conceptual framework that links skill development, agency, social capital, and ecosystem support to sustainable outcomes in enterprises led by women.

4. Conceptual Foundation

Women's entrepreneurship can be comprehended as the outcome of the interaction between individual competencies and the environment in which these enterprise activities are embedded. While skill development provides women with the basic knowledge and expertise needed for productive engagement in economic activities, the translation of these skills into sustainable enterprises depends on agency, social support, and various other conditions prevalent in the entrepreneurial ecosystem. As discussed through the literature review, the conceptual framework for this study adopts five interrelated constructs, namely: Capability Building, Agency, Social Capital, Ecosystem Support, and Sustainable Enterprise Outcomes.

4.1 Capability Building (Skill Development)

The process through which women gain the requisite knowledge—technical, managerial, financial, and digital—that is essential to initiate and manage an enterprise is known as capacity building. Skills develop the range of activities women can undertake and enhance their ability to produce, market, and deliver goods and services consistently. Training to gain knowledge about digital platforms, online payments, pricing, and branding is extremely relevant when market channels are diversifying.

However, skills represent **potential capacity**, not guaranteed outcomes. In the absence of any means to apply these capabilities in actual economic settings, the benefits are limited. Hence, capacity building can be considered as a foundational, yet incomplete condition for enterprise success.

4.2 Agency and Entrepreneurial Self-Efficacy

The ability to make a goal and then act upon it is agency. The belief in one's capacity to perform entrepreneurial tasks is considered enterprise self-efficacy. The prevalent socio-cultural norms, household dynamics, and exposure to role models shape agency. Similarly, proper coaching, mentoring, and peer support have been proven beneficial in strengthening confidence and risk-taking ability. Thus, agency functions as the **link** that allows skills to be exercised meaningfully in enterprise contexts.

4.3 Social Capital and Collective Support

Social capital refers to the networks and relationships that provide information, encouragement, trust, and cooperation. Group-based platforms like self-help groups, cooperatives, women's associations, and digital communities play a significant role in expanding access to shared knowledge and market connections. It also reduces remoteness, supports learning, and many a time substitutes for formal advisory services. It also strengthens agency by providing recognition and validation from peers. Stronger social capital ensures that women are more likely to engage with wider markets and pursue enterprise growth.

4.4 Entrepreneurial Ecosystem Support

The entrepreneurial ecosystem comprises institutions, market linkages, financial architecture, and policy frameworks, all of which influence enterprise formation and continuity. Access to credit, simplified regulatory procedures, digital infrastructure, incubation platforms, and mentoring schemes are achieved through ecosystem support. If the ecosystem is empowering, transaction costs are reduced and enterprise sustainability is incentivised. On the contrary, if the ecosystem is fragmented or insufficient, the benefits of skills and agency may not be translated into sustained enterprise activity. Thus, the ecosystem influences whether women-led enterprises remain merely survival-oriented or become growth-oriented.

4.5 Sustainable Enterprise Outcomes

In the context of this study, sustainability in women led enterprises refer to continuity, stability of income, improvement of livelihood, scalability, and ultimately contributing to community development. Ideal outcomes of sustainability are possible when skills, agency, social capital and ecosystem support reinforce each other. This perspective

Table 2. Key Constructs and Their Definitions.

Construct	Explanation	Relevance in Women's Entrepreneurship
Capability Building (Skills)	Acquisition of technical, managerial, financial, and digital competencies.	Enables women to undertake and manage enterprise activities.
Agency & Entrepreneurial Self-Efficacy	Confidence and decision-making capacity to act on entrepreneurial intentions.	Converts skills into active enterprise participation and risk-taking.
Social Capital & Networks	Peer groups, collectives, community ties, and professional networks.	Strengthens access to information, support, and market linkages.
Ecosystem Support	Finance systems, policy environment, digital platforms, incubation support.	Determines how effectively women can expand and sustain enterprises.
Sustainable Enterprise Outcomes	Stable income, continuity, adaptability and community-level value creation.	Represents long-term impact of entrepreneurship.

Source: Developed by the Authors

shifts the focus from entrepreneurship as a single act of business formation to entrepreneurship as a process of capability use within supportive conditions. The relationships between the framework constructs, their meaning and relevance in the context of women's entrepreneurship are systematically presented in Table 2.

5. Conceptual Framework

The proposed framework gives a reasonable explanation of the way skill development of women contributes to sustainable entrepreneurial outcomes upon receiving appropriate support from agency, social capital, and a conducive enterprise ecosystem. The logic of this framework is sequential, while it recognises the interdependence of personal capabilities and environmental support structures.

5.1 Capability Building as the Starting Point

Capability building refers to the acquisition of technical, managerial, digital, and financial skills relevant to enterprise creation and management. Women achieve the means to participate in productive activities, improve product or service quality, and manage business operations with greater efficiency because of skill acquisition. Skill development initiatives also introduce women to market-focused knowledge, such as costing, pricing, branding, and customer engagement. However, capability building alone does not ensure enterprise sustainability. There are instances of many trained women who do not enter entrepreneurship, and even those who start enterprises may remain limited to only low-revenue activities. The framework therefore positions capability building as a necessary but not sufficient condition, which requires further enabling factors to translate into meaningful enterprise performance.

5.2 Agency and Entrepreneurial Self-Efficacy as a Mediating Mechanism

As per the understanding of this study, agency and entrepreneurial self-efficacy mediate the transition from skill acquisition to enterprise sustainability. Agency symbolises a woman's ability to make decisions regarding the business, allocate resources, negotiate with buyers and suppliers, and take initiative in market engagement. Entrepreneurial self-efficacy reflects their confidence in handling uncertainty, interacting with customers, and solving operational challenges. Even when skills are present, limited decision-making power or low confidence may limit entrepreneurial action. Consequently, agency acts as the connection that enables the utilisation of capabilities in practice. Strengthening agency requires not only knowledge but also psychological confidence, recognition, and supportive social environments. Mentoring, exposure, and role-model interactions are also observed to support this development of agency more effectively.

5.3 Social Capital as a Moderating Influence on Agency

The effect of agency on sustainable enterprise outcomes is augmented through social capital. Surrounding networks, peer groups, and community organisations provide encouragement, shared learning, and access to suppliers and markets. Social capital reduces isolation and creates channels for business information and referrals. The confidence gained through agency is more likely to convert into productive entrepreneurial actions when women are part of active networks. On the contrary, women with agency but without access to networks may experience barriers while approaching new markets or negotiating business terms. Therefore, social capital strengthens the relationship between agency and enterprise sustainability by providing supportive relational structures and playing a moderating role in this framework.

5.4 Entrepreneurial Ecosystem Support as a Moderator of Capability – Agency Conversion

Entrepreneurial ecosystem comprises of policies, financial systems, market connections, digital infrastructure, regulatory environments, and institutional platforms. This support moderates the effect of capability building on agency. When financial services, formalisation procedures, digital marketplaces, and training institutions are accessible and responsive, women are in a better position to exercise autonomy and apply their skills confidently. When these structures are weak, even skilled women may be deprived of the means to channelise their capabilities. Thus, a supportive entrepreneurial ecosystem enhances the likelihood that skills translate into agency-driven enterprise participation. This study highlights the importance of aligning training programmes with credit facilities, incubation support, and simplified regulatory processes.

5.5 Sustainable Enterprise Outcomes as the Resulting Condition

Sustainable enterprise outcomes refer to the ability of businesses owned by women to generate steady income, sustain operations over time, acclimatise to changing market conditions, and create socio-economic value for different households and communities. Sustainability also includes non-financial achievements like prolonged decision-making power, mobility, and community recognition. The framework suggests that sustainability is most likely to prevail when capability building, agency development, social capital, and ecosystem support interact with each other constructively. This movement reflects a transition from subsistence-based enterprise activity to growth-oriented and durable economic participation.

5.6 The Integrated Nature of the Framework

The framework should be regarded as an integrated system rather than a linear progression as illustrated through Figure 1. Capability building influences agency, but agency also encourages further learning. In a similar fashion, social capital supports agency, but agency also happens to advance women's participation in networks. Ecosystem support strengthens all relationships, and sustainable outcomes translate into higher self-efficacy and recognition, thereby reinforcing agency and culminating in empowerment. The model captures this dynamic interplay while maintaining conceptual clarity through the primary and moderated pathways.

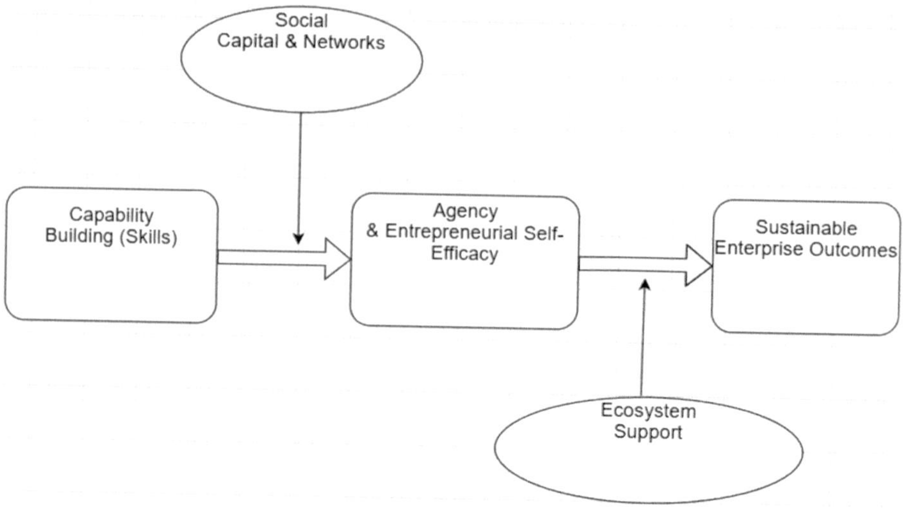

Figure 1. Showing the integrated Framework. Source: Developed by the Authors.

6. Discussion & Conclusion

Women's entrepreneurship has huge potential to advance inclusive and sustainable development. However, the transition from skills training to long-term enterprise sustainability still remains irregular. This study contends that capability building does not suffice unless it is accompanied by reinforced agency, supportive social networks, and an enabling ecosystem. The conceptual framework presented here contributes to the ongoing discourse by clarifying how these elements interact both linearly and through reinforcing relationships. The framework explicitly positions **agency and entrepreneurial self-efficacy as the mediating mechanism** through which skills translate into entrepreneurial behaviour, while **social capital and ecosystem support** operate as moderating situations that influence the degree to which agency may lead to sustainable enterprise outcomes.

This integrated perspective shifts the focus from viewing women's entrepreneurship as an individual endeavour to understanding it as **an interpersonal and context-dependent process**. Sustainable outcomes emerge not only from what women know and can do, but also from the degree of autonomy they hold, the networks they access, and the established environment that shapes the cost and feasibility of entrepreneurial action. By highlighting the reinforcing feedback between sustainable outcomes and continued growth in agency, social capital, and capability enhancement, the framework recognises that women's entrepreneurship evolves dynamically over time.

The chapter shows practical implications for policy and programme design, emphasising the importance of synchronized support mechanism that align training, finance access, market linkages, mentoring, and regulatory simplification.

The insights offered here contribute to a more holistic understanding of women's entrepreneurship and provide a foundation for designing interventions that foster **resilient, growth-oriented, and well-grounded women-led enterprises.**

References

Allendorf, K. (2012). Women's agency and the quality of family relationships in India. Popul. Res. Policy Rev. 31: 187–206.

Al Mamun, A., Fazal, S. A. and Muniady, R. (2019). Entrepreneurial knowledge, skills, competencies and performance: A study of micro-enterprises in Kelantan, Malaysia. Asia Pac. J. Innov. Entrep. 13: 29–48.

Balcar, J., Johnson Filipová, L., Brixiová Schwidrowski, Z. and Sinha, P. (2024). Networking increases the probability of women's start-ups in EMDEs. J. Dev. Stud. 60: 1071–1087.

Bandura, A. (1997). Self-efficacy: The Exercise of Control. W.H. Freeman, New York, USA.

De Bruin, A., Brush, C. G. and Welter, F. (2007). Advancing a framework for coherent research on women's entrepreneurship. Entrep. Theory Pract. 31: 323–339.

GEM. (2023). Women's Entrepreneurship Report 2023/24. Global Entrepreneurship Monitor, London, UK.

Ghosh, P. K., Ghosh, S. K. and Chowdhury, S. (2018). Factors hindering women entrepreneurs' access to institutional finance: An empirical study. J. Small Bus. Entrep. 30: 279–291.

GIIN. (2024). Gender Lens Investing Insights Report 2024. Global Impact Investing Network, New York, USA.

GSMA. (2023). The Mobile Gender Gap Report 2023. GSM Association, London, UK.

Hallward-Driemeier, M. (2011). Strengthening women's entrepreneurship. pp. 67–78. *In*: Africa Competitiveness Report 2011. World Economic Forum and World Bank, Geneva, Switzerland.

Hemalatha, M., Mohan, V. C. and Jasim, K. M. (2013). The antecedents of marketing success of women entrepreneurs. Int. J. Bus. Innov. Res. 7: 637–662.

Huq, A., Delaney, A. and Debney, B. (2022). Challenging the entrepreneurial discourse around women home-based workers' empowerment. Econ. Labour Relat. Rev. 33: 308–328.

ITU. (2023). Measuring Digital Development: Facts and Figures 2023. International Telecommunication Union, Geneva, Switzerland.

Kabeer, N. (1999). Resources, agency, achievements: Reflections on the measurement of women's empowerment. Dev. Change 30: 435–464.

Kuran, O. and Khabbaz, L. (2025). Women entrepreneurs in challenging contexts: The role of purpose and coping strategies in building resilience. J. Entrep. Emerg. Econ.

Minniti, M. and Naudé, W. (2010). What do we know about the patterns and determinants of female entrepreneurship across countries? Eur. J. Dev. Res. 22: 277–293.

OECD. (2021). Bridging the Digital Gender Divide: Include, Upskill, Innovate. Organisation for Economic Co-operation and Development, Paris, France.

Prasad, V. K., Naidu, G. M., Kinnera Murthy, B., Winkel, D. E. and Ehrhardt, K. (2013). Women entrepreneurs and business venture growth: An examination of the influence of human and social capital resources in an Indian context. J. Small Bus. Entrep. 26: 341–364.

Singh, A. and Paliwal, M. (2020). Skill development and women empowerment: Synthesis of review and policies. pp. 30–36. *In*: Bansal, R. (ed.). Skill India: A Catalyst to Nation Building. Empyreal Publishing House, Ghaziabad, India.

UN Women. (2022). Progress on the Sustainable Development Goals: Gender Snapshot 2022. UN Women, New York, USA.

We-Fi and World Bank. (2023). The WE Finance Code: A Global Framework for Advancing Women's Access to Finance. World Bank Group, Washington, DC, USA.

World Bank. (2022). Women, Business and the Law 2022. World Bank Publications, Washington, DC, USA.

World Bank. (2024). Women, Business and the Law 2024. World Bank Publications, Washington, DC, USA.

Yetim, N. (2008). Social capital in female entrepreneurship. Int. Sociol. 23: 864–885.

Index

For Product Safety Concerns and Information please contact our EU representative GPSR@taylorandfrancis.com Taylor & Francis Verlag GmbH, Kaufingerstraße 24, 80331 München, Germany